THE BUSINESS OF Communicating
SECOND EDITION

John Nutting   Gillian White

WITH
Malcolm Davies
Linda Kalle
Kerry Kreis
Rosamond Nutting
Keith Tronc

*fully block
open punctuation*

McGRAW-HILL BOOK COMPANY Sydney
New York St Louis San Francisco Auckland Bogotá
Caracas Hamburg Lisbon London Madrid Mexico Milan
Montreal New Delhi Oklahoma City Paris San Juan
São Paulo Singapore Tokyo Toronto

First published 1981
Reprinted 1982, 1984, 1985, 1986
Second edition 1990

**National Library of Australia
Cataloguing-in-Publication data:**
  Nutting, John.
    The business of communicating.
    2nd ed.
    Bibliography.
    Includes index.
    ISBN 0 07 452533 6.

    1. Communication in management. I. White,
  Gillian. II. Title.

  658.45

Produced in Australia by McGraw-Hill Book Company Australia Pty Limited
  4 Barcoo Street, Roseville, NSW 2069
Typeset in Hong Kong by Setrite Typesetters Ltd
Printed in Hong Kong by Dah Hua Printing Press Co. Ltd

Sponsoring Editor: Gillian Souter
Production Editor: Bettina Stevenson
Designer: Wing Ping Tong
Cover Illustration: Jenny Coopes
Cartoonist: Jenny Coopes
Technical Illustrator: Diane Booth

Contents

◀ PART 2 ▶
Developing communication skills

◀ PART 3 ▶
Writing at work

Preface

Few people in business today question the importance of communication skills in the workplace. Those who are effective communicators usually rise rapidly in their chosen fields because their superior communication ability aids them in countless ways. Like other skills, the ability to communicate clearly can be developed, but not in the same way that one learns accounting or statistical methods. We learn to communicate best by experiencing and experimenting. In the process we may make mistakes, but we also make many useful discoveries which enable us to communicate more effectively on later occasions. As a result, no act of communication is ever a complete failure.

To facilitate this learning process, this book offers a set of guidelines and practical examples.

There are no fixed rules that will ensure perfect communication: it is too personal and complicated a matter to predict how two people should deal with a particular issue. In each instance a communicator must consider many factors, the most important being the perspective of the person with whom you are communicating. We suggest that you use the concepts in this book as a framework on which to build a personal account of effective communication methods.

No matter who you are, you can improve. To communicate effectively is a challenging and rewarding experience, and one area of personal development that provides you with the opportunity for almost unlimited growth combined with advancement in your chosen career.

Acknowledgments

Apart from Gillian White, there are also others who are responsible for the success of this book. Special acknowledgment must go to Malcolm Davies, Dr Keith Tronc and Kerry Kreis who co-authored the first edition and whose work remains the basis of much of this revision. Dr John Damm and Bob Dick of the University of Queensland and Dr Leslie Button, author of *Discovery and Experience*, provided inspiration and learning and helped instil many of the central concepts from which my own ideas developed.

Two other people who helped make this book a reality deserve special recognition: Roz Nutting and Linda Kalle. Roz played a special role in creating, writing, researching and editing the manuscript, beginning in the 1970s when we worked together on the original 'Writing to Win' programs. In a number of chapters we built on concepts from her *Skills for Positive Living* (Pitman, Melbourne 1985) and her published papers, including those from *Experimenting with Personal Construct Psychology* (Routledge & Kegan Paul, London, 1989). Linda has a special ability as a writer. She knows how to explain key ideas clearly and simply. Having used my earlier drafts of this book in the classroom, she was able to provide practical, constructive criticism on style and content. In the end, she helped rewrite the entire manuscript in the form you see here. Linda provided much of the essential material on continuity in writing, study skills and corporate communication, and in countless examples and exercises.

I would also like to acknowledge the professional assistance of Eve Haywood and Justine Stewart for their encouragement and advice throughout the project and for permission to adapt material from their own work on communication. Special thanks are due to Gillian Souter of McGraw-Hill for her guidance, leadership and patience. Finally I want to record my appreciation for the enthusiasm shown by past students whose suggestions and comments greatly influenced the content and structure of every chapter.

John Nutting

PART 1

Making communication work

N23P

thursday   3-6

The process

Chapter 1 introduces many topics that will be covered later in more detail. In particular, it deals with the terms people use in talking about communication — for example, 'sender', 'receiver', 'channels' and 'messages'. Since you have been using communication skills all your life, some of the terms will be familiar, but others used to 'communicate about communication' will be new, or will take on new meanings. This chapter also gives a simplified, theoretical model of the communication process. It makes a good starting point, but you'll find that real-life communication is much more complicated.

Topics

What is communication?

It takes two to communicate

Main elements in the communication process

Communication variables

One-way and two-way communication

Making communication work

Assumptions about communicating

What is communication?

When you explain an idea to someone, you're trying to share that idea. If your communication is successful, and as a result you share that thought, it is then something that you and the other person have in common.

Communication is the means by which people share words, ideas and feelings. Sharing ideas helps people to relate to each other more effectively, to work together more happily and to get jobs done faster. Effective communication makes business work.

But is that all there is to communicating? What is really going on? When people say they are 'communicating', are they talking only about 'sharing ideas'?

Because the meanings people share are important, 'communicating' involves much more than just the simple act of sharing thoughts. Usually a relationship is affected — sometimes seriously — as a direct result of just one particular act of communicating.

'I've had a long day'

1. Think of someone you know really well — preferably a person you see daily. (This exercise works best if you think of someone you really like or dislike.)

2. Imagine a scene in which that person comes up to you and says: 'I've had a long day'.

3. Describe various ways in which you could react to the other person's communication.
   - What would you say in reply?
   - What tone of voice would you use?
   - What would you do physically?
   - What kind of expression would you adopt?
   - What emotions would you feel?
   Would all this 'communicating' have a positive or negative effect on your relationship with this person?

4. Repeat the whole exercise, this time imagining that *you* are saying 'I've had a long day' to someone. What responses would you expect? Consider:
   - what might be said in reply;
   - tone of voice;
   - any physical reaction;
   - a likely facial expression;
   - an emotional reaction;
   - the effect this 'communication' might have on your relationship.

5. In each case, would the time of day or the location of the conversation have any effect on the meaning of the words used?

6. What other outside factors could influence or alter the whole process?

This is a realistic example of what communicating involves and how complex it can become, involving a lot more than just an exchange of words. One quick body movement — a frown or a smile — could change the meaning of the exchange. The result can be influenced also by your feelings towards the other person, by time and place, or by outside factors that you know nothing about — for instance, ten minutes before your conversation took place the other person may have either lost an argument with someone else or just received a promotion.

How communication works

To keep things simple, start by imagining communication as though it were a much less complex activity. Figure 1.1 illustrates the concept in its simplest form, but this is not an accurate picture. For a start, it shows a message travelling in only one direction when in fact most communication involves two-way exchanges. What it does show is that there are two people involved: the sender and the receiver.

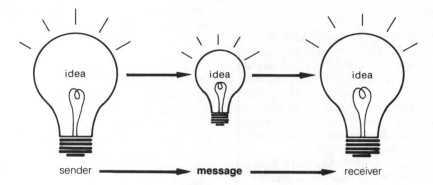

Fig. 1.1 *Communicating: a basic model*

It takes two to communicate

The word 'communication' and similar words such as 'community' and 'communion' all have Latin origins describing the idea of 'common-ness', the result of sharing ideas, having a shared understanding or reaching a common agreement. To be described as communication an exchange must involve two or more individuals, although not necessarily humans. Most living creatures communicate, and humans often share ideas with animals. But you cannot share ideas with a machine. Computers are used to communicate, but having no ideas of their own they cannot communicate with you or among themselves.

Main elements in the communication process

It is never easy to define either the steps involved in communication or exactly what happens while it is taking place, so perhaps it is wise not to start by laying down too many firm definitions. However, without some specific labels it would be impossible to talk about communication. The main parts of the process and the terms most commonly used to describe it are given below.

Who communicates?
    A sender
    A receiver
What do they communicate?
    Messages, codes and meanings

How do messages travel?
    Via channels
How does it happen?
    Sender has an idea
    Sender converts idea into message
    Message is sent or transmitted
    Message is received
    Receiver works out what message 'means'
What else happens?
    Receiver responds or reacts
    Sender gets feedback

The message

A message is a unit of communication, an imaginary package that carries a meaning. Some messages are portable; for instance, a memo being passed from one person to another. Others are transferred visually — a smile, or a raised eyebrow. A handshake travels by touch. All these are messages.

A message can be a phone call, a notice on a board or a stop sign. What are some other examples?

The sender

All communication begins with the sender. You have an idea that you want to share with another person. Until you send it (in a message), nothing happens.

The receiver

With whom are you communicating? As the example above illustrated, the effect of your message will depend on the character, mood and personal background of the person who receives it, and much more. As explained in Chapters 4 and 5, understanding often depends as much on what the receiver thinks you are saying as on what you actually say. 'Receiver factors' like these play a major part in the communication process.

Of course, a message often has more than one receiver, but it must have *at least* one. On many occasions messages are sent but not received, and in such cases, *no* communication takes place.

Sending or transmitting

Sending a written message, such as a letter, requires a series of physical actions. For instance, the sender types the words on a word processor, prints them out, puts the paper in an envelope and the envelope in the mail-tray. Each action helps to start the message on its trip from sender to receiver, so each is a part of the sending or transmitting aspect of communication.

Channels

There also needs to be a way of carrying your letter to the post office, across town and so to the receiver's desk. Messages can be sung, sent along wires and glass fibres, projected on a screen or bounced off a satellite. One particular message could be conveyed via a 40-metre sign on top of a building, a 30-second television commercial, or a note stuck in a door. All these are channels — physical or electronic methods for carrying messages.

Channels can be plain or complex. If you nod your head to indicate agreement the channel is a simple combination of your body movement and the receiver's vision. Other channels have many parts to them; the postal system is a complex one made up of letter boxes, post office sorting services, mailbags, vans and all the people who help transfer mail from senders to receivers.

While many channels employ mechanical and electronic devices, most start with basic actions — speech or body movement — and all involve at least one of the senses, such as sight, touch or hearing, at the receiving end.

Codes and meanings

Suppose you feel happy about meeting someone. To communicate this you need to convert your feelings into a word, a smile or some other form representing your idea of happiness. In communication terms this is known as 'coding' the message. The word 'Hi' and your smile are two well-known codes for 'happy to meet you'.

> A code can be a word, a ringing bell, a handshake. What are some other examples?

Interpreting meanings (decoding)

If people 'decode' your message correctly, by interpreting your smile and 'Hi' as meaning 'happy to meet you', they understand you; your communication is working. The business of coding and decoding is one of the main factors in making communication work.

Understanding and misunderstanding

Understanding is achieved if the sender's original idea is conveyed without alteration to the receiver, but no matter how carefully you choose your codes, all too often the message produces unintentional meanings; in reality, the meaning sent and the meaning understood seldom match perfectly. This is explained in more detail in Chapter 4.

Communication variables

Sender–receiver relationships

Suppose two people (whom you know well) both invite you to join them for a meal. How you interpret (decode) each invitation and why you think each person wants you to be his or her guest will differ according to the relationship you share with them. Relationship issues influence not only decoding and understanding, but also the willingness of the receiver to agree to a request, undertake a task or carry out an action. They play an important part in determining the success of your communication.

Background signals

When you communicate with another person, as well as the main message you often transmit other signals that define aspects of the two-way relationship between you and that person. Some — perhaps a smile — are obvious; others, such as failing to offer a chair, are the kinds people refer to when they say they 'read between the lines'. Because such signals are transmitted in the background, behind the main message and often on a different channel, the term 'background signal' is used in this book to refer to them.

Background signals can have a major effect on receivers' reactions to messages, because they help to indicate just what kind of relationships exist between people. Some — for example, keeping someone waiting for an interview — may not really be part of the communication process itself, but even so that action will have an effect on the relationship when the interview begins. In extreme cases a background signal may completely reverse the meaning of spoken or written words.

Apart from the common phrase 'between the lines', other terms used to describe the background signals include 'metacommunications', 'para-language', 'relationship signals' and 'modifying signals'. They too are explained in greater detail in Chapter 4, and because of their powerful effect on both written and spoken messages are also mentioned in many other chapters. Because background signals are associated with almost every message sent or received it is virtually impossible to avoid their influence.

The situation or context

How well your messages work also depends on conditions such as time of day and location. While not actually part of the communication process, the situation (context) certainly affects the outcome, adding just one more set of factors to increase the complexity of exchanges. Provided that you keep this in mind, however, you can make sure they don't interfere with clear understanding.

Think of three people. Imagine each one phones you late at night and says, 'Come over as soon as you can. There's something we need to discuss'.

1. What are some possible meanings that each one might want to share with you?
2. How much would your interpretation of the meaning be affected by the time of day and the meeting-place each sender suggests?
3. What other factors could help to change the meaning or affect understanding according to which person was calling?

One-way and two-way communication

One-way communication occurs when a message is received but there is no response or reply. Two-way communication is more complicated. When you respond by in turn communicating to the original sender, *you* become a sender. The original sender becomes a receiver (see Fig. 1.2).

During an ordinary two-way conversation, you (and others involved) can reverse roles several times a minute as you speak, listen and speak again. If several different channels are being used together (words, body movement, tone of voice), it's likely that you will be sending on one channel and receiving on another one at the same time! The process of communicating is much more complex than was suggested by the basic model given earlier in this chapter.

1. Reading this book is an example of one-way communication. What are some others?
2. Answering the telephone is an example of two-way communication. What are some others?

Feedback messages

When you reply to a message, the chances are that your response will include some reaction to or comment about the sender's original idea. You nod in agreement, give what was asked for, laugh or

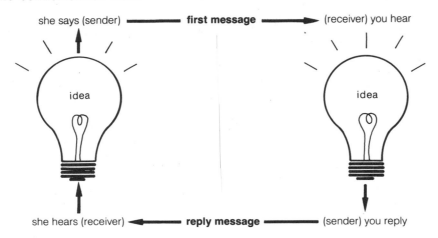

she says (sender) ━━━ **first message** ━━━▶ (receiver) you hear

idea

idea

she hears (receiver) ◀━━ **reply message** ━━━ (sender) you reply

Fig. 1.2 *Two-way communication*

frown, say 'Thanks', or post a cheque. If your response concerns the topic in the original message, it is called 'feedback', and the chance to share feedback is one of the main reasons that two-way communication is more effective than one-way. *Positive* feedback tells you your communication is working; *negative* feedback tells you either that it is not working at all or that there are problems with some aspect of it, perhaps with understanding. (Chapter 3 explains in detail the importance of feedback.)

Making communication work

Once you have an idea of the way communication works, you can organise your exchanges more effectively. Imagine yourself in the situation described below. Notice, as it develops, how the elements described in this chapter are involved.

You need to leave work at 5.00 pm on Mondays because you have a regular engagement at 6.00 pm (say it is a course on communication), but every Monday afternoon your supervisor seems to have some urgent job that holds you up, often until 5.30 or later.

1. Plan your communication

You communicate more effectively if you have a clear idea of what you want to achieve, and why. Before you approach your supervisor, spend a moment thinking about what is involved.

- Which channel? Which would be best: talking on the phone, or face to face? Face-to-face communication will give you a chance to use body language (a smile) and a cheerful voice. You will also get immediate feedback, which will help you gauge how effective your message has been.
- What style of communication? Should you be

as brief as possible? Would a detailed explanation be more convincing?
- When is the best — and the worst — time? Timing is important in all communication. Should you make an appointment or wait until next time you happen to meet?
- What else is involved? Look at the overall situation. Are others affected by your problem? Will they be pleased or concerned by your discussion with the supervisor?
- What barriers have to be overcome? Some of these may be beyond your control, but many can be avoided if you think about them in advance. In planning your message, the more you recognise the problems caused by communication barriers the better will be your chance of success.
- Have you a positive goal or purpose? Thinking positively about the outcome — and how success will help you — will make you feel more confident.

2. Sit in the receiver's chair

This is a technique using what is known as 'empathy', and is a vital skill that helps to create successful two-way exchanges (see Chapter 5). In this instance, consider how to encourage the supervisor to take an interest in *your* problem. If you explain that your studies are going to help you at work, you'll have a better chance of building agreement.

3. Code the message

Divide your message into sub-topics:

- How do you build up interest so the supervisor really wants to *receive* rather than just hear you talk? (This is known as 'switching the receiver on'.)
- How do you explain about your studies?
- Why are you delayed on Mondays?
- Can this be changed?
- What do you have to do to make the change possible?

Unless each point or topic is clear in your own mind, you'll find it hard to transmit your total message clearly. Focus on a description of the problem, and the need for action by the supervisor to solve it.

- Find the right codes. As you think and plan, your ideas and images link up to form patterns. They begin to take on an even more distinct shape as the words and meanings join to create the actual message. Thinking through a conversation in advance makes it easier to express yourself when the time comes.

4. Send the message

You are in the supervisor's office:

'I enjoy my work and don't mind working back to finish an urgent job. However, I've just started a course in management and I have to be at college at 6.00 pm on Monday nights. Somehow it always seems to be on Mondays that you ask me to work back. Is there some way you could arrange it so that I get off at 4.45? Could I work later on Tuesday afternoons to make up for it?

5. The message is received

The supervisor listens to your words and watches the way in which you convey your message. You look confident, you smile, your request is sensible and your tone is sincere. You have planned the exchange thoroughly, so its meaning is received and decoded clearly.

6. Build understanding and agreement

Listeners need to understand exactly what you are asking for and why. They also need to agree with you before they do what you ask. This step in the process is complicated, and is the point at which many breakdowns occur. In almost all business communication today it is worth the extra effort to build goodwill and create positive agreement rather than put pressure on people.

Your offer to work late on Tuesdays is a positive signal, one that helps to create such agreement (see Chapter 12, 'Creating co-operation').

7. Feedback

Suppose that in this case the whole process works out as you planned it. After some more discussion the supervisor agrees, and transmits positive feedback:

'OK. You can leave at 4.45 on Mondays. I'll tell the others about the arrangement so that there'll be no misunderstandings. And I appreciate your offer to work back on Tuesdays. How about staying until 5.15?'

8. Confirmation

Your communication worked (or did it?). 'Success' in terms of understanding and agreement is of limited value unless it is followed by something more than words. When you were thinking and planning, you had a goal or target. You now know that your idea has been received and understood: you have positive feedback in the form of the supervisor's 'Yes'. You may now feel confident, but when will you know for sure that your message worked?

9. Action feedback

The spoken feedback indicated that your message was understood, but action feedback — if you find you *do* get away from work at 4.45 on the following Monday — proves something far more important: your communication really worked. In business this is the result that counts, particularly if you are concerned with solving problems or making changes as in the example above.

Assumptions about communicating

There are a number of common assumptions made about communicating; having read this chapter, you will recognise some of them as being inaccurate. To clarify this initial explanation of the communication process, look now at some assumptions and compare them with reality.

Assumption 1: Anything you see, hear, or remember is part of your daily communication.

Reality: You can make an observation, notice something or remember an appointment, but it's not communication unless shared with someone else.

Talking to yourself is not communicating. Remembering is not communicating. Typing a confidential letter on a word processor or typewriter is not sharing ideas with the machine. If you leave the room and (unknown to you) two window cleaners look in and *notice* what you have typed, even that is not really communication, since you were not trying to share any thoughts with *them*.

Noticing or observing is not communicating. It is intimately tied up with the process of communication but is not communication, at least until the point at which you share your observation with another thinking individual. You may just *notice* someone walking past, but once even the smallest idea or feeling — even a background signal — is exchanged between you, *communication* has begun.

1. A person is looking at a clock and frowning. In what circumstances is this a case of communication? When would it not be?

2. You trip over a chair left in a darkened hallway! You have lots of thoughts you would like to share, and you put some of them into words! What else is necessary before communication takes place?

Assumption 2: Communicating is the same as understanding.

Reality: Even a total misunderstanding indicates that communication has taken place. It just didn't work properly.

Communication has taken place, as long as *some* meaning (even one totally unintentional) is created in the listener's mind as a direct *result* of receiving the message. In fact, the meaning that enters the receiver's mind will in most cases be a bit different from the one the sender hoped to convey (see Chapters 5, 6 and 7).

Assumption 3: Much communication is dull and unrewarding.

Reality: Unless it is rewarding, communication may not continue long enough to *become* boring.

People minimise effort in communicating once they are convinced it has little value for them, and avoid communicating altogether if they see no value in it at all. You could call this principle 'The First Law of Communication':

Communication continues only so long as people feel they are benefiting from it in some way. If they do not feel this, they switch off and stop communicating.

Faced with a speech they find boring or a memo they find dull, most people just think about things that interest them more. If someone complains that a report was 'unsatisfactory' try to find out how much of the document he or she really read. If the first law of communication holds true, active communication (in this case, reading and understanding) will have ceased at about the time the individual decided the report had no value. The reader may have gone on looking at the pages but will have taken in little meaning. This is why so much written communication is 'read', yet seems to produce no visible results.

Assumption 4: All kinds of communication work in the same way.

Reality: There are different kinds and different ways of communicating.

Each of the circumstances listed below needs different skills and techniques in communication, and in the following chapters you will discover many specific and appropriate techniques you can use in these situations.

- *Person to person* — reading a letter, making a phone call, dancing
- *In a small group* — planning, solving problems, making decisions
- *In a meeting* — presenting, bargaining, negotiating agreements
- *In an organisation* — writing reports and memos, using noticeboards, supervising, managing

- *Through the mass media* — speaking in public, on radio or television; writing for the media, in papers, journals, books; advertising and public relations
- *Others* — training or teaching, entertaining (art, cinema)

'CommunicatioN' and 'communicationS'

These are two different terms. The distinction followed throughout this book, and the one now accepted by most Australian authorities (including the *Macquarie Dictionary*), is as follows:

- The singular word, 'communication', refers to the process of communicating, which is the topic of this book.
- The plural word, 'communications', refers to the technology, the organisations that deal with message transmission, and the electrical and mechanical systems used to carry messages. *Example*: A new AUSSAT communications satellite will be launched next month.

Summary

1. Communication makes it possible to share words, ideas and feelings with other people.

2. A message is a unit of communication, like a package; it carries meanings from one person to another.

3. All communication begins with the sender — the person who has an idea and wants to share it.

4. Channels are the media or devices through or by which messages move. All at some stage involve basic senses — sight, hearing or touch.

5. In communication, there must be at least one other person to receive a message. That person is the receiver.

6. Most communication involves more than just sharing meanings. Usually it has a direct effect on the relationships between the people involved.

7. When a response is made to the sender of a message, it is known as feedback.

8. Two-way communication is far more effective than one-way because it allows feedback between both parties.

9. To share an idea or a message, the sender must first convert it into a code or symbol (coding the message). The receiver must then decode the message to discover its 'meaning'.

10. The meaning understood by the receiver is seldom exactly the same as the one in the sender's mind. Feedback helps to indicate how accurate the level of understanding really is.

11. Messages need to be planned. The effective sender thinks about *who* is receiving the message, *why* it should be shared and *how* best to share it.

Exercises

1. Is it possible for someone who died hundreds of years ago to communicate with someone who was born in 1970? If you think it is, give an example.

2. If two computers cannot communicate with each other, when would it be correct to say that you had used a computer to communicate?

3. What is the difference between the terms 'communication' and 'communications'?

4. When you shake hands, or give someone a hug, you are sending and receiving at the same time. What are some other examples of this kind of dual exchange?

5. List some of the communication steps that you went through to obtain this book.

CHAPTER 2

Choosing the channel

Any link that carries messages between a sender and a receiver is a channel, as was explained in Chapter 1. This chapter discusses the many different channels and the ways of classifying them.

Communication involves many things other than words, in fact the channels that carry words, although important, are greatly outnumbered by those carrying all kinds of non-word messages. Just as some forms of transport are better than others for specific purposes, so in communication some channels suit certain messages better than others. One of the main aims of this chapter is to develop your ability to understand the differences and to choose the best channel for any particular message.

Topics

Using your senses

Verbal and non-verbal channels

Choosing the right channels

Multichannel communication

Using your senses

One obvious way to identify different kinds of channels is to divide them according to which senses are used — for example, sound or sight.

Aural or acoustic channels

Conversation — using your aural sense — is ideal when you want immediate two-way communication with others, but there are many other aural messages such as a whistle, a doorbell or a public-address system.

Advantages

Aural channels are
- ideal when you need to attract people's attention quickly;
- fast and easy to use.

Disadvantages

- Aural channels are ineffective if receivers either are not paying full attention or hear what they want to hear rather than what you are actually saying.
- People are easily distracted by other sounds or by visual images, so aural messages are often not received as clearly as written ones.
- Even when the receiver pays attention, an aural message is not easy to remember accurately. Unless the exchange is recorded, there is no way to confirm the content of the message.

Visual or optical channels

Body movement — for instance, a smile or a shake of the head — is one of the fastest and most effective ways of communicating, but only if the receiver is watching the sender. This is why so many visual messages are transmitted in a permanent (recorded) form (letters, photographs, videos, posters, road signs, graphs, flags, architectural drawings and this book), so that they are available whenever the receiver wants to look at them.

Advantages

- Visual channels convey information more accurately than aural channels.

- Colour, which can only be transmitted visually, attracts attention and adds strength to most messages.
- Recorded visual messages can be duplicated, so that many people can receive the same version at the same time.

Disadvantages

Recorded visual messages
- are slower to send; often cost more to produce;
- are less likely to produce an immediate response (two-way communication).

Tactile or kinaesthetic channels

You shake hands to communicate trust, share a hug to express liking and appreciation. To communicate with children parents use touch — the first form of communication humans learn. Tactile channels convey messages by physical contact.

Advantages

- Tactile channels are better than words if you need to communicate feelings or emotions.
- 'Hands-on' training is more easily remembered than spoken instruction or information in a manual.

Disadvantages

- Many tactile messages are too personal or too emotional for use in business situations.
- Tactile messages are often misunderstood or misinterpreted.

Channels using taste or smell

Using taste and smell as a means of communicating may seem less applicable in business than in personal contacts. However, sharing a meal can use these channels (as well as the others) to help develop a better business relationship. Taking clients to lunch can be a very effective way of communicating trust, liking or appreciation. Recent studies show that people also emit natural substances called 'pheromones' that affect communication through the sense of smell.

Using combined senses

Rather than overloading the receiver, the use of more than one sense usually speeds up the transfer of meaning and reinforces understanding. Typical combinations include:
- visual/aural — audio-visual training programs
- visual/aural/tactile — 'hands-on' training courses
- visual/aural/tactile/smell/taste — celebration such as a party, with special food and drinks

Your favourite sense

Although people use all five senses in communicating, most have a 'favourite' sense. Whether thinking, planning, organising or remembering, they show their preferences by the style of communication they choose — aural, visual or tactile. This is explained more fully in Chapter 6, but here is one example of the effect of such preferences.

Say you and two others are planning an interstate holiday and are thinking about where to go. Kim prefers visual thinking — pictures and images. Leslie is a tactile thinker. You have a strong aural memory and are 'in tune' with sounds and words. Kim wants to study lots of maps and brochures before making a choice. You want to spend time talking to the others to 'hear' their opinions, or 'sound out' different locations. Leslie may be more interested in finding out what the weather will be like, and what kind of activities are popular at each venue.

Verbal and non-verbal channels

Channels can also be classified according to the type of signs (the 'language') used. This classification emphasises the distinction between verbal (word) and non-verbal (non-word) channels.

Verbal channels

A word is a verbal symbol; verbal channels include all forms of writing and printing, as well as speaking. For instance:

spoken: meetings, speeches, phone calls
written: reports, memos, balance sheets

Speaking obviously uses verbal channels. However, if you use the term 'verbal' to mean 'spoken' as opposed to 'written', it can lead to misunderstandings.

Numbers and symbols such as '$', '%' and shorthand are just other ways of representing words. So they also are verbal.

Non-verbal channels

A smile, a photograph or a flashing blue light can carry a message without using words. A sample of your most significant day-to-day communication patterns will confirm what you probably know already: that many of your most important exchanges occur via non-verbal channels. Managers and leaders in business know that skilful non-verbal communication is often far more effective than words.

Often messages are transmitted faster, more cheaply or more accurately non-verbally than verbally. Non-verbal messages are more effective when

- the message is too complicated for words (a quick sketch map is clearer than spoken words in describing a route from A to B);
- verbal channels are blocked (in a noisy factory conversation may be impossible, or a danger if misunderstood — sign language is safer);
- time is critical or a rapid decision or action is needed (alarms, sirens and flashing lights attract attention quickly and produce fast responses);
- deep feelings are being expressed (non-verbal messages are best for communicating emotions).

Chapter 4 explains more about these types of messages and their classification as non-verbal languages.

> Suggest some other occasions on which you would communicate non-verbally rather than by speaking or writing.

Body movement

A smile can be more effective than a two-page letter full of compliments. Messages that are conveyed physically may not always be accurate but can be very influential, because they have so much power over people's feelings. Most people attach more meaning to body language than to words. No matter what you *say*, if you say it with a frown people will take this as a sign of displeasure. Staying still when others want you to move can also convey a non-verbal message.

Vocal tone

Tone of voice is really a special form of body language. Consider the many different ways you can say, 'Thanks for telling me', and how each way might affect the meaning of the message. Vocal signals include the loudness, tone and pitch of your voice, and the rhythm and speed of speaking; each will affect the meaning given to what you say. Although these signals accompany verbal communication, they are treated as non-verbal because the meanings transmitted depend on the voice *tone*, not on the words used.

Pictures

Try turning off the television sound and looking only at the picture. You are still receiving messages, ideas and information conveyed as pictures, which are often more powerful than words.

Symbols

A wedding ring, a flag, a police officer's uniform and a siren are typical non-verbal symbols. (Remember that words too are 'symbols' but are of course verbal). Non-verbal symbols such as sirens are quickly interpreted and understood, so are ideal for exchanging information in times of emergency or confusion. Non-verbal symbols travel on channels as diverse as clothing, road signs, corporate logos and coloured lights.

Choosing the right channels

Different kinds of communication obviously need different kinds of channels. The distinctions between mass media communication and the more personal kinds are significant because of the different impression each kind has on the sender—receiver relationship. Make sure you choose the right channel for each situation.

Non-verbal language

Mass media

For one-way, impersonal communication — particularly messages for the general public — the obvious choice is the mass media (radio, television, newspapers, magazines and so on). (The singular word, 'medium', is just a technical term for any kind of channel.) These channels allow you to reach a large audience quickly and effectively, but since most only flow one way they are of value only if you want to give information rather than exchange ideas or share feedback.

Person-to-person channels

If you wish to communicate with only a small number of people — and provided you have the time to spend dealing with individuals — it's far better to choose a more personal channel. Face-to-face conversations, telephone calls and personal letters are more effective than impersonal memos or announcements over a loudspeaker. If you are trying to develop a better relationship or to create agreement you definitely need the opportunity for two-way message flow and for feedback, particularly if you are communicating with clients or colleagues you care about — people who could be upset if they heard from you only via less personal contacts. Person-to-person channels also make it easy to check that the receiver has understood and agrees with what you said. If there are problems, the more personal the channel the better you can deal with them.

Group-communication channels

There is an area between 'mass' and 'person to person' where the receivers as a group are well known to you but are too many to permit individual or personal contact. Typical ways of conveying a message to each member of a group include a photocopied memo, a form letter, a business report or an address at a meeting. These channels save time and effort but are less personal, so your ideas may be received with less enthusiasm or interest.

Be careful *not* to use group communication channels just to save time or trouble when the business relationship calls for a more personal contact. A canteen noticeboard is an ideal place for a reminder about the next staff outing, but not for advising individuals that they have been promoted or transferred! This may seem like an exaggeration, but in business many communicators fail to realise the importance of matching the channel with the relationship.

Intuitive communication — insight

You hear quite often of people who are unusually successful as decision makers. It could be due to good luck, but many such people say they are guided by what they called insight, 'gut feeling' or intuition. This is hard to define; possible descriptions are 'being sure, without knowing why', or 'knowing without being told'.

Using your intuitive skills involves a lot more than communicating, but one aspect of it is the ability to 'tune in' to other people's ideas, attitudes and feelings without using ordinary verbal or non-verbal channels. There is still much to learn about the process, but it is now accepted as quite normal and having nothing to do with mind-reading or gazing into teacups.

■ Almost everyone has to some degree the ability to communicate intuitively.

■ As with any other form of communication, the skills involved can be developed by practice and regular use.

Many business-oriented tests to assess job applicants now measure a candidate's level of 'intuitiveness' and list it alongside other routine abilities that employers look for. However, while it is appropriate to mention it as a special form of non-verbal communication, the topic is too broad to be covered in this text. For more information, see 'Additional resources and bibliography'.

Picking the best channel

Choosing the best channel for *your* message depends on

■ the purpose of the communication;
■ the size and type of receiver group you wish to communicate with;
■ the kind of relationship you want with an individual receiver or a group;
■ the nature and complexity of the message;
■ the time, cost and other resources concerned.

Multichannel communication

Since most verbal messages are accompanied by non-verbal ones, in most cases you will use more than one channel. As long as the different parts of the message complement or support one another, using a mix of different channels will result in

■ better understanding;
■ a stronger influence on the receiver;
■ a better chance of gaining agreement;
■ easier recall.

This is why television advertising, which combines words (both written and spoken) with visual images, body movement and symbols, is so effective, and why instruction manuals with examples, illustrations and diagrams are easier to follow than those with words alone. The use of graphs to illustrate a report helps readers to interpret complex data. A sample of your product in addition to a written description allows potential customers to understand more clearly what it can do for them.

Not all multichannel exchanges are successful. Suppose, when you arrive at a party, two people say they have been looking forward to meeting you (a verbal message) and then, after a short conversation, they rush off to meet someone else. Their non-verbal signals cancel out the verbal ones.

Summary

1. Be aware of just how many different channels there are. Recognise that most communication contains elements other than words.
2. Verbal channels (carrying words) are outnumbered by non-verbal channels (using codes other than words). Most messages use a combination of both.
3. Typical non-verbal channels include body movement, facial expressions, posture, clothing, symbols, colours, vocal tone and pictures.
4. Although people use all five senses to send and receive messages, most have a 'favourite' sense — aural, visual or tactile.
5. Mass-media channels are ideal for one-way, impersonal communication, particularly in carrying messages for the general public.
6. Personal channels are preferable for communication with a small number of people. They use more time and energy but create better relationships, helpful in bringing co-operation and agreement.
7. Do not use group-communication channels just to save time or effort if the relationship calls for personal contact.
8. Messages have a better chance of successful reception if transmitted via a combination of several channels.
9. Understanding how and why channels differ makes it easier to choose the best ones for each message.

Exercises

1. When would you choose non-verbal channels such as hand gestures rather than try to communicate by speaking?
2. Why do most people advertising accommodation or job vacancies prefer channels such as newspapers to radio or television?
3. Why do banks — and companies that handle finance or insurance — prefer to advertise on television and in high-class magazines rather than on radio or in local papers?
4. Why was cigarette advertising banned from television long before it was barred from other mass media?
5. Give some instances in which using several channels at the one time helps improve understanding or agreement.
6. Give an example of the use of several different channels at the one time which confuses people or results in loss of understanding. What is the reason for this?
7. Problems are likely to arise if a verbal message and an accompanying non-verbal message (or background signal) carry opposing meanings. Give some examples.
8. In the situation described in number 7, which of the two meanings (verbal and non-verbal) is more likely to be accepted?
9. Is writing verbal or non-verbal communication?
10. How many different ways are there to say 'Thanks for telling me'?
11. If you try to have a conversation with someone who is listening to *and* watching the news on television, what are your chances of success? Why?
12. In Australia the term 'verbal' is often given a different meaning from the one used in this chapter. What is this typical 'Australian' meaning? How does it differ from the meaning used in this chapter? What meaning of 'verbal' is given in your dictionary?

CHAPTER 3

Feedback

Feedback indicates how well your message is being understood; it helps to sort out communication problems and is vital for developing and maintaining business relationships. In fact, it is one of the most important parts of the communication process. This chapter explains its value, particularly in business, and the means to use it to improve your effectiveness as a communicator.

Topics

What is feedback?

Using feedback to hit the target

Aiming accurately

Feedback and the two-way relationship

False feedback

What is feedback?

Any reply to a message is 'feedback'. You ask the time, someone says '12.35' (receiver's feedback) and you say 'Thanks' (your feedback). Feedback can be classified in different ways. It can be

- verbal or non-verbal;
- positive or negative (error feedback);
- process or action;
- a combination of any of these.

Verbal and non-verbal feedback

Much feedback is non-verbal or includes non-verbal messages with words. In the latter case, if the two kinds don't match there are bound to be problems. 'Of course', says Leroi, 'come in and tell me about it. When my people have a problem I want to be the first to hear about it'. This verbal message offers positive feedback, but if Leroi keeps glancing at the clock, the non-verbal feedback throws doubt on the correctness of the verbal message. Just how interested do you think Leroi really is in listening to you and your problems? Usually, people put more faith in the non-verbal feedback.

Positive and negative feedback

Positive feedback

You advertise your car for sale for $12 000 and ten people phone you, all wanting to buy it. That's positive feedback, telling you that you have achieved the purpose of your message. A 'yes', a nod of agreement or a cheque in your mailbox are the same kind. Positive feedback lets you know you have no communication problem.

Negative or 'error' feedback

A reply that says your original message did not work is still useful feedback. If a caller in a public phone says 'A huge truck just went past. I couldn't hear a word', that's not positive but it's useful because it lets you know that something has gone wrong and that you need to repeat the message. At work, feedback like this often points to the cause of communication problems and suggests ways of fixing them (see 'Using feedback to hit the target', p. 21).

Action or process feedback

Whether verbal or non-verbal, positive or negative, feedback can also be classed as action or process.

Negative feedback

Action (GASFY) feedback

Remember the case in Chapter 1 in which you asked if you could finish early on Mondays? If you did finish at 4.45, you could 'see for yourself' that your communication was a success. This is called GASFY feedback, because instead of receiving a message from someone you 'Go And See For Yourself'. GASFY feedback can of course be negative as well as positive.

Process feedback

Instead of dealing with the outcome, process feedback tells you how the communication itself is working (or not working), or how to make it work more effectively. Say you are still trying to sell the car (the one in the example above). You run an advertisement in the 'Cars for Sale' column of a local paper.

1. *Message not received*: If your advertisement lacks appeal, or is too brief, process feedback (the lack

of calls) indicates the nature of the problem. You advertise again.

2. *Understanding*: Lyndsay, a potential buyer, phones but seems wary of your offer. After a few questions you get some process feedback: Lyndsay thinks you are a commercial dealer in used cars. You explain that you are selling privately, and Lyndsay immediately becomes more interested.

3. *Agreement*: You show Lyndsay the car. Lyndsay does not agree on your price of $12 000 but offers $11 750 (process feedback indicating willingness to negotiate). You suggest $11 800 and Lyndsay accepts.

Process feedback can be
- directive: 'Underline your headings', 'Please don't use such long words', or 'Could you speak a little louder, please?';
- open-ended, using questions to clarify understanding: '. . . and why do you feel that way?' or 'How sure are you of your figures?';

- diagnostic: 'I didn't get your message', 'I thought you meant that ...'.

Keep feedback channels open

For both you and Lyndsay, feedback has helped to overcome a number of problems standing in the way of the outcome you wanted. But what if Lyndsay then goes to the bank for the money, misses the bus and cannot return? Before you part, exchange phone numbers or contact addresses. This keeps the feedback channels open.

Communication often fails because of external factors, but a solution is still possible if the people involved remain in contact.

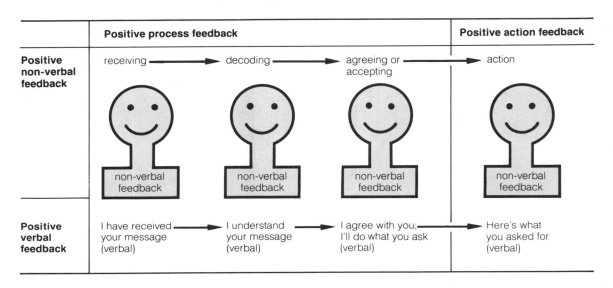

Fig. 3.1 *Positive feedback*

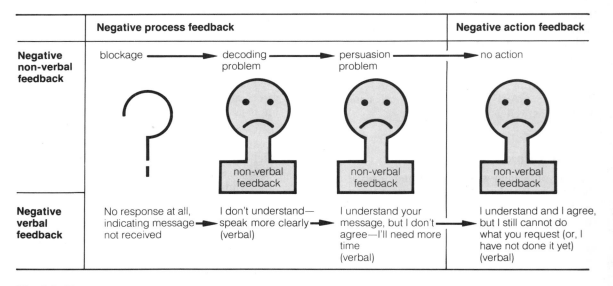

Fig. 3.2 *Negative or error feedback*

Using feedback to hit the target

In communication terms, negative feedback is like the 'error message' in a guided-missile system or a computer. In most cases it guides you towards improved techniques. You can only make improvements if you know

- your messages are going 'off target';
- whether you are far off target, or getting close;
- which direction to go in;
- what kind of errors to avoid.

For example, if you want to sell your car, negative or 'error' feedback can help you gain the best price. Suppose you started by advertising the car for $12 000. It didn't sell, but a number of people who looked at it told you it was 'just a bit too expensive'. That kind of error feedback points you towards a price you can expect: somewhere — but not much — below $12 000. If it sells quickly once you drop the price to $11 800, you can be confident you received top price.

Although described as negative, most error feedback isn't necessarily made up of bad news or unpleasant responses. Suppose you show a new employee how to work the photocopier and then ask, 'Can you manage it on your own now?' Which of these responses would be the more useful?

Positive feedback: 'Yes, sure!'

Negative or error feedback: 'I think so, but I'm not sure about how to clear a paper blockage.'

The trouble is that 'Yes, sure!' doesn't really tell you whether the employee

- is being completely honest and understands fully;
- wants you to stop talking — wants a chance to try working the copier to find out for certain if he or she *does* understand;
- is too shy to tell you that your instructions are unclear.

The second response is certainly more precise, it defines the area of misunderstanding and opens the way for you to focus on exactly what the trainee needs to be told. The more negative feedback of this kind the trainee gives you, the better, but you need to reassure people so that they feel confident in sharing error feedback with you.

Encourage error feedback

There are reasons why people avoid giving negative feedback. They may not wish to appear critical of others. By drawing attention to a mistake or problem, they could themselves appear to be at fault. Some just don't want to be bearers of bad news. You are unlikely to be given much error feedback at all unless people are sure you will accept it as constructive. You can encourage error feedback by making it clear that

- you recognise it as vital if you are to know what is working properly and what is not;
- you do not become upset or angry towards those who are prepared to share error messages with you;
- you believe in fixing problems rather than blaming or punishing those who report them;
- even when you are at fault, you value this kind of message more than 'cover-ups' or false praise;
- you encourage and support others who accept error feedback.

When you do this, you extend your effectiveness both as communicator and as problem solver. You will be able to pinpoint trouble spots faster and with more accuracy. Naturally, a climate in which there is open discussion of errors, mistakes and problems takes a little getting used to, but work groups soon become comfortable with it. It's an ideal foundation for positive problem solving because it

- promotes active thinking by looking more closely at problems rather than avoiding them;
- is more likely to be true, and probably more accurate than overly positive feedback;
- makes it harder for people to 'hide' problems (hoping you won't find out about them).

Don't make the common mistake of assuming 'everything is all right' just because there are no visible signs of trouble. It is wise to be a bit sceptical if you receive only positive feedback. Tune in to the bad news along with the good.

Food for champions

To appreciate error feedback is not to have a pessimistic view of life. Many outstanding leaders and managers encourage this kind of communication: it provides so much information necessary when things go wrong that it has been referred to as 'the food of champions'. On the other hand, there are famous examples of disasters resulting from leaders' refusal to tune in to negative feedback:

- the ANZAC campaign at Gallipoli
- the *Challenger* shuttle disaster
- the sinking of the *Titanic*

Think of some more — there are plenty to choose from.

Aiming accurately

You can make the most of feedback *only* if you know exactly what your message was intended to achieve. Different situations require different aims. There are broad ones, such as 'getting the work done on time', and specific ones: 'Get the $10 000 that Mearall Ltd owes us, before 3.30 pm this Friday'. A real estate agent might sum up his or her target in one sentence: 'Getting buyers and sellers to agree on a price'. A project leader would have more complex aims: 'Encouraging co-operation so that we get on with the job. Cutting down misunderstandings. Getting jobs done how and when they should be done'.

Four common aims

If you compare enough responses of this kind, however, you find four aims that apply in almost every case:

1. to achieve the desired result on time, how and where intended;
2. to exchange ideas and information freely and accurately;
3. to gain co-operation or reach agreement;
4. to establish or define the relationship between sender and receiver so that people know where they stand.

Each time a skilled communicator completes an exchange, he or she looks at the results. How successful was the exchange in terms of the four aims? Did the message hit its target? If not, how close was it? By encouraging and analysing feedback in this way you gain greater insight as to why each message succeeded or failed, and this is the starting point for developing many new and better ways of communicating, as you will discover in later chapters.

Encouraging feedback: the sender's part

- If you are talking, ask questions to see how much your listeners really understand.
- When writing, tell people how best to contact you if they have any questions.
- Encourage people to ask questions about your decisions.
- Do not assume understanding or agreement.

Don't use expressions such as 'You can't miss it'; they discourage feedback.
- Help others by making it easy for them to send feedback. If a standard reply is all you need, add a prepared reply slip.
- Show that you welcome feedback of any kind, whether good news, bad news, action or process.
- Visit every section, unit, branch or department under your responsibility regularly. Seek feedback from as many people as possible and from all levels — the control system known as MBWA (managing by walking around).

Encouraging feedback: the receiver's part

Do not wait to be asked for feedback — volunteer it.
- Tell the sender what you think you *do* understand as well as what you do not.
- Do not assume that your powers of communication are so well-tuned that you automatically understand others. Use feedback to make sure. Say, 'I think I understand, but could I go through that again and see if I have it right?'
- In face-to-face communication, do not allow a speaker to continue uninterrupted if you are in doubt about his or her meaning. Explain your confusion: ask a question.
- Phone the writer of a letter if its meaning is not clear and ask for extra information or clarification.

Follow-up feedback — keeping in touch

Keeping in touch is just another way of exchanging feedback, but the more of this kind you generate the better for your business. No matter what type of work you are connected with, you need to keep in touch with all who do business with you. In a retail firm you might make daily or weekly surveys of customers. If they are not ordering regularly, call to see if there is anything they need. If there is going to be a shortage, call your regular customers and suggest they stock up. In other cases, follow-up feedback may involve little more than an occasional phone call or a half-yearly visit. It still pays to keep in touch and to make sure that clients are happy with your products and your service. Follow-up contact should use two-way channels, rather than printed forms or brochures. Questionnaires are of some value but do not really meet the main aim, which is to maintain two-way contact (Peters & Waterman, *In Search of Excellence*).

Feedback and the two-way relationship

You have lunch with Kym so that you can compare ideas on a joint project. Kym listens attentively, questions you about your ideas, compliments you on the work you have put in so far. Kym is giving important non-verbal as well as verbal feedback, suggesting an unspoken bond of understanding and a positive relationship. You get the impression that Kym feels good about working with you. Feedback in relationships is like a game of tennis: the relationship is inclined to alter with each exchange. Each positive signal from the other person makes it easier to deal with problems; the very act of reaching solutions together reinforces the relationship. But as in tennis, one bad signal from either side can upset the balance and undermine the relationship.

Background signals in feedback

Apart from the main kinds of feedback, the background signals described briefly in Chapter 1 (and in more detail in Chapter 5) add to or modify the meaning of other feedback. These signals can be unintentional (for example, a blush or a frown), but can quickly influence people in situations such as job interviews or sales presentations. They may represent the only way you can find out what kind of signals *you* are sending. So learn to watch how others react when you communicate, and if necessary, change your style.

Consider this case: Last week you were introduced to Ginni, a new staff member, but had very little time to talk to her before you were called away to an urgent phone call. On Sunday you are at the beach with friends when Ginni comes up and says 'Hello'. Unfortunately you cannot remember her name, so you just say 'Hello, and how are you today?' and hope that as you talk her name will come to you. So far all your spoken feedback has expressed liking and genuine interest, but your non-verbal feedback is less positive. All Ginni knows is that at work you rushed off after meeting her and today you omitted her name when you said 'Hello'. As well, you have made no move to introduce her to your friends (because you are trying to think of her name).

Moreover, the discomfort you feel about forgetting Ginni's name is revealed in your body language. Not knowing the reasons for all these signals, poor Ginni assumes that you dislike something about her. She becomes more reserved and finally walks away, convinced that she is at fault. You will be correct in treating Ginni's walking away from you as negative feedback, but unless you are aware of her reasons, you can easily misinterpret her action as a sign that she does not like you. Next time you see her you will be more reserved, and she may respond by withdrawing further. However there is an immediate way to solve the problem:

Verbalise the non-verbal (open communication).

When non-verbal feedback gets out of control like this, switch to verbal feedback. Tell Ginni you can't remember her name, and explain how you feel about forgetting. This cancels out most of the misunderstanding and provides each of you with a chance to talk about improving communication (see 'Open and assertive communication', in Chapter 12).

False feedback

Not all feedback is an accurate representation of events or feelings. Some people will try to use it to distort your vision of what is really going on. One obvious reason for doing this is to get the sender out of trouble — as in the classic, 'Don't worry — I posted your cheque today'. However, there are reasons apart from intentional dishonesty for giving false feedback:

■ to avoid blame — a team member might mislead management about his or her part in a problem: 'Even if I *had* sent the samples, Jo still wouldn't have closed the deal';

■ to keep people at a distance — a supervisor might give cold negative feedback to avoid being caught up in a situation at work in which feelings are involved;

■ to avoid unpleasant reality — in the face of an impending takeover, members of a work group might say to each other, 'The change will not affect jobs in our section';

■ to 'play down' a problem so as to lessen others' concern — health officials might tell media representatives that there is 'absolutely no danger' of an epidemic occurring, when they are really not so sure.

Be wary of exaggerated feedback. If someone is trying to get you to share the blame for his or her mistake, that person may give you false feedback. To deal with feedback that is overly critical or loads all the blame on you (or anyone else), try some of the assertive techniques explained in Chapter 12.

Third-party feedback

Think of a time recently when a third party (call this person 'C') gave you negative feedback — for example: 'Ginni was really hurt at the way you treated her at the beach'. Where did 'C' get this information? Third-party feedback is usually inaccurate, and the longer the communication chain ('C' heard it from 'D', who overheard Ginni talking to 'E') the less reliable the content. If it's important, always check the message and, if possible, contact the original sender.

Summary

1. Any response to a message is 'feedback'.
2. Feedback can be (a) verbal or non-verbal, (b) positive or negative, (c) process or action.
3. One kind of negative feedback, error feedback, is especially important. Like a missile-guidance system, it tells you whether your messages are 'on target' and, if not, how to set them right.
4. Encourage error messages in order to find out exactly when and where problems are occurring.
5. Action (GASFY) feedback indicates how well a message is working to achieve its goal.
6. Process feedback gives knowledge of the communication process and advice on how to improve it.
7. Most communication includes some feedback concerning the sender—receiver relationship.
8. If non-verbal feedback is causing relationship problems, 'verbalise it'.

9. Use follow-up feedback to keep business relationships active.
10. Don't assume that all feedback is accurate. Some people use it to mislead you.
11. Be careful of third-party feedback. Check the source.

Exercises

1. Give examples of positive feedback.
2. Give examples of error feedback.
3. Give examples non-verbal feedback.
4. Give an example of negative non-verbal feedback.
5. If you found a television commercial particularly offensive or annoying, how would you give feedback to (a) the sponsor and (b) the station management?
6. Why might people give positive feedback even if it were not accurate?
7. How does a live theatre audience send feedback messages back to the actors? Is this verbal or non-verbal? Is it process or action?
8. How could you, as a reader, give feedback to the authors of this book?
9. Give an example of action feedback you have received recently.
10. What would you do to increase the flow of feedback where you work? What could you do to improve the feedback process at home?
11. Do you agree that 'The difference between a boss and a leader is largely a matter of how each deals with error feedback'? How would you react to a person who had difficulty accepting error feedback?
12. Compare communication feedback with the thermostat feedback system in a refrigerator. When the temperature in the fridge gets too high the thermostat sends a message to the motor, which starts the cooling system. When the fridge returns to the right temperature, the thermostat sends another message which switches the motor off. Which message is negative feedback? Which is positive?
13. Describe a situation in which the verbal does not match the non-verbal feedback. In your example, which form would you be more inclined to believe?

14. Discuss a recent experience you had with 'third-party' feedback. How accurate was the content? If it was faulty, where did the breakdown arise?

15. List some famous disasters that might have been avoided if people had been more prepared to listen to error feedback.

16. Describe any similar experiences you have had personally — or at work — when useful feedback has been rejected.

Case study 1: Keybooks Ltd

For the past five years Lee Kenny has conducted a very successful student bookshop at the Greenview Community College. Lee has had an excellent working relationship with students, staff and administration. Book prices have always been discounted to help students and Lee has a reputation for helping staff obtain 'hard to get' texts from overseas. Lee was always included in staff social gatherings and regarded the principal and many of the teachers as personal friends.

Some ten months ago Lee decided to open a second bookshop at nearby Greysides College and arranged for a close friend, Gil Cairns, to take over the Greenview College shop. Every few weeks Lee phoned the Greenview principal to find out how things were going under Gil's control; each time the principal assured Lee that there was nothing to worry about and there had been no reports of any problems. Book sales were down at the end of the first semester, but Gil said this was offset by the higher prices charged, so profits remained the same. Lee received a couple of phone calls from students who claimed that they failed an exam because their textbooks didn't arrive until the end of the semester, but she explained that the delay was the printer's fault, not Keybooks; and couldn't be helped.

However, when the time came this year for Keybooks to renew its contract with Greenview College, Lee was told somewhat bluntly by the administrator that a new contract had already been signed with an opposition firm. When Lee asked why, the administrator said it was policy to change booksellers every five years. (Lee knew this did not happen at other colleges.) Lee's enquiries among students and staff soon pointed to a more likely reason: Gil Cairns did not stick to definite opening times, many classes had not received books until halfway through the semester, and a number of staff had waited months for texts ordered through Keybooks. Gil had also reacted in an unpleasant manner when teachers asked about these delays.

1. Identify some of the different kinds of positive feedback received by Lee. Were any of these non-verbal? How accurate was the positive feedback?

2. At what stage did Lee start receiving error messages?

3. What other kinds of feedback did Lee receive?

4. What might Lee have done to help maintain Keybooks' position at Greenview?

Case study 2: Off to the doctor

Maureen walks into Maria's office and asks in an agitated voice if she can have the afternoon off to go to the doctor. Maria doesn't even look up from the desk, and continues reading the report in front of her. After a long silence, Maria mutters, 'OK, take the afternoon off if you have to', still without looking directly at Maureen.

1. What kind of verbal feedback did Maureen receive?

2. What kind of non-verbal feedback did Maureen receive?

3. Which feedback told Maureen most about the relationship between them?

4. If you were Maureen, what would you have done or said in response to Maria's answer?

CHAPTER 4

Understanding — what do you mean?

Understanding is reached if an idea is interpreted by the receiver as it was conceived by the sender. Chapter 1 explained how an idea is first converted into a message, then transmitted. This chapter looks at the process in more detail, particularly what happens at the receiver's end before real 'understanding' is achieved.

A receiver's hopes, wishes, expectations, past memories, current thoughts and emotions all affect and modify the meaning that develops in that person's mind, as does the need to 'make sense' of the message, to get it to 'fit' his or her way of looking at the world. Yet with care, you can still exchange ideas with accuracy and understanding.

Topics

Coding the message

Decoding

Dealing with misunderstandings

Standard and non-standard meanings

Developing your vocabulary

Language — a set of codes

Background signals

Coding the message

Coding an idea converts it into a transportable form. Ideas exist only in the mind: what is actually transmitted and received — seen, heard or felt — is not the idea but a code — a word or a non-verbal symbol.

In coding and sending a message:
- the sender starts with an *idea*;
- the *code* takes the place of the sender's *idea*;
- the *message* (made up of *codes*) is transmitted.

Codes

Any image, sound, sign, symbol or pointer can be used as a code, as long as
- it can be transmitted in place of the idea it represents;
- it can be picked up by one or more of the senses.

Once the idea has been coded, it can move outside the mind. It can travel round the world or into space; it can reach out to touch another human being. Usually a number of different codes or symbols are transmitted together; the combined package, as explained in Chapter 1, is the message.

Use accurate codes

What happens if a sender uses codes that are not clear enough or do not match the original idea? For instance, if a test question states 'You may, if you wish, use the diagram on page 93 of your textbook to help illustrate your answer', you could guess that the lecturer's idea was probably 'If you can remember the diagram on page 93 of your textbook, and draw it as part of your answer, you will gain a higher mark'. But what if a student 'wished' to open the textbook during the test and 'use the diagram on page 93' in the honest belief that this was what the words meant? Inaccurate coding is not the only cause of misunderstandings, but it is a common one, because it makes decoding more difficult.

Decoding the message

Decoding

Decoding is the process by which the receiver converts the coded message back into an idea. This can require one, two or more steps before understanding is achieved.

Primary decoding (receiving the idea)

If the codes used are clear and can have only one meaning, the idea formed in the receiver's mind can be very similar to the one that the sender wanted to share.

In receiving and primary decoding:

- the receiver gets the *message* (made up of *codes*);
- the *code* is compared with *meanings* in the receiver's mind;
- the receiver chooses a meaning that appears to fit the sender's *code*.

For instance, two police officers switch on a flashing blue light on the roof of their vehicle. You receive the message (see the light) and decode it by searching your memory for possible meanings to fit 'flashing blue light on roof of vehicle'. Your past memories of flashing blue lights suggest that there is only one that makes sense — namely, 'it's the police'. That's how primary decoding works. Understanding was quite easy in this case because there were no alternative meanings to worry about.

Secondary decoding (developing the meaning)

If there are several meanings that could apply to one message, secondary decoding helps you choose the one that 'fits' best. It also helps, by adding further meaning to the basic message, to interpret the initial idea. Your final 'meaning' for 'it's the police' will depend on where you are and what you are doing when you see the blue light; for example, you may be driving at well over the legal speed limit or you may be alone in a dark lane and about to be attacked by someone with a knife. In primary decoding, someone speeding, someone being threatened in an alley and a shady character with a knife *all* interpret a flashing blue light as 'it's the police', but the final meaning, after secondary decoding, will vary for each receiver ('I'm going to get a ticket for speeding', 'Thank goodness they're here', or 'I wish they weren't here'.)

Nobody can see or hear an idea, so whatever is coded, transmitted and decoded is likely to be altered in some way during the exchange. Words, symbols, signs and flashing lights can point to meanings, but none has a fixed meaning of its own. Notice how the final meaning in the example above depended on factors known to the receivers but perhaps unknown to the senders. This is what makes understanding such a complex business; any of the factors above, or all of them, can affect the receiver's reference system.

Dealing with misunderstandings

If there is a misunderstanding, analyse it; find out how it happened. Instead of treating the result as 'bad' or 'wrong', take steps to diagnose the cause.

1. Treat a misunderstanding as an everyday hazard rather than something to get angry about.
2. Don't blame others (or feel guilty yourself). Feeling bad doesn't make you or the other person any easier to understand, but it can freeze up further communication and block feedback.
3. Ask questions, exchange feedback and look for non-verbal clues that may help to explain the cause of the problem.
4. Identify the particular factors that influenced the decoding process. Some at least of the following may be connected with the misunderstanding:
   - the time and place (the context) at which the message was exchanged, as in the blue-light example above;
   - non-verbal background signals and other 'clues' observed by the receiver (reading between the lines);
   - thoughts already present in the receiver's mind, and memories of recent events — if these relate to the current message they increase understanding, but otherwise can cause confusion;
   - the receiver's need to make sense out of the message by 'filling in the gaps' — also called the 'oil painting' factor (explained below);
   - different styles of thinking, of the kind described in Chapter 6;
   - differences in motivation (needs and goals), emotions, education, family background, beliefs and attitudes (see Chapter 5);
   - expected outcomes — what people *expect* to happen *because* a message is received also affects their interpretation of its meaning.

The receiver's reference system (mental encyclopaedia)

All or any of these factors form part of the receiver's reference system, which is like a mental encyclopaedia in which messages can be checked for clarification. The trouble is that no two encyclopaedias are ever the same! So the kind of 'understanding' a receiver builds up by referring to his or her mental encyclopaedia is not always accurate. If, however, a message *appears* to make sense, a person assumes it has been understood — an assumption made stronger by the desire to understand and because any clear picture is preferable to being left in doubt. Two specific causes of misunderstanding arising from the variations in reference systems are the supplementary decoding processes known as 'filling in the gaps' and the 'oil-painting factor'.

Filling in the gaps

Decoding can stop once the receiver is sure the message is understood, and the more care the sender uses (choosing accurate codes, adding helpful detail) the sooner the picture becomes clear. The process can be compared to that of two people working at different times on a jigsaw puzzle. The more parts of the picture (the message) that A (the sender) has filled in, the easier it is for B (the receiver) to fit in the remaining pieces and complete the scene.

If first attempts at decoding do not produce a clear meaning, receivers don't give up and settle for a vague impression. Nobody likes being in doubt. Like the people working on the jigsaw, a receiver experiments, trying bits and pieces in different slots to see if they fit. Sometimes this works, but sometimes pieces of the jigsaw seem to fit in places where they don't really belong; it's the same with understanding.

The following example illustrates how, unless handled carefully, filling in the gaps at the end of the secondary decoding stage often increases misunderstanding.

'I need a drink'

You and Jo are on a bush walk together. It's a hard walk and you are feeling tired, but you try not to show it since Jo does not appear to be at all tired. It's only five minutes since you last stopped for a rest and a drink of water, and you want to stop again.

As casually as you can, you comment, 'I feel like a drink', meaning you want to stop *now* for a rest and a drink from your water bottle. You expect that Jo may prefer to keep going and have a drink at the kiosk at the end of the track, about 15 minutes away, and you assume that if so, her reply will make this clear.

Meanwhile, although you do not know it, Jo is thinking about drinks too, but her thoughts are focused on the cold drinks at the kiosk.

Primary decoding

Initially, Jo decodes the words 'I feel like a drink' and decides on a basic meaning that matches the phrase.

Secondary decoding

Jo considers the situation and checks your non-verbal communication (body language and background signals) for clues to confirm the meaning forming in her mind. If these indicated tiredness, Jo would tune in to them and realise you meant 'I feel like a drink *now*'.

Because you are hiding your exhaustion, Jo gets the wrong signals and assumes that you mean a drink at the kiosk, 15 minutes away.

Jo fills in the gaps

Any of the factors listed on page 28 can either clarify or confuse Jo's understanding. In this case the thoughts in the forefront of her mind at the time you speak can cause difficulties. She was already thinking about the cold drinks in the shop at the end of the track, and these thoughts will appear to be connected with your meaning. (Ideas already present in a person's mind don't go away just because you start to talk.) It's only five minutes since you last stopped for a rest and a drink. The memory of that recent event is still vivid, which (for Jo) adds logic to her reasoning that you too are thinking about something other than another drink from your water bottle.

Both recent memories and pre-conversation thoughts have the power to block or divert the meaning of a message. In this case, both help to convince Jo that you are thinking about the same idea as she is.

The 'oil-painting factor'

People not only fill in the gaps to make meanings clearer, they also tend to choose whatever meanings are most pleasing. They 'hear' what they would like to hear. They fill in the gaps not only with what makes most sense for *them*, but also with whatever most appeals to *them*. They 'improve' on your original message. If there is any room for doubt, Jo's idea of a cold drink at the kiosk will be more likely to jump into the 'gap' than your meaning which involves some warm water out of a flask.

The effect is the same as when looking at a rather vague picture, perhaps an oil painting. If you stand close to the painting you see a series of paint splotches, with no particular detail, so when you stand back you could expect the detail to be even less clear, since the splotches are further away. But what actually happens? Suddenly you see a 'clear picture'. That's because the image on the canvas is unclear enough to allow you to fill in the gaps for yourself. The missing parts of the picture you 'see' are filled in from *your* mental encyclopaedia. The outline of the picture is painted by the artist, but the detail depends on you. (Semitransparent clothing — or a veil — has the same effect; the lack of clear detail allows each individual to fill in the gaps in ways that appeal most.

Avoiding the oil-painting factor

The oil-painting factor is not limited to vision; *any* unclear message — spoken, written or non-verbal — that leaves room for people to fill in gaps is at risk, because it allows people to decode its meaning in whatever way appeals most.

- Don't leave gaps for others to fill in *your* messages — clear, accurate words, symbols and non-verbal signals all help to avoid the oil-painting factor.
- Exchange feedback — the less cause there is for others to fill in gaps the less chance there is of misunderstanding. If Jo is unsure of what you mean, instead of filling in the gaps she could ask questions and share feedback. Two-way communication is the most practical and sensible way to find out what people really mean.

The trouble with words

John Casson, in *Using Words*, claims that the meaning of a word changes *every time* it is used by a different person and in different circumstances. Some of the main reasons for this are connected with coding and decoding problems, but there are other causes of misunderstanding.

Word meanings are in people's minds (not in dictionaries)

Few (if any) words have just one meaning; many English words have two, three or more, and the 500 most used words in English have between them some thousands of dictionary definitions. Dictionaries contain lists of *best known* or commonly used word meanings, but in everyday use what a word means to a person depends very little on the meaning given in a dictionary. Using a dictionary will enlarge your vocabulary, but will not necessarily improve the accuracy of your own messages or your understanding of other people's.

Words leave gaps in understanding

Jackie writes to you, saying 'We have a new dog'. What she is thinking about is a brown Labrador whose name is Bobby, but to convey her thoughts (her idea) she used the code word, 'dog'. This saves time and effort for Jackie, but makes decoding harder for you. The written symbols 'd-o-g' certainly don't bear any resemblance to Jackie's idea, 'Bobby, the brown Labrador', nor to any other four-legged animals known as dogs that you have known in the past.

If there is a misunderstanding in this case, one reason will be the way you fill in the gaps in the message. The word 'dog' by itself is like a map that shows you some features of a region but leaves out many others. Your reference system (vocabulary) helps fill in some of the gaps, but the oil-painting factor can create a final meaning derived largely from *your* memories of dogs, and the meaning that appeals most to you. If Jackie had included a photo of Bobby, understanding would be much easier.

Words are not real objects

The words you are reading now are only black shapes on a sheet of paper. They are not real objects. Some words obviously relate to a visible object, such as a book or a table, but what if a lecturer says 'You should exercise more responsibility'? You can't see 'responsibility', there are no photographs, measurements or specifications you can refer to. What you do, of course, is try to fill the gaps using your reference system. You remember having heard others using the word, but there are no clear images to help as there were for 'blue lights' and 'dogs'.

You'll have memories (some factual, some emotional) associated with the word 'responsibility', but are any of them the same as the lecturer's memories? The wider the gap between your memories and those of your lecturer, the more meaning *you*'ll have to supply.

Concrete and abstract words

Concrete words are easy to visualise; they represent clear ideas or objects — for example: table, Epson LQ800 printer, textbook, police siren. When you use concrete words combined with examples and illustrations, the images you transmit will be clear, specific and easy to understand. Abstract words such as responsibility lack this clarity; it's harder to work out the user's specific meaning. An 'abstraction pyramid' helps illustrate this (see Fig. 4.1). The single word 'managing' at the top of the ladder is abstract, general and non-specific. Meanings become clearer and words less abstract as you move down the ladder.

Abstract words can cause problems in understanding if used excessively (see 'Reducing the fog level', in Chapter 18) but need not if used in moderation, especially if you add descriptions such as the one at the foot of the ladder. True, you use more words, but if this makes your message clearer, it's worth it.

Standard and non-standard meanings

When you need to sort out word problems it helps to know the formal terms used to classify verbal meanings.

Defined meaning (denotation)

This refers to all the meanings — objects and the different ideas — represented by a verbal symbol. If you look up 'drink' in a dictionary you will find all its defined meanings (in current use), but the actual image produced in your mind will depend not so much on the word's defined meanings as on the context and circumstances of its use.

Literal meaning

A literal meaning applies when a word is used in a straightforward, unemotional, uncoloured way. For

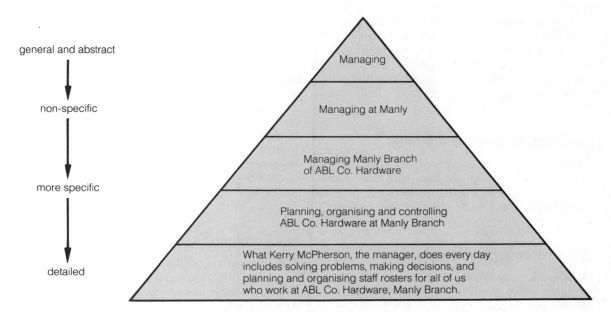

Fig. 4.1 *An abstraction pyramid*

example, 'Chris is a lecturer', literally means that Chris's job is to stand up in front of classes and give lectures. Words used literally are the most straightforward and therefore the easiest for people to understand.

Figurative (metaphorical) meaning

If you say 'Chris is a bit of a lecturer' because you want to indicate that Chris talks down to people in a formal way, allowing them little opportunity to respond, you are using the word 'lecturer' figuratively. Figurative meanings are usually also emotional, which suggests it is unwise to employ them when you are trying to present a logical, objective or unbiased case.

The other problem with figurative meanings is the confusion they cause to people learning English as a second language, because the metaphorical meanings seldom appear in a dictionary. Imagine the decoding problems for a recent migrant if you remark casually: 'They say the boss is a tight old bastard, but that's a load of rubbish. He's really been both father and mother to all of us'.

Emotional meaning (connotation)

Words create different meanings according to the feelings they convey. The word 'run' may produce quite different images and emotions for an athlete, a bank manager, a grazier or a computer programmer. Personal lifestyles and past memories about 'run' create a variety of interpretations and affect the final meaning the receiver attaches to the word.

Technical meaning and jargon

This can convey meaning very accurately *if* you belong to the group familiar with the terms. Otherwise it can be hard to understand or even 'meaningless' (see Chapter 19, 'Technical writing').

'Nice' meaning (euphemism)

Many speakers and writers feel nervous about using words that sound unpleasant, so they adopt alternative and usually unclear phrases that are supposed to sound more acceptable yet mean the same.

People are said to 'perspire' instead of 'sweat', to 'pass away' rather than 'die'. Garbage collectors become 'sanitation technicians'. Companies report on 'net income' or 'earnings' instead of 'profits'. A hire-purchase loan becomes a 'deferred-payment plan' and the insurance policy that will provide for your family if you die is 'life' insurance. Euphemisms do not help in communication, and can often make a message appear weak and ineffectual, especially if the words lack the precise meaning of the ones they replace.

Label words

In a similar way, labels such as 'computer problem', 'misunderstanding' or 'personality clash' are used to avoid issues or suggest they are not important when in fact they may be serious, involving bad programming, poor planning or ill temper. Words used in this way distract you from the real problem: concentrate on fixing the problems, not on the words.

Bias and prejudice

If you want to support someone you can use the words 'strong and determined'. An opponent may describe the same person as 'pig-headed and dictatorial'. Label words like these make it harder for others to judge for themselves the person described. They distort understanding, often causing people to react emotionally rather than logically.

If children grow up hearing derogatory labels used in reference to social groups — for instance, to migrants, Aborigines, Irish Catholics or New Zealanders — they will find it hard to establish a positive attitude towards members of these groups. If children of either sex spend their early years hearing people talk about business*men* and house*wives*, they will grow up with restricted views of their own career prospects and about 'men' and 'wives' in general.

Non-standard words

This description applies to words that, although commonly used, are regarded as slang or colloquialisms, or vary in meaning according to what part of Australia you live in. They may appear easy to understand, but the trouble is that being non-standard they often produce images of a very different kind, and also different emotional reactions, depending on who sends and who receives the words. This raises the question of who should decide what is 'standard' at any one time. Newspapers no longer adhere to standard English, but newsreaders on television and radio — particularly in the Australian Broadcasting Corporation — generally do. The Australian *Macquarie Dictionary* and its associated *Thesaurus* also provide up-to-date standard references.

Slang and colloquial terms

Non-standard words and slang are useful for attracting attention in advertising. 'Throw-away bargains at crazy prices — drop in today and get yours.' Some slang may be effective in notices and in casual conversation, but don't use it in business letters or reports. What attracts attention in a television commercial may spoil your chance of an interview if used in a job application. Slang meanings and usage also vary from one location to another, which adds to their unreliability.

Generic meanings

Over time, a word that once referred to a specific brand-name or product will come into general use as a label for all items of a similar kind. You blow your nose on a kleenex, taken an aspro for your cold, write with a biro and go for a drive in a utility. All these items were or are still brand-names, but they have taken on a general meaning.

Generic terms can cause confusion if used interstate or when talking to overseas visitors. Many are specific to Australia (even to one state), and most are really a form of slang, so use them with care. In Queensland and north-east New South Wales a suitcase is commonly called a 'port'; in the other states the term in this sense is almost unknown. In New Zealand you can go to a 'dairy' in the middle of town for a milkshake, but in Australia it's a milk bar. You'll sound more businesslike if you keep to standard words that convey the same meaning to everybody everywhere.

Positive and negative 'loadings'

Compare the terms 'half empty' and 'half full'. Whether you are talking about a box of chocolates or a fuel tank the proportion is the same, but the meaning is 'loaded' in a positive or negative way according to which phrase you use. Use positive words and attitudes when you deal with customers, employees and suppliers. Say that you would be 'happy to fill the order as soon as we know the colour required' rather than 'unfortunately we cannot fill the order because you neglected to advise the colour'. The second version may have the same 'dictionary' meaning; however, it carries far more negative loading than the first.

Developing your vocabulary

The list of standard verbal codes that you can use confidently (without having to refer to a dictionary or a textbook) comprises your vocabulary, an important unit in your mental encyclopaedia. A good communicator is constantly extending his or her vocabulary and one of the best ways to do this is to read widely and talk with as many different people as you can. Your vocabulary will develop faster if you keep both a dictionary and a thesaurus handy, either in book form or on an electronic memory system. There is, however, one point that needs to be stressed:

Longer words do not make a 'better' vocabulary.

Developing your vocabulary does *not* mean learning to use longer and more complex words, or learning five new dictionary meanings a day. Having a well-developed vocabulary means knowing the right words to use and when and where to use them. Unless a long word makes your message easier to understand, there is no justification for it. Short, simple words are vital for most business communication; however, longer words or specific technical terms used correctly can be more precise provided all users are familiar with them.

Spell-checkers and computer dictionaries

A *true* computerised dictionary is an asset, because you can check a word so quickly. However, what is called a dictionary disk (supplied as part of a word-processor package) is usually only a spelling-checker. Even this can be very useful (if you type your own words) because it keeps reminding you of your errors, but it has its limits. It tells you if you typed 'principol' instead of 'principal', but not if the word you should have used was 'principle'.

Using a thesaurus

A thesaurus is a useful and user-friendly publication. Rather than giving plain meanings it lists a variety of associated terms and phrases for a given word and leaves it to you to choose the one that suits you best. But use your thesaurus *only* to create clearer and more interesting sentences, not to find longer or more complex expressions.

You need no training to use a thesaurus; instructions are included in the book. Until a few years ago, the best known thesaurus was that edited by Peter Mark Roget, but the Australian publication (mentioned earlier) from Macquarie University is an excellent reference and very easy to use. It also gives opposite meanings. Computerised disk and compact disk versions are available.

Language — a set of codes

'Language' is the code word used to describe a collection of codes or symbols that have the following characteristics:

1. The codes used in a particular language have a common form (words, flashing lights, body movement).
2. The codes for a language are transmitted on a common channel (body language travels via body movement, writing via words recorded on paper or on a screen).
3. The codes that make up the language, though used by many different people, are regarded as having a common or similar meaning.

Verbal languages

The set of commonly used codes called 'English' (or Australian English) is a language that meets these guidelines. You might, however, consider how closely everyday Australian English meets the third condition ('similar meanings for every user').

Non-verbal languages

A collection of non-verbal codes can just as easily act as a language. You are familiar with the term 'body language'. Once you get used to the idea, it's just as easy to think of pictorial codes as 'picture language' and symbol codes as 'symbol language'. These three non-verbal languages match the types of non-verbal channels described in Chapter 2. Keep in mind that, as explained in that chapter:

- most messages are made up of a combination of verbal and non-verbal transmissions travelling together;
- if part of a message is sent in one code (words) and part in another (body language), the two must match, otherwise receivers become confused or distrust the message (and the sender);
- if more than one non-verbal language (say body movement and symbol) is transmitted in a message, then provided they agree in meaning they will give a more complete picture and make decoding more reliable.

Body language

This uses standard actions such as smiling, frowning, hitting and kissing, plus head, eye and hand movements and many more. All are part of the language as long as they imply the same or similar meanings to sender and receiver.

Picture language

Movies, photographs, building plans, holograms, paintings and diagrams are all included here. One advantage of this form of communication is the increased accuracy and understanding when it is used together with words.

Symbol language

There are so many different kinds of symbols they need to be divided into subgroups.

Status or power symbols
A judge's wig, a Rolls Royce and a manager's office suite each indicate something that the user wants to convey to you, something the user thinks indicates a special person, or a special authority. Status symbols are often used to mask reality: a small firm with little capital can rent a modern office with luxury

fittings. People surround themselves with symbols of this kind if they wish to impress or influence others.

Personal symbols
A wedding ring, jewellery, a particular style of clothing, very short or very long hair, a beard, a business suit, coat or tie — each transmits a symbolic message about the wearer. Either intentionally or unintentionally, symbols are used to make personal statements which may not be factual; as with power symbols, you can use them if you want to 'dress the part'.

Group or team symbols
A flag, a football jersey or a badge are symbols that help prove membership of (and loyalty to) a particular group. Trademarks (for instance, the Qantas flying kangaroo) or brand-names are used in the same way. If the group itself has special power or authority, a symbol such as a police cap or an army uniform makes this clear.

Control or action symbols
Flashing lights and sirens emphasise the action desired by the user. Their value lies in the speed and accuracy with which they can be understood in an emergency even by those who do not share the same verbal language.

Symbols work better than words for ideas that are hard to express, perhaps for conveying messages of trust, sympathy or friendship. A bunch of flowers, a card or a gift will carry this kind of message. If you are very busy and a colleague brings you a cup of coffee, that's a symbolic gesture of support and companionship.

Private or restricted languages
Not all languages and their associated codes have to be widely known. A special language can have meaning for small groups of people.
- Two people may share a private language made up of words, glances, gestures that hold meaning for them alone.
- A group such as a football team can have their own special language, a set of codes that have meaning only for them and only during a game.
- A computer-system operator may send a series

of flashing codes to warn users of the network that it is about to shut down.
- Technicians in any field develop their own special language. Often it is unintelligible to others, but in that group is generally more accurate and specific than ordinary words.

Background signals
Every time you communicate, in addition to the main message you transmit — even if unintentionally — background messages. As explained briefly in Chapter 1, these help people to 'read between the lines'. Background signals cannot move by themselves; they travel in conjunction with ordinary messages. While not really codes in their own right, and despite their vague background characteristic, they can have a powerful effect on decoding and the resulting level of understanding (or misunderstanding). For instance, suppose an associate comes towards you with hand outstretched, saying 'Glad you could join us'. The hand signals are deliberate and are intended to add meaning to the verbal greeting, but what if at the same time the associate is frowning? Though unintentional, the frown is a background clue about hidden feelings.

Background signals won't 'go away'
Background signals like these may not be accurate, but they are part of the total message and their effect on meanings and business relationships may be powerful enough to change the outcome of the message. They are a part of every act of communication. You cannot cross them out when you write because they are 'between the lines'. You cannot leave them out when you speak. So it is better to recognise them, be aware of them, and do what you can to manage them.

Relationships and background signals
One reason background signals are important is that they provide pointers to the nature of the relationship between sender and receiver. They have a profound effect in the area of business relationships. Consider this exchange:

Your supervisor, Glen, wants to talk to you about a suggestion you made recently for improving morale. Glen writes you a personal note suggesting a place where you can get together and talk. What meaning would you say Glen might be signalling (about the relationship) for each of the following possible locations?

- Glen's office;
- your normal working area;
- your lunch-room, in an informal meeting with others;
- a city restaurant, where you can talk alone;
- Glen's home, where you will have dinner and discuss the idea afterwards.

You can see just how much unspoken information about the relationship is contained in the background signal, which in this case is Glen's choice of a meeting place. 'Choice of location' is a common source of such signals. The verbal meaning of Glen's note can be altered completely according to the suggested location.

Background signals can be misinterpreted

The meaning transmitted via a suggested location will not be crystal clear, but it is significant and you will work hard to understand the clues it provides to the relationship. Sometimes, of course, people misread a background signal. This makes it all the more important for you to be conscious of the signals you receive, so that you can check the meaning you give them.

There can be a point, however, where a background signal exists only in your imagination. For instance, if the phone goes dead in the middle of an angry discussion you may feel sure that the other party has hung up, but the connection may have been broken by someone else. Unless you are certain, be careful about giving meaning to what may only *seem* to be a background signal.

Watch, too, for feedback from others which may indicate that *your* background signals are being misunderstood.

Sources of background signals

Choice of location

The places people choose to exchange messages can tell you much about the relationships involved.

Personal space

In moving towards each others, moving away, coming out from behind a desk to talk, sitting together or sitting on opposite sides of a table people convey significant meanings or information about their relationships.

Choice of timing

The time of day chosen for communication, the length of time spent in communicating, deliberate delays in responding — all these convey meaning about a relationship.

Frequency of communication

How regularly or how often messages are exchanged and any sudden change in the frequency or regularity are indicators of a change in relationship.

Choice of sequence

Whether someone chooses to interrupt you or waits for you to finish speaking shows how that person feels in relation to you, particularly in terms of power ratios.

Choice of channel

Do people choose to write to you instead of phoning? Would someone pay you a personal visit instead of writing a memo? You may have heard the expression, 'the medium [media or channel] *is* the message'. This is another way of saying that the choice of channel is so strong a signal that it outweighs the verbal message. Is this true or is it an exaggeration?

What background signals communicate

Power ratio between sender and receiver

Virtually every message contains some background clues to the ratio of power between sender and receiver. Most of these signs are low key and non-verbal, and most are transmitted only as background signals. Commonly any person in a relationship feels a lesser or greater proportion of power, and non-verbal signals will indicate the sender's position as he or she sees it. In most cases there is little or no verbal expression concerning degrees of power in a relationship; because power-ratio issues are usually 'undiscussable', the information is confined to background signals.

'Higher than you' signals

Long, relaxed pauses in speech; an expansive (strong, but casual) body stance; standing or sitting so one's eyes are higher than another person's; interrupting another person; organising someone else's timetable, furniture or personal papers; delaying reply or action wanted by someone; failing to share scarce resources or equipment — all these are 'higher than you' signals.

In writing, high power is signalled by the use of large areas of blank space, wide margins, blank lines between paragraphs and numbered headings to direct the reader.

'Lower than you' signals

Allowing interruptions, body leaning forward towards speaker, standing or sitting so one's eyes are lower than other person's, giving up scarce resources without expecting anything in return — these are 'lower than you' signals. In writing, pages are cramped, with narrow margins, and few (if any) strong headings.

'Both equal' signals

Two powerful figures — say two state premiers meeting together — may make a point of signalling 'high but equal power' by shaking hands and smiling. Two lovers may signal 'power is not an issue' by each making sacrifices for the other. More common examples include sharing food, sharing scarce resources (such as photocopy paper), sharing a difficult task, sitting or standing so one's eyes are level with others', co-operating and compromising to fit in with others, and helping others to solve their problems. In writing, the signal for equal power is the 'adult-to-adult' tone (see Chapter 6).

Positive or negative aspects of relationship

These are aspects of the communication relationship that many people are often reluctant to put into words. How are they communicated?

High level of trust (positive)

Sharing food, sharing results of research, sharing secrets and delegating responsibility are indications of this.

Low level of trust (negative)

Locking a door, avoiding questions and constantly checking on the work of other people are negative indications.

Empathy (positive)

This is expressed by showing care and concern, showing understanding for another's problems, extending help, perhaps by offering a cup of coffee as a sign of support at a difficult moment.

Level of interest or intensity in relationship

Avoiding contact and excluding people from gatherings imply negative feelings; positive interest is shown by regular contact, invitations to social gatherings, and shared meals.

High or low level of conflict in relationship

To support someone in a meeting is positive, whereas interrupting a person in a meeting, walking out of a meeting or hanging up in the middle of a phone conversation is negative.

Future of the relationship

Background signals can help you predict your chances of success in a business relationship. In negotiations, they tell you whether you are gaining, losing, or maintaining a steady position.

Background signals in written messages

The way a report or assignment is set out conveys background signals about
- the sender's level of interest in the receiver;
- power ratios between sender and receiver.

A document with a cover, contents page, open layout and illustrations suggests that the sender was thinking about the reader and wanted to make the message interesting and easy to follow. Leaving a lot of space on a report page signals confidence and strength on the writer's part, a significant power-ratio signal.

How would you see your relationship with a firm which sent you a routine computer print-out but disguised it in the hope of making it appear to be a personal letter? Would you trust and believe the contents? Or would you tune in to the stronger, non-verbal message — namely, that the firm deliberately chose a channel (the computer-based mailing system) to mislead its readers? Suppose another firm sends you the same letter, but it is handtyped on high-quality paper and ends with a handwritten signature. In this case the 'choice of channel' background signal helps assure you that both writer and message are worth tuning in to.

Convert background signals to verbal ones

Converting background signals into ordinary verbal messages helps to avoid incorrect decoding. However, it also offers a tactical lead to the person who makes the transfer *first*. For instance, Fred is sending you a lot of 'parent' messages which include background signals that he sees himself as more powerful than you. What if you respond verbally with the comment: 'You know, Fred, when you talk that way you sound like a cross old father talking to a naughty kid'? That's strong feedback, but it means that the power-ratio issue is no longer 'background' — it's now right out in the open. In this way you can better deal with problems arising from the kind of issue (such as power ratio) that causes real trouble if it remains 'undiscussable'. The fact that *you* raised the matter to the verbal level gives you a distinct advantage. This process is known as open communication, and is explained in Chapter 12.

Individual differences

In later chapters you'll learn of wide differences in the way that any two people think, remember, and make decisions. You have seen in this chapter that while it's natural for each individual to code and decode in different ways, it is equally natural that the outcome will be a loss of understanding. However, if you know about these differences you can code messages that match the other person's way of thinking *as well as* your own. Once you can do this, you will have achieved a major step towards greater understanding. When it comes to decoding, you'll naturally find the same skills working in your favour there as well.

Summary

1. Coding an idea converts it into a transportable form. What is transmitted and received is not the 'idea', but code — a verbal or non-verbal symbol.

2. Decoding is the process by which the receiver converts the message back into an idea. This can involve several steps before understanding is achieved.

3. Meanings are in people's minds. You cannot see or hear an 'idea', so by the time it has been coded, transmitted and decoded its meaning is likely to become changed in some way.

4. Each person has a unique reference system that works like a mental encyclopaedia, where messages can be checked for possible meanings.

5. Two causes of misunderstanding are the supplementary decoding processes known as 'filling in the gaps' and the oil-painting factor.

6. When meanings are not clear, a person's needs, experience, expectations and emotions influence the way the gaps in meaning are filled. People tend to 'hear' what they would like to hear.

7. Words are not tangible objects, but some are known as 'concrete' because they represent ideas or objects easily visualised.

8. Abstract words are broad, non-specific and harder to visualise, but are useful when you wish to generalise.

9. The defined meaning (denotation) of a word refers to all the meanings — the objects and ideas — represented by it.

10. Other kinds of word meanings are figurative (metaphorical), emotional (connotations), generic, 'nice' (euphemisms), slang, and colloquial.

11. There are both verbal and non-verbal languages. English is a verbal language.

12. If more than one non-verbal language (such as body movement and symbols) is transmitted together with words, decoding is more reliable and creates clearer understanding (provided all carry the same meaning).

13. Background signals (those 'between the lines') communicate information concerning the power ratio between sender and receiver, the positive or negative aspects of a relationship and the future of a relationship. Background signals cannot be 'written out'; they are part of every communication, travelling alongside the main message.

14. Verbalising background signals has a significant effect. The person who can do this openly enjoys a major advantage in communication.

Exercises

1. What different meanings might *you* attach to the sight of a flashing blue light? What meanings might others attach to this message?

2. What examples can you give of codes, symbols or words (for instance, laser or cassette recorder) that did not exist fifty years ago but are in common use today?

3. List some codes, symbols or words whose meanings have altered over the last fifty years. (Examples: grass, tape, blue, satellite.)

4. What are some special codes (symbols, words or signals) that you use at work or with your friends or family but that are not part of any standard language and would not be recognised by other users of the English language?

5. Here are some 'word labels' used to describe problem situations: personality clash, communication gap, age barrier, male chauvinist, unionist, government interference, rural conservatism. (Add more examples of your own.)
   What do you think each phrase is describing? (Check with one or two other people to see if they agree.)

6. Here are some figurative words: bird, fruitcake, garbage, foxy, mongrel, smooth. Think of some more.

7. Suggest some examples of generic words.

8. Words that should be avoided in business writing because they carry strong negative loadings include unfortunately, neglected, unsatisfactory, mistake. Suggest some more.

Case study: The sad story of Tom and Mary, Dick and Harry ... and Grudge!

There were once two islands, which for simplicity were called A and B. The map below will give you an idea of their size and shape.

Originally people travelled freely from A to B and back again, either by rowing across in boats or by walking over a narrow suspension bridge strung across a chasm that separated the islands in the north. However, a few years ago a bold young entrepreneur named Harry set up a ferry service between A and B. Harry's ferry was fast, efficient and cheap, and since he only charged 5 cents a time, people soon stopped rowing altogether and took the ferry instead.

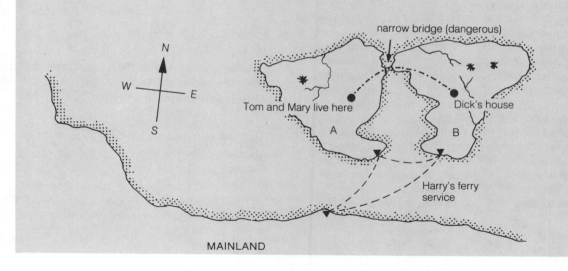

narrow bridge (dangerous)

N
W — E
S

Tom and Mary live here

Dick's house

A   B

Harry's ferry service

MAINLAND

Their own boats either became leaky through lack of maintenance or were sold, so that after a while the only means of crossing from A to B were Harry's ferry and the narrow suspension bridge. Harry, with an eye to increasing his profits, secretly employed a mentally unstable character named Grudge to spend his time scaring people who tried to use the bridge. Grudge enjoyed his work and gradually became more and more aggressive until eventually the bridge was used only in emergencies, and it too fell into disrepair.

At this point Harry, ever conscious of profit margins, increased the cost of a single ferry trip to 50 cents, which he said was necessary because of increasing fuel prices, and whereas in the past he had allowed credit, he now introduced a strict 'no credit' policy and placed a large sign at each terminal telling people that they could only use the ferry if they paid for a ticket in advance.

Now, on the island of A lived Tom and Mary, and a happier and more devoted pair you could not imagine — as far as their public appearances went. Under the surface, however, their lives were not quite so idyllic. Mary complained to Tom that he never talked to her when they were alone. Tom replied that Mary was not worth talking to, and a terrible fight ensued. After that they stopped talking to each other altogether and Tom started going off on visits to the mainland, often for days at a time, where (or so he felt) he was able to find consolation with someone who really was worth talking to.

Mary was bitter at first, but then decided that she could easily play the same game as Tom, provided no one found out about it. So whenever Tom went away, she too left the house on A and secretly went to visit a friend named Dick who lived in a secluded and very romantic hideaway on Island B. Mary, however, always made a point of getting home again before Tom, so that he had no way of knowing that she was visiting Dick. Dick, who was something of a male chauvinist, was more than happy with the arrangement. He listened to Mary's problems and he contributed in whatever ways he could, filling the gaps in her life that had arisen as a result of her fight with Tom.

The one thing Dick would not do, 'on principle', was to give Mary any money, since he said this would cheapen their relationship. Mary, on the other hand, felt that Dick should at least meet the cost of her travelling from A to B and back again, and to force the issue one morning she deliberately left home without the 50 cents for her return fare. She knew Tom would be back that night, so after an enjoyable lunch with Dick she asked him ever so sweetly for 50 cents for her return trip.

Dick refused to give her the 50 cents and Mary retaliated by calling him a lot of names. She then tried pleading with him, explaining that she had to get home before Tom arrived so he wouldn't find out about her visits to Dick. Dick still refused to give her the 50 cents and finally threw her out of his house, telling her to borrow the money from Harry, the ferry operator. Harry refused. He said it was just a matter of policy, but actually he had found out about Mary's visits to Dick and thought that if she were desperate enough he might be in a position to benefit in other ways.

However, Mary decided to take the other alternative — the rickety old suspension bridge at the northern end of the island. She calculated that if she hurried, she could get home just in time via the bridge. She ran all the way to the bridge and was halfway across before Grudge, the mentally unstable 'minder', saw her. Furious that someone had almost escaped his notice, Grudge started to shake the bridge harder and harder. Suddenly one of the old ropes snapped, and Mary fell into the sea. Grudge made no attempt to save her and she drowned.

THE END

Now that you have read the story, discuss the following questions.

1. Who, do you think was the person most responsible for Mary's death?

2. Who came next in responsibility?

3. Who was least responsible?

4. What are your reasons for these judgments?

5. What words in the story had the strongest influence on your decision?

6. What non-verbal messages in the story had the most influence?

CHAPTER 5

Tuning in to the other person

Tuning in begins at the point where you realise that the world as others see it not only looks different but actually *is* different from the world you see. Whenever you 'sit in the receiver's chair', 'walk a mile in someone else's shoes' or 'put yourself in another's position', you are developing your ability to tune in to others. Your success as a communicator will grow as you learn more about this special skill — as you develop 'empathy'.

This chapter explains how to develop this ability to tune in to others and how to assess the differences that separate you and understand the reasons for them.

Topics

The value of empathy

Needs, interests and goals

Attitudes and beliefs

Self-image and other images

Gaps and blanks

Two-way empathy — excellence in communication

The value of empathy

Tuning in to people adds to your ability to understand them and their messages. It helps you to

- understand what another person is really trying to say;
- forecast when and why misunderstandings can arise;
- avoid using a communication style that might cause disagreement;
- develop co-operation and agreement;

- work out in advance what will attract a receiver's interest.

Using empathy requires extra effort. You might ask, 'Why should I do all the work?', 'Why do I have to see things from *their* point of view? They should know what *I* mean'. The reason is that empathy helps people to agree with *you*. The harder you work at empathising, the greater the chance of agreement, which in turn makes it more likely others will do what you want done: finish your job on time, deliver the goods (the ones you want delivered), or fix problems when and how you want them fixed.

'Ought' and 'should' — unhelpful words

The more you tune in to other people the more easily you will avoid the problems that haunt those who think that everyone ought to see the world as they do. In communication it is a serious mistake to rely on the other person to get it right, and a mistake you often end up paying for. Two of the least helpful words in the communication world are 'ought' and 'should'. If you expect people to understand you without your having to use empathy, if you say that they 'ought' to have told you they did not understand or they 'should' have known what you meant, much of your communication will be marred by misunderstanding.

Empathy is not sympathy

Tuning in to and recognising another's position does not necessarily involve agreeing with that person. Don't confuse empathy with 'sympathy' (which means sharing the *same* feelings).

Kem (who has just beaten you for a promotion you were hoping for) may be full of pleasure at winning the position. But if she offers you a friendly

41

hand and says she understands your feelings, Kem is expressing empathy, not sympathy.

Needs, interests and goals

If you are familiar with the hierarchy of needs described by Abraham Maslow (see Fig. 5.1), you will be aware that as people's needs change, so they tend to change their level of interest in any particular activity. This affects every aspect of their communication, particularly message priorities. The topics they were keen to talk about last week have no interest now. They may ignore instructions about extra workloads but tune in to rumours about pay rises. They may forget completely what you tell them, yet remember every detail of a conversation

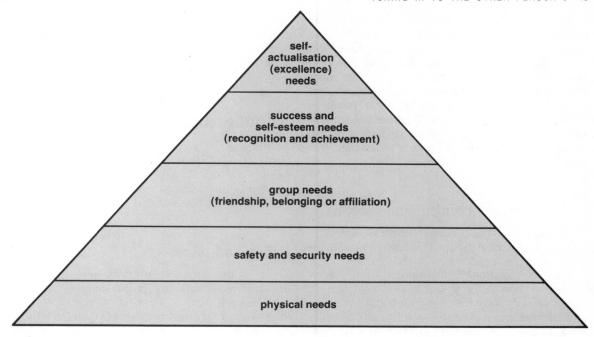

Fig. 5.1 *Maslow's hierarchy of needs*

with someone else. It all depends where they are positioned on their 'ladder' of needs. Tuning in to people helps you to work out what needs or goals will get top priority when you want to talk to them (or when they read your letters or reports).

Maslow's 'ladder' of needs may be neither complete nor accurate, but it helps you to identify others' communication priorities and to understand why it is hard to get and to hold people's attention unless they feel your message will help them to meet at least one of their current needs.

Physical comfort, safety and other basic needs

When you are hungry, messages about food will take priority. When you are cold or tired or frightened or in physical danger, messages about safety or protection come first. Provided that these issues are not a problem where you work or study, your priorities there will focus on other needs, but if the air conditioning breaks down or there is a bomb scare, messages of most interest will once again be those about physical comfort and safety.

Emotional security

People also need to have somewhere comfortable to live, be in good health, have a secure income, and be relatively free of serious worries or stress. Otherwise much of their time and energy will be focused on these needs until such time as they have been met or partly met.

The need to belong or to be part of a group

The need for friendship and a feeling of belonging, called the 'group need', is next on the priority list and usually remains dominant until it is satisfied. It can assume a most important place in communication at work and greatly influence your activities and the topics you like to talk about. Once this need is satisfied (you have a number of close friends, or you join a club), you will soon give priority to other goals.

Recognition

Being accepted as part of a group is good. Being recognised by the group as a popular or useful member is even better: withdrawal of such recognition is therefore a serious threat. The need to 'conform' (do what the group wants you to do) stands high on the list of communication priorities. It is very hard to communicate with someone about going against group standards (such as union rules) *unless* he or she can be sure that the result of defection from one group will ensure recognition from (and perhaps membership of) a more attractive group — for example, promotion to management level!

Self-esteem, achievement and success

good opinion of oneself

Messages that strengthen self-esteem are most important. One way of getting this kind of message is of course to be a success.

People communicate a great deal about success — how to get it and how to hold onto it; therefore, if a person has a need for both recognition and success and if what you want to talk about is going to help that person to meet these needs, you can be almost certain you will gain attention. Here is an example.

If you approach someone who is watching the news on television, he or she may not even realise you are speaking. It is no use just wanting the person to tune in to you. Suppose you are asking for help with a report you have to finish immediately, but the television is running a story on cuts in income tax. To encourage the person watching to tune in to you, you need to show that what you want to talk about has a direct bearing on his or her chances of future success, and one that offers more appeal than anything on television (see Chapter 13, 'The power of persuasion').

The need for excellence — self-actualisation

At the highest level of needs, after all other needs have been satisfied, people communicate less about material success and more about knowledge, justice and helping others rather than themselves. People at this level of motivation display a special interest in excellence, whether in art, architecture, styles of management, communication or cooking. The result is the form of individual behaviour that Maslow calls 'self-actualisation'. Such people have

little interest in needs such as belonging or recognition; to open up communication with them, one would talk about excellence (or similar themes) in areas of particular interest to them.

Attitudes and beliefs

Attitudes affect a person's understanding and interpretation of meaning, and influence the credibility given to a message. This in turn determines which incoming messages are selected as important, which ones are believed and which are rejected.

Beliefs and values

Some of the strongest attitudes people hold — drawn from personal beliefs and values — concern moral issues; what is 'right' or 'wrong', 'good' or 'bad'. Values vary from person to person but tend to be constant within the individual. They are seldom expressed in words, but may be indicated in messages about attitudes, and by how strongly a person communicates on value-related topics. If a firm's sales representative believes on Monday morning that the company is fair and cares about people, you can expect that he or she will still believe it on Friday. If an auditor had fixed views about the importance of honesty and accuracy when checking your books last year, you can expect to see the same values next year and probably thereafter. People's spiritual beliefs are also based on deeply held values, so faith tends to be a strong influence in this area.

Attitudes

Your attitude towards particular groups is another visible expression of your deeper beliefs and values. If you have a positive attitude to the police force, reflecting your personal values and your consequent respect for law and order, this will show in the favourable way you talk about the police, even if those around you express a different view. You *can* change your attitudes if you really want to, but you'll resist if others try to make you change.

Never underestimate the value of positive thinking and the power of positive attitudes. A person with a negative outlook on life will be influenced by it in most aspects of communication (and relationships) with others. A male colleague may not openly express his negative attitude towards women in positions of responsibility, but it will be conveyed by his non-verbal actions. Tuning in to such a person is harder if his negativeness makes you angry. Use empathy. Show that you can tune in to him even though you do not accept his views, then stress your own positive attitudes on the issue. In time you may get through. Both positive and negative attitudes are contagious.

Personal and family or ethnic backgrounds also have a profound effect on the individual. Lifestyle plays a very significant part in the shaping of beliefs and attitudes.

Projected image	Self-image
How people want to appear to others or think they should appear to others	How people see themselves— often they will try to keep this view hidden from others
External image	Unknown to others and unknown to individual
How people appear in the eyes of others (not always an accurate picture)	Hidden potential or abilities, undiscovered talents or faults

Fig. 5.2 *Different perceptions of a person (adapted from the Johari model)*

Opinions

Empathy helps you to determine whether people are just expressing opinions or indicating much stronger beliefs or attitudes, and knowing that it is very difficult to change deeper beliefs and attitudes can save you many wasted hours of argument. On the other hand if an individual is simply expressing an opinion, it's worthwhile sharing your point of view too.

Self-images and other images

People often think that others see them as different from their own view of themselves. It takes extra empathy to deal with the discrepancies between

- the way people see themselves (self-image);
- the way people want others to see them (projected image);
- the way people actually appear to others (external image);
- the unknown self (hidden potential).

The features that make up each image can have a powerful effect on the way individuals communicate and on their relationships with others.

Self-image

Some people may present a confident, self-assured image in public but privately feel uncertain or insecure. Naturally they will try to conceal this, and so help maintain the stronger, public image. This creates conflict in communication, since many of their messages will be aimed at masking the self-image and boosting the projected one.

Others may perceive themselves in a negative way, overemphasising weaknesses and ignoring positive personal qualities; negative messages from parents, teachers or associates will reinforce this. Such a person may refuse a chance of promotion when it is offered: though seen by others as able to do the job, the self-image is 'not good enough'. Empathy on your part, enabling you to recognise the barrier, is one of the ways of getting through to such people with the good news about how others see them.

Projected image

A person's projected image is controlled by the desire to look good to others. The form it takes is generally positive, depending on the roles the individual is expected to play when communicating. Most people have a number of different projected images associated, for instance, with the position at work, level of education, or social status. Tune in to the projected image. People react strongly if your communication with them or about them threatens to downgrade their projected image.

External image

This is a more shallow and often inaccurate image built up by others when communicating among themselves about a third party. People discuss external images with everyone but the individual concerned so you may not be aware of yours, yet every time you communicate with others, your external image influences the process (see chart below).

People's lives would be far less complicated if the three images were roughly similar, but this is not usually so. Most projected images will involve some kind of facade intended to impress others, and this deception — as far as the 'projector' knows — may appear successful. But quite often the external image, the one you know least about, is the one other people tune in to most frequently.

Too wide a difference between the three positions leads to major communication problems and misunderstanding of motives, as is illustrated in the chart below. Empathy, openness and trust are needed to help others to deal with issues like these, which have a serious effect on understanding and agreement.

The unknown self

Everyone has 'another' side — the undiscovered abilities (or faults), the hidden qualities of which neither the individual nor anyone else is aware. This fourth side is of interest from a personal-development point of view, but since it is unknown, it is unlikely to be involved in daily communication. However, in a time of great danger or crisis, or after a major change in lifestyle such as the loss of a job or a marriage break-up, a person often discovers

unsuspected powers of leadership or immense strength of character, or some other positive talent. (Sometimes, of course, the opposite occurs.) Sudden and apparently 'out of character' behaviour will worry friends, who may label it abnormal. It helps communication if you can recognise what is really happening.

Gaps and blanks

Experience gaps

If Hal has never been sacked from a job and Mal has been sacked many times, they will see the world of employment differently. If you have travelled overseas, your views may differ from those of someone who has never been outside the home state. Such gaps in experience can create barriers in communicating that empathy helps to overcome.

Lost or missing memories

People do not remember 'forgetting'. If a memory is lost there may not be any sign that it ever existed, in which case a person may really believe that every detail is remembered. Forgetting is something like erasing a computer file from a disk, but there is one difference: with computers, you are aware of the missing data. If you want the memory restored, you can use a backup disk to restore the erased file. When people are unaware that they have forgotten, there is no record of the erasure and no backup, so they convince themselves that they forgot nothing at all! You probably know all too well how this can

Self-image	Projected image	External image
I think I really am . . .	I want others to see . . .	Others actually see . . .
a person who has to work twice as hard as everyone else to be certain of success	a hard worker who can handle any given task	a workaholic who pushes him or herself twice as hard as necessary
a person who is unusually unlucky and misses out on things that come easily to others	someone who deserves extra help to make up for being so unlucky	someone who always complains about being unlucky to gain an advantage over other people
a person who is not valued or appreciated nearly as much as I would like	a valuable asset to my group, without whom they could not succeed	a person who tries to take all the credit for group efforts

affect a person's credibility and how the resulting loss of trust reduces the chances of co-operation and agreement.

Empathy is needed when someone has completely forgotten an arrangement made between you, particularly if the situation is made worse because the person denies that the arrangement was ever made. Empathy allows the situation to be rebuilt, and may help the other person to realise that he or she really could have forgotten.

It is a humbling thought to realise that all thinking is limited by the practical limitations of our memory systems. You only remember a fraction of all that you say and hear and do. By Wednesday you can recall only about 10 or 20 per cent of all you *heard* on Monday. What you *see* stays in your memory longer, but by Saturday you will still have lost (from your conscious memory, anyhow) about 95 per cent of the sights and scenes from earlier in the week. A communication that combines sight, sound and body language messages has two to three times more chance of being remembered. Memories tied to strong feelings stay longest — the birth of a child, a family break-up, a car accident, a holiday will be deeply (though not always accurately) imprinted.

Keep a record

Even though you too are affected by forgetting, at least you know that it is normal and happens all the time. Apply empathy in advance — keep notes of important discussions. As well as being a permanent record, written notes can act as a trigger, helping you recall other details that add to the total memory picture. People generally appreciate the need to record important discussions, so make notes openly. In many cases a tape of a discussion is an even better record. *Remember*, however, that you must have every participant's permission before taping a discussion, and that for the record to be of any value the given permission must be noted on the tape or put in writing.

Distorted and filtered memories

Forgetting can be a useful mechanism if it helps get rid of unpleasant or unnecessary memories, but the gap created can easily affect the way people interpret your messages. Even really important items (remembered initially) can be filtered; certain parts

are forgotten, while others remain. Moreover, what is recalled may be distorted. Empathy with the receiver will help you to recognise some of the factors that cause memories to be filtered or distorted.

Discomfort

Embarrassing or discomforting memories are often filtered. A sales representative will remember a mistake that lost a sale, but the details of the day are filtered so that the memory is less painful. The only thing clearly recalled will be that 'the client wasn't really interested, anyhow'. This helps reduce the discomfort and makes the mistake seem unimportant.

Fear and pain

Fear causes distortion, particularly loss of detail. There have been occasions on which (without any warning) a mock murder has been staged by professional actors in front of an unsuspecting crowd, to test this effect. Thinking the murder was real, the viewers would experience fear.

Statements taken afterwards from 'eyewitnesses' of these tests revealed alarming variations. Some said the person killed was responsible for starting the fight, others said the opposite. Many people thought the attacker was a 'foreigner' or someone whose skin colour was different from theirs, although in fact there was nothing in the staged murder to suggest this. The worst distortions concerned the words spoken by the actors — the longer the time between the event and the recollection, the greater was the distortion. Keep in mind that these people *believed* that they were giving important statements to police; they were trying hard to remember important details. Most were also sure that what they remembered was accurate. Very few said 'I'm not sure'. From this a question arises: How much does our legal system rely on memories of this kind?

Pain and anger also distort memories, for reasons similar to those above. If the pain is strong enough, the memory may be completely blocked.

Bias or prejudice

A manager may 'remember' the failures of a female colleague and forget those of a male team member, or vice versa. A supervisor may remember that a popular employee comes to work early, but forget the times when a less well-liked worker has stayed late to finish an important job.

Expected outcomes

If people expect something bad to happen, this affects their perception. The more negative their expectations, the more they will control what is actually 'seen' and 'heard', which in turn affects what is remembered. The actors in the experiments described above were not foreign, yet many witnesses said they 'remembered' that the killer looked like a foreigner. This perception matched their negative and discriminatory expectations regarding murderers.

If what people remember is distorted or filtered, then — as when using a corrupted program in a computer — whenever the affected part of the memory is used, the output will be distorted too. Only empathy can cope with this kind of misunderstanding.

Two-way empathy — excellence in communication

Empathy on the part of both sender and receiver makes for far better communication; in fact, it marks the difference between ordinary understanding and excellence in communication. The more you and your colleagues use mutual empathy, the more you can develop a sense of shared trust and openness, and this helps to remove so many other barriers. Communication problems become a point for discussion rather than one for conflict.

In many cases, however, it will be you alone who will empathise — it will be one-way empathy — simply because the receiver does not know how to use empathy or does not realise how beneficial it is. Although this may be frustrating, it does not prevent you from exercising your skills to the fullest; in fact, this is usually when you need them most.

Putting empathy to work

Often in business you need to reach agreement when the people on the other side of the table are in no hurry to agree with you. Empathy may well be one of your more valuable communication tools in such cases; use it to tune in to their prejudices, their fears, their lack of trust — the feelings that are working against you. Two-way empathy lowers these barriers and allows people to discover how co-operation benefits everyone.

Empathise with enemies

You do not have to like people to empathise with them, nor do you have to approve of their actions or agree with their opinions. You actually can (and should try to) exercise empathy when you communicate with your worst enemy, your most difficult customer, your most prejudiced opponent. The more you can tune in to these individuals, the better will be your chance of communicating effectively with them. While you do not have to agree with them or accept their points of view, it will help *you* greatly in your communication if you can recognise the differences between you and respond accordingly. Faced, for instance, with an opponent's biased view of accountants as a group, tune in if you can to the bias itself, and perhaps find out why it exists — then you'll have a better idea of how to deal with this particular kind of prejudice.

Empathy works just as well in less difficult cases, where feelings are not so much involved yet where two people still see the world differently. For instance: Ricky is on the phone trying to arrange a time to see Jerry. Jerry says, 'I'm too busy for a meeting this afternoon. Come over first thing in the morning'. The next day Jerry arrives at her usual starting time (9.15 am) to be met by a frustrated Ricky, who has been waiting since 8.30 am. Neither could 'see' the meaning of 'first thing' as the other saw it.

You become a better communicator each time you consciously stop to think about your receiver before you communicate. Ricky could have realised that people's ideas of 'first thing' usually differ, and asked Jerry what time she had in mind. Jerry could have realised that Ricky started work at 8.30, and changed her message to 'Let's get together as soon as I get in tomorrow morning'. If mornings are a busy time for Ricky, Jerry could also suggest, 'That's usually a busy time for you. I'll phone you as soon as I get here and find out what time suits you'.

In the following chapters you will be reminded many times about sitting in the receiver's chair — when you are talking in a meeting, speaking on the telephone, writing a letter, using a public-address system or being interviewed by reporters from the media. Use empathy not only in spoken or verbal communication, but in written and non-verbal messages; for instance, in drawing a map, designing an advertising layout or putting up a sign.

Summary

1. Tuning in to people (using empathy) adds to your ability to understand others and helps others to understand you.
2. Your empathy also encourages others to agree with you by showing them how your message will help them to meet *their* current needs.
3. It is hard to change beliefs and attitudes, but opinions can be altered. Empathy helps you to decide whether people are expressing only an opinion, or strongly held views based on beliefs and values.
4. People see different 'images':
   - the way they see themselves (self-image);
   - the way they want others to see them (projected image);
   - the way they actually appear to others (external image);
   - the unknown self (hidden potential).
5. People react strongly if your communication with them downgrades their public (projected) image.
6. Empathy helps you to recognise how memories can be filtered or distorted, and events forgotten.

7. Keep a record of important communication, particularly discussions.
8. Empathy on the part of both sender and receiver marks the difference between ordinary understanding and excellence in communication.
9. Use empathy in communicating with difficult customers or prejudiced opponents. You do not have to like people or agree with them in order to empathise with them.

Exercises

1. What are the dangers of using the words 'ought' and 'should' when communicating? How might they affect empathy?
2. The following topics will attract people's attention if you start talking about them, so they obviously have the power to motivate people to communicate. Do you think they fit the standard categories listed by Maslow or might they point to other needs apart from those Maslow identified? Why might this be so?
   - gaining more power at work
   - making more money
   - love and/or sex
   - a picnic or barbecue
   - travel
   - a comedy show on television
3. Why might people filter or distort things they are trying to remember, yet not realise they are doing so?

CHAPTER 6

Style and fashion in communication

Communication styles differ from person to person because people are individuals. Styles also vary from situation to situation. A team leader adopts a friendly and open style while explaining the job to a newcomer. Two programmers adopt a serious style while working on a computer system, but switch to happy informal communication over lunch. No two people communicate in exactly the same way.

This chapter looks at

- the range of styles available to you as a sender;
- the range of alternative styles you may encounter as a receiver;
- how different people recall and process information, and how this variation affects communication;
- how differences in style create problems and tensions that affect interpersonal and group activities;
- styles people adopt to express power or feelings — the 'family' roles;
- how to develop the power of your communication by combining the best of each different style.

Communication styles can be divided into several categories. Some of the terms used to label these will be familiar; others have been drawn from disciplines such as psychology and sociology, but most are now in common use in Australian business circles.

Understanding different styles, being able to identify them and to use them how and when you want to, adds new dimensions to your skill as a communicator. Your day-to-day communication style is influenced by which one of *each* of the styles you use, so the end result is a unique combination . . . *you*. Nobody else will think, remember or communicate in quite the same way.

Topics

Your natural communication styles

Linear and lateral approaches

Visual, verbal and tactile approaches

Personal communication styles

Family-role communication styles

Other communication styles

Your natural communication styles

The ways in which you think, remember and understand are as unique as your voice and the shape of your face (but not quite as hard to change). Why should you change? People are different. No one should expect you to alter your style just to match theirs, nor should you ask them to change for you. But sometimes there are advantages in changing.

Trying out new fashions

Some of your communication styles may be old ones handed down from parents, teachers or other influential figures in your past. These need changing if

- they are out of fashion;
- they do not fit your needs as an adult.

Like clothes, you can change your communication style if you find a better one. Throughout this book you will find suggestions for new and up-

to-date ways of communicating. Try them on. If you find a new style works better for you than those you used in the past, practise it until it becomes familiar and ready to use when you need it.

Copying styles and fashions — take care

The best styles to copy are those that help you to adjust to new ways of working or to solve problems more effectively. But be choosy about the communication fashions you borrow from others around you. A person may wear the same kind of coat as yours but choose a hat that is not your style, and you know how you would react in that case if advised to 'get a hat just like mine'.

If you do decide to change a style, make sure you have a sound reason for doing so and are making the change because *you*, as well as others, will

benefit. In business, some superiors expect everyone working under them to copy their style and are upset if this is not done, but unless your superior's style is comfortable and meets your needs, it is probably the wrong one for you.

Strengths and weaknesses

Every style of communication has its strong features. Recognising the strengths in yours helps you to look for the kind of jobs where they will be most in demand. You can also team up with another person (or a group) so that their strengths and yours complement one another and any gaps in your style, and in theirs, are filled or at least minimised. If an audit team finds a sudden rash of human errors in the monthly invoice statements, the strengths that help to spot accounting errors may miss some of the human issues behind the trouble. A 'facts and figures' type of investigation may have little chance of finding out the real reason people are making so many mistakes. If you are good at communicating about 'people problems', you are the kind of person who can help here. You may be weak at figures, but if you join the team at this point, adding your strengths to theirs, the whole group becomes more effective and finds better answers.

Linear and lateral approaches

How do you think? How do you solve problems? How do you classify ideas in your head? Some people have a basic preference for thinking in a logical and linear way (in a straight line). Others find they get better results using lateral thinking, which is broad-ranging and more creative. Both styles are normal, but the words you use, the way you speak and write and the way you think and plan your communication will all vary according to your natural preference for linear or lateral style.

Linear-logical thinking

Linear thinking is ideal for complex problems that require data to be rearranged or organised into a logical sequence. Your ability to use this form of thinking has a major influence on your decision-making and management styles. It is a practical and reliable style that helps you to

- communicate about facts and remember names, dates, telephone numbers and similar specific data;
- organise ideas and meanings into a structured message, such as a report or submission;
- use numbers, symbols, codes and formulae in place of words.

Linear thinkers often find it hard to understand why everybody does not operate as they do. They support the use of rules and standards in communication and administration. They tend to see 'good' writing as that which adheres to the rules of grammar, punctuation and spelling. If these qualities are missing, a linear reader may downgrade your message, even if it contains important ideas or data.

Think of someone you know who shows strong linear-logical thinking behaviour. What other characteristics does that person display in his or her communication style?

Lateral-creative thinking

This kind of thinking (also discussed in a section of Chapter 11, 'Thinking and reasoning') follows new and often different paths towards solving problems. It makes the most of imagination and intuitive skills. Many inventors, explorers and experimenters are lateral-creative thinkers.

- Although a lateral style may be less useful than linear thinking if you want to analyse a page of facts and figures, it offers many advantages when it comes to understanding people.
- It is good for 'sitting in the receiver's chair'. A lateral-creative thinker can see things from another's point of view — has the ability known as empathy (see Chapter 5).
- It is more suitable for thinking about ideas than about objects.
- It sees the total picture more quickly, but is not as reliable in focusing on small but important details.
- It is useful in solving complex management problems that contain a mixture of issues involving people, machines, policies and goals.
- It works best in communication systems that are not restricted by too many rules or too rigid a structure.

Lateral thinkers are natural innovators and entrepreneurs. Many achieve success in life even though they appeared to lack ability at school. This is more likely to be so if schools attended used mainly linear-logical tests such as multiple-choice questions and essay writing. Today there is a growing appreciation of the need for educators to put equal emphasis on both linear-logical and lateral-creative thinking (see Linda Williams, *Teaching for the Two Sided Mind*, 1984).

Think of someone you know who shows strong lateral-creative thinking behaviour. What characteristics of style does this person display in communication?

Using both together

Even the most advanced computers still cannot handle lateral-creative thinking. Decision making based on what computers (or linear-logical thinkers) alone suggest as the 'best' solution to a problem is usually incomplete. On the other hand, a combination of linear-based computer analysis and lateral-creative thought can turn up an outstanding solution. Learning to use both styles *together* is a powerful step forward in developing your total ability as thinker and communicator. There are a growing number of books available on the subject. Guidelines for developing lateral-creative thinking are included on page 114.

Visual, verbal and tactile approaches

As explained in Chapter 2, some people remember verbally, but just as many think and remember sucessfully using mental images. A third type thinks in a tactile way; these people remember best by recalling physical actions, touch, movement or feelings.

1. Verbal or aural thinkers
   - think and remember in words, sounds and numbers, so usually find it easy to put words on paper — they like to 'discuss' ideas in their minds before communicating;
   - are good at grammar and punctuation and usually spell well, but their written messages are often too long and their pages may be overfull of words and lacking in visual appeal.

2. Visual thinkers
   - think and remember most clearly in pictures and images — a visual thinker is often described as having a 'photographic memory';
   - tend to use colourful, descriptive language;
   - prefer photographs, drawings and diagrams to long, wordy explanations;
   - are attracted to pages with strong eye-appeal and open space, and avoid reading anything that looks dull or cluttered;
   - often fail to give sufficient verbal detail when speaking because the image is so clear to them ('Just do it the way I do; it's easy').

Of course, visual thinkers are conscious of words, too, just as verbal thinkers can visualise pictures. It's a matter of preference. Thinking visually encourages lateral-creative thinking, and vice versa. At school Albert Einstein was labelled as weak in mathematics by teachers who could not follow his visual way of thinking; in later life Einstein explained that his most important mathematical ideas came to him only when he thought in pictures. If you are a verbal thinker discussing ideas with a visual thinker, both of you need to 'show' as well as 'tell'. Write key ideas on a board, on paper or on a screen so that they can be easily seen; draw a picture or show a video.

If you are a visual thinker and want a verbal thinker to understand you, it will be necessary to expand the detail of your explanation to present the picture as you see it.

3. Tactile thinkers
   - think and remember best when memory is based on actual experiences — they prefer active, hands-on learning to being told or shown;
   - use people's feelings and actions as a basis for analysing communication, and are good at appreciating other people's points of view;
   - may have been identified as poor writers by teachers who were linear (and verbal) thinkers;
   - can be very successful if given the opportunity to communicate in their own style (one of the authors of this book is a tactile communicator);
   - may have difficulty organising words and ideas into a logical sequence, and need numbered headings to make the sequence clearer.

sense of touch

The words used by people who have strong tactile memories are related to touch, actions and emotions rather than to sounds or images. To get through to them, talk about actions rather than ideas, give a demonstration, use a computerised simulation, or best of all let them experience directly what you are talking about in a 'hands-on' situation.

Even using 'active'-sounding words helps you to get through to a tactile thinker. They will remember what you write if — rather than using long sentences — you summarise vital points and close with a strong 'action ending'.

Which is the best style for remembering?

Imagine the three memory styles (aural, visual and tactile) set up like drawers in a filing cabinet. If your visual memory is strongest, it acts like a top drawer, but once you have accessed a visual memory you use it to connect up sounds and feelings from the other drawers. This means that much of the time you use a combination, but your top-drawer style is the one that feels most natural and works best for you. Your style will vary also according to whether you are in a linear- or lateral-thinking mode.

Different study styles

Linear-logical writers who are also strongly verbal or visual thinkers have a special advantage when answering written tests, writing essays or working with figures, because they can plan so much of what they want to say without putting anything on paper.

Asking others — tactile or lateral-creative thinkers — to organise ideas (in the mind) *before* putting them on paper creates serious writing problems, such as 'writer's block'. Chapter 14, 'Writing in four easy stages', shows how to avoid this by using a mixture of linear and lateral thinking when writing, and by starting with a series of rough drafts (or using a word processor) rather than trying to write 'correctly' straight off.

Personal communication styles

Personal communication styles are similar to the personality types first identified by Carl Jung (1923) and updated by Isabel Briggs Myers and others (*Gifts Differing*, 1980). There are a number of commonly used tests that identify the styles, but you can probably tell from those mentioned below which are most like yours. Notice that each style is 'opposed' by an alternative or contrasting style. However, the contrast is not in fact always as strong as in these examples, which are used to highlight the differences.

show a difference
— when compared

The outgoing versus the self-contained communicator

Outgoing communicators work well in a group or team. They like to talk to people about whatever they are doing and welcome the chance to participate in meetings and to give and receive feedback.

Self-contained communicators like to think through a problem until they understand it fully before they communicate about it. They are happy to work quietly on their own rather than draw attention to themselves, avoiding group activities as much as possible. Even in meetings they will be quieter and less noticeable than the outgoing communicator. As they usually communicate more effectively if they first work out alone what they want to say, it's understandable if they use memos or letters to convey their ideas rather than address a meeting.

These differences sow the seeds for potential disagreement on issues such as the frequency of meetings and how much time to allow for discussion before taking action. Problems arise when leaders (or lecturers) expect a self-contained communicator to work with others on a team project, or submit a jointly written paper.

Specific (factual) versus creative-intuitive communicators

immediate understa... something without reaso...

Specific-fact communicators look for accuracy and detailed logical reasoning. They are inclined to believe numbers rather than words, and look for specific data as a basis for decision making. You'll see the obvious link between this and the linear-logical style of thinking described at the start of the chapter. If a report lacks factual detail, it will be seen as unreliable. If a proposal has even small errors in grammar or arithmetic, this type of reader will spot them and then be less inclined to trust anything else in the document. Factual communicators may not wish to experiment with new communication styles. They prefer the safety of standard communication methods that worked for them in the past.

Creative-intuitive people are imaginative, forward-thinking, and like working on new and original projects. They see the broad picture clearly, but may miss small details, which can cause clashes when it comes to problem solving. Intuitive reasoning works surprisingly well for them, and as a result they often attain a better record for decision making than their specific-fact-oriented colleagues. They buy just before prices go up, spot hidden potential in people and products, or win when everyone was sure they would lose. Often they cannot explain the basis for their successful choices, or give specific facts and figures to support their intuitive, gut-feeling approach. The link between this style and the lateral-creative thinker is obvious.

The analytical versus the feeling communicator

Analytical communicators think in a logical, linear manner, often with a verbal emphasis. They are good speechmakers and report writers, so are likely to be promoted to executive positions. As receivers, they like discussions and meetings that concentrate on logical analysis; they find it hard to trust a decision that cannot be supported by a clear, well-analysed argument. They may not be particularly sensitive to other people's feelings, and when solving a problem choose the most logical solution rather than a compromise that would restore morale or maintain harmony.

Feeling communicators are orientated towards people. Because they are more sensitive to other people's feelings, they have an advantage when it comes to establishing business relationships. Their choice about what is fair and right will depend not only on facts and logic, but also on the effect on people of any decision taken. Because they weigh up 'people' issues and values alongside facts, they can make popular (and often very sound) decisions.

The decisive communicator versus the flexible communicator

Decisive communicators prefer to base decisions on immediate evidence, expert opinions or even intuition, rather than on lengthy debate, and once the decision is made they resist attempts to change it. Decisive communicators are results-oriented. They judge the success of their communication by its effect on others. If there is no visible outcome, no feedback, they feel their messages are not working. Decisive types set fixed time schedules and work hard to meet deadlines. They do not like sudden changes or alterations to plans. Decisive writers dislike editing and rewriting. They like to get reports or assignments finished in 'one go'. They can appear to others as impatient, or as willing to sacrifice quality for speedy completion.

Flexible communicators like to leave themselves in a position where they can move freely to meet differing situations. This has many advantages in business, but it can also lead to problems. If they keep too many of their options open at the one time, they appear to the decisive person to lack clear goals. They may have trouble completing a project by a set date, as they keep adjusting to changing conditions.

Their flexible, spontaneous style of communicating means that they are more tolerant of other people's differences, and find it hard to understand when they are not granted the same understanding in return. This applies particularly to their lack of 'time consciousness'. Decisions made by a flexible-style communicator, though often late, tend to be better thought-out than those made by decisive thinkers. However, the flexible person's lack of concern for deadlines and time schedules leads to communication breakdowns if they have to work in partnership with decisive communicators.

As writers, they like to produce a number of rough drafts, adding extra information, editing, improving and rewriting, all of which raises the quality of the finished work but may result in it being late.

Your overall personal style

Each person will demonstrate a particular combination, one style out of each of the four groups, so there are sixteen possible combinations. Try to understand and appreciate the strengths and weaknesses in each style, and its opposite. All sixteen are normal; there are no 'bad' styles, but often people mistakenly assume that the style that works best for them must work best for everybody. They react against your choice because it opposes theirs.

Airing differences

Although fixing clashes in style is not solely your responsibility, you can expect a long wait if you expect others to change their styles to fit in with you. You will benefit more by demonstrating your adaptability, and your capacity to understand and appreciate others' strengths and support their weaknesses. When you do this, other people are encouraged to do the same.

If two people discuss their different styles, they can develop simple bridging techniques to help create clear understanding and encourage agreement. This is easier if you can each recognise the other's individual style as being normal.

Modifying your styles

These styles are not as much a part of your natural personality as those described previously. Rather they are preferred styles that you have chosen through years of trial-and-error experiments. You will be convinced that some (your opposite or 'shadow' styles) are definitely not 'comfortable' for you, while others (your preferred styles) 'fit' better, but this does not necessarily mean that your chosen style is the most effective or productive. It is possible to change, but only if you are convinced that the alteration benefits you or increases your level of 'comfort'. For instance, if any of your styles clash too much with those of people you care about, it is worth trying to modify them. If you are a polisher, you can develop your latent decisiveness: you can learn to use time management methods so that you meet important deadlines. If you receive a promotion as soon as you start getting your work done on time, this adds to the 'comfortable' feeling and you continue to develop your shadow style; if nobody notices the change, you will soon move back to your preferred, polishing style.

Personal communication styles and team building

If people accept their strengths and weaknesses and then blend them with the talents and strengths of others, the result in terms of team work can be a powerful, effective and co-operative team. Imagine that you have to form a working group to discover why production levels are falling. The leader, responsible for overall planning and for meeting the deadline, should be a decisive, outgoing communicator. The person who carries out the first informal interviews with workers might be someone with intuitive skills and the ability to recognise people's feelings. Later in-depth interviews could be conducted by a specific-factual thinker, to pinpoint the cause of the problem. Someone with strong linear-logical thinking should decide how the findings are to be presented. If a report has to be written, the whole team should be involved in preparing it. The factual content might be put together by the logical thinkers, but the analysis and discussion on proposed changes ought to involve someone with feeling ability who can appreciate how people are likely to react to the recommendations. The final document should of course be checked by a specific-factual member who can spot any errors or omissions.

Family-role communication styles

When you communicate, you can adopt one of three styles similar to those used by family members. These were first defined by Eric Berne in *Transactional Analysis in Psychotherapy* (1961). Since then, many other writers including Robert Ball (1977) and Amy and Thomas Harris (1970, 1985) have looked at the styles and in particular at their powerful effect on the personal relationships between sender and receiver.

Role	Style
Parent	Critical or protective
Adult	Rational, analytical, impartial *fair*
Child	Angry or compliant

These roles have nothing to do with age or family status; the descriptions refer only to the communication style and its effect on the sender–receiver relationship. Nor do people stick with one style. In a minute — or less — a speaker can use all three.

Parent-style communication

Any communication, verbal or non-verbal, in which the sender is criticising or sitting in judgment on other people's behaviour is 'parent style', so called because it is similar to the way a dominating parent communicates with a child. Typical parent phrases include 'It's not your job to worry about that' or 'You will have to do better'. Parent messages use information as a means of forcing agreement, as if to say 'Those are the facts. You have no choice'; they may include warnings about what will happen if orders or rules are not obeyed or if deadlines are missed, often with the added implication that any punishment will be well deserved. There are other characteristics:

- One-sided judgment: 'You're wrong', 'You're late', 'You were rude to that customer'. Without hearing your side, the speaker decides that you are at fault.

- Negative labelling: 'You are so inefficient' or 'You're all thumbs!'. When you think how inaccurate they are, label messages like this should be easy to disregard, yet they are often quite hurtful. Learn to reject them. They have no basis in fact.
- Allness: 'All employees are lazy' or 'You university types all think you know the answers'. The word 'all' and similar words ('never', 'every time') are used to reinforce the criticism.
- Protective: 'That's a difficult problem. You'd better let me fix it for you, so you won't get into trouble'.

Parent-style messages like these often lead to feelings of anger and stress for those on the receiving end, which harms the sender—receiver relationship. If you are the receiver, it helps to identify the source of your anger as the parent style instead of worrying about the words. If you can do this, you can stay calmer and concentrate on solving the real problem.

The most successful way of dealing with parent-style messages is to respond with adult-style replies, as explained below. A more permanent way of dealing with critical (and manipulative) parent messages is to use open assertive communication, as explained in Chapter 12. Use of the parent style makes it easier to dominate a discussion or meeting: the user takes a superior position, and makes judgments and decisions on behalf of the whole team. It can simplify decision making, but decisions made this way may not get much support from those who are expected to carry them out and the 'parent' figure then has to resort to even less popular measures to force obedience.

Adult-style communication

Adult-style messages are analytical and deal with facts. They are often stated as questions in order to avoid any suggestion of an attempt to control the listener or dominate the relationship. They can express ideas and opinions as long as these are free of feelings or prejudice. They use phrases such as 'I can see your point of view', 'Let's look at it carefully', 'What reasons are there?' or 'Why do you think that is so?'. This kind of communication

- avoids judging the behaviour of others, or labelling behaviour as right or wrong;
- uses rational analysis to solve problems;
- helps people to settle misunderstandings and

reach mutually satisfying agreements or compromise.

Adult-to-adult communication

If both parties communicating use adult style, it leads to better problem solving and sound co-operation. Adult-to-adult messages are positive relationship-builders because they signify equal status, respect and recognition. An adult response to criticism of a draft letter might be 'Can you tell me why my wording is unsuitable so I can rewrite it?'. This encourages the critic to move down from a negative, parent position and communicate on a constructive, adult level. This works well in situations when you

- are replying to criticism or anger directed at you;
- are unsure of your situation or of the people you are dealing with;
- want an adult response from someone else;
- know the other person is deliberately trying to raise your stress- or anger-level for manipulative reasons;
- need to keep your emotions under control.

Adult messages need not be uninteresting just because they avoid emotion, but do not use them all the time. They are, however, the best response at work if you need to block emotional reactions (either by others or from yourself) that would get in the way of clear understanding. They are not appropriate if you want to express strong feelings of liking, trust or appreciation about others. Your feelings may be sincere, but if the message lacks emotion (as it tends to do with the adult style) it can sound as though you don't really care.

Child-style communication

Child-style messages often exaggerate feelings and emotions and distort information. This helps the communicator to

- avoid getting into trouble;
- avoid feeling stress, or worrying;
- avoid having to face up to problems;
- feel that he or she is 'right', regardless of the facts.

Decisions expressed in the child style often indicate jealousy or rebellion: 'I don't care who says so, I'll do it my way!'. This understandably creates a negative reaction in others and makes co-operative problem solving difficult. By becoming emotional, the user avoids facing responsibility or even having to discuss issues. If decisions are made, they are likely to centre more on choices that will reduce stress rather than develop a sound solution.

Positive child messages

Many child messages, however, are concerned with feelings other than anger or agreement. You say 'We made the sale!', 'Now everybody knows we're the best'. Positive forms of child communication are a sound way to share good feelings at work. There is nothing 'childish' in using them as long as they are appropriate to the situation. Honest and open expression of feelings at work is appropriate; it strengthens friendships, improves customer relations and lifts morale (see Chapter 12).

Adaptive or co-operative responses

For the sake of peace, or for other reasons, you can react by adapting your role to suit the sender of a message sent in another mode. The child-style response, 'I'm sorry you don't like the recommendations in my report. I'll get onto them and change them straight away', is probably just the reaction the parent communicator wanted, so the two styles complement each other. The child agrees with the parent and communication channels stay open, because both parties accept the relationship as it is defined by the exchange. If, however, your personal rights are given away or denied as a result, this is likely to create new problems (see Chapter 12).

Sometimes a child message may be the only way to communicate your distress, and at such times a protective, parent response may be far more welcome than an adult one. But most adaptive messages signal compliance — agreement to do what is wanted whether it is right or wrong. They often seem to represent a desire to be liked or needed rather than a willingness to co-operate.

Crossed reactions

If a child message stirs a negative or angry parent response the transaction is no longer complementary, but 'crossed'. The message may be a genuine call for help, but if the 'child' exaggerates the problem to gain unwarranted sympathy, it can quickly 'hook' a strong parent response: 'Look! There's nothing wrong with the computer. Stop wasting my time and go and read the operator's manual'.

Mixed-role messages

Mixed messages occur when a person switches from one style to another in a single communication. 'If these delays in delivery continue, you're in big trouble. I'm terrified of what will happen unless things improve. Tell me honestly, just what do you intend to do about fixing things?' The speaker is criticising (parent), expressing fear (child) and asking for information (adult).

Other communication styles

There are many other styles, behaviour patterns and fashions in business communication. Some of these, mentioned here briefly, will be explained in later chapters.

Assertive, competitive, aggressive and manipulative [*handle cleverly*] styles

Assertive and competitive styles are strong forms of communicating and both have their place in business, particularly when you are negotiating, bargaining or defending your position against aggressive or manipulative communication (see Chapters 12, 13 and 24).

Open and closed styles

Closed communication is impersonal and is used — intentionally or unconsciously — to keep people at a distance. Open communication is based on mutual trust, honesty and respect (see Chapter 12).

Formal and informal styles

The level of formality affects the relationship between sender and receiver. It is particularly important when you are using written rather than spoken communication. In business organisations, a distinction is also drawn between formal and informal communication channels (Chapter 25).

Polishing style [*become smooth*]

Of the many different combinations possible between linear and lateral thinking, aural, visual and tactile remembering and the other styles, one in particular is of special interest. A lateral-creative, intuitive thinker who is also a flexible communicator will exhibit an overall communication activity known as 'polishing', referred to in Chapters 14, 18 and 30.

Don't let labels tie you down

As you read about these styles of communication, you will certainly identify with some of them. Naturally, names and labels must be used to refer to them, but be careful in the ways you use such labels. They are useful as a means of defining behaviour, but *not* as names for individuals who adopt the behaviour style. You may prefer 'visual communication'. This does not make you 'a visual'. Labelling yourself or anyone else (instead of just behaviour) tends to

- limit expectations about what a person can or cannot do well;
- provide an easy excuse for behaving in a particular way;
- reduce motivation for trying new, alternative (or more effective) styles.

Summary

1. Communication styles differ from person to person and from situation to situation.

2. To be an effective communicator, you need to know which styles are most natural for you and which help you best to achieve your aims.

3. Tailor the way you communicate to fit in with the way you think and remember.

4. Use your knowledge of style differences to develop better understanding between you and others.

5. Some people have a basic preference for thinking in a logical and linear way. Others get better results using lateral thinking.

6. Some people remember verbally; some prefer mental images. A third type thinks in a tactile way.

7. Apart from the thinking and remembering styles listed above, there are four overall styles used in day-to-day communication. Each one has an opposite side, or 'shadow':
   - the outgoing versus the self-contained communicator
   - the specific versus the creative-intuitive communicator
   - the analytical versus the feeling communicator
   - the decisive communicator versus the flexible communicator

8. Another well-known classification compares communication styles to those followed by family members:
   - Parent — critical or protective
   - Adult — rational, analytical, impartial
   - Child — angry or compliant

9. If two communicators both use adult style it leads to improved problem solving and co-operation because it emphasises equal status and mutual respect.

10. A skilled communicator understands and accepts the strengths in styles other than his or her own.

11. Learning to use different or 'opposite' styles, and combinations of styles, adds to your ability as a thinker and a communicator.

12. If two people can discuss their different styles, they soon discover bridging techniques to help create clear understanding and encourage agreement.

Exercises

1. Describe a recent situation in which someone became upset or said that you did not 'understand', but in which you think the problem was that your communication styles did not match.

2. You have several staff members who want to learn a specific skill, such as using a new computer or fax machine, or driving a forklift truck.

   (a) What different ways of communicating can you use while training them?

   (b) What methods would you use for someone who is a feeling person but who remembers best in a tactile form?

   (c) How would you train a linear thinker who remembers best in visual ways?

3. Some people use communication styles to avoid facing personal doubts or fixing mistakes they should be dealing with. Kay discovers that when she uses an analytical-parent style people are more inclined to obey her without questioning her decisions, so she uses this style when issuing instructions.

Describe a recent incident in which someone used a particular style to avoid discussion or avoid questions on an issue that was important to you.

4. Ask someone to spell a difficult word, to recall a phone number or address, or to do some simple mental mathematical calculations. Watch the person's eyes, at the very moment of remembering. A person who looks upwards is probably using a 'visual' memory. One who looks to left or right is using an aural memory. Looking down suggests a tactile memory.

People who look down when spelling or doing calculations may make more errors, because they are trying to decide if their answer is 'good' or 'bad' (right or wrong) in a tactile way. Try getting a person who does this to look upwards instead, and ask the same question again.

5. When people speak or write they naturally use words and phrases that reflect their particular thinking and remembering styles. Suggest two or more probable styles indicated by each of the following:
   (a) What do you say to this suggestion? I'll call a meeting so that we can all get together and talk about the problem.
   (b) Don't sit around feeling sorry for yourself. Come up to my office and we'll hammer this problem out together.
   (c) The logical answer is to strike while the iron is hot and stop the opposition before they get started. I'll send out a memo on it next Monday.
   (d) Don't tell me it won't work. I've been using this system for years and I don't intend to change now.
   (e) I have a new record; come over tonight and I'll show it to you. We can look through my collection and see what else there is there that catches your eye.
   (f) Nobody cares about me or how I'm coping with the job. I just sit here by myself and do it as best I can.

   (g) They'll tell us about their side of the problem, then hear what we have to say. Then we can talk about a compromise solution.
   (h) It's people like you who cause road accidents. I don't know how you ever got a driver's licence!

6. Non-verbal patterns of behaviour reflect a person's style in terms of how they think and remember. Non-verbal behaviour also provides clues about personal communication styles. What might the following indicate about a person:
   (a) Although Leroi's desk/workbench is cluttered and untidy, he can 'put his hands on anything he needs'. If someone tidies it up for him, he gets upset.
   (b) Robin's refrigerator is sparkling clean. Items on each shelf are arranged in a fixed pattern and all standard foods have a fixed location. Robin gets upset if anyone puts things in the 'wrong' place.
   (c) Ricky is very conscious of his personal appearance, and physical fitness. He likes being noticed by others, and wears bright strong colours and stylish fashions. He also loves going to parties where there are lots of people, and is usually the last to go home.
   (d) Frances prefers pastel colours, and smaller parties with just a few close friends. In a meeting she takes lots of notes, but prefers not to say anything. She is brilliant with figures, and loves crossword puzzles.
   (e) Ken sets high standards and expects everybody to work as hard as he does. He doesn't come out of his office or talk to people very often, because he is so busy himself. He doesn't delegate as much work as he should. If someone makes a mistake Ken calls the person in and quietly and positively discusses the problem and how it can be fixed.
   (f) Vivian is not a popular boss. If you do not meet her expectations, or if you make a mistake, she yells at you or insults you in front of everybody. People with personal worries know it is no use expecting sympathy from Vivian.

7. Think about a recent occasion on which you enjoyed a really good meal with several other people. Try to recall the situation in detail.

What can you 'see' in your imagination? Can you recall colours, the clothes people wore and so on? Can you recall some of the sounds involved, the names of those present, the conversation? Can you 'hear' sentences as though they were being replayed on a recorder? How hot or cold was the food? How did it taste? Can you remember emotions you were feeling at the time? Can you recall where people sat in relation to you?

Which of these memories were the most powerful? Which were the weakest? What does this suggest in terms of your aural-visual-tactile memory style?

8. Someone you know well and care about has a communication style that you find very annoying. This is also affecting your ability to get your work done. What are some possible ways in which you could try to deal with this situation?

CHAPTER 7

Communication breakdown

This chapter will help you to diagnose communication breakdowns and work out ways of getting things moving again. Once you can identify a problem, can describe it (in words, symbols or pictures), you are on the way to solving it. The breakdowns that are hardest to fix are those that people

■ do not understand;
■ find it difficult to talk about.

The better your diagnosis, the better will be the chance that you and others can get together, analyse the cause, and work out a solution.

Topics

Communication barriers

Breakdowns in understanding

Personal barriers

Anger — the five-way barrier

Other barriers

Diagnosing breakdowns

Communication barriers

Physical barriers, like closed doors, affect transmission. Language barriers reduce understanding. And even if a message is received, personal barriers can reduce co-operation and agreement. You will be able to find a way round most barriers, but it usually means spending extra time, effort or money.

Distance

Distance is a significant barrier in Australia. Instead of a face-to-face meeting, you may have to make do with a phone call or a letter. You still get through, but the time and cost involved in bridging the distance is likely to reduce the amount of two-way communication and feedback. This in turn creates other barriers. In a national organisation, for instance, the staff in the far north or the central west may feel that 'no one in head office understands what it's like here'.

Face-to-face communication helps to reduce barriers. While business trips interstate or around the country may appear as a 'perk', they can (and should) in fact be used as team- and trust-building exercises, breaking down distance barriers and dissolving prejudices.

Social and ethnic barriers

The more people have in common, the more easily and effectively they communicate with each other. People speaking different languages may use an interpreter or a multilanguage dictionary; they may draw pictures or — if the matter is important enough — one may learn the other's language. They can achieve understanding if they have to, but it may involve more effort and time than they are prepared to give.

When it comes to negotiating with overseas businesses — writing business letters, sharing ideas in a meeting — a lack of knowledge of the other national cultures is a handicap; for instance, most Japanese would consider it ill-mannered if you tried to discuss business deals during a meal; while many Japanese managers are familiar with our customs, we know very little of theirs (see 'International communication', in Chapter 25).

Rank, status and power barriers

Distance between two people is an understandable barrier if they work in different states, but an even

greater 'distance' sometimes separates individuals working in the same building. This is the result of differences in rank, status, or the amount of power each holds in the system, and the greater the extent of these differences, the less people tend to communicate.

People at lower levels may be discouraged from initiating direct contact with top management, while upper levels may simply be 'too busy' to tune in to those at the front counter or on the production line — the places most important to the welfare of the enterprise.

Power

People who worry about their power or status set up barriers between themselves and those they see as junior to them; most communication contains background signals about who has the most power or status. An 'account overdue' letter may be rejected if written by a credit clerk but paid immediately if signed by the general manager. When Magda asks her secretary to call Rae's office to arrange a meeting there should be no status barrier if Magda's secretary talks to Rae's secretary, but if either secretary talks directly to the other's boss, difficulties can arise. Senior staff don't want to be seen agreeing too readily to requests from those with lower status.

'Why wasn't I told?' (filtering and gatekeeping)

Sometimes a particular official decides whose messages get through and whose are blocked, according to who is favoured, or who has power or status. This barrier is called filtering, or gatekeeping. To beat it, find another channel that bypasses the gatekeeper. Write a report (see Chapter 16) and send a copy to the appropriate people.

Find a common channel

Chapters 25 and 30 explain how to establish common channels — committees and special types of meetings — through which management and workers can overcome barriers and communicate openly. Use a report (another common channel) to draw attention to the need for a joint meeting.

Send equal status signals

If you have more power or authority than your receiver but want to reduce this barrier, do so with clear and visible actions or words rather than vague signals that may be misinterpreted. Move well away from your desk. Use an adult-to-adult rather than a parent-to-child style (see Chapter 6).

Noise, interference and distractions

If you can't use the phone because of the jackhammer working next door, you do not need to study this chapter to diagnose the problem. Many experts on communication, however, use the terms 'noise', and 'interference' to refer to a much wider range of barriers than just loud sounds. Any distraction that affects your concentration will have the same effect as the jackhammer. You will either miss parts of the message or mistake one word for another. Transmission problems classed as caused by noise include

- a ringing phone or a loudspeaker announcement while you are talking to a group;
- an interesting television commercial diverting you from a conversation; or an attractive member of the opposite sex distracting a client while you are trying to make a sale;
- technical problems such as a copier or printer producing hard-to-read copies;
- people wanting to see you urgently while you are trying to read an important letter.

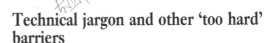

Technical jargon and other 'too hard' barriers

Technical language may create great respect for the sender's vocabulary, but the message may not get through and the job not be done if the effect is to set up a 'too hard' barrier. 'Insert the magnetic media unit into the rectangular orifice' sounds impressive, but if the sender only wanted a disk put in a slot, it would have been better to say so.

Writing that produces a 'too hard to read' feeling creates a similar barrier. Letters loaded with old-fashioned jargon, pages that are cramped, poor handwriting and misspelt words are typical examples.

Receivers 'switched off'

Often you need to 'switch receivers on' to overcome barriers set up in advance by people who are sure they know what you are going to say. Instead of listening to you, they are already thinking about their replies. How do you switch listeners on?

- Ask a question. If your listener's attention seems to be wandering, the question 'If you had to decide, what would you do?' politely demands attention. Asking questions makes it harder for the receiver to assume in advance what you are going to say.

- Switch channels. If you dial a customer's number but there is no answer, switch to another channel. Send the message by fax, so that it will wait on the receiver's desk. If your fax gets no reply, pay a personal visit.

A 'switch-on' opening adds life to routine writing such as overdue account letters. It's no use saying people ought to read them. You are the person who wants a cheque in the mail so creating the interest is up to you (see Chapter 15, 'Australian business letters').

Breakdowns in understanding

You know already that in most communication some variation of meaning normally arises in transmission. If this difference is too wide, however, there will be a breakdown in understanding. Some of the main causes of breakdowns are

- unclear purpose in communicating
- ambiguity (multiple meanings)
- YCMI (You can't miss it) communicators
- communication chains

One of the difficulties with breakdowns is that it may at first seem as if the message has been safely transmitted. This makes misunderstandings harder to identify; neither party may be aware of them.

Unclear purpose

If you are unsure about the purpose of your communication you can expect your receivers to be unsure too. In preparing a job application, think about whether your aim is really to

- get the job;
- be given an interview; or
- persuade the receiver to read your résumé.

Choosing the correct goal helps to have your application placed on the short list. A letter explaining only why you want the job is more likely to end up in the wastepaper basket. One that aims to convince a busy reader (with a hundred other applications to follow yours) that you are one of the people to be given an interview must have a clearer aim (see Chapter 21, 'Getting the job you want').

People speaking to a group make similar errors if they don't first clearly determine who they are talking to, why they are talking and what result they want (see Chapter 29, 'Having your say').

Ambiguity

Ambiguity arises when a word or a message offers a choice of meanings. The well-known 'I am pleased to advise that your husband, who has been listed as a missing person for the past six years, has now been confirmed as dead, at your request' is a classic example. The sender of course meant that confirmation would smooth out legal problems such as payment of life insurance or settlement of the estate, but the wording was ambiguous. Ambiguity allows the receiver to decode the meaning in more than one way. The trouble with ambiguity is that

- senders are usually not aware of it, or they would change the wording;
- receivers too may be unaware of alternative meanings (as Chapter 5 explained, people naturally assume a meaning that makes sense to *them*).

For instance, a senior manager says, 'I'll see you all first thing after lunch'. Does this mean, after his or her lunch or after your lunch or at the end of the lunch period? Does the manager really want to 'see' you — or 'talk to' you? And where? Because senders are less likely to recognise ambiguity, receivers can help by giving very specific feedback. A response such as 'We'll meet in your office at 1.45 pm — OK?' would detect any variation in understanding by either side.

Phrases with too broad a meaning

Ray says, 'Take care of the bad debts this week'. Should you send reminder letters, file the accounts, phone the firms concerned, call a debt collector, or what? 'Take care' has too broad a range of meanings, just as 'very little extra cost' has in money terms. 'It won't take long' and 'as soon as possible' are similar causes of ambiguity. Avoid them all.

Long or vague words (generalisations)

Short, sharp, specific words create fewer misunderstandings. Written communication *can* be less ambiguous than speech *if* you take the time to choose the clearest words. Confident writers do this; writers who are not sure what they are communicating about often use long words with very broad meanings to cover their lack of understanding.

Overuse of 'that' and 'there'

Not all short words are easy to follow. Two small words, 'that' and 'there', belong in the high-risk category. Asking 'What happened about that urgent order?' does not make it clear which order is meant. Instead of 'that', choose words showing precisely what you are talking about. Descriptive words help the listener to see exactly what you see. Say, 'What did you do about the McPherson order that had to go out on Friday?'.

Leaving out parts of the message

Some senders find it hard to see a message from the other person's point of view, so they forget to fill in the details. They use a kind of verbal short-hand: 'Go to the usual room, and bring the book in my top drawer'. They assume that you visualise the same room or the same book as they do. As a receiver, you can help in such cases by asking for additional data. 'What is the title?' 'What room number is it?'

The responsibility for a clear message rests with the sender, so choose the best and clearest codes you can. Avoid words, phrases and any non-verbal codes that could hold different meanings for different people or could vary in meaning according to the context.

The YCMI (You can't miss it) communicator

People who feel that misunderstandings are always 'the other person's fault' are difficult to deal with. They tend to be defensive about 'their' meanings, so that even when you point out a misunderstanding they assume you must be to blame.

YCMI communicators really believe that *all* their messages are easy to understand. Because they picture their messages clearly, they assume that the pictures *must* be received just as clearly by others, and anyone who doesn't understand is either not paying attention or not trying! They say things like 'Why should I explain it again? I've just told you what I wanted', or 'Straight down the road for a couple of kilometres, left at the big tree, over the creek, and keep going till you see the roof of the hayshed. You can't miss it!'.

Instead of accepting the reality that there is always some difficulty in exchanging ideas, the YCMI sender adds to the error rate by rejecting feedback and the need for two-way communication as a waste of time (or an insult to his or her ability as a communicator). In a way, YCMIs deserve sympathy — they have a serious problem.

Communication chains

What are the chances of success when a spoken message is passed first from A to B, then from B to C, from C to D and finally from D to E? Four senders plus four receivers add up to eight places where things can go wrong. There is little chance that any message passing through a chain of this kind will remain unchanged. For instance: 'Sal? Mike here — thought I'd call on the two-way radio and save you a trip back here. There's a note on your table from Miffy. Sam called on the intercom and asked her to tell you when you got back that Blackfords want you to go over to their factory urgently. Finish what you're doing, then get on your way'.

By the time Sal gets the message it has been transmitted first by Blackfords on the phone to Sam, the manager, then retransmitted four times:
1. spoken via an intercom;
2. written by Miffy and left on a desk;
3. read by Mike;
4. spoken on two-way radio to Sal.

If a message reaches you through a chain of this kind, be suspicious of its accuracy. Check back to the original sender, or at least as far along the chain as you can. If you must send a spoken message via a chain, keep its content as simple as possible: 'Get Sal to call Blackfords. Tell her it's urgent'.

Personal barriers

You can usually work your way round the kind of everyday barriers described so far, but the more personal the barrier, the more caution it warrants.

Denial barriers — not wanting to hear the message

Denial barriers are among the most difficult to get past because they form part of an individual's 'defence mechanism'. These are behaviour patterns

A communication chain

that almost everybody uses (largely unconsciously) to block messages they find painful or disturbing.

Addicts of all kinds, smokers, alcoholics, workaholics, and people with eating disorders are all inclined to deny that they have a problem. Older people beginning to lose abilities that brought them status in the past use denial barriers to hide this from themselves and others.

The 'shame' core

Old Mac's work skills are falling behind the times, yet he refuses to take the offered retraining course to upgrade them. People like Old Mac often reject messages about change or reorganisation. At the core of many such barriers is a sense of shame associated with whatever the individual is denying (Shirley Smith, *Set Yourself Free*, 1990).

Sometimes really hard talking can break through a denial barrier, but trying to do this before the individual concerned is ready can increase the sense of failure. First help the person to deal with the feelings of shame or guilt.

Bias or prejudice

Prejudice (meaning prejudgment) is a way of maintaining a barrier that is more imaginary than real. Prejudice is often expressed by individuals who want to maintain a public image of strength and superiority and who hold strong feelings about the importance of rank or authority in an organisation. They can, for example, refuse to believe that rank-and-file employees are capable of sharing responsibility for solving problems at work. By maintaining such a bias, the authority figure maintains power.

People who are unsure of themselves are often those who express the strongest bias against weaker minority groups (the aged or the disabled, for example). To express equality would make the insecure speaker seem less strong and powerful than the public image he or she wants to maintain.

To accept as equals people who have always been prejudged as inferior also means admitting a mistake — another reason for maintaining a biased position. One effective technique for overcoming this form of prejudice is to let those who deny reality experience it for themselves.

Who'd employ a married woman?

During World War II there was a major shortage of male factory workers in many parts of southern USA. Most firms found, however, that they could hire single women to take over jobs on the production lines.

As the demand for workers increased it was suggested that married women could also work on production lines, but most factory managers and supervisors refused to consider the idea. Despite evidence to the contrary, it was commonly believed that married women with children were not capable of handling factory work or would want too much time off work to attend to family matters (prejudgment).

Finally one company found a way of overcoming the prejudice barrier. They arranged a meeting between the factory manager, the male supervisors and a university research team. The 'research' involved a study of married women in factory jobs to measure just how much less reliable they would be in comparison with single workers. To do this naturally meant putting some married women on the factory floor for the trial period. After six months the supervisors' prejudice finally broke down, as they discovered that in fact married women were far less trouble to supervise, worked harder, and had a lower absenteeism record than any other group in the factory.

People who dislike or distrust each other can experience a lowering of barriers if they can be persuaded to share a meal and a few drinks. Other ways of developing trust and openness between people (and reducing prejudice) are suggested in Chapter 12, 'Creating co-operation'.

Pain or illness

People who enjoy good health forget that physical pain or discomfort can act as a communication barrier, affecting
- the desire to communicate;
- the ability to understand clearly;
- the ability to reason logically in response to a message;
- the ability to solve problems or make decisions about the content of a message.

Somebody with a bad headache or a cold will simply not be able to handle these aspects of communication as well as they might wish to.

Guilt, shame and stress

With a little empathy anyone can understand the effect of a cold or a headache and accept the sufferer's difficulty in handling two-way communication, but other less obvious problems can have the same effect. Anxiety, guilt, shame, nervousness, despair — all these create emotional stress. Individuals in this kind of situation may have little or no control over their communication barriers and should not be held to blame for poor performance or misunderstandings. In fact, criticism only sets up a situation in which blame, shame, guilt and stress chase each other round in a circle.

It is possible, however, to overcome these barriers, if both sender and receiver really *want* to communicate and can use empathy, stress management skills or similar techniques.

Fear of change

People who are worried about change are better able to communicate their fears if they are given a part to play in planning the change — for instance, given the basic outline for the new plan and then asked to work out

- how and when the change can best be introduced;
- where new equipment or personnel will be situated;
- what could be added to the new program to make it more effective.

You may need to reduce anxiety barriers first, however, before any worthwhile communication can take place.

Anger — the five-way barrier

Anger is one of the most serious communication barriers and one of the least understood. Anger or aggression is confusing to deal with, because it can stem from different sources.

Anger can be a *positive force*. Sometimes you need to take strong action against others who refuse to deal with you honestly or fairly. Assertion (see 'Open and assertive communication', in Chapter 12) is preferable, but as Shirley Smith emphasises in *Set Yourself Free* (1990), you have every right to express your personal anger as a way of protecting yourself from threats to your position or your *positive* feelings. Be sure, however, that you are directing your anger at the correct person. Do *not* start trying to solve the problem until your anger has cooled (see Chapter 23, 'Decision making and problem solving in a group').

Anger can be a *signal* that people are under stress. If people are anxious, ashamed, frustrated, worried, guilty, insecure or hurt, they may try to hide these feelings by expressing anger.

Anger helps a *powerful* individual express strength or authority. Used this way it is an effective way of getting others to obey or comply. An angry 'Don't ask why, just do it — or else . . .' is a management tool that gets results quickly and requires little or no skill. It can also save having to communicate or justify reasons. As a short cut therefore, anger may help bosses get a job done, but it also blocks communication between them and the receivers.

Anger can help a *weaker* person to gain power. How? By harnessing the remarkable ability of anger to create a sense of guilt or shame in another person (even when that person has done nothing wrong). Although unjustified, such negative feelings can be very real; consequently, an innocent party often makes concessions or gives up power to reduce the 'shame' (see 'Dealing with manipulation', in Chapter 13).

Anger helps to keep barriers in place. Individuals — weak or strong — who do not want to face facts or who want to keep people at a distance can use their anger to maintain that distance. Some go one step further. If they can first make *you* angry, then your anger strengthens the barriers. This is particularly common in the case of denial barriers.

Since nobody is likely to tell you which of these reasons are behind the anger expressed, you will need special strategies for dealing with anger in communication. (See Chapter 12, 'Creating Co-operation'.)

Other barriers

Priority clashes

Sometimes a message is clearly understood and the receiver intends to co-operate, but other messages get in the way. You ask someone to do an urgent job for you. They promise to do it immediately. But as soon as you leave another client calls with an even more urgent problem, and this is done instead. To avoid this you need to establish the priority of your request. While explaining what you want done, state clearly

- when it is needed (give a fixed time);
- why it is important;
- what could happen if it is not fulfilled on time.

Leave no gaps in your communication for others to fill. Arrange to be contacted immediately if the job cannot be completed on time.

Negative anticipation

Helena was reprimanded by Vivian a week ago for an accident that was really no one's fault. The next time Vivian speaks to her Helena will be half-expecting the same kind of message, so when Vivian walks by and casually remarks, 'Your work is really improving', Helena misses the positive note and takes the comment as yet another reminder of the previous episode.

Instead of the bare comment, 'Your work is . . .', Vivian would have been wiser to start with some preliminary conversation, to 'switch on' communication and re-establish a positive two-way relationship; it would have lowered Helena's negative anticipation barrier and prepared her for a positive message.

Lack of credibility

Barriers that arise from distrust or disbelief are hard to overcome. Make sure your body language, facial expression and background signals all match your words. People will not trust someone who says 'Yes, I'm quite happy with your work' if the speaker's face and tone of voice fail to signal enthusiasm or warmth. A client's 'yes' will mean little if his or her eyes and body are saying 'no'; the non-verbal message is 'louder'. In written communication, correspondence by computer, particularly if unsigned, will create little trust.

Different goals

Whether you are writing a letter, speaking in a meeting or bargaining over prices, if you want agreement it helps to compare goals and show that you and others have a common purpose; then use this as a foundation for co-operation. A clash of goals at work can have a serious effect on co-operation (see Chapter 25, 'Corporate communication'). If management and unions each see the other as having totally different goals, this maintains low trust. Communication slows down and agreement becomes more difficult.

No common interests

If people play different sports or work at different jobs, the lack of common interests can be a similar barrier. To overcome this barrier, show an interest in a person's way of life. Say 'I can see you are really interested in . . .', and then ask questions.

Unpopular channels

Similar barriers arise if other people do not like a particular communication channel that you happen to prefer. Recognise this and adjust to it. If you call a formal meeting and no one else turns up, change to an informal get-together with sandwiches and coffee.

Diagnosing breakdowns

As explained in Chapter 3, sharing feedback helps to pinpoint communication breakdowns and therefore to select the best solutions.

Using feedback to diagnose breakdowns

1. Ask 'how?' instead of 'what?'
Ask what procedure the listener intends to follow in carrying out your request. The response will give you a better idea of what they have really understood.

2. Ask the receiver to repeat your message.
Some are happy to do this; some are not, since your request could imply distrust, but with friends — or someone you are helping — this is an excellent way to avoid misunderstandings.

3. Explain why you need feedback.
Since you are studying communication breakdowns, it will help to get open and direct feedback about misunderstandings as often as possible. Explain this to receivers, and ask for their co-operation in providing it.

4. Do *not* ask 'Did you understand?'
Questions like that add to the problem. Few people will openly admit failure to understand, especially if they are trying to impress you. Instead, ask new employees, for instance, to repeat the skill you have been demonstrating.

5. If you are the receiver, don't wait to be asked for feedback.
Volunteer feedback. Say 'Let's see if I can remember it all. First I have to . . .'; this also encourages others to do the same.

Summary

1. Anything that delays a message or makes it harder to convey meaning to another person is a communication barrier.

2. You can overcome most communication barriers if you are prepared to spend extra time, effort or money.

3. A breakdown in understanding involves a variation of meaning between the thought the sender wanted to share and the thought produced in the receiver's mind.

4. People who are not clear about their purpose in communication usually send unclear messages that lead to breakdowns.

5. The YCMI communicator is one who thinks misunderstandings are always the receiver's fault.

6. Stress, fear, shame, guilt, pain or illness are all likely to lead to personal communication barriers affecting the desire to communicate, the ability to understand clearly and the ability to respond logically to incoming messages.

7. Denial — a result of unwillingness to receive the message, or bias or prejudice — also leads to blockages and barriers.

8. You can reduce fear of change (a common barrier) by allowing people to take part in planning the change.

9. Anger can help to keep barriers in place, or keep people at a distance. Anger is often a form of self-defence when someone is feeling anxious, ashamed or guilty.

10. Use feedback to diagnose breakdowns, and don't wait to be asked; when communicating, give feedback as a matter of course. This encourages others to do the same.

11. Use empathy: 'sit in the receiver's chair' to discover the causes of misunderstandings and breakdowns.

Exercises

1. Give some examples of a noise barrier that you have experienced recently. How would you overcome this kind of barrier?

2. You need an important file that you gave to Lorrie late yesterday. If you say 'Lorrie, could you bring me that file, I need it again', what kind of problems can arise? Why? How could you avoid them? *which file* *specific* *the file*

3. In the example on page 66 a message to Sal was sent through a communication chain. If you were Sal, and knew that the message had been through four or five links in the chain, what would you do to clarify it?

4. Describe occasions on which you experienced filtering or gatekeeping. How did you overcome it?

5. Describe a case in which you had to communicate with someone who was just not interested in your message. How did you handle the 'not interested' blockage?

6. Some people say the best way to overcome a denial barrier is to force the individual concerned to 'face the facts'. Do you agree or disagree? *impartial*

7. Give other examples of bias or prejudice barriers you have experienced recently. How can people overcome these barriers?

sculptor
Gulf war
religious
politics
gender / male
partial = part of a bit
← female I am partially disabled
partially affect
a very strong will
impartial
racial bias/prejudice

PART 2

Developing communication skills

CHAPTER 8

Face-to-face communication

Let thy speech be better than silence, or be silent.

Dionysius the Elder (fourth century BC)

A vital aspect of business communication is knowing how to make the most of daily discussions, particularly at work. You know how to talk and listen already, but do you know about 'timing' a discussion, how to tune in to non-verbal signals as well as to words? Can you tell when it's best to stay silent (and listen) and when to speak? Because you spend so much time each day talking and listening it's easy to assume you already have the necessary skills to handle any kind of discussion, but there are many ways of improving both talking and listening.

This chapter looks at some practical techniques that will help you to take a more active role in discussions with clients and colleagues, and with people at higher levels in the organisation. Some special guidelines for taking part in interviews and for on-the-job training are included at the end of the chapter.

Topics

Active listening

Discussions at work

On-the-job interviews

Training, instructing and giving directions

Active listening

Active listening is a skill you learn by practice. It takes more effort than plain 'hearing', but the benefits make it well worthwhile. How do you become a more active listener?

Active listening – guidelines

1. Know why you are listening.
If you don't know why you are listening, you won't gain as much from communicating as you will if you have a definite purpose in mind.

2. Listen with your whole body.
Active listening involves you physically and mentally. Read the sender's body movements, and exchange non-verbal feedback. Look directly at the sender, express interest with your face, eyes and hands.

3. Give feedback, respond to the person.
The best listening also involves talking, as you respond verbally to what you hear. If you agree, say so; don't leave the other person guessing. A comment which confirms that you have heard and understood is better than just a 'yes' or a nod of the head.

An ideal response is to rephrase the speaker's words, indicate support, and then ask a question: 'I agree with you about needing more operators. Should we train some of the present staff or advertise for outsiders?'.

4. Show empathy.
Make it clear that you understand the other person's point of view, even if you do not agree with it. Active listening requires sensitive judgment about when people want to talk and when they don't. Use one ear to listen to meaning and the other to listen to feelings (like reading between the lines). Remember that words often mask real feelings.

5. Encourage the other person.
If a sender is shy or nervous, suppress your own ideas or feelings and instead offer support: 'That's interesting; tell me how you . . .'; 'So what happened then . . .?'; 'I see what you mean . . .'.

Face-to-face conversation

6. Forget about talking while you are listening. If you're thinking 'Wait till I tell her what I heard about the new supervisor . . . she won't be so happy then!', that thought takes priority and you lose the other person's ideas. You can't listen properly while you are planning what to say next.

7. Match your mood to other people's moods. If they are excited, be excited too. If they are formal, don't be too casual. If they seem tired or worried, show them you recognise it (see exercise 7, page 84) and determine four responses according to their needs.

8. Listen to the whole message.
Assuming that you'll hear nothing worthwhile or that you've 'heard it all before' shuts off active listening.

9. Put the other person at ease, then relax yourself.
Helping people relax encourages them to talk, but relaxed speakers also use fewer, better chosen words. You'll learn more, and will be regarded as easy to talk to and an excellent listener. If you are impatient, or stressed, it will affect your listening.

10. Look for positive points.
Judge the message, not the person. Concentrate on its positive aspects, not its faults. Nervousness or poor dress sense may irritate but does not prevent a person from having something worthwhile to say.

Benefits of active listening

- You enjoy two-way benefits. When people notice how well you listen to them, they usually reciprocate and try to understand you better.
- Relationships within a group improve. Members develop a more positive attitude towards each other, so personal support and teamwork is strengthened. Friendships develop and deepen.
- You receive more accurate information. People explaining a problem are more inclined to give you the whole story. The more confident they are that you are listening, the happier they will be to share facts they would not reveal to a poor listener.
- People encouraged by your active listening often discover solutions to their own problems. The opportunity to talk things over in depth — or just the chance to put a problem into words — is all they need to see the issue in its proper perspective.
- You get on better with people. Disagreements are more easily settled when people listen to each other. Active listening combined with empathy makes it easier to solve problems or at least reach a compromise.
- You can find out not only what people are saying, but *why* they are saying it. You acquire vital information and discover more about what is really going on.

Limits on listening

Interrupting
You may disagree with what is being said; however, it pays to hear the other person out. Interrupting to inject a counter-argument is a non-verbal signal. It suggests that for you, scoring a point of disagreement holds a higher priority than finding what issues you agree on. If you listen without interrupting and *then* in turn make your point, the other person will be more inclined to listen to you.

Letting your emotions control your listening
If you get too emotional you'll be more inclined to jump to conclusions or interpret words and actions wrongly. This distorts the discussion and hinders clear understanding.

Listening with your fears instead of your ears
The more anxious you are and the more stress you feel, the more likely you are to make serious errors in listening. Put your fears aside long enough to hear what the other person is really saying. If you cannot do this, try to postpone the discussion. It's better to walk away from a high-stress situation than to continue if you are getting angrier by the minute.

Selective hearing
If you 'screen out' what you would prefer not to hear, you must finish up with an incomplete picture. If you then fill in the gaps yourself, you have even less understanding of a message.

Inadequate background knowledge
Often when people begin to speak they assume you know exactly what they are referring to. If this appears to happen, stop the speaker and ask for clarification.

Blaming the speaker for listening problems
Everyone can develop better listening skills. Beware of people who say that they don't have listening problems — that the fault lies with the speaker.

Understand what you hear

As you listen, you'll need to extract the main ideas from among the other points. People cannot always serve their spoken messages to you in neat, organised packages; that's why they write important messages — to sort out ideas before presenting them.

Listen for key 'topic' ideas. They need not always be facts. Facts, data and examples may have been added only to support the main topic, which might be non-factual but vitally important — for instance, how others feel about a controversial issue.

The average person speaks at an average of 100–250 words a minute. You can hear and understand over 400 words a minute and can think at an even faster rate. Use this spare thinking time to concentrate on summarising main points, clarifying meanings and checking non-verbal signals.

Consider the context in which you are listening, the power ratio and other background signs before deciding what the *main* topic really is. The guidelines explained in Chapter 4 (understanding), Chapter 5 (empathy) and Chapter 9 (comprehension) will help you to isolate the main points. Then use feedback to find out whether what you *think* you understand is in fact the key issue.

One-way listening

Practising one-way listening is important too. Many active-listening skills, while intended for two-way communication, can be used to develop your one-way listening in situations such as lectures or meetings. Ten minutes spent each day listening to and watching current affairs and documentary programs on television will improve your ability to collect important data in this way.

Discussions at work

How often, when you need something done in a hurry, have you said 'I'll go and talk to —— about it myself'? Personal contact gets results faster because problems can be identified quickly and decisions made on the spot. The aim of most discussions is the exchange of ideas and information, and usually some persuasion as well.

Personal discussions — guidelines

Personal discussions take place in many and varied situations, as diverse as selling your house, arranging for a colleague to do your work while you are on holidays and lunching with your manager and an important client. How do you make sure personal discussions are a success? Most involve two-way communication, so you find yourself acting alternately as sender and receiver.

Starting off

Clarify the relationship
Establish an atmosphere in which all parties can share ideas, information and feelings openly and comfortably. Exchanging friendly greetings helps break the ice. So does a cup of coffee, a drink or a meal together.

Show interest and empathy
The less doubt about the relationship, the more successful the discussion. If anyone is unclear about the power ratio between those present the atmosphere is dampened. Some basic aspects of the relationship are of course defined non-verbally — for example, by shaking hands. It's better, however, if one or both parties establish empathy more clearly by putting it into words: 'I feel I can trust you to give me the right advice'.

Build a bridge
Having a similar interest draws people together. Whether it's fishing, classical or popular music, computers or work interests, just recognising the connection is one of the best ways of creating the atmosphere for a successful discussion. Spend a few minutes finding out about other people's interests before launching into the main topic.

Respect rituals and formalities
There are some unwritten rules or behaviour patterns that you should observe before starting a personal discussion, especially with anyone who is not well known to you — for example, when entering someone's office, remain standing until you are offered a seat. Rituals vary from situation to situation, but if you ignore them you may put the other person offside. If the discussion is with a person from overseas, call the appropriate consulate or

embassy in advance for advice on the correct way of conducting introductions, and other protocol.

Establish the purpose

Although personal discussions tend to be informal and spontaneous, it pays to have an outline in mind. You usually can't prepare in detail, but think in advance about what you are going to say.

You may already have an idea of what you hope to get out of the discussion, but *both* parties need to be clear about its purpose if it is to work properly. Even if you're talking with someone you know well, never assume without checking that you both have the same topic in mind. Make a remark that will draw a response from the other person which will either confirm the topic or indicate doubt. Ask a question: 'Do you know when the new offset press will be ready for use?' or 'Have you ever had to do a submission for the board?'.

Exchange information – clearly

The more specific, straightforward and factual data you can share, the better is your basis for agreement. Prepare your facts and arrange them clearly in your mind.

Use non-verbal communication to help understanding

Though discussions are based on verbal messages, you need to supplement speech with complementary body movement. Consider facial expressions and hand gestures. Tune into the non-verbal transmissions and background signals communicated by the person you are talking with.

Verify important data

If you have relevant evidence — photographs or samples — use them. When seeking information, ask questions and check reliability. If the other party relies on generalisations, sweeping claims and doubtful assertions, the case presented may be weak.

Keep the discussion moving

Be flexible

You'll have some idea of what course the discussion should follow. If you find it wandering, try not to overreact. Listen to what others want to talk about, then slowly redirect the topic to the main point with a statement like 'Is this as important as our earlier discussion, when you were saying ...' or 'I was particularly interested in something you said earlier' or 'I would like to go back to something that you said before'. In each case, you are referring to something the other person said or something you discussed together; in this way you avoid creating the impression that you are only interested in directing the conversation towards your particular goal.

Ask open-ended questions

Ask questions that will invite an exchange of useful information and encourage other people to talk about themselves, their feelings and their opinions.
- What do you like most about this plan?
- What do you think will happen when the new boss takes over?

Build agreement

The techniques involved in creating agreement vary according to the situation. If you have solid facts to build on, then a logical and well-reasoned argument of the kind described in Chapter 11 may be sufficient. In other cases you might need also to communicate support, friendship or appreciation. (Other persuasive techniques are described in Chapters 13, 14, 22, 23, 24 and 31.)

Express your feelings

A discussion needs to be about more than facts and figures. The way you speak — the tone of your voice — helps others tune in to your feelings. But if you are not happy, words are easier for others to follow than body language. Explain the situation, so that the other party is not left guessing.

Use your whole body *total meaning*

Look at the other person. Eye contact is a non-verbal signal indicating trust, openness and a high degree of interest. While you are speaking, monitor your non-verbal messages, too. Nod in agreement, use facial expressions and maintain an alert body posture to show that the other person has your attention.

Be natural

Show 'the real you'. Be prepared to acknowledge any lack of understanding and be helpful if the other person has a similar problem. Use your normal voice, and 'adult-to-adult' language. Chapter 6 outlined the dangers of the parent message and its negative effect on agreement.

Give feedback

Let the other person know how the process of agreement is working: 'Let's see if this will work ...', or 'Can I summarise what we have discussed so far?'.

Listen more than you talk

A discussion is a two-way affair; allow time for the other person to express views freely. You have two ears and one tongue, use them in the same proportion. Taking up more than your 'fair share' of discussion time is a power-ratio signal that says 'I am the more important'. Others will avoid communication with you, even on vital matters.

Don't try to dominate

Avoid showing anger or impatience. If differences arise, discuss them calmly and logically and be prepared to admit your own mistakes. Don't build a verbal wall around yourself as protection from ideas you don't agree with. Be open-minded and prepared to change your point of view, or at least to modify it in the light of logical argument.

Avoid direct contradiction

It's better to appear to accept an initial claim, before directing the other person's attention to what may be wrong with it. You might say, 'That's an interesting idea, but do you think that all staff will be able to carry it out without extra training?', or 'Yes, I may have some difficulty in handling the increased responsibility, but this is just the kind of experience to help me learn how'.

Closing the discussion

Don't go on for too long. After a certain period, you will feel the pressure of a two-way active conversation. Learn how long you can spend in active discussion before losing concentration; for many people 15 to 20 minutes is the limit. It is better to end before your lack of concentration becomes obvious. Set limits in advance — 'I only have half an hour, but let's talk until 3.30'. Watch for non-verbal signs — such as increasingly longer pauses — that the other person wants to stop, but don't make

it appear as though, having got what you wanted, *you* want to rush off. It is good if the other person makes the first definite move to conclude.

A successful discussion ends with both parties feeling it achieved what was intended. Restate the original aim and summarise the discussion to show clearly *your* view of what you have agreed to: 'Well, John, that solves it as long as you agree to ...', 'Great, now we have decided to ..., we can ...' or 'That's a good idea, Penny, I'll go ahead and ...'. If there is a need for another get-together, arrange it before you leave and close on a note that suggests the next discussion will be as useful as this one.

Choosing times and places

If you are planning a discussion, check first to see whether the time and place are convenient for others. If you want to avoid interruptions, plan a meeting away from the work environment. 'That's a good idea. Let's go out and talk about it over lunch.'

If someone else wants to talk and the time doesn't suit you, explain why: 'That's important to me, too, and I've got some time free this afternoon. How about getting together at 3.30 when I'll be able to concentrate on it?'. Stress your willingness to discuss the topic, but only when you can give it your full attention.

Group discussions

A group of workers sitting around a table discussing a problem — or a group of supervisors discussing the introduction of a new procedure on the shop-floor — may divide into small groups to discuss some aspect of the matter. Group discussions can be similar to other face-to-face discussions considered in this chapter, but they are often subject to a number of specific influences (see Chapter 23, 'Decision making and problem solving in a group').

On-the-job interviews

On-the-job interviews are used to collect information and deal with all kinds of problems. In a typical interview one person acts as leader or interviewer, the other as interviewee, but in some cases there is more than one interviewer and occasionally more than one interviewee. It is just another form of conversation or discussion, but knowing how to communicate in an interview is an important skill. (Employment interviews are covered in Chapter 21, 'Getting the job you want'.)

Performance or appraisal interview

Interviews help in assessing or appraising skills, performance and progress on the job. Appraisal interviews may also be part of a technique in promotion assessment; the interviewer may point out weaknesses and suggest how they could be corrected. Welcome this kind of interview, and count yourself fortunate if you work in an organisation that uses this method to help staff get ahead. (You are always entitled to see a report of the interview.)

Information gathering

This kind of interview is used to collect data for use in a report, as part of an opinion survey, or to explore any special interest (see Chapter 31).

Police interview

After an accident or a robbery you may be interviewed by police. There is no need to fear the interview. Police need the help of honest citizens to do their job. Give the plain facts and avoid dramatic statements. Remember that you may be called months later to repeat the information in court, so take detailed notes of exactly what you say. If a statement is typed by the police and you are asked to sign it, *insist* on receiving a copy for your own records.

Grievance interview

If you are being unfairly treated or subjected to harassment of any kind, you may find that 'nobody wants to know about it'. One way to handle this problem is to request a grievance interview; this makes the problem 'official' and puts senior staff in the position of having to take action.

An interviewer looking into a grievance needs to be a patient listener. Some take all the details and put them in a report, but in many organisations the interviewer may be a member of the personnel section and can therefore help you — for example, by moving you to a different work area.

If you are the interviewee, be completely open and honest; give both sides of the issue, not just the one that favours you. Sometimes the other person involved may be brought in and you will be required to restate your complaints face to face. Be prepared for this.

Exit interview

This is the final fact-finding step taken when someone is leaving a job. When it comes to saying just what it is that enhances job satisfaction and morale and what causes dissatisfaction, a departing employee may speak far more frankly than those remaining, and may without hesitation explain the decision to leave. The end of the interview is a good time to present a loyal employee with a specially written reference.

Discipline or reprimand interview

This is a variation of the appraisal interview, but differs in that the aim is to resolve a problem that will otherwise lead to dismissal. There should be a frank and clear warning to the employee of the consequences if he or she cannot meet required standards. A signed record must be kept by both parties, so that in the event of a subsequent dismissal the employee cannot claim that no warning was given.

Counselling interview

This special form of interview can prove of great assistance to anyone with a personal problem that is affecting his or her work. Most problems are easier to solve if they are not faced alone, so the counsellor's purpose is to help the client put his or her worries into words rather than keep them bottled up. In contrast to other interviews, the details are completely confidential.

Counsellors do not tell people how to solve problems, they are more like good friends who suggest possible solutions, help clients try them out but leave it up to clients to handle their own lives in their own way. Given a little sound counselling, most people have a far greater capacity for coping with personal problems than they realise.

In some cases an employee may be urged, for his or her own benefit, to make the facts known to the immediate supervisor. Counsellors will help with this if clients are worried about doing it alone.

You as the interviewer

If you are to conduct an interview, think of it as just another face-to-face discussion, but one for which you need to plan ahead. This includes reading relevant files.

The opening — establish the relationship

Your first task is to establish rapport, to put the interviewee at ease. One way of doing this is to ask the person to summarise his or her reasons for coming to the interview.

Describe your purpose

Once the interviewee is feeling relaxed, it is easier for you to provide a clear statement of your objectives. Explain the timing and procedure you plan to follow.

Exchange information and build agreement

Ask and answer questions. Keep alert — pick up relevant points and pursue them with further questioning; this, of course, means using your active listening skills.

Maintain control of the interview

Listen attentively but selectively to assess the genuineness of each comment. Some interviewees can put on a show in order to impress you; on the other hand, nervousness can obscure a person's qualities. Be aware of non-verbal background signals and the value of intuitive, gut-feeling assessment. While not a substitute for thorough investigation, an interview often provides the leads you need to discover the real person underneath the mask.

The close — emphasise the required action

Before closing the interview, allow a short time during which the interviewee should be encouraged to ask questions. End on an active note. You can signal that you want to end the discussion by saying, for instance, 'Now, to finish, I'd like to summarise what you have told me and the steps you intend to take'.

Keep a record
Always make a written record. Note your intuitive impressions as well as the facts — a prepared checklist is a help if you conduct many similar interviews. If it is not possible to take notes as you go along, record your impressions while they are still fresh in your mind — leave time between interviews for this.

Training, instructing and giving directions

These guidelines apply in particular to training in manual skills. However, the same points apply (perhaps with the exception of number 8) when giving almost any kind of order, instruction or direction at work.

1. Prepare people by putting them at ease.
Spend time relaxing the listeners. If people are not at ease, they find it hard to pay attention.

2. Get people interested.
A good way to do this is to show the importance of a task. Every job has a place in the overall plan. Explain how the one you are describing fits in.

3. Find out what people can do.
You do not want to waste time teaching people something they already know, but you cannot assume they have skills or knowledge without first asking them. Make sure, also, that what a person professes to know is correct and not just said to impress you. If someone claims to be familiar with any aspect of the task, ask a specific question; for instance, 'Last time you worked this cutter, what was the first thing you had to do to get it going?'

4. State the task.
Describe each stage of the job clearly, in chronological sequence, and in sufficient detail for anyone to recognise what to do and what not to. Avoid statements such as 'Of course, you are familiar with this part of the job', 'I'm sure you know this' or 'I

know you've done this before', implying that if the trainees do not have this knowledge they are at fault. Even if this is not so, they may be reluctant to admit to lack of knowledge once you have shown you expected more of them.

5. Give full and complete directions.

When giving directions, explain not only *what* you want done but also where, when, how and why. Only then will you be properly understood. Your instructions should include

- when you want the work completed;
- who is to be involved;
- where it is to be done;
- which machines or other equipment are to be used;
- what not to do; and, above all
- why the job needs to be done.

One of the best ways of clarifying any instruction is to put it on paper and include a diagram. Nobody objects to this kind of clarification, even after you have explained something personally.

6. Ask for ideas or suggestions.

The old-fashioned idea that workers were supposed to do as they were told without questioning the reasons or policies involved is no longer acceptable in the well-managed organisation of the 1990s. No matter how interested they may be at the start, everyone's level of involvement in the job will increase if they feel they are able to contribute ideas as well as effort. Even the newest employee can have ideas worth listening to. If suggestions are not acceptable, explain why, avoiding outright rejection if possible.

7. Encourage questions.

A good instructor knows how to stimulate questions. Do not talk all the time. Don't give the impression that you haven't time to answer questions. Good questions indicate that people are really thinking about the job.

8. Ask for feedback.

Ask a trainee to show you what he or she has learned. Depending on the task, try to get either a verbal summary or a demonstration — or better still, a combination in which the trainee goes through the entire process in front of you, explaining what is being done and why. If you have given only general instructions, the feedback could be less detailed.

9. Follow-up.

A wise instructor always checks progress a week or two after a training session. Even if you explained what, where, when, how and why, and you had sufficient feedback to be sure you were understood 'perfectly', situations can alter. Other people, with the best intentions, can give your trainee different instructions; the job itself may change. Even if everything is running smoothly, the trainee will appreciate your follow-up.

Summary

1. Active listening is a skill you learn by practice; it doesn't develop naturally. It encourages others to listen to you and helps them talk more freely.

2. Know *why* you are listening. If you do, you'll get more out of the discussion.

3. Use one ear to listen to meaning, the other to listen to feelings. Try to judge when people want to talk and when they don't. Tune in to what they are really trying to say.

4. Don't think about talking when you should be listening; you can't listen properly if you do. When it is your turn to talk, show you've been listening by responding first to the other person's comments rather than talking about your views.

5. Read the other person's body movements and exchange your own non-verbal signals.

6. Listen for 'topic' or 'key' themes, not just words. The main point of a conversation might not be facts and figures. It might just as easily be how people are feeling about an issue.

7. Always keep a written record of an interview. Record as you go or as soon after as possible, while your impressions are fresh.

8. When giving instructions, a good way to create interest in a task is to show how important it is.

9. Add clarity to instructions by putting them on paper. clearness

Exercises

1. Listen to a radio news broadcast, but don't take any notes. Afterwards, list four or more of the topics covered and write a very short summary of each. When you have done this a

few times, extend your list and summaries to cover six or more items.

2. What is the most interesting piece of information or statement you have heard during the last two days?

3. Who among your friends or colleagues is the best listener you know? What does this person do to create that effect?

4. List six 'do's' and six 'don'ts' as guidelines for good listening.

5. The typical Australian worker is said to spend much more time in face-to-face communication than in reading or writing. How do the following figures compare with your own experience?

   65–80 per cent of time in face-to-face communication (speaking, listening, body language)

   10–20 per cent of time in writing

   5–10 per cent of time reading

   1–5 per cent of time in thinking about communicating

6. Why would you expect to take part in more face-to-face communication as you move up the organisational ladder?

7. You drop into Roz's office to toss around a few points on a new marketing plan that is forming in your mind. Roz listens for a moment, then snaps, 'You don't seem to have thought it out very thoroughly yet. Let me finish this report and come back when you have it worked out more clearly'.

   What is Roz really trying to tell you? How should you respond, as an active listener?

8. List some of the benefits of active listening.

9. What are some of the guidelines for giving instructions?

10. What are some of the 'rituals and formalities' that accompany the start of face-to-face discussions in Australia?

11. What are some of the main types of interviews?

12. Why is it important to keep a written record of an interview?

CHAPTER 9

Reading for understanding

Faster reading with understanding is a skill that with practice you can develop quite easily. Guidelines are suggested in this chapter, which also cover the important issue of 'comprehension'. Critical comprehension involves more than just understanding. It adds depth to the words you read and helps you to interpret non-verbal content and background messages more accurately.

Topics

Selecting, scanning and sorting

Reading for detail

Faster reading

Critical comprehension

Selecting, scanning and sorting

Efficient readers start by working out in advance what they are looking for — what they need and do not need to know. This saves time immediately, since much of what appears in front of you at work does not need to be read at all, and of the remainder a great deal need only be scanned to pick up essential points. The 'S' techniques (Select, Scan and Sort) help you to make the initial choice and determine the level of reading needed for items containing wanted information.

Selecting — 'Why should I read this?'

Establish the real value of the item. Read nothing until you have a clear purpose in mind, and know *why* you should read it. The most productive business readers are those who dispose of unnecessary papers quickly. If an item is not important and a copy will be available whenever you need it, why read it today? Administration sections send out lots of memos on procedures (staff transport, expense claims, using the photocopier). If they concern you directly, read them last (not first); if they don't, for the moment just note that they exist. Use the same method when looking through books in a library or bookshop.

Scanning — 'What are the main points?'

Of the items that need closer examination, begin with a quick overview to get a general idea of what each contains.

- If there is a table of contents, read it first.
- If the text includes headings and subheadings, scan them to make a quick summary.
- Scan the opening and closing paragraphs in each section.
- Scan the rest — keep your eyes moving rapidly, on the lookout for useful information but ready to skip unimportant sections.
- Watch for key words or phrases — sentences beginning 'the main point is' or 'in summary' or 'in conclusion'.

Higher level executives often spend only 30–50 seconds scanning an item before deciding whether it is worth reading in detail. If by then the document does not seem sufficiently important, it will be passed down the line for someone else to read. (When you write, remember that *your* readers may do this too.)

Sorting — 'Which items will I read first?'

Whether you are reading books, letters or memos, the same principle applies: scan only as much as is necessary to allow you to rank the material in order of priority. The time you save by selecting, scanning and sorting allows you to devote more energy and attention to detailed reading of the items that are most important to you.

Reading for detail

Even when you read for detail, start by running your eye once again over the main headings to get an overview of topics and how they are connected — how major points in each chapter relate to subtopics; for example:

$$
1 \quad \text{Major point} \begin{cases} 1.1 \quad \text{topic} \begin{cases} 1.1.1 & \text{subtopic} \\ 1.1.2 & \text{subtopic} \\ 1.1.3 & \text{subtopic} \\ 1.1.4 & \text{subtopic} \end{cases} \\ \\ 1.2 \quad \text{topic} \begin{cases} 1.2.1 & \text{subtopic} \\ 1.2.2 & \text{subtopic} \end{cases} \end{cases}
$$

$$
2 \quad \text{Major point} \begin{cases} 2.1 \quad \text{topic} \begin{cases} 2.1.1 & \text{subtopic} \\ 2.1.2 & \text{subtopic} \end{cases} \\ \\ 2.2 \quad \text{topic} \quad 2.2.1 \quad \text{subtopic} \end{cases}
$$

Once you can see this relationship it becomes easier to grasp the topic as a whole. If there is a summary at the beginning or end of each unit or chapter, read that next.

Reading for detail — guidelines

- Set time aside for detailed reading. Understanding a complex argument or familiarising yourself with new ideas requires concentration.
- Stop all calls, refuse interruptions and give the job of reading your full attention. Recorded music in the background helps concentration, but radio can distract you if it includes commentaries or commercials.
- Treat reading as an *active* process. Be comfortable, but don't relax too much.
- For full understanding it is essential to read material once to gain an overview, then perhaps twice or more again to develop deeper understanding and comprehension (see 'Critical comprehension', pp. 88–91).
- During second and third readings, write short notes to summarise each point. These act as keys

for later recall. There is no rule that says that 'remembering' has to be achieved without notes.

- Highlight or underline important points.
- Do not guess at the meaning of an unfamiliar word; write it down, to be checked in a dictionary (but remember that the dictionary may not give the meaning that was in the writer's mind).
- Note technical terms, and find out what each one actually describes. If it's a term that you could use in your work, add it to your vocabulary.
- Before starting a new section, scan previous material related to the topic.

Faster reading

The speed at which you read depends on

- purpose (study, business, legal, general interest, relaxation);
- level of difficulty (academic, technical, abstract, financial);
- level of interest (personal, professional);
- level of motivation (genuine interest or just necessity.

As you move upwards in your career you will find more and more situations in which you need to scan large numbers of reports, files, memos and so on. The more information you can discover (and remember) in this way, the greater will be your advantage as a decision maker, leader or manager.

In the business world, however, there is more to reading than speed. If you average about 200 words a minute you are a reasonable reader; faster reading is a success *only* if it brings with it the benefits of improved comprehension and the ability to remember what you read. Learning to read faster is the first step. The next is to develop your ability to comprehend what you read.

Special speed-reading and comprehension courses are available at most colleges and universities. Many are self-paced and employ computerised audiovisual or mechanical aids to train your eyes and brain to handle words at a faster rate. Apart from these, there is much you can do for yourself that will improve your speed.

Test yourself

First, as a matter of interest, test your present reading speed. Time yourself and note how many seconds it takes to read pages 99 and 100, which

Speed reading

contain a total of 1288 words. Test your rate again after you have practised the exercises below.

1. Decide first what and how much you are going to read. Know in advance where you will stop.

2. Once you start, do not reread anything even if you are not sure of meaning or you know you have missed a point or two. Keep moving forward until you come to the end. Rereading *after* you have read the unit in full is more efficient.

3. Read groups of words rather than individual words. Run your eye along the top of the line rather than focusing on the centre of each word.

4. As you swing your eye along each line, try to use wider and wider sweeps, taking in larger groups of words.

5. Keep extending the area of vision until you can zigzag down the middle of a page, letting your eyes pull in the words at the edges.

6. Match your speed to the content of the message. Slow down for a heavy part, speed up for straightforward bits.

Note: Make sure you are not 'reading' out loud. Mouthing the words (moving the lips soundlessly) can slow your speed by 50 per cent. Even pronouncing words mentally makes reading slower.

Critical comprehension

No matter how fast you read, if an item involves important decisions that affect your business or your career you need to take time to decide whether you agree with what you read and how you ought to respond.

Benefits of critical comprehension

Critical comprehension helps you to clarify the real message — as distinct from one the writer may want you to receive — and to decide if the action proposed is in your interests. Be especially cautious if you know a writer is trying to persuade you to make a decision or take action that will cost you money, or to adopt a position you are not happy about. Some writers may deliberately distort their messages — play upon your emotions or make exaggerated or unfounded claims about a product — to gain support for a point of view. Critical comprehension helps to protect you in these situations.

Critical comprehension — guidelines

To achieve full comprehension you may need to make a deliberate and conscious assessment of some or all of the points given below, though not necessarily in the order suggested here.

1. What is the relationship between you and the writer?
Do you know the writer personally? Have you communicated with this person before?

2. What is the writer's aim or purpose?
How you comprehend a message may depend on whether the writer wants to take you to lunch, sell you a used car, give you a promotion, help you communicate more effectively or canvass your vote. People write business messages for many reasons, but always with some goal in mind.

Because you can't share two-way feedback or ask questions to clarify meanings, you'll usually need to think carefully about the writer's real purpose, and to identify any hidden motives in the message. Are you expected to benefit as well as the writer?

3. What is the context?
How much do the circumstances of writing (or reading) affect your interpretation of the message? Could background signals such as the power ratio between you and the sender influence your decoding?

4. What effect does the writer's style have on you?
Is it practical or emotional, organised or unstructured? Is the sequence obvious? Do thoughts flow in a logical way or do they seem muddled?
■ Does the writer build up to an action ending that clarifies the aim or purpose of the message?
■ Are some points discussed in full and others treated briefly or ignored? If so, does this suggest that you are not getting the full story?

5. How reliable is the channel (method of transmission)?
Was the message sent directly or passed through several hands?. Is what you are reading all or only part of the original? Has it been rewritten, edited or otherwise filtered by others?

If the transmission process seems too unreliable, ask yourself if it's worth continuing to read. There's no point in trying to comprehend a message if the process is unreliable. Wait until it has been confirmed.

6. Does the non-verbal content convey extra meaning?
What style has the writer used? Was the message signed or unsigned? Does the page layout suggest

that the writer is showing empathy (by making it easier for you to follow), or does it indicate a 'don't care' approach?

7. Is your reaction logical or emotional?

How do you feel about the message? Often your initial gut reaction tells you something worthwhile; sometimes it is a warning that you are being diverted from the real issues by manipulative writing.

- Is the writer trying to create a shock effect, to horrify, astonish or amaze rather than convey facts — for example, in media presentation of news items?
- Does the writer allow facts to speak for themselves or have they been 'coloured' with emotional terms? Some people use the distance between writer and reader, as an opportunity to vary the truth more than they would if communicating face-to-face.
- Have emotional or manipulative techniques been used deliberately to override your judgment? Is the writer working deliberately to get you to respond with a specific emotion (guilt, shame or anger for instance) to steer you towards untimely action?
- Were any writing 'tricks' or devices used to try to influence your point of view?

8. How credible is the message?

Writers tend to give less detail than speakers. You get less of the picture. Is the overall communication reliable and valid? Should you accept or discount the information as it is presented?

Short cuts

In many cases, by step two or three it may be obvious that the message is not important enough to require such extensive analysis, and you do not work all the way through to the end of the list. This applies particularly if you feel someone is trying to feed you unreliable information or to manipulate you. On the other hand, if the issue involves you personally in a $100 000 deal or is concerned with your future promotion prospects it may be necessary to work through every step to make sure that you have achieved complete comprehension.

Choose your response

With much business writing you need to respond to what you read. How should you respond? What is your overall reaction? If you are writing, what will you say? If you need to make a choice, what will your decision be?

Critical comprehension in practice

If comprehension sounds like a complicated process, the case studies below may help to show you that consciously or unconsciously you have been using this process for years. What has been described at length above often happens in a matter of seconds.

Case 1: At an intersection

As you drive towards a busy street intersection you see a six-sided metal sign saying 'STOP'. It is red with white lettering.

Comprehension

The context in which the word STOP is being used is obvious because of its location. The sign exhibits strong non-verbal components that add credibility. The writer's intention is obvious. It takes only a moment to comprehend such a message and to work out the writer's goal or purpose. You note that the writer is not using any unfair or emotionally biased wording to sway your opinion (although a colleague of the writer may be round the corner on a motorcycle, checking to see how well your comprehension is working!).

Reaction

You believe and accept the message and you respond by stopping your vehicle, indicating understanding, agreement and acceptance of its content. And it all happened in half a second.

Case 2: Stop and buy

You are driving in the country when you see another stop-sign. 'STOP NOW!' it says, adding underneath, 'Buy our delicious farm-fresh fruit and vegetables. Bargain prices!' This sign is also painted in white letters on a red metal background, but in this case the metal is rectangular and looks suspiciously like a sheet of old roofing iron. The writing appears to have been hand-painted and is not very neat. The background signals tell you this is a different type of stop-sign.

Comprehension

Consider the intention behind the sign. You comprehend immediately that rather than road safety, this sign is concerned with selling. The writer's purpose is obviously to persuade you to stop long enough to buy farm produce.

- What effect did the choice of channel (hand-painted on a sheet of roofing iron) have on the quality of the message?
- What effect did the context (location beside the gate of a farm) have on its credibility?

Reaction

If your reaction is to stop and buy some fruit it may be either because you wanted some anyhow or because you were attracted by the promise of a bargain. Your response in this case will depend far more on *your* wishes than those of the writer.

Notice that you are again following the same steps for critical comprehension, without even having to think about them. However, as you observe longer and more complex messages it pays to be consciously more aware of the comprehension process you are using, so that you can monitor the outcome.

Case 3: Letter to the editor

Highly persuasive messages often appear in the 'Letters' columns of newspapers. People write these to express their opinions in the hope that others will support them. Some are biased and some base their arguments on feelings alone, with no supporting facts. Such letters provide an opportunity for you to practise your critical comprehension skills.

Start by scanning the following letter. Notice the style of language, the lack of factual content and the overuse of emotionally coloured words.

Dear Editor,

It is a pity that the old myth of the only good snake being a dead one still persists. Your report of a 2.4 metre carpet snake being killed simply because it came into a yard for a minute simply shows the ignorance of some people, and resulted in the death of a beautiful and completely harmless creature.

In fact carpet snakes do a tremendous amount of good by killing rats and mice. The vast majority of snakes are harmless, and the few who are not will never attack, only defend themselves if necessary. Our house is only ten metres from open land with long grass, but we have never seen a rat as we have left the snakes alone.

As our whole town area is a fauna reserve and no snake may be killed unless someone is in danger, the law has been broken, and it will be interesting to see if any action is taken to have the killers punished.

'Snake Lover'

Comprehension

Read the letter again and think about the writer's intention in composing it. Then follow through the steps for critical comprehension, as previously explained. The following issues are probably the most significant.

- *Credibility*: Does the writer appear to be an expert on snakes? (What facts were presented to suggest knowledge or expertise? Do the general claims made about 'all' snakes seem reliable?)
- *Writer's style*: Are words or arguments repeated? If so, what is the writer trying to emphasise? Despite a lack of ability as a writer, is this person trying to say something important?
- *Emotional appeal:* The writer uses one particular word twice in the first paragraph to emphasise the alleged 'ignorance of some people'. What is the word? Does its repetition contribute to or detract from the power of the argument?

Reaction

At this point, consider whether you would
- agree that most snakes are harmless;
- consider encouraging snakes as a means of controlling rats;
- agree that most people are ignorant about snakes;
- agree that all snakes attack only in self-defence and should therefore be left alone;
- support prosecution of the killer;
- remember that the town is a fauna reserve next time you want to attack a snake;
- when killing snakes in future try harder to discriminate between those that are dangerous and those that are beneficial to humanity;
- do nothing at all;
- react in some other way.

As a result of your comprehension you will have noted that the letter lacks credibility because it fails to present a clear argument. You may respond by taking no action at all, but if you do; how much of your reaction would be motivated by your own views rather than those in the letter?

Summary

1. To save reading time, have a clear aim. Work out in advance what you need to know and what you don't.

2. Scan selected items to obtain a quick overview.

3. Sort items into order of priority. Then give the most time to the ones at the top of your list.

4. Read important material more than once — first to gain an overview, again to develop understanding and comprehension.

5. During the second and any later readings, take notes.

6. Critical comprehension involves full understanding of the words used, but also considers non-verbal background signals, the context, and other factors that help to develop a total understanding.

Exercises

1. Read the article below, using the guidelines for business comprehension and understanding. (Chapter 20, 'Summarising and condensing', will show you how to reduce this article to a 150 word summary, using business-condensation techniques. To achieve this you will be asked to identify the main ideas in the article, so as you read and comprehend, make a note of them.)

Youth Unemployment in Australia

A generation of young Australians is growing up with many of its age group unable to find work. The total number of 15 to 18-year-old school leavers looking for full-time work represents 18.7 per cent of that age bracket. They make up more than a third of the total number of unemployed and face an average wait of five months after leaving school before they find some form of part-time employment. Many have yet to work in any kind of full-time job and a percentage have been out of work for longer than a year.

Some stay at school until a job comes along even though they would rather be in work. Some have given up looking for work altogether and adjusted their lifestyles to the point where they seem able to exist for ever on unemployment benefits. Some become involved in voluntary community work in return for meals and handouts. Even those who study and gain qualifications are not immune. There are cases where young graduate scientists are working as gardeners, while qualified accountants sell ice-cream.

As the average length of time out of work increases (along with the number looking for jobs), it becomes progressively harder to motivate the young unemployed to keep on looking for work. Today, thousands of young Australians seek apprenticeships unsuccessfully; that means there will be a chronic shortage of trade technicians during the 1990s and beyond.

Experts cite many causes of unemployment. Inflation and economic recession have reduced the opportunity of industrial expansion in areas which would have absorbed large numbers of workers. Some blame increased unemployment on the high birth rate of the 1960s and the consequent spill into the workforce of larger numbers of young people. Many see technology, particularly computerisation, intruding into a widening area, particularly in offices and retailing. As the school-leaving age increases, many employers argue that this actually reduces the employability of school-leavers when they enter the workforce at a later age but with no work experience.

Speaking at a Youth Employment seminar in Sydney last week, Australian Consolidated Credit's National Manager (Dr Lyn Baldwin) told participants that the problem of youth unemployment had two important contributing factors.

'Current wage scales for juniors act against school-leavers gaining employment', Dr Baldwin said. 'The pattern of most awards was established many years ago when most young people left school at the age of 14 or 15 and had some years of work experience by the time they turned 18 or 19. Juniors at that time received a low rate of pay for a start, but by the time they reached 19 the gap between their pay and the adult wage was quite small.' Their work experience made them worth their increased pay rate. Today young people enter the workforce at 18 with no experience, yet expect to start on high rates of pay.

But the main cause of youth unemployment, according to Dr Baldwin, is the increased participation of mature-age women in the workforce. 'This', said Dr Baldwin, 'is the most significant change in employment patterns in the last thirty years'. Dr Baldwin quoted Australian Bureau of Statistics figures to show that mature-age women now occupy 27 per cent of jobs which at one time would have been reserved for juniors. Women are often preferred to juniors because of their training and work experience. They are also more stable as long-term employees. 'Remedies are not easy', Dr Baldwin said. 'It is naive to think of reducing the wage levels of juniors to give them an economic advantage in the job market. This ignores the realities of the industrial relations system. It is illegal to discriminate against women in terms of employment and it would be against Australia's best interests socially and economically to discourage women from maintaining their present role in the workforce.'

National TAFE Research Officer Pat McPhee, who also spoke at the seminar, said planning was going on continuously to find new ways to ease youth unemployment. Additional emphasis was being placed on the problems experienced by students in handling the transition from school to work. Schemes that enabled students to gain work experience while they were still at school had been partly successful, but by far the best results had come from TAFE programs that focused on giving school-leavers the practical skills they needed to get jobs.

Other suggested solutions include government- and industry-funded traineeships, and a modernised apprenticeship system for the skilled trades. Greater emphasis is now being placed on compulsory community service for those on unemployment benefits or not undertaking full-time study, to help them maintain their working skills and avoid the negative stigma (often associated with unemployed youth) of having no useful role in the community.

Adapted with permission from an article originally published in the *Courier-Mail*, Brisbane

(a) What was the writer's motive, aim or purpose? How do you think that you and other readers are expected to react or respond after reading the article?

(b) How reliable is a news report like this? The information appears to have been rewritten or edited. Has anything been added? What has been left out?

(c) What (if any) significant facts are ignored or missed by the writer?

(d) What (if any) points are exaggerated or overemphasised?

(e) What (if any) writing techniques might help to create an inaccurate picture or colour meanings in one direction?

(f) Does the context in which the article was presented have any effect on its importance or credibility?

(g) Do your feelings about the topic affect your reaction to it?

(h) How relevant or important is the article to *you*? What was your first reaction? What is your reaction now?

(i) What (if any) non-verbal content is there that could affect your reaction or alter your decoding and interpretation of meanings?

2. Choose a full-page article in a newspaper or magazine on a topic you are interested in. Time yourself as you read it as quickly as possible, then write down four of the main ideas it contained.

Time yourself again as you read it a second time, but this time read for detail and at your normal speed. Count the number of words in the article and calculate your normal-reading and fast-reading speeds.

In the two readings, how much difference is there in your recall of the main points? Did you miss any important information when you read rapidly?

CHAPTER 10

Studying and learning

A positive approach is your most powerful learning aid: the more you believe in your ability to learn, the more you will learn. This chapter will show you how to develop a positive approach both in class and when studying alone. You also need to know how to make the most of your time. This helps reduce your stress level and increases your effectiveness as a student.

Topics

Approaches to learning

Class work

Personal study

Assignments

Examinations

Approaches to learning

The better prepared you are, the more you gain from any learning situation. Develop confidence in yourself and your ability to learn. Forget past evaluations. Many people who think they are 'below average' students do well in practical areas such as communication and management. School results may not be reliable indicators of how successful you'll be in business and other tertiary studies, nor in business itself.

Establish your study goals

The clearer a goal, the more power it has to motivate you. Positive objectives make studying more rewarding. Choose study goals that are specific and realistic.

1. Tell lecturers about your aims.

Aims put into words do more to motivate you than those you only think about. Lecturers can help you if you discuss your aims with them. They respond to students who have a positive outlook and a drive to succeed.

2. Put your goals on paper.

Goals you write down are more powerful motivators than those you only talk about. Draw up a personal goal plan (with *your* name on it). Divide the plan into stages, showing what you will have achieved in three months, six months, one year and five years from now.

> **Goal plan: Kelly Stewart**
> By the end of this week I will have achieved:
> By the end of March I will have achieved:
> By June I will have achieved:
> In one year from now I will have achieved:
> In two years from now I will have achieved:
> In five years from now I will have achieved:

Keep the chart where you will see it every day — on your desk or mirror — and update it regularly. It's not necessarily a good idea to make personal goals known to family and friends unless you are sure of their support — associates and some fellow students may even belittle your aims, which won't help to motivate you.

3. Picture your goals.

Goals displayed as actual *images* are the most powerful motivators of all. Put up pictures — of the car you want or the house or holiday you'd like — near your goal plan.

Picture yourself as a successful student. Imagine the advantages of success. Regularly visualising a positive image is a powerful force in establishing new learning habits or discarding old ones (see Rosamond Nutting, *Skills for Positive Living,* p. 35).

4. Personalise your goals.

High motivation is linked to personal goals. Make another list — this one showing all the things you want as rewards for finishing your course.

- travel, and new friendships
- more money
- a new car
- job satisfaction
- promotion, power or status
- increasing self-esteem and self-confidence

A strong personal aim, such as getting that one special job, motivates you more than studying just to get a degree or a diploma, or to please your family.

5. Review your plans and goals.

Cross off your list those either achieved or no longer appropriate. Add new ones. Be realistic; don't worry about the ones you can't reach.

6. Give yourself rewards for studying.

Rewards are positive motivators. Give yourself a break or an outing; buy yourself a small gift each time you hand in an assignment. Promise yourself some time pursuing your favourite activity after a goal has been achieved. You don't have to study all the time.

7. Be persistent — stick at it.

Most people who complete set assignments and tests in a subject *do* pass. Students who fail are rarely those who give it their 'best try', but rather the ones who decide for themselves they cannot succeed, and give up. They fail not because they lack the ability to pass, but because they tell themselves they are going to fail. Think positively.

Plan your time

The most efficient use of time is achieved by planning — not (as many people think) by being punctual or by clock-watching. Knowing in advance what you plan to do and the order in which you will do it saves time and mental energy; you don't have to stop and think about what to do next. Planning helps you fit as much as you can into each twenty-four hours without stress. Here are some pointers.

1. Establish priorities.

Decide: 'What will the consequences be if I do/don't complete this item today or this week?'. Arrange jobs in order of priority on paper, in a diary or on a computer. The more you stand to gain by doing each individual task — or the more you stand to lose by *not* doing it — the higher its priority will be.

2. Plan specifically.

Plan in clear, practical units; for instance, 'I will answer these five questions before lunch' or 'I will read Chapter 6, then watch a video', rather than 'I will study law today'. You'll feel a stronger sense of success because you can see yourself reaching your planned objectives regularly.

3. Organise regular jobs.

A fixed routine or sequence for repetitive jobs saves time, especially in those parts of the day when time is shortest. Trying to get dressed, make breakfast and pack your bag all at once wastes time. Work out how many minutes each routine task takes, then see if you can improve on your 'personal best'.

4. Divide large tasks into smaller ones.

Tasks such as writing assignments should *not* be completed in 'one go'. Dividing them into smaller units with clear stopping points allows you to finish one step at a time, as suggested in point 5, with breaks in between.

The four-stage writing method (see Chapter 14) is ideal for this purpose. If reading a whole chapter will take a long time, plan ahead; study the first three or four points, take a break, then go on to the next three.

5. Complete one (short) task before starting another.

Having divided a long job into short, easily completed units, don't try to do several at once. The more half-finished jobs you have to think about, the more stress you will feel and the more time will be wasted moving backwards and forwards. If others want you to stop in the middle of your task because they want help with theirs, tell them to wait.

6. Use the same time slots each week for routine study.

Study the same subject at the same times and on the same days. Program personal study to be done just before or just after lectures in the subject concerned.

7. Match daily study time to fit appropriate activities.

When fresh, tackle difficult tasks. Walking and

creative thinking go together, so if you want to think of new or different ways of tackling a project, take a walk and think as you go. Learn routine formulae on a train or bus. Driving in traffic gives you time to review points in your head.

8. Allow yourself free time.

Leave a single block of, say, half a day free of work or study or family commitments every weekend. Use the time for unforeseen situations, or just for relaxing.

9. Set aside time for leisure activities.

Rather than give up a favourite activity, drop its priority level. Program it to fit in with your study plan, not the other way round. Choose a time for it at the end of a concentrated study period, so that enjoyment is a reward for hard work. Don't leave heavy study to be done at the end of a day of recreation.

10. Prepare timetables.

Planners like those suggested in Figures 10.1 and 10.2 help you to see where you are heading. Don't

buy expensive wall charts; a small one that you draw up yourself and which fits in a folder is better.

Use a similar type of planner to work out daily schedules or to keep track of any tasks where you need to follow a routine pattern.

Stay flexible in your approach to time. Don't overorganise; leave some spare slots for unforeseen interruptions. Remember that most human beings *underestimate* the time it will take to perform any task. Allow for this, and your plan will be more effective.

Blocks to learning

Anxiety and stress

Some people work well under pressure. They like deadlines and the excitement of meeting them. They can manage more work 'at the last minute'. Other people find stress a real barrier to learning. Ask your counsellor about stress-reducing strategies.

Monday 10th	Tuesday 11th	Wednesday 12th	Thursday 13th	Friday 14th	Saturday 15th	Sunday 16th
Economics assignment due in 5.00 pm		Maths test 11.00	Start work on report plan	Give talk in class		
Monday 17th	Tuesday 18th	Wednesday 19th	Thursday 20th	Friday 21st	Saturday 22nd	Sunday 23rd
Study for letter-writing test	Letter test 2.00 pm		No classes— study at home		Farm visit for report	

Fig. 10.1 *Weekly study planner*

Time	Monday	Tuesday	Wednesday	Thursday	Friday	Saturday	Sunday
5.30							
6.00							
7.00							
7.30							
8.00							

Fig. 10.2 *Daily study planner*

Overcoming study problems

Distractions

Many students find that background noise — especially music with a particular beat or rhythm — helps them to study. Others need absolute quiet. People who are not studying are one of the worst sources of distraction; try not to study in places where they can contact you. Studying in a park or on a bus or train may be easier than at home.

Personal problems

Personal problems affect study, concentration and motivation. Whatever the trouble is, *do not* try to handle it in secret or on your own. Talk to a friend or your college counsellor, join a group where others have the same worries, seek spiritual counselling — anything is better than bottling up your anxiety. If your worries are related to such issues, Chapter 7, 'Communication breakdown' and Chapter 12, 'Creating co-operation' can help.

Class work

Educators have tried for years to find a study environment that would improve on class learning. Self-paced programs, teach-yourself computer packages, and study kits all have a place. However, faced with a choice of external study or live classes, most students prefer an active class situation.

Make the most of class time

The value of class learning is enhanced if you prepare beforehand, listen effectively and participate actively.

Preparation

It is easier to understand any topic if you prepare in advance. Find out exactly what reading, what assignments, what kind of practice and what level of participation is required for each subject. Ask for details of requirements for each assignment. Find out in advance what topics are to be covered in each class. Read something about them, even if it is only a 10-minute skim through a textbook while you eat. This helps you to focus on what is being said.

Preparation is essential for participation in group discussions, but you also need to be ready physically. Rush and hunger create stress that interferes with concentration; evening students in particular need to prepare for the night's program — try to relax for even a few minutes, and always have something to eat before a night class.

Active listening in class

Listening is important for learning, but it is a skill you need to learn and practise. Tune in to words and phrases such as 'the first point is ..', 'the main point here is that' and 'in summary' (see Chapter 8 — 'Active listening'). And just listening is not enough; take plenty of notes too.

Taking and making notes

Good notes help you to recall important points quickly and easily. Keep them brief — a matter of 'more think, less ink': by taking fewer notes you allow more time for thinking about what is being said or planning questions that will add to your understanding. Explanations in response to your questions will add to your understanding.

Learn how to select what to write, and how to write it. Your notes must provide shape and structure, and tie all points together.

1. Use your own words rather than the words of the speaker.

2. Develop a 'note-hand' — your own particular shorthand taking; for instance, shorten terms such as 'interpersonal communication' to 'inter/p com/c'.

3. Write essential details — figures, dates, times, technical terms and names — in full.

4. Ask for formulae and key words to be written on a board or screen. Do not write them the way they sound.

5. Make your notes easy to follow. Number important points; use headings to help organise items.

6. Leave spaces at intervals so that you can add extra points. Many students keep the left one-third of the page free as well, for later summaries or extra comments.

Leave this area free for later notes or summaries.

Main topic _____

1. First point _____

2. Second point _____

   2.1 Subtopic _____

   2.2 Subtopic _____

   (Leave space here for later items.)

3. Third point _____

   3.1 Subtopic _____

   3.2 Subtopic _____

---

7. Look for connections between different ideas or lines of thought. Attach a new idea to something you already know, such as building up a jigsaw puzzle. Ask, 'What do I already know

about this?' or 'Where does this new idea fit in?'.

8. Patterns help you to remember data. *Examples*: (a) Breaks in telephone numbers — 242 658 is easier to recall than 242658. (b) It is easier to remember three points in favour of X and three against X than just six points about X.

9. If there is something you don't understand, don't put it in your notes! If possible, stop the speaker and ask for an explanation. Otherwise, make a side note to ask later.

10. Revise and edit your notes as soon as possible after taking them, while the ideas are fresh in your mind. Summarising your notes is one of the best ways to increase understanding and learning. Reread notes regularly. Regular recall strengthens understanding and plants ideas more firmly in your memory.

11. To make notes more interesting and easy to follow:
    - use colour or highlighter pens to emphasise key ideas;
    - add diagrams or drawings;
    - add stars (asterisks) or underline for extra emphasis;
    - add extra summary notes in the margins;
    - rearrange key points to make them easier to recognise.

12. Try to record lectures you cannot attend, but obtain advance approval from the lecturer. Recording while you are in the room (instead of taking notes) tends to discourage active listening, but offers advantages if you have difficulty following spoken English, or have a hearing disability.

You and your lecturer

A good student–teacher relationship is one of the surest roads to success. Develop this by participation both inside and outside the classroom. Help your lecturers to get to know you (by name) as early as possible in the life of the class. In business and tertiary courses you are expected to have your own views, and to be prepared to express them in class discussions. Ask a question at the start of the class to show you have done advance reading and to emphasise your interest.

Disputes

Teachers and lecturers aren't perfect. They have personalities that may or may not be compatible with your own particular learning style, as explained in Chapter 6. Some may appear to have unrealistic expectations about what you ought to achieve in a given time; sometimes they are wrong, but often you will be surprised at what you can do when challenged. Lecturers who never push you to the limit are not helping you discover your real potential. If you are sure too much is being asked of you, or if a teacher is treating you unfairly — for example, if you have been sick but are still given the same penalty as others for a late assignment — ask for an appointment to speak privately to the teacher concerned. If this does not resolve the issue satisfactorily, don't raise it in the classroom and don't ask other teachers to 'take your side'. Ask a non-teaching third party, such as a counsellor, to help.

The teacher is not 'the subject'
Some teachers may not be very good in one subject, but excellent at others. If a subject is important to you, don't allow poor teaching or a clash with a teacher to stop you getting the most out of it.

Personal study

As your new drive to study and new study habits start taking effect, your confidence will improve too. It is amazing how success leads to success, and there are still other ways in which to develop your learning skills.

Techniques

Practise regularly

If you want to complete a trial balance, write a report, answer a question in an exam or cut someone's hair, you need hands-on (practical) experience. If you do anything often enough, you'll develop the ability and confidence to repeat it even under stress. For instance, say you're in a hurry and need money from an automatic teller machine, but you can't recall your PIN number. If you have practised keying it in regularly, your fingers will probably press the right buttons (they'll remember, even though you can't).

This is why it is important for you to do all the assignments and exercises and trial exams you can. They provide practice for your ears, eyes and fingers as well as your mind, and at test time it is the fingers and ears and eyes that help your memory work. Practise answering questions by asking yourself:

- 'What are the five points in the diagram that define X?'
- 'What does —— mean?'
- 'Why is —— better than ——?'

Get all the feedback you can

Athletes who watch videos of themselves for feedback on style and performance find that their skills improve immediately. Feedback on tests and exercises will work the same way for you. You are entitled to it, so if a teacher does not give you enough written comments, ask for more. Request feedback on your communication skills from your workmates, colleagues, friends and customers, as well as from teachers.

Night or morning?

Decide for yourself how and when you can best study, rather than let others set times for you. Late night study is good for some; others prefer the early morning. Avoid using your most active thinking-time for leisure activities, then struggling to study in the time that's left. Schedule outings for your 'slow thinking' time.

Counselling

If you still feel that there is a negative barrier affecting your ability to study, a talk with a counsellor or educational psychologist is often all that is needed. Most people know of 'battlers' — students who start with everything against them, people with physical disabilities and learning blockages — who yet manage to succeed because they never give up. If they can do it, so can you.

Revision

What you learn in class is only an outline, a set of skills, a collection of points or details. To learn in the real sense, you need to put all the pieces together yourself. This is why revision is as important as anything you do in formal learning situations.

Alone or in company?

If you are a quiet person, you will probably revise better on your own. If you are outgoing and love to have people around you may find that revision with another person or a group is more stimulating and rewarding. Choose for yourself; don't let others make you follow their methods.

Form a study group

Many students benefit from getting together on a regular basis as a study group. Provided the group is organised and keeps to the point, team study can develop understanding far more than working alone.

- Start with a general discussion, or just share ideas.
- Let each member present a short summary on one topic.
- Finish with a general discussion over a meal.

When studying with others, however, set guidelines in advance to make sure you meet specific study needs for each person.

Reading to learn

When you read as a student, your goals differ from those described in Chapter 9. However, many business reading techniques can be adapted for study purposes. You can certainly use methods such as speed reading, but it takes more training to remember what you read at high speed. It's better not to go too fast.

If you need only to identify main ideas from a book or a journal, try the scanning method explained in Chapter 9. If the material is excessively heavy, scanning reduces boredom and stops you getting bogged down.

- Read introductions, summaries and tables of contents.
- Scan headings, and opening and closing paragraphs.

As you do this, ask yourself, 'What is the main theme in this book?', 'What are the most important points in this journal article?', 'What key issues does this report deal with?', and at the same time, 'Are these issues related to the topic I am studying?', 'Is the topic I want to discover more about covered here in depth or only in brief?'. If the coverage suits your needs, read the relevant chapters in detail. Make notes as you go. Also record:

1. Author's name
2. Name of article, journal or book
3. Publisher and place of publication
4. Year of publication
5. Chapter titles, page numbers and so on

You'll need these to cite references either in the body of the text (business style assignment) or in your bibliography (academic style). Refer to the section 'Quotes, references and acknowledgments', in Chapter 18.

Using your library

New library technology is being introduced at such a rapid rate that there is no need to feel embarrassed about asking for help. Librarians are happy to give advice or show you how to locate information on particular topics. Apart from using standard library references, extend your research into other areas such as business and industry reports, records of speeches, current affairs articles in the media and so on. Chapter 31 explains more about using library resources as well as other kinds of research.

Assignments

Chapter 14 explains about 'Writing in four easy stages', a system that makes assignment writing a less difficult task. In brief, the four stages are as follows.

Think and plan

Allow time to think about the subject before you begin writing. Work out the broad aim, the kind of information you need, how much library research must be done and so on.

Timing

Work out how much time you have between the date on which you are given the assignment and the due date. Allocate time on the following basis:

30% Planning and research: read, research, make rough notes, adjust plan if necessary
10% Write rough draft, and outline
30% Reorganise — final outline — main draft
20% Revise, rewrite
10% Check, edit, condense

_____

100%

Capture ideas

As you think of ideas and topics for the assignment, jot them down. Don't try to connect all your thoughts at first, unless the grouping is obvious. For many people, this process (random writing) works as well as or better than mentally connecting words and ideas.

Develop the structure

Organise your ideas in a logical sequence. It helps at this stage if you write a brief outline — that is, a list of the main topics or headings. Draft an introductory paragraph explaining how you plan to cover the topics, then write the body of the assignment. End with a summary that refers to the question posed (and to your introduction). State what conclusions you reached from your reading, thinking and analysis of the topic.

Editing and proofreading

As well as proofreading and checking for accuracy, allow time for rewriting and, if possible, for extra 'polishing' (see Chapter 18, 'The final polish') to add extra quality to your work.

Presentation and packaging

Fix the assignment inside a cover, preferably plastic, but do _not_ insert individual pages in clear plastic envelopes. The front page should contain the topic of the assignment, your name and student number, the name of the lecturer, the class and other information. Number every page. Always keep a photocopy (or disk copy) of the assignment in case the original is lost.

Short cuts and timesavers

If you are running short of time on an assignment, or in an exam:

Divide the work into subtopics

If you are stressed or tired, divide the subtopics further into minor points. It is much easier to write a few lines about many specific points rather than a lengthy discussion about a few broad ones. You may gain a lower mark than if you had put more work in over a longer period, but it is hard to fail a question completely if your answer — even if it is just a series of small units — is correct and the ideas well-organised. Conciseness and structure help make up for lack of content.

Write about only one aspect of the topic

You are supposed to write in detail about problem X (unemployment or alcoholism). If you cannot cover the topic in broad terms, write about individuals who have had experience with the problem. Or write about problem X as it affects you or your community. This may be enough to earn you a pass.

Examinations

Success in examinations depends mainly on regular study and revision throughout your course. You can improve your chances as well if you

- answer past papers without looking at any notes and within a set time limit — this gives you a better idea of what the real exam will be like;
- ask your lecturer about the material to be covered and the type of questions to expect (lecturers may stress areas that they think are important, but don't concentrate on these alone);
- settle examination nerves, which can completely block your thoughts in the exam room — college counsellors have a series of exercises you can follow for several weeks before an exam, to reduce pre-exam stress as well as stress in the examination room (if this has been a problem in the past, you will find these exercises very effective).

In the examination

Before you write anything, read the exam paper several times. Make sure you really understand the questions. If you have a choice, select the ones you will answer and cross out the rest.

Budget your exam time

As you read the questions (and *before* you start writing), allocate time for each question. If you have a 3-hour paper (180 minutes), first deduct 20 minutes in which to read through your answers, correct errors and check spelling. Allocate the remaining 160 minutes according to the value of each question. A total of 100 marks means 1.6 minutes per mark, so allow a maximum of 16 minutes for a 10-mark question.

Decide which questions you will answer first

It is better to begin with those you are most confident about. Watch the time; if you spend 30 minutes on a 10-mark question, you may impress the examiner but will still not get more than 10 marks!

Make rough notes

Set aside a section of the answer book for rough notes; use it to jot down key ideas as they come into your mind (even while answering other questions) — otherwise they can escape. Rough out headings you can use as an outline for a longer answer. Doing this on paper is far easier than in your head.

Answer at least part of every question

It is far better to have answered half of all questions than to complete two-thirds of the paper and write nothing about the remainder. A one-minute outline of seven or eight key headings shows that you know the main points but did not have time to fill them in. No matter how short of time you are, write at least that much for every question.

Write simply and keep to the point

Make sure you are answering each question exactly as it is asked, not as you'd hoped it would be asked.

What the question means

Different words describe different types of assignment or examination approaches.

- **Summarise**
  Pick out the key points or topics from a lengthy message (whether a book, report, chapter or speech). Rearrange these key points, if necessary under headings. Write one to ten lines on each point, according to the total length. Ask the lecturer whether you are expected to comment,

evaluate or analyse the ideas selected or need only give a straight summary.

■ **Analyse**
Divide or separate a complex topic into subtopics, then discuss each one. If necessary, evaluate particular points. End with a clear conclusion or summary.

■ **Discuss, examine or consider**
As in an analysis, start by breaking the topic into subtopics. Choose which of these you want to discuss in detail. The less significant a subtopic, the less time you spend writing about it.

■ **Discuss or examine critically**
This is similar to ordinary discussion but places more emphasis on expressing opinions, choices or judgments (either for or against) about selected subtopics. Opinions expressed should include a mixture of your own and those of recognised authorities. Take a stand, rather than a 'middle of the road' position.

■ **Evaluate**
At the start, this is similar to a critical discussion but requires more emphasis on your own opinions, choices or judgments. Support them with opinions from other people.

■ **Compare**
List the similarities and differences between two topics or two issues, then analyse or discuss them as described above.

■ **Contrast**
List the important differences between two topics or two issues, then analyse or discuss as described above.

■ **Define or describe**
Give a detailed description or explanation, but remain objective. Do not offer judgment, criticism or evaluation.

Other key words give you clues as to what is required. If the direction is 'make a list', it is pointless to write an essay. Other words such as 'reasons', 'outcomes' and 'implications' pinpoint different ways in which you should organise your answer.

Note: The section 'What the question means' was adapted from notes written by Eve Haywood. Reproduced with permission.

Summary

1. See yourself as a person who can learn successfully. Think positively; develop a drive to succeed.

2. Set specific and realistic study goals. The more visible a goal, the more power it has to motivate you. Written goals are the most powerful.

3. Work out in advance what you plan to do and the order in which you will do it. Set times for study and leisure. Manage your time.

4. If you practise regularly, you will find you can perform any task even under stress.

5. Form a study group. Get together on a regular basis to share study activities.

6. Take notes to help you recall important points, but keep them brief.

7. When writing assignments, follow the four-stage writing process explained in Chapter 14.

8. In examinations, budget time for each question as you read it and *before* you start writing.

9. Answer at least part of every question. It is better to answer half of all questions than to complete two-thirds of the paper and write nothing on the rest.

Exercises

1. Draw up a time-planner, using the model on page 100 or one of your own design.

2. Find out where and how past examination papers can be obtained in your college.

3. Form a trial study group to meet outside college hours.

CHAPTER 11

Thinking and reasoning

Reasoning and other kinds of thinking add depth and meaning to the world around you. You can think in pictures or in words, silently or aloud. Some thinking involves you in clarification of current ideas, some requires new ideas to be created. Thinking can be logical or emotional. Different ways of thinking and reasoning include logical analysis, judgment (evaluation), ethical and lateral or creative thinking.

Topics

Fact or opinion?

Objective information — facts and data

Tests for objectivity

Subjective statements — opinions

Logical reasoning

Inductive and deductive reasoning

Alternative ways of thinking

Fact or opinion?

Most messages are a mixture of fact and opinion. Distinguishing one from the other is essential if you are to think clearly; however, separating the two is complicated by decoding and other understanding problems, such as the tendency people have to select meanings that have most appeal, rather than meanings that are the most accurate. It's common, for example, for people to treat an opinion as if it were a fact because it appeals to them, even though there is no evidence to confirm its 'truth'. Consider the following case.

Case study: Which way to go?

Brendan is in the second year of his course in engineering. He had planned, after graduating, to start work in his family's engineering business. However, although his marks are above average in science, mathematics and engineering, he finds he is getting less and less satisfaction from this kind of study. The subjects he really enjoys are management, marketing and business communication. In the last round of tests he topped the class in all three subjects.

Brendan talks to his parents about this. His father tells him it's a 'fact' that he (Brendan) will make far more money in the long run if he sticks with the family business, and that he should therefore complete the course in engineering.

Brendan's mother says it's a 'fact' that the secret of most successful businesses lies with the skill of their managers rather than their engineers. She says he's already 'proved' that this is where his real ability lies, and suggests that he switch to a course in marketing and management. Brendan comes to you and asks your advice.

1. How would you suggest he think through the problem?

2. Should he persevere with engineering, switch courses, or are there other solutions?

3. What facts are there on which he might base his decision?

4. Which opinions should he consider? Which should he ignore?

Brendan's problem illustrates the difficulty involved in thinking about complex issues where personal goals, emotions, predictions and factual

data are involved. Statements that seem factual may really be opinions, a prediction (only an opinion today) can prove to be fact in two years' time.

Of course there is no clear answer to Brendan's question. However, for a start he could divide the statements he is dealing with into two groups:

1. objective information — information that he knows is correct or about which he has no doubt as to its accuracy and reliability;
2. subjective statements — opinions, conclusions and predictions about which there is less certainty.

Analysing information into these two groups is essential if you intend to use a logical approach to think about any situation of this kind.

Objective information — facts

Take something that really exists, such as two $A50 notes. You can see and touch and count them. When you say 'My two $A50 notes are worth as much as your $A100 note' you are making an objective statement, and one that should mean much the same, regardless of who you are talking to or what their opinions are about money.

There are plenty of examples in science, in nature and in business when you can tell quite clearly if information is objective:
- The sun rose in the east this morning.
- Canberra is Australia's capital city.

Simple statements like these can be shown to be true or false by direct observation, research or measurement. Regardless of what anyone thinks or feels about the topic of a simple objective statement, what is described really does exist, really did happen or measures up to the specifications given. In these circumstances the statement is either 'true' and 'factual' or it's 'false'.

Other levels of objectivity

In real life, the level of objectivity of a statement often lies somewhere in between 'true' and 'false', depending on *how* closely the statement reflects the real situation. This is the problem with many kinds of day-to-day business information whenever
- nobody knows just what the 'real' situation is;
- several different statements are available, some of which appear to be more objective than others.

The solution in this case is to sort each statement into a different class according to its degree of objectivity:

Different classes of objective and subjective statement

1. *OBJECTIVE INFORMATION — FACTS*
   1.1 Specific and accurate, 'first-hand' information
      - Results or findings from your own research
      - Personal observations of specific events or situations
   1.2 Accurate and detailed information, from reliable sources
   1.3 Information said to be 'factual' or true (but without an explanation or evidence to support the claim)
      - Evidence or affidavits given in court
      - Statutory declarations
      - Ordinary 'factual' statements

2. *SUBJECTIVE STATEMENTS — OPINIONS*
   2.1 Logical opinions
      - Expert judgments
      - Expert opinions
      - Logical conclusions
      - Logically sound predictions
   2.2 Unsupported opinions
      - Assumptions
      - Inferences
      - Personal points of view
   2.3 Biased opinions
      - Exaggerations
      - Prejudiced or overly emotional statements

As illustrated above and in Figure 11.1, most kinds of information fit into one of these categories. If you sort statements this way before you make decisions, you'll find that it helps you think and reason more effectively.

Specific and accurate, 'first-hand' information

Information that you gather by personal observation or, as it is often called, GASFY (Go And See For Yourself) research, is likely to be very objective. It might include, for instance, stock figures or measurements of a building. If you are able to base most of your reasoning on this kind of information, you have a powerful advantage in persuasion, bargaining or negotiation.

Accurate and detailed information, from reliable sources

Provided the source is reliable, the information appears to be logical and there is evidence to support the claim, most people believe and accept information collected by another person. It won't be quite as objective as GASFY data, but usually it's close enough.

Information said to be 'factual' or true

Often people make statements which they say are 'undeniable facts'. The claim as stated may well prove to be objective and the information quite true, but you will need to investigate further to be sure. Sometimes, for example, in a statutory declaration or a witness's statement in court, the information will appear to be highly objective. Even so, this kind of message should not be taken as correct without questioning or asking for supporting evidence.

Tests for objectivity

There are several tests you can apply to help you classify information and decide just how objective or subjective it might be. The more tests that attract a positive answer, the more objective the information. If some of the answers suggest that the information is unreliable, treat it with caution. In most cases, questioning also clarifies the meaning.

1. How reliable is the source?

The more objective the source and the more reliable the channel used, the more likely it will be that the information is objective. A bank is usually a source of objective information about the money in your account. Its computer (the channel) usually transmits this information without error.

2. Are 'key' meanings communicated in a clear and accurate code?

Key words in a statement are the ones that help define accuracy and objectivity levels. 'Perth is more modern than Melbourne' may or may not be an objective statement. This can be determined only after the key term, 'more modern', has been defined. Does it refer to the buildings, people's attitudes, the night life or something else? Information expressed in precise codes is more likely to be objective.

3. Does the statement match up with previously known facts?

New data that is consistent with previous objective data about the same topic is also likely to be objective. Provided you have made only one deposit of $100 and if your latest bank statement shows a credit balance of $150.60, compared with $50.60 last month, this suggests the data is reliable.

4. Is there supporting evidence?

Compare the bank statement with the figures on your cheque butts. Does their evidence confirm the bank's figures?

5. Is there conflicting evidence?

Suppose this month's bank statement shows you have a credit balance of $150.60, but last month the balance was $1506.00 and you have not made any deposits or withdrawals. The similarity of the figures suggests that the bank's computer may be having trouble with its decimal point.

6. Can you 'Go And See For Yourself' (GASFY test)?

If you can make your own observations or test a statement personally, you can be more confident about its reliability. Go to the bank and see how much you can draw in cash. Often, just the knowledge that the information *is* able to be verified is enough to give you confidence about its reliability.

7. Is the message free of bias?

A message that is free of bias, prejudice, emotion or exaggeration is more likely to be objective than one that has emotional overtones.

Subjective statements — opinions

Subjective statements can take many forms, but each in some way lacks the essential factual qualities of objective information. Subjective statements vary widely in terms of meanings and reliability, depending on who sends and who receives the message and how each individual feels about the topic. For instance:

- Canberra's streets are better laid out than Adelaide's.
- Melbourne is hotter than Townsville in midsummer.
- Your $A100 isn't worth as much today as it used to be.

Just what each statement means depends on how you decode words such as 'better laid out', 'hotter', 'midsummer' or 'worth as much'. However, subjective statements too can be clarified by asking for key terms to be defined or explained, or by asking questions similar to those listed above as tests for objectivity.

While it is possible to distinguish between objective and subjective information, it is harder to classify different kinds of subjective statements. Even the words used to describe subjective statements are often interchanged. Inferences are called assumptions or insinuations, assumptions are called implications, predictions are described as conclusions and so on. However, although they vary widely in their level of subjectivity, the following types play a significant role in problem solving and decision making at work.

Logical opinions

Developing a sound opinion requires logical thinking (explained in the next part of this chapter). The sounder the reasoning, the stronger the opinion. Logical opinions include the following.

Expert judgments

Judgmental thinking by an expert draws on evidence, logic, past experience, training, and creative-intuitive thinking too. The result is the most reliable of opinions. In many cases an expert judgment might even be treated as objective, provided it is supported by sufficient evidence and the person expressing the judgment has had extensive past experience — for example, a doctor's diagnosis.

Judgments like these rely heavily on experience as well as logic, so they should be accepted only if made by someone with training or expertise in the area. Expert judgments are not reliable just because they come from an expert. Remember the case at the beginning of this chapter where Brendan was considering his future? Dr Roe, a world authority on marine biology and a friend of Brendan's father, advises Brendan: 'A career in marketing will never be as rewarding as one in engineering. Finish your engineering course and then study marketing part time'. How much weight should Brendan give to this 'expert judgment'?

Expert opinions

Expert opinions are similar to judgments, but lack the support of strong evidence. However, if they make sense and are supported with sound logical reasoning by a qualified expert, they can prove most helpful in day-to-day decision making.

Logical conclusions

A well-thought-out opinion, even if not supported by evidence or expertise, still has value if it is the outcome of logical reasoning. 'Conclusion' of course means 'end point', hence the name. A conclusion, though the result of careful analysis, is still a subjective opinion. If you don't have enough objective data and you need to make a decision, at least a choice based on a logical conclusion is better than one with no logical basis.

Logically sound predictions or recommendations

A prediction or recommendation is an opinion about something that will happen later, or something that needs to be done in the future. This special form of opinion appears in business reports or submissions when the writer makes predictions about future outcomes to support his or her proposals. Be careful not to treat them as objective, even if you agree with them. They are obviously subjective when first presented, even though they may later prove to be absolutely correct.

A new employee's performance in terms of her first month's sales figures is objective data. A prediction that she will double these figures as soon as she has had some training is subjective.

Unsupported opinions

Opinions that lack the support of logic or evidence are more inclined to be influenced by the tendency (described in Chapter 5) for people to fill in the gaps, to assume a statement is correct because it is what they *want* to hear or because it makes sense to them.

Assumptions

A new manager calls the staff together and tells them that there are going to be major changes in the way the firm will run. One assumption the staff members could make is that the manager does not agree with the way the firm has been managed previously. Another assumption might be that the manager prefers the current system but has to make changes to meet budget cutbacks. Assumptions like these seem to be based more on past experience and expectations than on logic.

Why not ask the new manager to explain the 'real' position? As with other subjective statements, many assumptions can be proved or disproved by questioning. If the answers confirm that an assumption is correct, then what started out as subjective becomes another item of objective information.

Underlying assumptions

A main assumption is sometimes based on a series of secondary assumptions that 'lie under' it. A main assumption might be: 'If students who pass an entrance test are the only ones allowed to enrol, the number who don't finish the course will be reduced'. The underlying assumptions (that you must assume before you accept the main assumption) are that

- there is a test that can identify students who will be successful and those who will fail;

- all applicants can be tested under the same conditions;
- the main reason students don't complete a course is that they can't pass tests.

If these underlying assumptions are not valid, the main assumption about testing students to reduce later failures will also be unsound.

Inferences

Opinions or expectations arising from less reliable analysis are more accurately described as inferences or insinuations. For instance, if three students submit very similar written assignments a teacher could draw an inference that they had not worked independently. This may be consistent with the teacher's past experience, but there is no evidence to support the inference. It is equally sound to infer that each student copied the same data independently but from the same book. If, as in this case, a person's reputation is at risk, then inferences — no matter how 'true' they appear to be — need to be questioned and confirmed before being treated as reliable.

Personal points of view

These are often less reliable than other opinions. However, they may be the 'best available' information at the time. They may also, in the future, prove to have been quite correct. Treat them with caution, but don't ignore them.

Biased opinions

Any opinion that reflects bias or prejudice is too risky to have value in business communication. Beware of such statements.

Exaggerations

Exaggerations are obviously biased, especially if they feature 'general' words such as 'never', 'always', 'everyone' and so on (see 'Generalisation', p. 113).

Prejudiced or overly emotional statements

Most statements made in a highly emotional way reflect the sender's joy, fear, anger, excitement or other feelings rather than any useful data. Claims that 'You are the most wonderful person in the world' or 'You are quite mad' may occasionally turn out to be factual, but you need to question emotional statements thoroughly before treating them as anything other than an indication of another person's feelings.

In some situations, of course, a little emotion increases the believability of a statement. A cold, emotionless statement, 'I appreciate your advice', will appear less believable than if the words are delivered with feeling. This still does not alter the subjective nature of the statement.

Presenting objective and subjective statements

Being able to distinguish between objective statements (facts) and subjective statements (opinions) is an essential basis for clear debate. It is hard to have a logical discussion unless the parties involved recognise the difference.

Keep facts and opinions separate

- If you are communicating factual data, say so, and include supporting evidence.
- If presenting an opinion in a discussion, say 'In my opinion we should . . .', so that people can tell you are talking subjectively.
- In a written document such as a report, allocate different sections for each: a findings section for the objective and analysis section for the subjective.

Objective statements vary in their level of reliability according to your choice of codes. Ideally, they should be expressed in words, figures or images that are clear and specific and will hold very much the same meaning for any receiver. The more accurate the terms used, the more easily people will be inclined to accept the statement.

Logical reasoning

Logical reasoning uses structured, step-by-step thinking to compare and analyse objective data from reliable sources. The result is often described as a logical argument, although it bears no similarity to the kind of verbal 'argument' that may arise when people clash over whose turn it is to do the

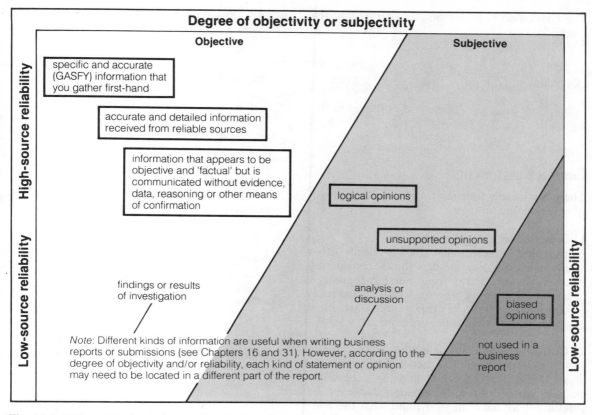

Fig. 11.1 *Different kinds of objective and subjective information, statements and opinions, and their value in business decision making*

washing-up or which team will win next Saturday's match.

Logical arguments can be simple or complex, strong or weak. You can think of one to support your position during a 10-second break in conversation, but a complex argument for use in a business report may take weeks to develop.

Conditional arguments

The strongest arguments are based on conditions that are proven facts: they are expressed as condition or 'if' statements followed by a conclusion, a 'then' statement.

Condition statements

Condition statements usually begin with words such as 'if', 'because', 'since' or 'unless'. If you don't

need to emphasise the structure of the argument, you need not include these words as long as each condition is obvious.

Conclusion statements

A conclusion is a logical outcome that follows from the expressed condition. It often starts with 'then' or 'therefore':

Condition: *If* Sydney has a larger teenage population than any other city in Australia,
Conclusion: *then* the markets for teenage fashions in Perth and Adelaide will be smaller than in Sydney.

The conclusion is sometimes stated ahead of the condition:

> **Conclusion:** (*Then*) It is Ken's turn to buy lunch today
> **Condition:** (*because*) Marie bought it yesterday.

Complex arguments

There are usually four main steps in developing a complex argument:

1. Describe aim or purpose.
A structured argument should always begin with a clearly stated aim. For instance, you are considering whether to buy petrol from Service Station A (2 kilometres away) at 60 cents a litre or Station B (4 kilometres away) at 55 cents a litre. Your aim is to decide which is the more economical.

2. Gather information or evidence.
In this example, as well as fact-finding you might also ask other people for their opinions, a secondary but very useful form of information. However, be careful not to make up your mind what the conclusion is going to be and then collect only information that supports that view. If there are two or three possible conclusions, a sound thinker looks for information supporting each one.

3. State the conditions (the 'if' statements).
Begin by stating one or more conditions based on the information you have collected.

> **Condition 1:** *If* petrol is 5c a litre cheaper at Station B and
> **Condition 2:** *if* driving the extra distance costs 50c,
> **Conclusion:** *then* as long as I buy more than 10 litres, I am better off buying petrol at Station B.

4. Determine the most logical conclusion.
Notice how the conclusion is derived from the two conditions. In reality, few cases are as straight-

forward. Reaching a conclusion becomes more complicated as other conditions are added:

> **Condition 3:** *If* I need 50 litres of petrol,
> **Condition 4:** *if* I am short of cash, and
> **Condition 5:** *if* Station A takes credit cards and B does not,
> **Conclusion:** *then* I am better off going to Station A.

Other conditions that might alter your conclusion could be:

> **Condition 6:** *If* Station B gives a free ticket in a prize draw to each customer for a Gold Coast holiday ...
> **Condition 7:** *If* I can earn $12 an hour at home plaiting genuine leather hand-made hatbands, and if I use up an extra 20 minutes travelling to and from Station B ...
> **Condition 8:** *If* the manager at Station A takes me to lunch once a week ...

Inductive and deductive reasoning

Deductive and inductive reasoning are two well-recognised but very different forms. Which one is the more convincing depends on the topic and the kind of people you are reasoning with.

Inductive reasoning

To reason inductively, start with a number of similar examples or observations taken from a larger group or 'population', then use these to develop a broad, 'general' conclusion about all such situations:

$$\left.\begin{array}{l}\text{Specific examples}\\\text{or observations}\end{array}\right\} \rightarrow \left\{\begin{array}{l}\text{General conclusion}\\\text{about any similar case}\end{array}\right.$$

As an example, suppose that yesterday, when the power went off, you lost everything you had typed into your computer. The same thing happened to you last week on another computer. A fellow student next to you had an identical experience. These are *specific observations*.

It does not take a great deal of inductive reasoning to develop a *general conclusion* about computers, namely that the data in a computer's memory is lost when the power goes off.

Individual examples for use in inductive reasoning can be gained through measurement, questioning, listening, taking samples, surveys, experiment or direct observation. The more individual examples you have to support your argument the more easily you can extend your reasoning to the point where it becomes a general conclusion. Sometimes, as in the case above, a few examples are enough to support the general rule; if the issue were about *human* behaviour, you would need many more samples before a general conclusion could be treated as valid.

Jumping to conclusions

A common error with inductive reasoning is to make a general conclusion as a result of only one or two isolated observations, as in this example:

Individual cases: Every time Mel skipped breakfast this week she got a headache.
General conclusion: *If* Mel eats a good breakfast she will not get headaches.

Drawing too narrow a conclusion

If you look at only one aspect of a problem, you can draw a conclusion that is too narrow and misses the real point.

Individual cases: We cashed ten pension cheques this week and seven of them turned out to have been stolen.
General conclusion: Most pension cheques are cashed by thieves.

This conclusion ignores a number of other important conditions. Instead of looking only at 'cashing cheques', the speaker should also consider what kind of people cashed the stolen cheques. A more reasonable argument might be:

Individual cases: We cashed ten pension cheques this week without asking for any form of identification, and seven of them turned out to have been stolen.
General conclusion: It is not wise to cash pension cheques without positive proof of identity.

A similar mistake is to draw a general conclusion that anything that has happened regularly in the past will continue to happen in the future. This can lead to severe financial problems in any kind of business operation.

Making too wide a conclusion

Another error in inductive reasoning is to draw too wide a general conclusion in relation to the individual sample. A sample of 100 Saturday-morning shoppers in a Collingwood store are asked whether or not they use Swishex detergent. If eighty say 'yes', the researcher may reason inductively as follows:

Individual cases: *If* eighty out of a sample of 100 Collingwood shoppers say they use Swishex, and because Collingwood shoppers are Victorians and Victorians are Australians,
General conclusion 1: *then* eighty out of every 100 Victorians use Swishex.
General conclusion 2: *then* 80 per cent of Australians use Swishex.

This is far too wide a conclusion to be drawn from the restricted sample. Can you identify other errors in the way the question was asked?

The best inductive arguments are based on scientific testing. You set up an experiment, observe and record results carefully, and analyse *every* possibility before coming up with a general conclusion that follows logically and is only as broad as the sample used in the experiment (see 'Experiments', Chapter 31).

Deductive reasoning

Deductive reasoning starts with a 'general condition' that is known to be true or that most people agree is so. It then looks at just one or two examples from within that general group, and makes a specific conclusion that matches the general condition.

$$\text{General condition} \rightarrow \text{Specific sample or condition} \rightarrow \text{Specific conclusion}$$

Consider the following cases:

> **General condition:** *If* all registered accountants are qualified to handle tax returns,
> **Specific case:** [and] Jean Vecchio is a registered accountant,
> **Conclusion:** *then* Jean Vecchio is qualified to handle our tax returns.

This is logical, because the particular example (Jean Vecchio) is one of the class of people (registered accountants) defined in the general statement. The following deduction, however, is not as certain.

> **General condition:** *If* all registered accountants are qualified to handle tax returns,
> **Specific case:** [and] Mal O'Hare is qualified to handle tax returns,
> **Conclusion:** *then* Mal O'Hare must be a registered accountant.

The particular example (Mal O'Hare) does have tax accounting qualifications, but he may or may not have the same ones as Jean and other accountants. Unless the specific example is a member of the general group, the deduction is faulty. On the other hand, it may be the general condition which should be questioned:

> **General condition:** *If* all snack bars make good profits,
> **Specific condition:** and *if* the El Muncho is a snack bar,
> **Conclusion 1:** *then* the El Muncho is a good credit risk,
> **Conclusion 2:** *then* it is safe to approve its owners' application for credit.

The specific condition, 'El Muncho is a snack bar', is easy enough to confirm. However, is the general condition true? Do 'all snack bars make good profits'? Even if this is so, is their profitability a direct result of their being snack bars? If their profitability is due to other factors, such as the long hours snack-bar owners and their families work without claiming wages, then the general condition is not valid, so no conclusions can be drawn.

Complex reasoning

In everyday life an inductive argument may become the basis for further deductive reasoning. There may be branches where several different chains of reasoning converge to form a final argument and this, in turn, supports one final conclusion. For example:

> **Condition 1:** *If* Sydney has a greater population than Brisbane, and
> **Condition 2:** *if* Melbourne also has a greater population than Brisbane,
> **Conclusion 1:** *then* Sydney is a larger market than Brisbane,
> **Conclusion 2:** *then* Melbourne is also a larger market than Brisbane,
> **Conclusion 3:** *then* Brisbane is the smallest market of the three.

Oversimplifying the argument

People who worry about problems look for ways to keep them 'simple'. It is not, however, logical to suggest that one idea is sound because it is simple and reject another because it 'adds complications'. Investigate simple solutions, by all means; some do have value, but they will be supported by logical reasoning. Watch for oversimplification arising from prejudice, lazy thinking or intentional distortion. Deliberate oversimplification is a common strategy in business meetings and unless examined closely can be used to lead the group into making a quick and easy (but unsound) decision (see 'Groupthink', in Chapter 23). Among the more common examples are generalisation, stereotyping and information blockout.

Generalisation

Robin says, 'All our troubles are caused by high taxes. Cut them in half, and everything will be right'. It is easy to agree with simple and attractive proposals like this, but be wary of any argument that uses words such as 'all' or 'every' in place of 'some' or 'many', and 'never' in place of 'not often'. These and similar phrasing ('any', 'always', 'none', 'every time') block logical thinking.

Stereotyping

This is a result of a simplified belief that all members of a group (Aborigines, TAFE students, accountants, women in management, migrants, footballers, alcoholics, ex-prisoners) act or think in a common way. It saves having to use logical reasoning before making decisions about individual members of that group. Unfair treatment is often experienced by members of a minority as a result.

Information blockout

If you avoid consulting others who have important information or ideas on any topic, it naturally makes thinking on the topic easier. 'It's no use asking the staff — they'd never agree.' 'No point in consulting the student committee, it rejects everything we suggest' (generalisation). In issues where many people are affected, the more individuals you consult before making a decision the greater the chance of finding an acceptable and practical solution.

Selective reasoning (filtering)

Filtering allows one argument to be accepted without full examination if it appears to confirm what the person already believes (the oil-painting effect, explained in Chapter 4). Opposing arguments are rejected not because they are unsound, but because they do not support a preferred point of view.

Alternative ways of thinking

Although logical thinking is important as a means of effective decision making, there are many business situations in which alternative ways of thinking can be used in combination with logic and reason. Balancing logical thought with ethical, lateral and other ways of thinking can lead you to a better solution because you gain access to a much wider range of ideas.

Ethical reasoning

Decisions based on ethical reasons are clearly subjective, since they depend on one's views about issues such as what is fair or unfair, right or wrong. The outstanding feature of ethical thinking is the emphasis it places on the effect a decision will have on others. Each time you pay a higher price for biodegradable products; recycle glass, timber or paper; leave your car at home and take an electric train, or make a similar choice that avoids polluting the environment, you are using ethical thinking, putting the good of the community as a whole ahead of your own physical comfort or personal profit. An ethical decision might appear to be lacking in 'logic' from a business point of view, yet still prove sound if it

- can improve the firm's public image;
- can raise morale;
- will clearly benefit the environment.

More and more business decision makers are coming to the realisation that ethical thinking is just as important as logical reasoning if they want their enterprise to survive in the coming years.

Lateral-creative thinking

Lateral-creative thinking often produces better solutions to problems than does straight logic. It can be ideal when new and original solutions are needed or when conditions are changing rapidly. The ideas developed are broader and relate to the whole situation rather than to details or sections of a problem. A simple example will help to illustrate the difference between lateral and linear reasoning.

Question: What is the easiest way to add all the numbers from 1 to 9?

The logical way would be to add 1 and 2, add that result to 3 and the next result to 4 and so on. An alternative way is to add 1 to 9 (equalling 10). Then add 2 and 8, which also equal 10, as do 3 and 7, and 4 and 6; the four pairs therefore add up to 40. Add the middle figure, 5, and the correct answer, 45, is obtained. The second method works just as well if you want to add all the numbers from 1 to 99: $1+99=100$, $2+98=100 \rightarrow 49+51=100$. That's 49 times 100, plus 50. Total 4950.

Because lateral-creative solutions seldom fit standard patterns, they are not as easy to think of if you are stuck in a logical-linear thinking mode. However, lateral-creative thinking can be learnt.

Developing lateral-creative thinking – guidelines

1. Ask 'what if?' and 'why not?'.
Make a deliberate effort to find answers that are different or unusual. Adopt a provocative approach. Challenge any suggestion that an idea 'can't work'; question limitations and constraints.

2. Avoid thinking in a logical mode.
One of the best ways of avoiding the logic trap is to do what Edward de Bono calls 'thinking in the opposite direction'. For instance, a company introduces a new sales-training program, but within a few weeks many of the newly trained team resign. Logically, it would seem that the training program has failed; however, consider whether from a lateral point of view the course might have been too successful! Is the real problem that the trained sales staff are being pirated by opposition firms?

3. Remind yourself that there are many 'correct' answers.
Don't accept the most obvious solution as the best. Think of at least two alternatives.

4. Don't take your thinking too seriously.
Laughter encourages imaginative thinking. So does breaking established rules and patterns. Explore new and different approaches for fun, without worrying where they will lead you.

5. Treat mistakes as useful learning experiences.
Learn how to turn an apparent disadvantage into an advantage. Shops often find they sell far more stock than normal if they advertise a special sale of 'scratched and damaged' bargains.

6. Use analogies.
Look for similarities in apparently quite different topics or ideas. Chapter 14 describes how pointless phrases such as 'I am sending this letter to you . . .' help to generate creative ideas when you write. The analogy in this case is highlighted by calling such phrases 'jumper leads', since they help to get a stalled idea up and running.

7. Think in pictures as well as in words.
This allows your imagination and intuition more freedom.

Believe in your ability to think creatively even if you are by nature a logical thinker. With a little practice, anyone can learn to think laterally.

Integrated thinking

Logical thinking, as described earlier in this chapter, is linear: it follows a fixed, visible sequence, moving step by step from condition to conclusion. If used exclusively, however, it blocks alternative thinking. Suppose a branch store is losing money; it would appear that, logically, it should be closed since if selling goods makes profits, and if sales fall, then profits must go down. This view is too limited. It ignores the 'people' factor and other aspects of the total picture. Equally, to use lateral-creative thinking alone is not a sound approach in the business world. Planning and decision making are most effective if creative, logical and judgmental thinking are integrated.

Computerised reasoning

As computers take over routine thinking tasks that used to occupy people's minds for much of the working day, more opportunities (and more time) are available for integrating all kinds of thinking. A spreadsheet, for example, gives you the time to try out all sorts of experimental 'what if' ideas, with the computer doing all the linear-logical calculations needed to confirm the results.

Do not, however, leave all the reasoning up to the computer. Many people still tend to think that any argument is somehow stronger if it comes out of a computer. It may appear sound, but is open to question because

- computers can process objective True/False data, but cannot judge different levels of objectivity or consider ethical issues;
- computers cannot evaluate an opinion, nor process information that relates to 'people' issues such as morale and leadership.

This may change in the future, but be very wary of any claim that your computer's AI (Artificial Intelligence) level has been developed to the point where you can safely hand over logical decision making without closely integrated human involvement.

Summary

1. Most messages are part fact and part opinion. Distinguishing one from the other is essential if you are to think clearly.

2. Objective statements communicate information about objects that really exist or ideas that are factual.

3. Subjective statements (opinions) vary widely in meanings and reliability, according to who sends and who receives the message and how each feels about the topic.

4. Logical opinions are built up over time out of your past knowledge and experiences. They are your personal estimate of what should be true or what you logically expect to be true.

5. 'Expert' opinions are an important kind of judgment, but should still be critically examined.

6. Other kinds of opinions that vary more in terms of reliability include assumptions, inferences, conclusions and predictions.

7. Logical reasoning uses a structured, step-by-step sequence to compare and analyse objective data from reliable sources.

8. Inductive reasoning takes a number of similar examples or observations from a larger group or 'population' and uses them to develop a broad conclusion about all such situations.

9. Deductive reasoning starts with a 'general condition' that is known to be true or that most people agree is so, then takes one or two examples from within that general group and makes a specific conclusion about them that matches the general condition.

10. Evaluative or judgmental thinking fills gaps in information by drawing on past experience, training and creative or intuitive thinking.

11. Lateral-creative thinking often produces better solutions to problems than does straight logic.

12. Reasoning, planning and decision making are more effective if creative, logical and judgmental thinking are integrated.

Exercises

1. Which of the following arguments uses deduction and which uses induction to reach a logical conclusion? Which are valid?
   (a) All Martians are green; the creature in the box is a Martian, therefore (*conclusion*) it must be green.
   (b) The creature in the box is green; all Martians are green, therefore (*conclusion*) it must be a Martian.
   (c) The creature in the box is a Martian; the creature is green, therefore (*conclusion*) some Martians are green.

2. You are a detective investigating a safe robbery at Bondville. Fresh, muddy footprints around the open safe are of a particular type of soil found only in the suburb of Lower McGerkinshaw. It rained yesterday at Lower McGerkinshaw, but not at Bondville. What conclusions can you draw? For each conclusion reached, say whether you used deductive or inductive reasoning, or both.

3. Consider the reasoning involved in each of the following statements. Are the specific examples and conditions sound? Are other aspects of the reasoning reliable? How sound and logical are the conclusions?
   (a) People who are tense and nervous also smoke heavily. Studies show that heavy smokers are more likely to get cancer and heart disease. Therefore cancer and heart disease are really caused by nervous stress and tension.
   (b) Stealing means taking something that does not belong to you and not giving it back. Copying computer programs is not stealing because you leave the original program exactly as it was, intact and unharmed. Since nothing has been taken from it, there is nothing dishonest about copying programs.
   (c) Tests by the University of New South Wales confirm that Type A person worries about being late for important appointments, while Type B person does not worry about being on time. Type A people are known to be much more likely to have heart attacks than Type B. Therefore you can reduce the risk of having a heart attack by not trying to be on time for

things such as appointments and classes.

(d) The XYZ political party is made up of trendy school teachers, academics, lawyers, rich landowners and feminists. These individuals have nothing in common with the average person, so the party cannot claim to be representative of the community.

(e) A recent opinion poll showed that 61 per cent of the public hold the teaching profession in high regard — on the same level, in fact, as engineers and police. Only doctors, dentists and bank managers gained a higher score. This proves that people are generally satisfied with the job teachers are doing.

(f) It is a scientific fact that next winter Australia will face the threat of the worst ever epidemic of viral hydatiditis. Unless the government takes immediate steps to introduce a mass immunisation program, the population will be left totally unprotected.

4. What is the structure of the argument in each of the following cases? Which of the four is valid, and why?

(a) Each time Fred is late for work, his pay is docked. Fred was very late for work today. Therefore, his pay will be docked.

(b) Each time Fred is late for work, his pay is docked. His pay was docked today. Therefore, he must have been late.

(c) All bosses have authority. Freda has a boss. Therefore Freda's boss has authority.

(d) All bosses get angry. If there is someone at work who gets really angry, that person must be Freda's boss.

5. A young investor buys shares and sells them at a profit on ten different occasions, then makes a general conclusion that one always makes a profit buying and selling shares and immediately buys a Porsche on hire purchase! What other conditions did the investor ignore before jumping to the (wrong) general conclusion?

6. Name some large business organisations that you have noticed exercising ethical reasoning in their planning and policy making. Name some other firms or organisations that have lost public support — or even gone out of business — because it was discovered that they were not prepared to use ethical judgment.

7. Give some examples of statements that are highly objective.

8. Give some examples of statements that are subjective.

9. You are told that 'Sydney is the largest city in Australia'. What questions would you ask the speaker to help decide the credibility level of this statement?

10. How many different ways are there of cutting a 400 mm square sheet of cardboard into four pieces *identical* in shape and area? There must be no waste.

Examples:

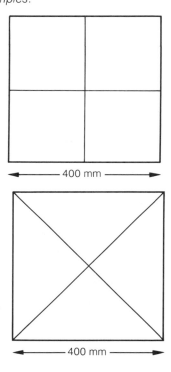

Hint: If you use linear thinking, you will probably only think of six to ten ways. If this happens, reread the guidelines on lateral-creative thinking (p. 114) and then try again, because there are actually well over fifteen quite different ways of cutting the square, and hundreds of variations of each of these ways.

Case study 1: Margaret's day out

Imagine that the following incident actually happened just as it is described.

Margaret Welch was going into town last week when her vehicle and a Holden sedan (driven by an off-duty nurse) were involved in a minor collision. (She was backing out of a narrow laneway at the time.)

Margaret called the police by phone, but they did not arrive at the scene until nearly 55 minutes after the collision had occurred. They told her not to drive her vehicle, so she had it towed to her local garage and called a taxi.

The main damage was on the left side of the vehicle. Two experts in crash repairs gave Margaret written quotes on the estimated cost of fixing it; both said it would be over $800. Margaret was not too upset by this, as she expected the full amount to be paid by her insurance company.

You are preparing a short report on the incident, and you interview Margaret, the other driver, witnesses and other people who were involved. The following statements were made variously by these individuals:

1. Margaret's vehicle was damaged in the collision.
2. The police arrived almost an hour after the collision.
3. Margaret was driving her vehicle when the accident occurred.
4. Margaret was not driving any vehicle when the accident happened.
5. Margaret's vehicle was parked at the time of the collision.
6. Margaret's vehicle could not be driven safely, according to the police.
7. Margaret's vehicle had to be towed away.
8. The police told Margaret she was not allowed to drive.
9. The other car reversed out of a narrow laneway.
10. Margaret's vehicle reversed out of a narrow laneway.
11. Margaret has written quotes from two different repair shops.
12. Margaret's vehicle was damaged on the passenger side.
13. Margaret will not have to pay anything towards the repairs.
14. The accident resulted in over $800 worth of damage.
15. Margaret's vehicle had at least $800 damage.
16. The police did not hurry to the accident after they were called.
17. The driver of the other car was to blame for the accident.
18. Because both drivers were female, they probably were equally to blame for the accident.
19. Since the collision was 'accidental' no one was to blame.
20. The other woman should have been more careful.
21. Margaret does not own a car.

Giving your reasons in each case, state which of the above statements you would treat as

1. objective — true and factual;
2. logical, and therefore likely to be true;
3. expert opinions or judgments;
4. assumptions, ínferences or conclusions that you would like to question before making a choice (list the questions you would ask);
5. unreliable statements — unlikely to be true.

Case study 2: Tom, Dick, Mary, Harry and Grudge

Reread the story in Chapter 4 about these five characters and their problems. This time consider the story from a logical point of view rather than in terms of words and meanings. Discuss it in your group as well, before answering the following questions.

1. Logically, who more than any other was the one person most responsible for Mary's death?
2. Logically, who was the least responsible?
3. What method of reasoning did you follow in reaching your conclusions?

◀ CHAPTER 12 ▶
Creating co-operation

The term co-operation suggests positive outcomes for those who work together, so it is easy to assume that co-operation is worthwhile. However, this can lead to a second and less certain assumption: any method that creates co-operation is justifiable. Chapter 12 considers whether this is so, and asks these questions:

■ What communication methods should you use to persuade people to be more co-operative?
■ What communication methods should you avoid?
■ If someone is being unfair by refusing to co-operate, what can you do about it?

Topics

Co-operation ethics

Personal rights

Open and assertive communication

Closed communication

Co-operation ethics

The better you are at communicating, the more often jobs are done properly and on time. In business terms you are a good manager, leader or organiser because you use persuasive communication to create co-operation (see Chapter 13, 'The power of persuasion'). How fair is this to other people?

Ethical persuasion should respect the rights, goals and emotions of everyone concerned. Creating co-operation must not include overriding other people's needs and getting whatever you want at any cost. Consider the following questions.

■ A team leader wants the group to accept a new roster. The leader knows the new system will benefit everyone, but to begin with no one else agrees. How far should the leader use powers of persuasion to make the group co-operate and accept the plan?
■ It is fair to use your skills as a communicator to persuade people to co-operate by paying their accounts on time. Is it fair to use the same skills to sell an encyclopaedia to a customer who cannot afford it or does not need it?
■ Sometimes people who have your best interests at heart try to stop you doing something that could get you into trouble. How far should they go in using persuasion to prevent your doing it?

Why people do not co-operate

There are two sides involved in any act of persuasion. If receivers agree with people sending the messages, they co-operate. If not, they do not. If you are not getting the results you want from your communication, one of the first things to check is whether lack of co-operation is part of the problem. Indeed, the experienced communicator learns to expect and plan for some opposition in a large proportion of business situations, and there are four main things to be considered here.

Different goals

If people have goals that differ from yours or even if they *think* their goals are different, they will oppose you. Chapter 13 is largely concerned with showing people that in fact you share similar — or at least complementary — aims. You can also build agreement by logical reasoning (see Chapter 11).

Indirect opposition

Some people will resist or reject your requests without offering any clear reason or suggesting an

alternative. They may be upset just because you and they don't agree, which makes it harder for them to co-operate. Persuasion based on sentiment or emotional appeal can help to overcome such opposition.

Justifiable opposition

On some occasions people will have valid reasons for failure to co-operate. It is vital that you discover these reasons; if they are justifiable, perhaps it's your turn to co-operate.

Unjustified opposition

Some people have selfish or unfair reasons for unwillingness to co-operate. They are not interested in what you want.

Open assertion (explained later in this chapter) is a method that can help you to deal with these situations by clarifying your goals and defending your rights. It is such a powerful technique that quite often it results in other people deciding to co-operate willingly!

Personal rights

Learning to make the right judgment in situations like those given above is easier if you apply a set of standards commonly known as 'personal rights'. Personal rights exist apart from legal and democratic rights, such as the right to vote.

Decision-making and problem-solving rights

The right to be consulted

People who are making decisions that affect you personally should talk with you before making such decisions. Failure to respect this right indicates a lack of regard for you as an individual — a common cause of stress. Others have the right to expect the same from you.

The right to decide 'yes' or 'no'

You should not be put under pressure or harassed because your response does not suit someone else. There should be no such thing as an offer you 'cannot refuse'. Even in tough business negotiations the right of each party to accept or reject an offer must be recognised.

The right to a reasonable explanation

If you hear phrases such as 'None of your business' or 'You don't need to know about that', or if people become angry when you question them, it suggests that perhaps someone's rights are being undermined. You have the right to ask questions and to request information from anyone, including those more powerful than you. (If there are legitimate reasons why data is confidential, people will usually give them.)

The right to try new or different problem-solving methods

Don't accept that the way others solve their problems is necessarily the best method for you. Reasons such as 'That's how it's always been done' should be questioned. There is of course some danger if you defy advice such as 'It's against the rules', but check the truth of such claims. People do invent 'rules' and 'policies' to help them get their own way.

The right to learn by making your own mistakes

Do not worry about criticism, and do not feel silly or guilty if results are not what you expected. So-called mistakes often provide valuable feedback that points you in the right direction. If others stop you from making a mistake, they may also be stopping you from learning how to correct mistakes. Note, however, that this should *not* extend to trying out anything that puts others at risk, is illegal or involves a risk to mental or physical health (drug-taking, for instance).

The right to decide who will fix what

Helping others is a fine and worthwhile activity, but it cannot be demanded of you. It is your right to decide for yourself

- whether you will help others to solve their problems;
- which problems you will help with;
- when you will help.

This also applies in reverse, in situations when others insist on telling you how to fix your private problems. Listen to the advice, but don't be pressured.

The right to establish priorities

Use time-management techniques (see Chapter 10) to decide which jobs deserve the most attention and the order in which you will handle them. Friends, family and people at work often want to help you decide your priorities, but in many cases their judgment may not be as good as yours. You should also be free to decide for yourself just what constitutes 'success' and 'failure' in terms of your career, and how far you want to go in that career.

Relationship rights

You also have rights concerning what can be asked or expected of you in relationships with others.

The right to 'equal openness'

You may or may not want to communicate with others about your feelings. Nobody should expect you to be completely open on such issues all the time. What can be expected is that people will match your degree of openness and be as honest and accurate in describing their feelings to you as you are with them. Closed communication makes it harder to solve relationship problems and leaves the way open for manipulation (see Chapter 13).

The right to resist emotional appeals

Tears and anger are often used as a way of limiting people's rights. If you respond too easily or too often to this kind of pressure, you can expect it to be repeated. Be cautious about any appeal that places too much emphasis on emotions, whether it be in face-to-face situations, meetings, memos, advertisements, reports or phone calls. If other people's emotions — even when genuine — put your own rights at risk, be prepared to resist the pressure.

The right to manage your own feelings

Other people cannot 'make' you feel guilty unless you allow them to. Why hand control of anything as valuable as your feelings to someone else? It is your right and yours alone to decide how you will feel. Fight to maintain it.

Feeling guilty uses tremendous amounts of mental energy. Even if you are responsible for some mistake, your energies can be better used by trying to correct it than by fighting guilt.

Exercising your rights

People who exercise personal rights lead more satisfying lives, with less stress, and find it easier to work happily with others, to agree and co-operate. However, unless you communicate openly about your rights, others tend to assume that

- you don't care about your own rights;
- you will not complain, no matter how much your rights are violated.

Suppose that a particular person came up to you at the same street corner every payday, threatened you with a gun and took all your money. Suppose you continued to accept this, without telling anyone or even going home another way. Most people (including the thief) would see you as non-assertive. Of course, this wouldn't happen: people speak out when they are robbed — yet they often keep silent when personal rights are taken from them.

Talking or writing openly about your rights helps you to maintain and defend them; not doing so makes it easier for others to undermine them. And if you don't communicate on the subject at the time, it may be too late afterwards. One way to bring the issue out into the open is to use open and assertive communication.

Open and assertive communication

Open assertion, based on respect for and understanding of personal rights and feelings, is an active process that helps people communicate effectively about their rights. If you'd like to practise it, however, it's better to begin slowly.

1. First develop your ability to communicate openly.

- Become a more active listener, tuning in to people's non-verbal signals and 'feeling' messages, as well as to their words, in their communication about rights and feelings.
- Try being a little open for a start by expressing friendly or positive feelings in safe situations, such as letters and phone calls.
- Notice the improvement in working relationships when you share open and honest messages about personal rights and the feelings that go with them.

2. Then become more assertive.

The most important time to be open is when your rights or the rights of others are under threat. This will seem difficult at first. As with any new or unfamiliar style of communicating, it requires regular practice. As in learning to drive a car or to work a computer, you develop the real skills of open assertion through hands-on — or in this case face-to-face — practice. Here are some ways you can begin.

- Stand up for your own rights when they are under threat from others. Begin by just stating a particular right clearly and firmly. Stay calm and use positive words.
- Avoid angry or parent-style messages of the kind described in Chapter 6. Once you become emotional or negative, you are no longer using assertion.
- Work together to find mutually acceptable solutions when two people's rights and feelings do not match.
- Encourage openness in others. If others are using too many closed messages (in small group meetings, or in an interview), help them to reduce the barriers.

You can read more about open assertion in books such as the Australian best seller, *You and Stress* (Montgomery & Evans, 1984). There are also many excellent assertion training courses available, and you have nothing to lose by giving one a trial.

How you treat others has a major influence on how they treat you. Keep in mind that open assertive communication involves you in helping others to maintain their rights and feelings as well as in maintaining your own. If you fail to remember this, you are not going to have much success as an assertive communicator.

Different kinds of assertion

For people you like, or know well

These are the methods that can be used when there is a bond of friendship between you and the receiver, especially if you both have experience in open communication. Because they are fairly gentle, however, they may not be effective against aggression or anger.

Consensus

Suggest ways that allow everyone to maintain rights and self-respect. 'Let's agree to share the loss equally. If we each put in five dollars, that will pay for the replacement.'

Clarifying reasons

Explain honestly and openly your real reasons for agreeing or disagreeing. If refusing a request, for instance: 'I'd prefer not to lend you my car because it's not insured and I know that if anything happens you can't afford to replace it'.

Negative feedback

You know from earlier chapters that negative feedback helps pinpoint answers to difficult problems. Make it clear that you welcome error messages — even if they involve *your* errors — and that you respect everyone's right to discuss problems openly and equitably with you. At the same time, say that you expect equal rights in return. 'I know some of you disagree with our new policy on promotions. I'm happy to listen to you if you can tell me about specific cases where staff have been treated unfairly. Then I'd like you to listen to me while I explain my side of the issue.'

Mutual change

Suggest an agreement under which both of you change, but both also benefit. 'I feel left out when I'm expected to mind the switchboard while the rest of you go to lunch on Fridays. Is there some way we could work out a roster so each of us takes turns to stay behind?'

For people you don't know well, or for total strangers

These styles of assertion are most useful with strangers, shop assistants, sales representatives, people in car parks — anyone with whom you have no emotional bond. It is not appropriate to use them with close friends or family members.

Conditional

Quietly but firmly state your rights. 'Before I answer any questions over the phone, I'd like to know your name and who you represent.'

Information exchange

Share information about your feelings. Ask for information about your rights. 'It worries me when you say I'm not allowed to question the bank's decision. Please could you show me the rule, so I can read it for myself.'

Empathy

Acknowledge respect for other people's rights and feelings before talking about your own. 'I know that the delay will cause you some problems, so I'll arrange to deliver your order as soon as you pay last year's account.'

For angry or aggressive people

Assertion will not perform miracles. However, when you are facing people who are angry or aggressive (whether close and distant in terms of the relationship), the first thing is to defuse the situation. The following methods will help to achieve this where perhaps no other would succeed.

Personal feedback

Use phrases such as 'I can see that you are very angry' or 'You sound pretty annoyed . . .'. Personal feedback helps calm an angry person. If you are expecting trouble, you can even work the words out beforehand and rehearse them. Avoid 'You are . . .' — it's too direct. 'I can see that you are . . .' is more adult and therefore more likely to be accepted.

'Can you tell me . . .'

Once you have given feedback, ask for some in return. 'I can see you are very annoyed. Is there something I can do to help fix the problem?' It is much harder for people to maintain anger while answering questions or exchanging factual information. Avoid a direct question. Don't ask, 'Why are you angry?'.

Repetition

If the two previous techniques have had some success but the other person is still angry, try repeating them. It is a simple yet very effective way of maintaining your position when you cannot think of anything else to say. By repeating statements calmly over and over, you yourself keep calm. This helps you to persist in the face of anger, and quiet persistence makes it hard for the angry person to remain 'on the boil'. Sticking to one point helps you to avoid manipulative baiting and sidetracking.

'You could be (partly) right . . .'

Accept the possibility of some truth in angry criticism, but remain the judge of just how much is true. This makes it easier to respond to meaningless insults, negative labelling ('You are a . . .') and so on without your feelings being involved. When you say 'You could be correct', you also show a lack of interest in having an argument. It does not, of course, mean that you agree. If the criticism is justified — for instance, if someone has a complaint about poor service — your polite agreement makes it easier to reduce that person's anger and find out the facts.

Developing your assertive skills

You can develop your assertive skills in several ways.

Persisting

If you don't get through at the first, fourth or tenth attempt, keep talking openly about the same rights and feelings. Repeatedly stating your own position is not aggressive, but it helps to maintain your confidence and makes it harder for others to dominate the exchange.

Practising

Try to use some degree of open assertion at least once every day. You won't be short of opportunities.

Letting too many chances slip by is almost like practising non-assertion.

Exchanging information

Ask questions and share information, including open information about how you are feeling. Give feedback on what you think other people are feeling.

Changing old habits

As a child you learn naturally to get co-operation by copying what you see others do. If you grew up hearing and seeing members of your family using threats or anger to get what they wanted, you will be inclined to do the same when your deeper feelings are aroused. On the other hand, if you grew up with people who 'suffered in silence', this may be your natural style. Practising open assertion helps you to move away from old habits.

Dealing fairly and positively with your own mistakes

Defending mistakes is not the same as defending rights. If you are at fault, express your respect for others' rights and accept your share of responsibility. Saying 'Sorry' is fine if you really mean it, but devote the most time to talking about how to fix things. If you are not to blame, use assertion to make this clear rather than argument or denial, both of which are non-assertive.

Believing in what you are standing up for

Whatever kind of co-operation you are aiming for, the outcome must be fair and just for all concerned. The more you believe this, the more powerful will be your assertion and the more readily people will co-operate.

Working for equality

Open assertion succeeds best when there is equal respect, equal caring and equal openness on both sides, but it can succeed even when only one party believes in equality and the value of personal rights.

Choosing not to be open or assertive

Open assertion is a powerful technique, but on occasions you can choose *not* to exercise this kind of power. Use assertion only in those places and at those times appropriate to the people and the situation involved. People who are elderly or those who are shy, sensitive and insecure may experience difficulty in coping with open communication unless introduced to it gradually.

Knowing the right time and place

One way to show a lack of respect for other people's rights and feelings is to pick the wrong time or place to be assertive. Check first. 'I've been waiting for a good time to talk about ——. Is it OK now?' Choose a place where both you and the other person will be comfortable and where you will both be free from interruptions.

As a general rule open assertion is harder to use effectively with people you care about, because your feelings and theirs get caught up in the exchange. Provided they are not causing you too much worry, be careful about using it when close friends ignore your rights — at least until you have taught them to understand its benefits. This takes time. Children seem to have a natural ability to handle open assertive messages from adults and, in fact, to appreciate the style, but may need help if they are to use assertion themselves.

Avoiding assertion

You can talk yourself out of being assertive by saying things like this.

- I tried it once and it just got me into more strife.
- I can't remember how to be assertive at times when I need to most.

These reasons may be valid, but make sure that it is not lack of confidence that is holding you back. Remind yourself of the story of the thief on the street corner. If you are shy or lack self-confidence, you are the kind of person who

- is most likely to lose out on personal-rights issues;
- stands to gain most by using open assertion.

The other reason some people avoid (or even criticise) assertion is that they find other methods are working very nicely for them. Such people know that for them it is better to rely on

- anger and aggression;
- active competition; or
- manipulation.

These are the very people who hope you too will choose not to be assertive. Don't give them the satisfaction they seek.

What can go wrong?

Open assertion, no matter how well it works, is a short-term solution. To deal with extended aggression you may need to reinforce your position through negotiation (see Chapter 24). Moreover, open assertion won't always work: problems can arise.

Conflict between cultures

Some cultures use open communication only in close family situations. Be careful in using it with overseas associates unless you are sure it will be accepted and appreciated.

Accusations of dominating a situation

If you use open assertion you cannot, of course, be pushy or dominating, but when you succeed in defending your rights against attacks by really pushy, dominating people, you can get nasty reactions. You are dealing with individuals who know only negative ways of getting co-operation.

Underneath, many such people are sad, frightened and insecure. Many of them won't know anything about personal rights, but only that they are losing control over you as you become stronger in defence of your rights. It can appear to them as though you have found a new 'trick' to stop them getting their own way, and if they know only how to be aggressive, competitive or manipulative, they mistakenly assume that you and your 'trick' must work in the same way.

Turning up the volume

This can lead to a reaction called 'turning up the volume' as the individual in question, trying to maintain control, increases use of the previously effective control pattern: more anger, more competitiveness, more tears, more pressure on you to feel guilt or shame and so on. At first this can be successful, but sooner or later (if you persist with your open assertion) the other person will run out of 'volume'. This is why you need face-to-face training before going too far in your use of assertive communication. Once you have acted out trial sessions in class in which someone else plays the 'volume up' role, you will find it very much easier to handle the situation in real life.

Closed communication

Open communication is not always appropriate. Some people find closed communication works best for them. When you practise closed communication, however, you
- restrict the topics you discuss with others;
- talk mostly about 'safe' issues such as money, cars, clothing, animals or television;
- discuss the past rather than the present or the future;
- avoid discussing controversial issues such as business ethics;
- avoid discussing issues that relate to feelings, personal rights or similar subjects.

On some occasions at work, closed communication is the appropriate style. It might not be wise to be too open when meeting the general manager for the first time, when chairing a formal discussion of the annual balance sheet, or in correspondence on legal matters. But once a person's rights are being affected, it's time to start opening up.

Pseudo-assertion

People who have had years of success with anger or manipulation find it hard to become assertive. Why? Because in the short term it means loss of power as they relax their grip on other people's rights. Even if they take part in assertiveness training, there is a danger that they will switch to a kind of pseudo-assertion in which they continue to use competitive or manipulative methods but in a quieter voice, mixing assertiveness with the same old behaviour. To create a real change you need to demonstrate the benefits of assertion: reduced stress, closer friendships, and happier, more effective working relationships.

Summary

1. One of the essentials of good management is to have people working together happily and efficiently. They should achieve goals according to plan *and* on time. This is much more likely to happen when people are willing and co-operative.

2. Co-operation and agreement occur more often when people use persuasion and open assertion rather than power or pressure.

3. The skill called 'open assertion' helps your communication about your personal rights and the decisions you make based on them. It is particularly useful in the face of unfair opposition.

4. Open assertion may appear to be quiet and passive, but is actually a very powerful way of communicating; for this reason it must be used with care.

Exercises

1. You are running late for a meeting when to your great delight you see a parking space directly ahead of you. You drive past the space and prepare to reverse into it. Suddenly a car appears from behind, and turns nose first into 'your' vacant spot. What do you do?

2. Rehearse and role-play in class the following situation:

   You are waiting to be served at a counter when someone rushes in and demands to be served immediately. What do you say to this person? If the shop assistant seems to be about to serve the newcomer, what would you do or say?

3. Each day at the canteen you buy a salad roll. It's a healthy lunch, the roll is always fresh, and the proprietor puts heaps of salad in it. Today you buy the roll, go outside and take a bite only to discover that the bread is stale and there is hardly any tomato in the salad. You take it back, and ask to talk to the manager.

   Imagining each of the following as a separate situation, what would you do and say if told by the person at the counter that
   (a) the manager is too busy to talk to you;
   (b) since you have taken a bite of the roll, it is too late to make a complaint;
   (c) there was plenty of tomato in the roll and you must have eaten it — you are well known as a trouble-maker and your name

will be given to the principal unless you go away;

(d) it is the baker's fault that the bread is stale;

(e) you can shout as loud as you like, but there will be no refund;

(f) you should be grateful — there are children starving in Africa who would be glad to eat the roll.

With another person, role-play one or more of the above.

CHAPTER 13

The power of persuasion

Throughout this book you'll notice an emphasis on positive methods of persuasion — communication skills that encourage people to agree and co-operate willingly. This chapter looks at the many different ways in which you can employ persuasion to create willing agreement.

Topics

A strategy for persuasion

Developing appeal

Persuasion through power

Appeals to reason and logic

Emotional appeals

Personal appeal

Other forms of appeal *80 for a decision*

Overcoming resistance

A strategy for persuasion

Persuasion succeeds best when it points out the advantages and benefits (the 'appeal') of co-operation. This is easier to do if you have a step-by-step strategy to emphasise the appeal. The following steps are well recognised as a format for this purpose.

1. Create interest.
Get attention. Ways of switching on people's interest are explained in later chapters on letters, reports, public speaking and using the telephone. If interest must be aroused quickly, pictures or practical demonstrations work better than words.

2. Discover a need or a desire.
Before you can connect what you want with an offer of reward or benefit, you need to pinpoint a need or a desire in the receiver. Don't decide too soon what this need might be — let the other person *tell you*. Ask questions, and listen carefully for clues to unfulfilled needs. Earlier chapters that looked at different personality types and levels of motivation can help here.

Look for alternatives. If you want to sell chocolate to someone who says that she doesn't eat chocolate, ask if her family likes it. Do not, however, try to create a need or a desire where one does not exist.

3. Show how the need can best be satisfied.
Once you know a client's needs, you can work out what kind of benefit will hold the strongest appeal. Then, to develop the appeal, explain the connection between
- the client's agreement with your idea or request, and
- the satisfaction he or she will gain in return.

This step is the heart of the persuasion process.

4. Balance the deal.
A skilled persuader 'balances the books' as part of the overall appeal. To gain the promised benefit a client may have to give up free time, exchange money for goods or goods for money, or make some other form of 'payment'. No matter how attractive the benefit, if it costs too much in these terms a person will back away from it. Convince the client that he or she is getting a fair deal.

Rather than real (tangible) benefits, it is often the emotional appeal that has the stronger effect when it comes to balancing the deal. The best balance, of course, is created by a combination of both real *and* emotional benefits so that the willing agreement that starts in the heart is reinforced by logical agreement in the head.

5. Get action — a response or movement.
Co-operation or agreement is not complete until

the other person makes the move you are seeking. Ideally, have the promised benefit (a suitcase full of cash, the new car, the immediate promotion) ready for exchange the moment the other person says 'yes'. If this is not possible, present a strong and clear mental image of it. Discuss the promised reward in detail, to help the other person visualise it clearly. Ask 'What colour would you like?', 'How soon can we start?'.

6. Follow up.
All persuasion loses its effect over time, and ignoring people speeds up this process. To keep agreement at peak level, you need to maintain contact. A quick phone call every few weeks or a visit to talk over the issue will alert you to any problems that might hinder continued co-operation.

Developing appeal

While the strategy you use may remain constant, you'll need to work out what kind of appeal is needed for each individual. Appeals can be based on
- needs, wants and desires
- any kind of power
- reason and logic
- fair exchange
- sentiment or emotion
- competition
- avoidance
- personal appeal

The goal of any appeal should be willing and positive agreement rather than pressured co-operation. If this is not possible, however, you need to employ a tougher approach involving bargaining or negotiation, and although negotiation can involve persuasion, the ground rules and techniques are very different (see Chapter 24, 'High-power communication').

Needs, wants and desires

Most people have their basic needs (food and shelter) satisfied by the time they come to work, and as explained in Chapter 5, a satisfied need has little value as a motivator. However, if you are in a position to help someone meet higher level needs (self-esteem, recognition, achievement) you have an effective basis for persuasion.

Desires are more complex than needs, and more bound up with emotions. They are also more specific, more personal and often unique. For instance, someone might have a strong desire to own a vintage MG sports car, but none at all to own a new Porsche. If you know of a specific desire *and* are able to fulfil it, you have a very strong foundation for a persuasive appeal.

Persuasion through power

One of the commonest forms of persuasion involves the use of power — the ability or potential to make something happen. Provided you use power in a fair, honest and positive way it offers a valuable and legitimate means of achieving co-operation; it is also an important function of 'high-power communication' (negotiating or bargaining) as well as of persuasion (see Chapter 24). One reason for looking at power in this chapter is that the more you understand about it and the more accurately you can identify each kind and where it comes from, the better use you can make of it. This will help you to
- choose the best kinds of power to use, depending on whom you want to persuade and how, when and where the persuasion is to take place;
- recognise what kinds of power you are up against, when others are persuading you.

Some forms of power, of course, carry with them the capacity to meet people's needs and desires, which adds to their appeal.

Reward-penalty power

You know from experience that people in a position to hand out rewards and benefits have power; money equates with power because it provides a means of offering rewards. Inflicting punishment or penalty is simply using power in the opposite way — for instance by
- withholding rewards (delayed promotion);
- cancelling rewards (dismissal);
- reducing the chance of future rewards (transfer); or
- making life less rewarding (verbal abuse, harassment).

This explains the term 'reward-penalty power', but usually the term is shortened to 'reward power'. It is one of the best kinds to use in persuasion; it is the basis of most democratic systems of government, law and commerce, and is easy to apply in combination with other kinds of power.

Authority (or position) power

Authority power is based on official position in an organisation or rank in a formal system. Usually the position will be accompanied by a name or title, and often also by non-verbal symbols which confirm the authority — a rubber stamp, a uniform, a type of desk or an office of a certain size. The extent of the power is usually well-defined (power to spend up to $2000, but not to spend $2010). The possessor usually has a book or a letter setting out just what powers are involved, and the terms and conditions of appointment to the position.

- Authority is the least personal of all powers and therefore is hard to use in negotiating or bargaining.
- Authority is hard to gain; you cannot buy it, and since positions are limited you may wait a long time to achieve the level you want.
- Authority is one of the easiest powers to delegate. Delegated authority is described quite accurately as 'power on loan'; it belongs to the delegating person or organisation, and when you cease to hold such authority it returns to the original owner.

It is also easy to lose authority, since the power is vested in the office or position, not in the individual. For example, at the 1988 World Expo in Brisbane many students worked as voluntary crowd-control officers. Once in uniform they had considerable authority, which between 30 April and 30 October was used to control the movements of millions of people — but *only* between those two dates and *only* in the Expo grounds. The rest of the time they were ordinary students.

Expert power

Anyone who is skilled in a vital technique, such as knowing how to program a computer, has extra power. You might have expertise in selling, sport or romance, or just have a general reputation for being a winner. Valued skills, knowledge or expertise, especially those in short supply such as medical training, leadership, management or accounting, are all sources of expert power. Such power can also be gained through possession of personal attributes: strength, height or physical fitness.

An important area of expertise is the ability to communicate effectively. You might be the only person where you work who is expert in chairing a formal meeting, or you may be the best at direct selling or report writing. Expert power is one of the easiest to attain early in your career through study and training. The more you increase your reputation as being good at your job, the more this kind of power increases.

The weakness of expert power is that if used alone it is hard to negotiate against someone with greater expertise than yourself. It is a power best used in combination with other kinds.

Affiliate power

Your good friend Glen Black has just been appointed to fill a casual vacancy in the Senate in Canberra. Suddenly you will enjoy special recognition, status and power, and will be able to influence people favourably, all because you are a friend of Senator Black. Affiliate power has nothing to do with personal qualities — other than an ability to make friends. It comes through your connection or friendship with others, particularly those with authority. If they lose power, so do you. Affiliate power is seldom permanent; it is personal and unofficial, and therefore not very effective in bargaining. It can, however, hold a strong persuasive appeal.

Other kinds of power

Special information

An individual with information that no one else in the immediate group possesses also holds extra power. Special information can be used to advantage in dealing, bargaining or negotiating.

Seniority or referent power

An elderly office assistant, a grey-headed lecturer, a grandparent — in fact, any elder of a group (or someone who has been a member far longer than anyone else) — is often consulted for guidance by those with less experience.

The older person is seen as a 'point of reference', which allows that individual to wield considerable power that is distinct from any other power or authority he or she might hold.

Contracted or shared power

If you share a house or flat with a group you will recognise shared power. By agreement or negotiation, specific powers are allotted to selected members. One controls the budget and another hygiene; one arbitrates and settles disputes, one organises household clean-ups and waste recycling. By common agreement each one holds power over the others in some particular area, but not in others. Participative management (worker democracy) is based largely on this type of arrangement.

Force and pressure

While any type of power can be misused, those listed so far can all be used positively and productively. This does not apply to force and aggressive pressure. They have no place in business, nor are they legitimate means of persuasion.

Charismatic and manipulative power

These are twin forms of power. While capable of exerting a very strong influence, both are based on the belief held by others that the 'power' figure has special strengths or abilities. As long as people believe in the power, then the strength of that individual is maintained. Once people stop believing a charismatic leader holds special powers, his or her ability to exercise control falls dramatically.

Most people with charismatic power use it in positive ways. Manipulative power, by contrast, relies on false belief by people that *they* have little or no power to resist another person's manipulative control. Between adults, particularly at work, its use is non-productive and often harmful.

Dealing with manipulation

The term 'manipulation' does not apply to every situation in which people are forced to do something they don't want to. It refers only to a range of emotional appeals that are used in dishonest ways to persuade and influence others or gain agreement and co-operation.

The process of manipulation is tied in with deliberate strategies adopted by those communicators who want to win regardless of the moral issues involved. If you are facing an angry boss who is threatening you with dismissal over an unfinished job, it's understandable if you feel fearful and offer to work during the weekend to finish it. But suppose that your failure to finish was the result of poor planning by your boss and that even so you did your best to finish by Friday afternoon. Your boss is trying to manipulate you if he or she wants you not only to accept the blame, but also to feel (unjustified) shame for 'your failure' *and* work over the weekend too! However, many people in these circumstances *will* feel they are at fault, take the blame on their shoulders and offer concessions to make up for their 'bad' behaviour. They are being manipulated.

The following are some typical signs that may assist you to identify manipulation.

■ There are two parties: (1) the active manipulator whose actions, whether intentional or not, gain an unfair advantage; (2) the victim, who may not even be aware that he or she is being manipulated.

■ As well as the threatened loss of tangible items (money, time, privacy, promotion, personal freedom), the victim's feelings and personal rights (see Chapter 12) are also at risk.

■ An appeal or benefit is offered in return for co-operation, but it turns out to be practically worthless or non-existent. As in the case above, a typical 'benefit' in return for co-operation is nothing more than regaining something taken away at the start of the manipulative process (you fear losing the boss's respect, you co-operate with the boss, you regain the boss's respect).

Note, however, that should a person be fully aware of the attempted manipulation, doesn't like what is being suggested, but agrees under pressure to co-operate in return for a real benefit (such as *not* getting the sack) this is *not* manipulation.

Manipulation is a form of cheating, a bluff or underhand strategy that gives one person an unfair advantage over others who choose not to employ the method. You face cases of manipulative communication daily and possibly use similar methods yourself on occasions. Watch for the following common forms.

1. Guilt and blame manipulation.

'Don't worry about me. You go off for the day and enjoy yourself. I'll just carry on working by myself.'

2. Stress manipulation.

A supervisor talks of pending dismissals (though none are planned) and hints that those who fail to co-operate will be the first to go.

3. Authority manipulation.
The public servant claims to have authority to say 'yes' or 'no' on issues that affect you when in reality the position carries no such power.

4. Expert manipulation.
A computer expert claims that a problem is due to a computer error when in fact it is the programmer or operator who made the mistake.

5. Blemish manipulation.
Small faults or mistakes are blown up out of proportion as a means of applying increased leverage for co-operation on other issues.

6. Role manipulation.
The individual acts out a role that hides the real self (or real motives) from others, making it easier for the player to gain co-operation. For instance, a nervous supervisor puts on a tough and aggressive front so that people agree with whatever he or she says.

7. Personal crisis manipulation.
Treating an ordinary problem as a personal 'crisis' helps the individual to pass the problem on to others, a pattern known as 'learned helplessness'. You may notice that the 'victim's' problems occur when the people who habitually come to the rescue are close by.

Manipulative games

In a surprising number of these 'crisis' situations, two people repeat a similar set of victim—rescuer activities on a regular basis. Each person plays the same role each time, and both somehow seem to be unconsciously hooked into repeating the event a week or a month later. This is known as a 'manipulative game'. Such games can continue only as long as you remain convinced that you must join in or that to refuse to play would cause harm or suffering which would be your fault. The best defence is to recognise and identify the process. If you think you are getting caught up in such a situation

- do not try to rescue a person while he or she is caught up playing a 'victim' role (especially if you are being held to blame for a problem that was not of your making);
- avoid becoming emotionally involved: try an 'adult-to-adult' response — use open assertion;
- do not accept the false idea that a person with a

problem has the right to insist that others share it;
- stop responding altogether: walk quietly away from the situation — it takes two players to keep the process going;
- remind yourself that you have the right to control your own feelings — do not give this right away to anyone, especially manipulative-game players.

Avoid labelling

Try *not* to use the word 'manipulator' as a label for people who use the method. While they may choose to use a dishonest form of persuasive communication, they are still people. They don't manipulate all the time, and hanging the label on them does nothing to help fix the problem.

Try also to distinguish deliberate manipulation from the unconscious kind. Many people discover only by accident that manipulative strategies work better than other methods, and so are less conscious that what they are doing is manipulative. What you see as artificial may have become real to the unconscious user, because it is so successful. In these cases, take care that you do not allow yourself to believe it is real too!

Legitimate and non-legitimate power

Whether power is legitimate or not depends on why it is used as well as on the type it is. For example, reward power is normally used honestly, but not always: as well as its use in business, government and the law, it is wielded in the areas of corruption and crime. However, because reward power is one of the easiest to identify and to measure, you can usually tell whether it is being used legitimately or not.

- A person exercising legitimate power is using that to which he or she is entitled, and does so fairly and openly.
- A person using illegal or improper power certainly has the ability to exercise control, but has gained it dishonestly or is using it illegally or unfairly. This includes the use of power to violate personal rights. Illegal power may, of course, also be applied to an honest purpose.
- A person using bluff or manipulation may exercise real control, but only as long as others believe that the power exists and think it is legitimate.

Giving power away

Recognise the difference between legitimate and non-legitimate power. If you allow others to exercise the latter to persuade you, it must be to your disadvantage. If in communication you restrict the use of your everyday legitimate powers in the belief that it is 'not quite nice' to use them in a business situation, you are really just giving them away — a costly but common mistake.

Power in personal relationships

Using power in a relationship between yourself and others does affect the relationship, though not necessarily in a negative way. However, the closer you are emotionally to another individual, the less you can (or should want to) use power as a means of handling problems between you. A mixture of open assertion, caring, sharing and consensus is a better formula.

Appeals to reason and logic

The most acceptable and reliable forms of persuasion are those that stand up to detailed discussion and analysis — the kind you would expect to find set out in a business report or put forward at a board meeting. You can respect people who use logical persuasion to gain your agreement, and they will respect you when you follow the same pattern. Reason and logic are very effective when used to emphasise advantages of purchasing goods or services; for instance:

- convenience: promoting a waste-collection service that may seem expensive, but when considered logically in relation to the time saved (by your not having to take the rubbish away yourself) is worth the cost;
- effectiveness: emphasising the benefit of a machine, a product or a system that works really well (used in this book to encourage you to try new communication techniques);
- efficiency: stressing ease of operation, simplicity or reduced operating costs — a logical approach that will help to persuade the people who control your budget to let you buy new equipment;
- value for money: persuading people to buy early, before next month's price rise;

- excellence or achievement: stressing benefits of outstanding quality in production even at a higher-than-usual cost in time and effort — an appeal often used by lecturers when setting assignments.

Logical appeals are ideal for use in written communication such as reports and submissions, because you can develop your argument while you write, but they also work well in committee meetings, debates and speeches (see Chapters 29 and 30). Appeals to reason recognise the individual's right of choice and similar personal rights — another point in their favour.

Fair exchange

Another form of legitimate and logical appeal is to offer a fair exchange. This interests most people. Often known as the 'If you do X, I'll do Y' appeal, it is one of the oldest forms of persuasion.

> Gil and Andre share a flat, with their pet dog Grishka. Gil prefers cleaning to cooking and Andre the opposite, so it's easy to imagine them working out a comfortable agreement for this part of the household management. Gil is also good at financial management, Andre is not. Gil offers to look after the household accounts if Andre agrees to wash the dog each weekend (a job Gil hates), but Andre is not convinced that this is a fair bargain. To gain agreement Gil may have to add other incentives to make the exchange more attractive.

Persuasion based on a fair exchange is useful if people are having trouble agreeing (see 'Compromise', in Chapter 23). During the bargaining stage those involved hammer out the issues causing disagreement, so that there is more chance of eventual and lasting satisfaction on all sides. As a form of persuasion it is often overlooked by managers looking for co-operation, yet it is fair, open and honest, and is a theme with several variations.

Mutual support

There is an old Japanese saying that 'if a firm looks after the things that most worry employees, then employees will look after the things that most worry the firm'. This kind of bargain between workers and management is now recognised as one of the reasons for Japan's economic success.

Common interest

When applying for a job, show that you and the employer have a common interest. Begin your application by saying, for instance, 'I was interested to learn you have a vacancy for a trainee manager, as I have just completed a Diploma in Management at Greenlands College'.

Incentive to co-operation

An offer, for example, of a promotion in return for special help or co-operation is an exchange most people find hard to resist.

Fair exchange appeals rely on honest and open communication. They cannot be as effective if some players won't 'put their cards on the table'. If one party keeps vital facts secret or uses threats to gain an advantage, the process is no longer 'fair', nor will the result be willing co-operation. At that point the process will move from persuasion to negotiation.

Emotional appeals

Appeals to sentiment emphasise the emotional advantages of saying 'yes', showing how agreement will help people feel happier, raise their self-esteem, and offer greater pleasure. Whether you are persuading someone to buy a new car or accept a promotion, it is important to stress the emotional as well as the logical advantages. Emotional appeals may not stand up to logical analysis, but they have a powerful effect *in combination* with appeals to reason. Among hundreds of such appeals, the following are typical.

Typical emotional appeals

Good relationship

This appeal, based on the desire most people have to get on well with others at work, can be used by managers who want to develop good teamwork. Speeches, reports, letters and phone calls all have a better chance of gaining agreement if they begin with an appropriate form of 'good relationship' appeal. The same approach is used a great deal in personal relationships.

Visual appearance and good health

This may begin as a logical appeal, but is strengthened by adding the emotional aspect of looking good to others and enjoying a healthy lifestyle. It is much used in marketing real estate and luxury cars.

Good-time appeal

This emphasises the very real appeal of fun, enjoyment, entertainment and laughter. The growth of commercial fun parks in Australia suggests that this benefit is highly valued by many adults as well as by children.

Moral appeal

This stresses the benefit of 'doing the right thing', or co-operating for the common good; it urges support for what is best for the majority. Americans call this the 'motherhood and apple pie' appeal, meaning that it is used to gain support for issues that no one can afford to criticise.

Respect or approval

With emphasis on the benefit of making a choice that other people will see as 'respectable', this appeal is based on the desire to be looked up to and respected by others as a 'good manager', a 'good citizen' or a 'good parent'. An example would be to seek support for a community project or persuade a firm to employ a student for work experience. A similar approach is used to encourage people to pay overdue accounts.

Change or variety

This suggests that there is a benefit in trying something new or different, or that any change will probably lead to improvement. An example of this was the ALP's 1972 winning electoral slogan, 'It's time'.

Emotional persuasion can also be used to distort your judgment; a past example of this was the advertising used to glamorise smoking. Emotional methods are also used by less ethical operators; be particularly careful of any appeal that includes:

- an offer of rapid or enormous financial gain, especially if you are told that you have been selected as one of only a few lucky people to share the benefit;
- an overdramatic appeal for sympathy, accompanied by tears, anger or a suggestion that you should accept full blame (or feel guilty) for a problem;
- criticism of a person rather than an attempt to solve a problem.

Competitive appeal

People can be quickly persuaded if they feel that co-operation will improve their chances of sharing in a limited number of benefits. For example, if there is only one position as branch manager available, there will be lots of competition for it; hopeful applicants will be easily persuaded to take on extra duties. It would be hard, on the other hand, to gain their support for a go-slow campaign.

Positive versus negative persuasion

Persuasion works best when people feel positive and slows down when they feel negative. A smile gets more co-operation than a frown and creates a far better response than do threats, coercion or abrupt orders. Chapters 14 and 15 draw attention to a similar mistake — that of using negative words in an attempt to make a written message more persuasive. From a business point of view, positive persuasion is far more effective.

Even when you are examining the disadvantages of not co-operating (avoidance appeal), move quickly from negative to positive. Stress the advantages of co-operation rather than the risks of non-cooperation.

Avoidance appeal

The basis of this is that co-operation offers the best chance to reduce or avoid risk.

- The appeal of protection stresses the value of products such as toothpaste and deodorants that 'protect' you from embarrassment or ill health. Sellers of encyclopaedias emphasise the value of an expensive set of books as a way to avoid 'not knowing the answer'.
- Insurance and guarantee contracts use a similar appeal, offering protection from expense or loss if things go wrong.
- Public exposure as a form of avoidance appeal is used, for example, in current affairs programs against firms which act unfairly or refuse to co-operate on matters of community concern. Most firms will try to avoid exposure of this kind. If you deserve a refund and the person behind the counter refuses to give you one, try saying in a louder than usual voice: 'But your advertisement on TV says you will refund my money within seven days — it's only five days since I bought this. *Why won't you keep the promise you advertised?*' Repeating this several times can bring a dramatic change in what was previously an inflexible attitude.

Avoidance appeals can backfire if used in association with forbidden or dangerous items. Attempts to have a book banned will stress the danger of allowing it to be read, but the extra publicity generated usually increases sales. Political campaigns can make much of the risk of a change from the party in power, but this may cause more people to think about a change than a positive campaign.

An avoidance appeal can also worry people, and its value is lost if it is presented as a threat. A section manager might raise the question of staff transfers, hoping that this will improve staff co-operation. Instead, many of the best staff resign and take up more secure jobs elsewhere, to avoid the transfer threat.

Personal appeal

Your power of persuasion depends on how much people accept you as a credible communicator, and will be strongly influenced by various facets of your personality.

Knowledge

The more you appear to be an expert, the more training and qualifications you have, the easier it is to be persuasive even on matters outside your area of expertise. People with titles such as 'doctor' or 'professor' are often seen as experts on a wide range of topics. Is this necessarily so?

Similarity of appearance and voice

Those who dress as you do, whether in a business outfit, jeans or skiing gear, will find you more persuasive than those who dress differently. The way you speak — your accent and pronunciation — has a similar effect.

Relationships

What kind of relationship do you have with the people you are trying to persuade? Do they like you? Do they trust you? If you are known to be an active supporter of a particular football team or political group, others with similar leanings will find you more persuasive than those who support different associations. If you play golf with the general manager, your power of persuasion at work will be stronger; if you play cards with the truck drivers, they will be happier to accept your personal appeal for co-operation than one from the general manager.

Self-confidence plus sincerity

If you appear to know what you are doing and have a reputation for sincerity, you will be more persuasive than those who act uncertainly or hesitantly.

Use body language, signs and symbols that project confidence. Show a personal interest in others. Overacting or exaggeration, however, suggest a lack of sincerity.

Ability to praise freely

Messages of thanks, appreciation and praise for past co-operation set the scene for future agreement. People who are mean with compliments (but generous with criticism) find persuasion particularly difficult and usually resort to less positive methods.

Ability to handle pressure

How much time do you have? Is this a competitive situation? If so, what do you need to do to meet the appeals being offered by the competition?

Other forms of appeal

Reverse appeal

Reverse appeals in theory should not work, since they appear to downgrade or criticise some aspect of a product. In practice, the effect is often to increase demand.

- A 'No frills' slogan suggests that the best is too costly and the second-best almost as expensive but that third-best, though plain, is so cheap it offers the top value — for instance, 'Rent a Wreck' hire-car services.
- Self-criticism, when handled correctly (usually by a well-known comedian), can produce an immediate increase in sales. Some people may be drawn by the appearance of total honesty shown by the advertiser, others by the humour and novelty. The association with a popular media figure helps, too.

Matching responses

There are limits to how far you can go with positive persuasion. If an individual just won't respond to a positive approach, switch to more direct methods. Try assertion (see 'Open and assertive communication', in Chapter 12), but if that does not work

the most appropriate answer to negative responses may be to match them. However, as soon as the other person shows signs of becoming more positive, match this response in turn.

Overcoming resistance

Persuasion usually means attempting to change or modify others' ideas. However, people often worry about anything unknown or unfamiliar, and this can create a major barrier that stops them saying 'yes' to a suggested change. You can use various means to overcome this kind of resistance.

1. Tell a story.

A short story about real people showing how much they gained from similar changes is one of the best ways of reducing these fears. If you cannot find a real-life example, however, try to give logical illustrations which will demonstrate that there are no sound alternatives to co-operation.

2. Show as well as tell.

Hand out pictures and diagrams; show a video. Use drawings or illustrations as well as words, especially when presenting key facts.

3. Make advantages clear and visible.

You are encouraging staff to support the introduction of a new and more efficient computer. Don't just say that the new system will be 'easier to use'. List advantages one by one on a board. Reduce fear of change by explaining that everyone will get full training (say just when and where and for how many hours each person will be trained — this helps people feel that the training offer is genuine).

4. Use non-verbal communication.

Words work quite well for everyday persuasion, but when it comes to major decisions such as choosing a career or a partner, deciding which insurance company offers the safest cover or which college or course of study has the most status, there is no doubt that non-verbal appeals exert a more powerful effect. They are estimated to be three to four times more influential in situations such as job interviews and sales presentations, and to have twice the influence in letters and reports.

Summary

1. Persuasion works by comparing the benefits of co-operation and agreement with the disadvantages of a lack of co-operation.
2. Positive persuasion is a very effective way of creating co-operation and getting people to do what you want.
3. There are many different 'appeals' that can be used to encourage agreement. The skilled persuader chooses the appeal that is best for each situation.
4. Persuasion involves more than just using words. Your personal communication skills and non-verbal communication also affect your power as a persuader.

Exercises

1. What is a persuasive 'appeal'?
2. What qualities make a person more persuasive?
3. Why do positive forms of persuasion work better than negative ones?
4. List the names of people you know who would be representative of the different kinds of persuasive power.
5. Why is authority called 'power on loan'?
6. One of the rewards that people need at work is information. Messages of value to a person, such as advance news of a job vacancy or a possible sales lead, can be a source of power. Give examples of power being exercised in this way.
7. Nikala has been employed for a week, on a trial basis. After two days, the boss tells Nikala, 'Unless you make fewer errors, you'll be out of a job on Friday'. If you were the boss, what would you say to Nikala?
8. Ashleigh, a successful young solicitor, is looking for a sports car. In casual conversation with Robbie, the car sales representative, Ashleigh mentions that a good friend has just bought 'a really smart-looking soft top XZJ for only $32 500'. If you were Robbie, what appeals would you now stress that would help to sell Ashleigh one of your cars?

PART 3

Writing at work

CHAPTER 14

Writing in four easy stages

Writing at work means communicating for people and with people. It's an excellent way to exchange information, but equally important is its ability to create bonds of understanding.

Recognise the power of written words to develop and strengthen business relationships. And the better the relationship between you and your readers, the more often your writing will get the results you want.

Many people think writing has to be hard work. It doesn't have to be: if you go about it the right way, business writing can be productive and enjoyable.

Stages	Task	Result
1. Thinking and planning	Deciding why you are writing and what you want to achieve	A list of ideas or topics
2. Capturing ideas on paper	Jotting down ideas as they occur to you	A rough draft
3. Organising shape and structure	Developing a layout and a logical sequence of ideas	A second draft with headings and outline
4. Editing, revising and proofreading	Rewriting, improving language, style and tone; proofing for errors	A final draft, then the finished version

---

Topics

One stage at a time

Stage 1: Thinking and planning

Stage 2: Capturing ideas on paper

Stage 3: Organising the shape and structure

Stage 4: Editing and revising

Rewriting

Proofreading

Tone and style

General guidelines for business writers

Stage 1: Thinking and planning

Think of yourself as the engineer, architect or designer of your written message. How can you build a worthwhile letter or report if you don't have a plan? It doesn't matter how many words you actually put on paper during stage 1; when you do start to write, you'll work far more effectively if you have a plan to work from. You need to understand

- the situation (context) in which you are writing;
- the topic you are writing about;
- the person or reader group you are writing to;
- what you really want to tell them;
- why you want to tell them this.

However, *your* understanding is not enough. When readers receive your finished letters or reports, *they* need to understand

One stage at a time

One way to make writing easier is to break the job into stages and give your full attention to one stage at a time. Writing involves at least four different activities: when people say they find it difficult, it's usually because they are trying to do all four at once!

- the situation that led you to write;
- what you wanted to tell them, and why.

Plan your writing with these needs in mind.

What is the situation?

What are you aiming for? What are your *reasons* for writing? Remember the four aims listed in Chapter 3 as the aims for all communication:

- Create action — get results.
- Exchange information.
- Use persuasion — build co-operation.
- Establish the relationship.

The RIPPA formula

Here's a useful formula to help you plan any kind of writing. Its steps cover the four aims (above) and there's a fifth step (paint a picture) which increases the chances of agreement. The initial letters of the key words give the formula name, *RIPPA*.

1. Establish the RELATIONSHIP ⟶ R
2. Give the reader INFORMATION ⟶ I
3. Persuade POINT by POINT ⟶ P
4. Strengthen the argument with a PICTURE ⟶ P
5. Close by asking for ACTION ⟶ A

As an example of how to use the formula, consider the case of a mythical writer, Karl Bluntski, who doesn't believe in planning (nor in writing in four stages). When he decided recently to write to Calshop (a mail-order firm that sells special business calculators), he grabbed his pen and wrote the following letter.

Dear Calshop,

I am a 28-year-old student, doing a business course at Greenwood College and I've got a bit of a problem. My business maths exam has been brought forward to next month, instead of the end of the year. I was going to order a special calculator before then but now I need it in a hurry.

It doesn't matter what one you send as long as I get it fast, but it has to be one that will do all the business maths formulae in our course. I think that sort cost about $30 to $35, but I suppose I could go a bit higher at a pinch.

Let me know how you want the money — bankcard, cheque or money order?

Thanks,

Karl Bluntski

Now imagine that you are planning a similar letter to Calshop. Your exam is only three weeks away. You know that the test will include exercises on compound interest and stock ratios, and you need a calculator that handles these calculations. Here's how you could use the RIPPA formula to plan your letter before you start writing:

1. **Relationship:** Because time is so short, I want Calshop to choose the calculator for me. Other students say they are very helpful, so I'm confident I can leave it to them.

2. **Information:** The calculator I need has special function keys for compound interest and stock ratios. I'd better give them the exact formulae we use, to avoid any confusion.

3. **Point-by-point persuasion:** I expect to pay between $30 and $35, but if necessary up to $40. I'll give them my credit card number to save them having to contact me about payment.

4. **Painting a picture:** I need to have the calculator here ten days before the exam. I can make that picture clearer by giving the date of the exam (the 25th); I'll *show* them what I want and why, rather than just asking them to supply it.

5. **Action ending:** I'll close by asking Calshop to make sure the calculator reaches me by the 15th. I want to be sure they send it priority paid, not by ordinary mail. The best place to mention that is at the end, so they'll remember it.

Note: When you write, translate 'I want' into 'can you', so that your letter does not sound like Karl's.

Hit the bull's-eye

Imagine the first four topics on the list (Relationship, Information, Persuasion and Picture) as the rings of a target. The action ending is the bull's-eye.

Develop the relationship first

You'll hit the bull's-eye more often if you first deal with the two-way, reader—writer relationship, then exchange information, then persuade or build agreement. This makes it much easier to create agreement, especially if you build a relationship that encourages co-operation.

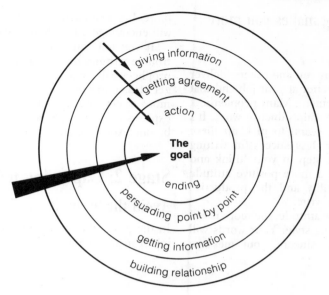

Fig. 14.1 *Hitting the bull's-eye*

Sit in the reader's chair

Spend time thinking about your readers. Otherwise your writing will tend to be cold and distant.

- People like to know where they stand in any kind of relationship.
- The more confident people are about the relationship, the easier it is to build agreement.
- A relationship that relies on power or threats may get results, but will not build co-operation.

Old-fashioned, 'business-like' writing was intentionally impersonal. It ignored the existence of a relationship. Today this cannot get you off to a good start, and won't encourage co-operation.

Defining and developing relationships — guidelines

1. Lay a foundation for your message.

The best base is a positive bridge of understanding between you and your readers. Apart from your words, your non-verbal writing style (background signals) communicates this.

2. Respect your reader.

Today's writers cannot assume an attitude of superiority as in the past. People prefer to do business with someone whose writing is user-friendly.

3. Help your readers to understand.

Anticipate questions. In the example given above, think about what else the people at Calshop need to be told.

Answering questions in advance shows readers that you understand they are busy and you want to reduce the chance of misunderstanding. People treat this as a compliment, and that makes them feel happier about helping you.

4. Consider readers' feelings.

The more you tune in to your readers, the easier it is to write to them and the better they will tune in to you. Sitting in the reader's chair helps you choose the best writing style (pp. 155–6) and the right level of empathy (see Chapter 5, 'Tuning in to the other person').

5. Estimate a reader's 'page limit'.

There is a limit to the number of pages a person will read before losing interest. Each reader will have a different 'page limit', so estimate the length likely to be most acceptable. A short memo read from start to finish is more effective than a long one half-read. Empathy helps you understand why one reader may find a six-page report 'too long' while another feels that twenty pages on the same topic is ideal.

Be positive — writing makes you more productive

Because your writing helps you and others 'deliver the goods', you become better at your job and that opens the door to advancement. Many people think of writing as unrewarding, unproductive work. It's quite common, over the years, to pick up these feelings based on earlier, less successful writing experiences. So the final step in your 'think and plan' stage is to develop a more positive attitude towards your writing ability and the productive value for *you* of what you write.

The more positive your attitude, the more it will be reflected in your writing style. Your words will sound warmer and more sincere, your message more direct and active; your own positive approach will encourage a matching response in the reader.

If you tell yourself that you are going to have trouble writing, there is a strong chance that your prophecy will come true. Anxiety makes it harder to get ideas into words; the more relaxed you are, the more freely your ideas will flow. The next section explains just how easy (and rewarding) writing can be once you take a positive approach

Stage 2: Capturing ideas on paper

Avoid the 'write it once' approach

In the past, when most writing involved pens and ink or manual typing, making changes to a finished

Capturing ideas on paper

page was always a problem. Naturally, writers tried to work out a message mentally and write it only once. With today's electronic writing systems this is no longer necessary, but even if you use a pen or pencil it's best to discard the 'write it once' approach. It happens to be one of the most restrictive practices you can adopt.

Trying to organise whole paragraphs in your head plays havoc with your thinking; so many ideas get lost while you try to think of the right words and put them in the right order.

Begin stage 2 by getting some thoughts down on paper or (if you are using a word processor) on screen. Sketch rough ideas first; organise them later. Any of the following methods will help.

- Make a shopping list.
- Take the complete-outline approach.
- Start with the interesting parts.
- Use the 'random writing' method.
- Try a 'jumper lead'.
- Take the opposite view.
- Use a word processor.

Make a shopping list

Make a list of things to write about. What points do you need to cover? What do you need to say to gain the reader's agreement? The example below lists five topics around which you would then build the letter.

1. Remind Mal that I support his position (*Relationship*).
2. Tell Mal the facts concerning the contract (*Information*).
3. Explain to Mal why he should sign (*Point by point*).
4. Show Mal advantages for him if he signs now (*Picture*).
5. Ask Mal to return signed contract (*Action*).

There is no need to start at the top. Begin with any topic you wish (see 'Start with the interesting parts', page 146).

The complete-outline approach

While many writers like a short list, others prefer to draft a complete outline as in the example below. A detailed set of headings helps you develop a better understanding of the overall topic.

A complete outline will list every topic you intend to deal with, and probably most subtopics. It may cover half a page, one page, or several pages. This approach is the one commonly recommended by teachers, professional writers, and authors of books on writing. It helps to keep your writing relevant and your ideas in order, and saves time. On the other hand, it reduces flexibility and restricts creative thinking.

Sample writing outline

Title: Worker democracy in Australia

Part 1: Introduction and definitions
　　Define: worker democracy
　　Worker democracy takes several different forms:
- Sharing profits
- Sharing control of decision making
- Consultation and consensus-type meetings used to make decisions and solve problems
- A mixture of all or any of these

Part 2: Worker democracy in practice
　　Two case studies
　　2.1　Study A: Westland Manufacturing Ltd
　　　　2.1.1　The basic structure of the company
- Management
- Administration and accounts
- Sales and marketing
- Manufacturing
- Transport
- Other sections

　　　　2.1.2　The democratic decision-making system at Westland
　　　　2.1.3　Profit-sharing procedures in use at present
　　　　　　　Example A
　　　　　　　Example B
　　　　　　　Example C
　　　　2.1.4　Proposals for the future at Westland
　　2.2　Study B: ACE Welding Works
　　　　2.2.1　The basic structure of the company
- Management, administration and accounts
- Factory
- Stores
- Other sections

Start with the interesting parts

The kind of person described in Chapter 6 who likes to be very organised will usually start with an outline similar to the one above and work through the list in order, but it makes just as much sense to begin with any one of the topics if it is already clear in your mind or you are already interested in it. If you find it helps to write the ending first, do so.

In a report, why not begin by writing up some test results you already have on hand or roughing out some of the recommendations you think will go at the end? Write a section that uses a similar approach regardless of the topic, such as the introduction to an assignment or the middle paragraph of a 'please pay' letter. Many people find this technique superior to writing sequentially. It is not a sign of untidy thinking; in fact, many experienced writers (including the authors of this book) find it actually speeds up the creation of a more organised structure.

The 'random writing' method

Trying to get ideas 'straight' and the right words organised too soon is a common cause of writer's block. If your mind is active it will come up with more thoughts than you can write down at one time, and this creates a traffic jam of ideas. Once you know the cause, however, you can avoid the blockage. The problem lies in the belief that words should be organised in your head. This is not so!

An associated cause of writer's block is worrying whether people will approve of your ideas and the way you express them. Keep rough drafts private and confidential — if you know that no one else will see them you can write more freely. As long as you do this, you will find the technique called 'random writing' among the best of all methods for avoiding writer's block.

Random writing — guidelines

1. Do not worry about choice of words.
Don't worry at first how they sound or whether they make sense. Dump them out of your head as fast as you can.

2. Skip the rules.
For the time being, do not worry about grammar or spelling, or the way sentences are put together.

3. Do not worry about sequence.
To begin with, write down your thoughts as they come to you. Just capture the ideas on paper or on the screen of your word processor.

4. Do not try to work out specific details.
Unless they come readily to mind, leave them until later.

5. Use diagrams, shapes or symbols.
They're often faster to use than words when you want to capture an overall idea.

6. Do not worry about appearance.
Draft writing doesn't have to be neat and tidy.

7. Keep it 'for your eyes only'.
As explained above, worrying about criticism is a source of blockages, so don't let anyone see your first draft.

8. Allow yourself freedom.
Make as many alterations and corrections as you like.

Advantages

Once your thoughts are on paper, it is easier to judge their value. If they are what you want, keep them; otherwise discard them. Some of the points you reject will have value in other ways.

- After the first random dump you will find it easier to think of more new ideas, some of which will be closer to what you were looking for.
- Among the phrases you reject you'll often find

one or two words that are worth using in other places.

- Observing rejected ideas may help you to clarify what you do *not* want to say, which helps to work out more clearly what you *do*.

Try a jumper lead

Jumper leads can consist of words that are unnecessary or totally incorrect or anything at all as long as they get your ideas moving. A writer's jumper lead works in the same way as the ones used on cars — it gets an important idea running. For example:

- I am writing this letter to advise you of serious difficulties that have arisen regarding . . .

Of course, an opening like this shouldn't appear in a final letter or report; like the automotive variety, jumper-lead phrases must be disconnected (deleted) once they have played their part.

Take the opposite view

Edward de Bono, in his books on lateral thinking, suggests a technique for creating ideas. He describes it as 'thinking in the opposite direction' and explains why it helps to overcome blockages in thinking and writing. Making a list of what you do *not* want to write is a surprisingly effective way of generating ideas about what you *do*.

For instance, you have to write a report on 'How to increase motivation' and you cannot think of even one way to motivate anyone! But, says de Bono, if you begin by making some rough notes on 'Ways of reducing motivation' you will soon find yourself thinking of profit-making ideas, including some that might have escaped you if you had concentrated only on the topic of profit 'increase'. A look in the opposite direction also increases your understanding of the topic as a whole.

Try a word processor

The four-stage writing method is ideal when you use electronic word-processing. You can move, add and delete sentences; insert headings; correct spelling; punctuate and so on until you are happy with the quality of the product. The computer has all your ideas on record, so as long as you keep a file copy you can recall, re-edit and recycle previously written material. Writers who switch to word processing report a major increase in both quality and quantity of words within a few weeks.

Stage 3: Organising the shape and structure

Organised text is set out in a step-by-step sequence. People need to see not only each idea clearly, but also the connection between one topic and the next. The rules for organising ideas and grouping topics according to their content can be summed up in two lines:

- Keep similar topics together.
- Keep different topics apart.

If it is obvious that two or three ideas belong together, put them in the same section. While working on your first draft you probably started sorting topics in this way. Keep on doing this.

Each shift in the way you think about a subject — and each change of topic — should be clearly marked by a new heading or a new number. Separate

- factual from non-factual, objective from subjective;
- data with differing levels of objectivity;
- well-documented data from unreliable material;
- negative items or bad news from positive topics.

Will your page turn a reader 'on' or 'off'?

A well-arranged page has a positive effect on the way your readers perceive you and your business. Before they read a single word, they will be influenced by its appearance; it suggests that you are a clear thinker, and this creates reader confidence. People look forward to reading such a page, knowing it will be easy to follow, and feel more positive towards both you and your message. Whether handwritten or typed, the appearance of a page can either attract attention (a 'switch on') or create a negative feeling (a 'switch off').

To show just how seriously a poorly arranged page affects the person in the reader's chair, read the paragraph below, set out in traditional 'essay format'. Imagine that you have been told to read it and remember exactly what it says. Concentrate on the meanings of the words. Try to gain a clear understanding.

In today's busy world, words alone cannot create clear communication. What you write must also look attractive. From the very first glance, your readers should be convinced that what is in front of them will be easy to read, easily understood and easy to remember. However, if you use a more attractive page layout, such as business format, you have a far better chance of getting your message through to busy readers. Use one topic per sentence or paragraph. Leave a blank line between paragraphs to show where each topic starts and ends. Use numbered headings to help people follow your topics in a step-by-step sequence.

- How easy was it to follow the message? Did it hold your attention?
- How many times would you have to reread it before you understood it clearly? How many of the important points can you remember now?
- What were your feelings towards the writer?

Contrast what you have just read with the item below, organised in business format. How does it compare for clarity and readability with essay format?

The Importance of Attractive Writing

1. *Give your pages 'eye appeal'.*

   In today's busy world, words alone cannot create clear communication. What you write must also look attractive.

   From the very first glance, your readers should be convinced that what is in front of them will be:

   - easy to read;
   - easily understood;
   - easy to remember.

2. *Use business format.*

   To get your message through to busy readers:

   - Use one topic per sentence or paragraph.
   - Leave blank lines between paragraphs to show where each topic starts and ends.
   - Use numbered headings to help people follow your topics in a step-by-step sequence.

Notice that this is the same message (almost word for word) as in the essay format example, yet the meanings seem much clearer and the flow of topics easier to follow. Therefore, what made the previous example so unattractive must have been its layout, rather than the words used.

Of course, the long sentences in the essay format made the problem worse. In business format — so-called because it is so commonly used in presenting business information — you tend to write shorter sentences, which are easier to remember and easier to find if you need to reread them.

Using business format — guidelines

It is quite easy to give your pages a businesslike, well-organised appearance with strong eye-appeal if you observe the following points.

1. Write about only one topic in each paragraph.
Think of a paragraph as a box. Think of each topic as something that you can put in that box. When you write, it's like 'packing' your topics so that they can be transported to other people's desks.

Readers have to unpack the boxes by themselves, and it's harder to unpack someone else's thoughts if the writer has put three different topics in one paragraph. A reader who is having trouble working out which topic is which usually skips the whole paragraph and the report, job application or memo that you were depending on is only half-read.

2. Use blank lines to separate paragraphs.
Blank lines, margins and the other parts of the page that are free of print are referred to collectively as 'white space'. Allow at least one line of white space between each paragraph (in addition to any line with a heading on it).

These spaces are 'topic separators'; they help both readers and writers to see where one topic ends and another begins. The visual effect is a 'white box' around your topic, identifying it as a single thought.

White space has a powerful psychological effect, drawing the eye to the page and increasing the reader's span of attention. It also has a positive effect on reader confidence. This is one of the reasons that the test layouts in the left column (the first using essay style with no white space, the second using business format with 'open' layout) produce different reactions.

How has white space been used in this book? Does the layout make it easier to read?

3. Use headings as signposts.
A label on the lid of a box describes what the box contains. A heading works in the same way, indicating the contents of the paragraph. A series of headings are like a set of signposts, directing the reader through the text, pointing out the way the writer is thinking.

Write headings on separate lines, beginning the actual paragraph on the next line. As your draft develops you can add subheadings to show that the main topic has been divided into subtopics, as illustrated in the example below, taken from a longer document. Here is topic number 5 which has required three subheadings.

5. USING HEADINGS
Headings tell you at a glance where a topic starts or stops. As you run your eye down a page, they also provide a quick summary of the contents.
5.1 How many headings to a page?
You do not have to use a headline for every paragraph, but each page of a long document should contain two or three.
5.2 Underline your headings.
Underline all main headings. Minor headings or subheadings need not be underlined.
5.3 Use subheadings.
Group a number of minor points along with a main topic. These may need subheadings to identify them as units of the central topic and to show how they are related.

After dividing and regrouping, you usually find you have some leftover topics. Combine them all under a final *blanket heading*, such as 'Other problems' or 'Other meetings'.

1. EASTERN STATES GROUP
   1.1 Sydney
   1.2 Melbourne
   1.3 Brisbane
2. CENTRAL AND WESTERN GROUP
   2.1 Adelaide
   2.2 Perth
3. OTHER BRANCHES (Blanket heading)
   3.1 Darwin
   3.2 Canberra
   3.3 Port Moresby

4. Number important headings and subheadings.
Numbering is a powerful aid to understanding. Numbered headings help the reader navigate by
- identifying a particular point;
- indicating how many parts there are to a topic;
- showing the order of the topics.

Numbers also help you, as the writer, to think more logically about the sequence you are using and to see whether or not each point is in sequence. Numbers do not create logic, but they do help others to follow a logical progression of topics, which encourages understanding (see 'Numbering headings', in Chapter 16).

Change margin widths

Another way of using white space is to vary the width of your margins. The more important the message, the wider margins can be. Generous margins give an impression of confidence and power. Narrow margins have the opposite effect. Experiment with margins wider than those you have used in the past.

Indenting margins

A step-by-step indentation of the left margin creates interesting white-space patterns, adds eye appeal and individuality to each page, and can also be used to identify subtopics:

A wider *left* margin (like this one) is a practical way of showing that the (indented) paragraph deals with a subtopic within a larger topic.
In this paragraph, widening the *right* margin also adds further variety to the white-space pattern. As long as you don't overdo it, this is another way of adding eye appeal.

List short items vertically

Some information may consist of only one, two or three words yet still be an important and individual topic. To maintain consistency, such topics should have their own 'paragraphs'. Do not put them all horizontally in one sentence; instead, list them like this:
- each on its own line
- each in its own small 'paragraph'
- one under the other

Use a star or a dot rather than a number to the left of each item. A small extra indent can add to the visual effect.

Boxing special items

Business format allows wide scope for other variations in layout.

> Create 'boxes' by ruling lines around important paragraphs. These contrast with the other shapes and the white-space patterns described above, adding further eye appeal.

Advantages of business format

As well as organising your ideas for the reader's benefit, all these techniques help you to write more effectively. Business format uses more space, but helps you to

- think more clearly about the whole subject;
- recognise each topic as a separate unit;
- recognise the best sequence for arranging topics;
- keep track of both simple and complex (or branching) topics, even though these may extend over several pages.

Knowing that your pages have a stronger appeal and that your message makes good sense adds to your confidence in your writing ability. Because the format makes reading easier and topics are displayed more clearly, you and your readers find the message easier to remember.

Stage 4: Editing and revising

Your final message needs to be clear, concise, correct, and easy to understand. Read it right through and change anything that does not meet the standards you have set.

- Check your language. Concentrate on the quality of the words. Change vague, abstract phrases into short, straightforward and direct ones. Give top priority to improving what you have written. Leave the addition of new ideas until last.

- Proofread every line. Check grammar, spelling and punctuation. Double-check numerical data.
- Review the tone and style — the non-verbal aspects that affect the way people relate to you and your whole message. This is explained below (pp. 154–6).
- Check for other faults. Look for minor yet annoying points of style such as passive sentences (see p. 151), repetition and redundancy (see p. 152).

Seek feedback

It is an excellent idea to involve others at this stage, to balance your own view. Ask for comment, criticism, or help in making improvements. Most sections of this book have been rewritten several times, following critical assessment and suggestions from teachers and students. As a result of their feedback, what you are reading today contains more useful information yet is far shorter than the original.

Business language

If you study business writing closely you will notice that Australian business language is developing a style of its own — one that differs from that used in countries such as Britain or the United States. Our writing is more direct and to the point, and sounds much as though the writer is addressing the reader face to face, something most Australian readers welcome.

Avoid out-of-date language

Why do some people, who speak normally, persevere with out-of-date language when they write? One reason is that people who are not sure of themselves or what they are writing about try to cover up this fact by

- writing overlong sentences;
- using longer words, believing that the result will sound more 'educated' (usually with the opposite effect, particularly if the words are unfamiliar and the writer uses them incorrectly);
- adding extra words, thinking that this will make their language seem more impressive (but generally only adding bulk);
- copying other people's words, particularly familiar phrases that appear to be correct because

in the past they have been used often to convey negative messages.

If you write in this way, it must affect the reader's perception of you. Dated language gives the impression that you are perhaps a bit out of date yourself. Negative phrases make you sound like a negative person. When you use any style that is not really your own, people will naturally be more inclined to doubt your objectivity.

Reject traditional phrases

There are no special phrases selected by writing experts as 'correct'. The only 'correct' words are those that carry your meaning clearly and accurately. Once-popular phrases — for instance, 'do not hesitate' or 'at your convenience' — are *not* correct, because they are not what you would say in face-to-face discussions or in telephone conversations. They are not *your* words.

Use your own words

The most powerful words you can use are your own words, because they sound sincere and believable. What you write should reflect your personality as well as your thoughts. Develop a style of your own. Writing which sounds natural sounds real. Doing this is easy if when you write you follow this rule:

■ When writing to people, use the words you would use in talking to them.

Be direct and natural, but not too informal. The ideal style is similar to that used in talking to a slightly more senior business colleague.

Do not become too casual

Do not become too conversational or 'chatty' in your business correspondence. How would you react to a letter like this one, written in a style recommended by some overseas writers as a form of 'personalised' business correspondence?

Good morning, Joe,

I'm writing to you personally, Joe, to ask if you can get to work on that overdue account of yours. Please, Joe, how about popping your cheque in an envelope today?

Inserting the reader's name mid-paragraph sounds artificial — more like a 'sales pitch' than a request for payment of an account.

Use words that fit your reader's vocabulary

Most business writers have specialised knowledge in their own field. Tied to that knowledge is a specific language — the technical terms and jargon used by experts to communicate on their particular subjects. An auditor reporting on a balance sheet to another accountant might well state that 'there are indications of impending liquidity problems', but for the average reader it would be better to say, 'There are signs that the company will soon be short of cash and may have difficulty meeting day-to-day working expenses'. Terms such as 'cash' and 'working expenses' fit most readers' understanding of business finance; 'liquidity' may not.

Change negative phrases to positive

The more bad news, complaints or criticism in a message, the more likely it will be to provoke a negative reaction. That reduces your chance of gaining the reader's agreement. The section 'Say "No" as softly as possible', in Chapter 15, explains in detail how to deal with 'bad news' in business correspondence.

Active and passive sentences

When you speak, you use active sentences such as 'I am very interested in your submission'. It makes sense to write this way, too. When someone writes 'Your submission has attracted considerable interest', that's passive. The effect is passive because emphasis is 'passed' away from the action and from the person involved. The action is focused on the submission, and just who actually is interested remains a mystery. The style suggests a distant and formal attitude, which has a negative effect on a business relationship.

Identifying a passive sentence

A telltale sign of a passive sentence is the complex verb consisting of two or (usually) three words, one of which will *always* be a form of the verb 'to be' (is, was, were, am, are and so on). When you see in your writing verbs such as 'will *be* kept', 'are *being* made', '*was* not received', consider whether an active sentence could be better.

Passive sentence: The contract is *being* signed on Monday by the client.

The sentence, though short, is impersonal. The contract (*an inanimate object*) is being signed (*action*) by the client (*the person taking the action*). What happens if, instead, the sentence starts by naming the person taking the action?

Active sentence: The client will sign the contract on Monday.

Notice the improvement in style and tone, as well as the shorter sentence. Passive sentences, however, can be useful at times.

- To distance yourself from a decision: 'Your application has been unsuccessful' rather than 'We have rejected your application'.
- To put an intentional emphasis on the object: 'Payments can be approved only by an authorised officer'.
- To provide variety in a long text: Too many active sentences together can be overpowering.

Watch for repetition

Repetition can be useful as a form of emphasis in speaking. In writing it is better avoided unless you want particularly to emphasise a point — for example: 'You can see the improvement; you should be able to hear the improvement too'. In this case, the wording has style. Compare it with this sentence, which has not, because the word 'work' is overused: 'Before work can start, a work permit is required authorising the work'.

Redundant words

It's a waste of time to use two (or more) words in the same phrase, if either one can convey the meaning quite clearly. For example: 'The *two* twins met *together* to celebrate their *joint* birthday'; '*Unfortunately* we cannot approve your application'. The words in italics are redundant. Everyone uses a redundant word occasionally, but it does weaken your writing.

tautology

Rewriting

Rewriting, as the name suggests, involves rephrasing — changing a word here and there, or the order in which they are written. If you have the time and like experimenting, try different arrangements of ideas and different styles.

Move the cream to the top

Try moving paragraphs around. The more you write about a subject, the more knowledgable you become about it, so you often find your most powerful ideas at the end of a section. If you think a later statement would have more impact at the start, move it. For handwritten or manually typed material, this may mean rearranging with scissors and sticky tape; it's a trial and error method, but quite often results in real improvement, so it's popular with writers who want their work to achieve the highest possible quality. If it doesn't work, put things back the way they were.

Many writers say that using a word processor results in a major improvement in the quality of their writing. With the ability to rewrite and reprint pages faster, you tend to become more critical of your own writing and to make improvements more often. That certainly makes you a better writer.

Rewriting letters

Letters particularly benefit from rewriting. Notice how the example below becomes clearer and more positive. (This does of course take time, so allow a period for rewriting when planning your letter.)

Original
Thank you for your letter. We refer to previous correspondence and now confirm our proposal to pay out the balance of the lease and enclose payment for this amount. It would be appreciated if you would confirm and advise what further action is required regarding MRD registration to note the transfer of ownership to us.

Rewrite 1
Thank you for your help and advice in sorting out our lease problem. If you agree, we are now willing to purchase the truck for the pay-out value of $12 040.00 and enclose our company cheque for this amount. Could you please confirm and advise so we can take action to notify MRD in regard to registration (due in May) concerning transfer of ownership to our firm?

Rewrite 2
AGC Lease 876−34−093 — Toyota Prime Mover Regn RHD-874

We agree with your suggestion that the best solution is for us to pay out the balance of the lease, $12 040.00 (cheque enclosed). Thank you for the advice and for your helpful suggestions.

Registration on the truck is due on 21 May. Could you please confirm the transfer before then, so we can advise the MRD Office of the change.

Rewriting reports and assignments

The longer the item, the more opportunity you have to rewrite. Reports and assignments are best written part by part and over a longer period than letters; write one unit, put it aside and write other sections, then come back to the first and rewrite it.

Use phrases in place of sentences

If three or four words will work just as well as a sentence in a report, why not use them? Listing items point by point is usually clearer. Consider the example below.

This report expresses major concern about the problem of under-age drinking, and the effect this has on the current rate of accidents involving inexperienced teenage drivers.

This combination of alcohol and lack of experience in driving motorised vehicles is undoubtedly one of the major factors leading to the present excessive road toll in this state.

This version contains a form of comment known as 'editorialising' — the words in italics. Such comments are out of place in business writing, so they are deleted, and salient facts are given in point form. Notice the improvement.

The report emphasises two points about teenage drinking:
1.1 The effect of alcohol on inexperienced drivers
1.2 The increase in road accidents as a result

Problems with rewriting

- If you rewrite two or three times and each version looks better, you may be tempted to try a fourth, fifth and sixth revision and find that with each successive improvement the urge to rewrite grows stronger. Set a deadline and stick to it.

- Rewriting can increase the length of a text if extra points are added to increase clarity or reinforce an argument. Make sure that the finished document does not exceed the reader's page limit, so that the benefit is lost.
- Rewriting almost always results in such an obvious improvement that you could safely scrap the old text, but occasionally it is not successful. *Never* discard earlier versions (or overwrite them on a disk) until the project is complete.

Proofreading

If you need to check spelling or figures by yourself, work backwards (from the bottom of the page up, and from the right end of each line to the left). This stops you 'reading' too rapidly and helps you to focus on individual words rather than on sentences.

- Checking grammar: Mistakes in sentence construction are easy to overlook yet create a very poor impression and reduce credibility. It's hard to see your own grammatical errors, so if possible have someone else check for you.
- Checking spelling: It is also easy to miss your own spelling errors, so it's useful to have someone else check this too. Computerised spelling-checkers are a help, but limited in their ability. They will not identify mistakes in figures or tell you if you have used 'effect' when you should have written 'affect'.
- Checking figures: Errors in numbers are easy to overlook, but one missing decimal point can destroy the credibility of the entire document. Double-check all figures and calculations.

If someone else types your work it is a fatal mistake to rely on that person to check your writing. Neither can you rely on the typist to pick up all his or her own errors. Check every word yourself. If you use a word processor, check the printed version too. Many errors that are unnoticeable on screen can be quickly seen when the text is printed out.

Sometimes, after correcting, rewriting and proofreading, you may feel that your work is still not ready to send to the reader. It may need condensing (see Chapter 20, 'Summarising and condensing'). If the structure is too loose, you may need to put in more work on the unity and continuity, reducing the fog level or reconstructing paragraphs (see Chapter 18, 'The final polish'). But perhaps all you need to do is change the tone and style.

Tone and style

Everything you write is a mixture of verbal and non-verbal meanings. Ideas that you want to state explicitly will be in words. Those you may wish to imply will be conveyed non-verbally through background signals and such writing characteristics as tone and style (the meanings people read 'between the lines'). Readers tune in as much to these as to the words themselves. You cannot leave them out, and they do have a powerful effect on the interpretation of your message. They can change the relationship between reader and writer in either a positive or a negative way.

Writing tone

The word 'tone', used to describe sound, is appropriate here because writing tone affects the way a message 'sounds' to the reader, helping to signal the kind of writer–reader relationship you want to establish. Letters can have a friendly tone, or a formal tone. They can sound angry, sad, happy, gloating, respectful, loving or bored. The tone of a report can make it sound like a parent talking to a child, or the other way round.

A letter may through its tone project trust and personal respect for the reader, yet the words 're-spect' or 'trust' may be nowhere in the text. Tone may depend on the choice of words (and the way they're put together), but may just as easily be conveyed by words that are left out; this is why tone is classed as a non-verbal characteristic. Typical words and phrases that signal tone are shown in the chart below.

Perhaps you will need words like these to project the precise non-verbal tone you want to convey. But be careful! If you write this way, your feelings are showing.

Fine-tuning your tone — guidelines

1. Adjust your tone to the situation, the topic and the reader.
If you are writing to someone in a position of authority, who appreciates formality, use an appropriately formal tone. If you are inviting a local sporting figure to open a new shopping centre, use an informal tone.

2. Where possible, personalise tone.
Keeping point 1 in mind, try to be sure that what you write is recognisable, through its tone, as your own individual message, presenting a true picture of your personality and reflecting the way you feel about people.

3. Be wary of a critical writing tone.
A critical or parent tone is more likely to produce a negative response than an adult one.

4. Be cautious about words not your own.
Copying words and phrases used by others means copying non-verbal content as well. If you must use someone else's words, check that the between-the-lines meanings are appropriate to your message.

Tone	Signals	Examples
urgent	imperative statements timing adverbs	'it is essential that' 'immediately'
informal	abbreviations colloquial phrases	'let's', 'you'll' 'I'll get in touch'
distrustful	extra-polite phrases qualifying phrases mitigating adjectives	'I must ask you for confirmation of' 'if, in fact,' 'your alleged accident'
negative	bad news to follow criticism of reader	'unfortunately' 'you neglected to'
pompous	outdated, pseudo-legal jargon overlong words	'the above-mentioned persons' 'quintessential'

Writing style

Your writing style will affect its tone; the two are closely related, but whereas tone is perceived non-verbally and may be variously interpreted by individual readers, style is based on well-recognised classifications and grammatical forms. Some of the most significant styles are identified by the way in which you use personal pronouns.

- First person (I, me, we, us, mine, ours): 'I need production figures for my report. Can I have them this week?'
- Second person (you, yours): 'Your production figures are needed this week for the May report.'
- Third person (he, she, him, her, his, hers, they, them, theirs): 'The committee needs production figures this week for the May report.'
- Impersonal (no reference to any person): 'Production figures for the May report are due this week.'
- 'You' and 'us' together: 'Please would you send me the production figures for our May report by 20 April.' The most effective writing usually combines 'you' and 'us' words, since this promotes a positive image of the relationship.

Each style has advantages and disadvantages.

The first person — the 'us' or 'me' attitude

This style emphasises the writer's position and personality. First-person style is best reserved for memos, personal correspondence and less formal submissions or assignments. However, too many I's too close together suggest that writers see themselves as more important than their readers. (Karl Bluntski wrote this way.) This style is best varied according to your purpose.

Writing about your responsibilities — use more 'I'

Emphasising the first person projects a stronger image of the writer as a leader. A person who is afraid of criticism might write 'It has been noted that there has been a reduction in sales'. If it is your job to make this kind of statement, then let the reader know you are confident. Write 'I notice that sales are down'. Minimise the use of 'I', however, if writing about your own achievements.

Expressing agreement — use more 'I'

If it is important to show people that you are a decision maker, or if you are expressing agreement, use 'I' or 'we' to personalise the approval. Write: 'I have decided that ...' rather than 'It is the conclusion of the writer that ...'.

Report — use no 'I' or 'we'

Report writers are supposed to be objective, not promoting themselves or their own views. Proposals and recommendations stated in a direct and impersonal way also sound more confident. Rather than 'We think the changeover should be at the end of March', write 'The changeover should start on 31 March'.

The second person — the 'you' attitude

This style projects a warm tone and sounds like one adult talking to another. Much of this book is written in this style. Because 'you' is personal and can refer to either male or female, it is also an excellent way to avoid any hint of discrimination in your writing.

The third person — the 'they' attitude

Third-person writing helps to maintain a polite distance between writer and reader. It allows the writer to appear impartial, which is useful when presenting factual information that must be considered objectively and free from personal involvement.

The user might refer to himself or herself as 'the writer' or 'the team leader' and to the people in the writer's team as 'the staff training unit' — not as 'my unit' or 'our unit'. When issues such as planning or policy making are involved, this unemotional and formal tone is preferable. The third-person style is correct when recording decisions reached at formal meetings, or in official memos and policy booklets. It is also used often in student assignments.

Impersonal style

It is possible to avoid using any personal pronouns at all. Instruction manuals and policy books are usually written in this style; for example, 'Section managers are responsible for approving all expenses'. It emphasises facts rather than people, which maximises the impact of important data. It works well in reports to upper-level management, press releases, prepared speeches and policy statements in which the writer wants to project stability and confidence. It is also preferable for a personal résumé. Direct-style messages must have high credibility — the backing of evidence or the support of a reference from a reliable source.

'You and us together' style

Linking the first and second person in the same sentence helps to emphasise a positive relationship. It shows readers that you and they share collective goals or interests. It is then logical to suggest mutual co-operation in reaching your shared goal.

The 'you:us' ratio

Compare the numbers of 'you' words and 'us' words in one paragraph. This is the 'you:us' ratio.

> **Unbalanced you:us ratio:** Although *we* have the parts in stock, *we* cannot send them until *we* receive payment. Please forward *us* a cheque so that *we* can mail them (zero 'you' words:five 'us' words).
>
> **Balanced you:us ratio:** *We* can send the parts *you* asked for as soon as *we* receive *your* cheque for $1267.89. They will be mailed the day *your* payment reaches *us* (three 'you' words:three 'us' words).

You may need to talk more about yourself in the body of a letter or a memo, but try to maintain a balanced you:us ratio in both the opening and the action ending. In a report, however, the ratio should be zero:zero, as explained above.

'One' used instead of 'me' or 'you'

Avoid using this as in 'One must be prepared to do one's duty'. It is more poetic than practical, and does not fit in well with business writing today.

Other writing styles

There are other writing styles you can use according to whether you want to write in a direct or an indirect way. This is illustrated in the following chart.

Direct . . . . *versus* . . . . . . *Indirect*	
organised	unstructured
short and concise	lengthy
specific and detailed	generalised
concise	wordy
open and confident	closed or uncertain
persuasive (builds agreement)	informative (just facts)
informal	formal

General guidelines for business writers

1. Simple words suit important messages.
The most important ideas can be best explained in short, simple words.

2. Write naturally.
Using everyday words helps to break down barriers. Artificial language, jargon and unnatural grammar rob your message of its sincerity.

3. Use empathy.
Your ability to see things from the reader's point of view is a powerful skill that helps you gain agreement and achieve the results you want. Business firms, government departments and computers cannot read, so write to the people who operate the computers, who run the firms, who work in the government departments. The most successful writers are those who write with an image of the other person clearly in view.

4. Use your writing to build relationships.
Friendly writing helps to develop the relationship between you and your clients and customers.

5. Develop your own way of writing.
Personalise your writing style. If you are signing your name to a message, make the words sound like

your words. Avoid 'traditional' phrases that sound as if they have been produced by a computer.

12. Tone and style affect responses to the content and meaning of written messages. They also help to signal the state of the writer–reader relationship.

Summary

1. Write in four stages, giving full attention to each stage. Think and plan first. Once you have captured your ideas on paper or screen, they are much easier to organise. After that — check, correct, clarify.

2. Sit in the reader's chair. The average reader prefers to do business with someone whose correspondence has a personal approach, is friendly, and appears to be written with the receiver in mind.

3. Some writers begin with a writing outline — a detailed list of every topic they intend to write about. Others find more open methods, such as 'random writing', are more effective.

4. To develop a more creative style, try 'thinking in the opposite direction' when you write.

5. People need to be able to see each idea clearly.
   - Write about only one topic in each paragraph.
   - Use blank lines to separate paragraphs.
   - Use headings as signposts.
   - Number important headings and sub-headings.

6. Check your final message to make sure it is clear, correct and easy to understand. If you can, get someone to help you proofread.

7. Is the language concise, descriptive, accurate and up to date? Concentrate on the quality of the words as well as on grammar, spelling and punctuation.

8. There are no special phrases selected by experts as 'correct'. The only correct words are those which carry your meaning clearly and accurately.

9. Avoid passive sentences; they signal a distant and formal attitude, which usually has a negative effect on the business relationship.

10. Tone is judged by the way written messages 'sound' to the reader.

11. Style is identified according to well-recognised classifications, and by the use of grammatical forms such as 'first person' or 'second person'.

Exercises

1. Make a list of twenty or more related items — towns, suburbs, railway stations, brands of clothing, items of food, animals, countries or cities around the world. Rewrite the list, this time grouping the items according to the rules for organising ideas (similar together, different apart).

   For each group write a numbered heading, *above* the first item but on a separate line. Finally, number each of the individual items under the heading.

2. Use the random-writing method to capture some ideas on paper for use in writing a two- or three-page assignment about
   - the history of your family over the past 200 years;
   - motivation and management;
   - discrimination at work;
   - any other topic of your choice.

3. Prepare a detailed outline for the topic you chose in exercise 2.

4. The paragraphs below have many different faults. Consider what the writer is trying to say, then write a new version that conveys the same meaning. Improve the clarity and the tone, and remove any errors. Convert passive sentences to active form. Replace jargon with clear, descriptive business language. Brief editing will not be sufficient — you'll need to change many of the original words.
   (a) Your letter has been received by us. Hearing from a regular client such as yourself is a pleasure for us, and we must thank you for same.
   (b) Before extension of the lines to your house can commence, your personal permission for us to lay the lines on your own private property is required.
   (c) Payment by cheque should be avoided as this unfortunately results in delays in processing of orders by our office.

(d) Good morning Kym, We're as sorry as you are about the cancellation of your loan. Anyhow, could you please call and drop the outstanding amount incl. interest back here by the end of the next fortnight? (That's $22 906.66 by the way!)

(e) Until authorisation has been confirmed by our Head Office, this account is not to be operated by persons other than yourself.

(f) Transfers of sums of more than $5000 are not to be made without prior consultation with (and subsequent approval by) the Director.

(g) An anticipated increase in profits has already been referred to by the Board in its Annual Report and this prediction has been further confirmed by the recent upturn in sales figures, also reported therein.

the loan of 22906.66

Only authorized account

CHAPTER 15

Australian business letters

Despite the many changes in communication technology, the most up-to-date electronic communication is seldom as effective as an ordinary letter when it comes to persuading people to accept a point of view, or getting action. Personal letters to customers, staff, clients or friends get results where reports, memoranda or notices may not.

This chapter shows you how to write a letter that Australian readers will see as up to date and effective, using language and layout that fit the business communication style of the 1990s.

Topics

Why letters work

Letter writing in four stages

The letter opening

Subject lines

The body of the letter

Say 'No' as softly as possible

The action ending

Editing and revising

Word processors and business letters

Letter layout

Standard business letters

Why letters work

You gain in several ways when you write a letter rather than communicate face to face or over the phone.

- You have time to think about what you want to say. You can redraft and improve the wording — something you can't do on the phone or in a meeting.

- A letter is a permanent record. A person cannot say 'I wasn't told' or 'I thought you said . . .'.
- You can make copies. Any number of people can see exactly what has been said or agreed. When conversations are reported verbally, the details often become distorted.
- Letters are harder to ignore. When you are dealing with government departments or large organisations, a letter often gets better results than a phone call or a face-to-face enquiry.

Well-written business letters have a powerful impact on the reader's relations with the writer. If the effect is positive, the result can be a new client, settlement of a debt, or similar financial benefits. Benefits that are less measurable, but also important, can include improved customer relations, increased turnover, higher morale, favourable publicity or reduced delays.

What letters do best

Well-written business letters are personal and persuasive. They can communicate in ways not possible in reports, memos, brochures and other kinds of written communication. If you want to exchange straight information, there is no need to write a letter. But if you want to build agreement or cooperation, to encourage people or gain their support, there is no other form of writing that does the job as well.

Are letters worth the cost?

Letter writing takes time. To decide how much is worthwhile (or cost-effective), think about the resulting profit if a particular letter achieves its goal. If the expected outcome is another $500 or $1000 in corporate income, it is sensible to spend at least an hour or more composing a letter. If the gain from a special 'one-off' letter could be a $200 000 contract, it is obviously worth investing the time needed to guarantee a quality production.

Letter writing in four stages

Chapter 14 explained the four-stage writing method. The same four stages apply when you write a business letter:

- Thinking and planning
- Capturing your ideas
- Organising shape and structure (opening, body, and action ending)
- Editing, revising and proofreading

Working in stages like this helps to avoid the pitfalls of writing in a hurry. The first two stages are discussed below, in brief. Stages three and four make up the main portion of this chapter.

Thinking and planning

Sit in the reader's chair

When you are planning what you want the reader to do, put yourself in his or her place. The more you can describe the required action from the reader's point of view, the more successful the letter will be.

What is the letter about?

What is the purpose of the letter? What are the main topics? First, think about the general aims listed in Chapter 14; they apply to virtually all letters.

- *strengthening* the relationship between you and your reader;
- *sharing information* that will make it easier to reach agreement;
- *getting agreement* from the reader so that he or she will be more inclined to respond in the way you want;
- *creating* action or movement.

Second, decide what you want in terms of specific *action*. What kind of response do you expect? Exactly what do you want the reader to do? When and how do you want it done? As you answer these questions, start making rough notes. When choosing the main theme, remember that it is a mistake to communicate about two totally different topics in one letter.

Write two letters, even if they go in the same envelope.

Decide on the length

Set a limit and stick to it. For most readers, this should be under two pages. Only key facts need to go in the letter. Information in business format is far easier to read than in letter form, so if you need to include detailed facts such as an itinerary, a résumé or a list of expenses, make sure that the bulk of the material is *attached* to the letter, not *part* of it.

Capturing your ideas

Concentrate on getting your ideas down in any order, either on paper or on a word processor. Don't try to compose the letter in your head — you need to capture ideas quickly, before they get away. Worrying at this stage about choosing the right words or the right sequence blocks the flow of ideas. (Refer to Chapter 14 for idea-generating techniques such as random writing, p. 146.)

Organising shape and structure

Once you have your rough ideas written down, you can rearrange them using the RIPPA sequence as a check-list. Organise the various points so that they form a logical and coherent plan that fits the three different sections of the letter.

Example A: Account overdue

Opening	■ Remind reader about our agreement.	R
Body	■ List outstanding amounts.	I
	■ Explain why payment is needed now.	P
	■ Note advantage of keeping account open.	P
Ending	■ Ask for a cheque before 27th.	A

Example B: Job application

Opening	■ Note my special interest in *this* job.	R
Body	■ List my qualifications for job.	I
	■ Support my case by pointing to résumé.	P

- Suggest a meeting to clarify picture.   P

Ending   ■ Suggest phone call re interview time.   A

The letter opening

The greeting or salute line (salutation)

Using first names is now quite acceptable for many kinds of business correspondence. If someone uses your first name on the phone or in writing to you, it is an indication that he or she would be happy for you to do the same in return. It is worth the effort, if necessary, of finding out a person's name in preference to using 'Dear Sir', which can cause significant problems.

Do you have to say 'Dear…'?

Many people still prefer a salute that starts with 'Dear …', and this is no problem if you feel comfortable continuing the custom. Many others, however, find it unnatural, since they don't use 'dear' on the phone or face to face. Examples of alternative salutations now in popular use include

- 'Lyndsay' (no 'dear' or 'hello') — using the receiver's name alone, just as you would in a memo or at a meeting;
- 'Hello Sam' (but not 'G'day Sam') — there is growing acceptance of this option, particularly if it is the way you would address Sam on the phone or in conversation;
- 'Good morning Gil' — this is fine if you would normally say 'Good morning' to Gil on the phone (if not, it may sound less natural than 'Hello');
- a strong subject line by itself (no salute line) — in this case the reader's title and position (and name if known) are highlighted *above* the subject line, either in the address or in a separate attention line (see p. 166);
- 'Sales Office, Myer Stores' — using the name of the division or of a staff position, you can of course use 'dear' too — 'Dear Personnel Manager' — or just begin 'Myer Stores', or 'Dear Myer').

A salute line that uses only a surname, 'Dear Miss Pinare', is impersonal and often appears 'incorrect' in the reader's eyes unless you know the latter's preference for Mrs, Miss, Ms or Mr. If any of the alternatives suggested above are acceptable, use them. If you do not know who the reader will be, *never* assume the person to be male or use 'Dear Sir' unless you know for sure. The mixed salute, 'Dear Sir/Madam', is out of date, impersonal, and does nothing for the reader–writer relationship. Use it only as a last resort.

The first paragraph

Begin with two or more 'subject lines' (see p. 166), followed by the first paragraph. To get your letter off to a good start the opening should

- show readers where they stand with you;
- refer to the main topic or purpose of the letter;
- switch the reader on — build interest;
- express appreciation and acknowledgment.

Show readers where they stand with you

Describe, define or develop the relationship. Use positive phrases and try to maintain a balanced mixture of both 'you' and 'us' words (see 'The you:us ratio', p. 156). Let people see clearly where they stand and their position in relation to you and the topic of your letter.

Describe an existing relationship

Do you already enjoy a good relationship with your reader? Show that you were thinking about this when you wrote the letter: 'I am contacting you, as one of our regular customers, to let you know that …'. Notice the balance — two 'you' words and two 'I' and 'our' words.

Define a new relationship

Are you are writing to someone who does not know you? Begin by defining the type of relationship you seek. Make it clear whether your approach is personal or official, formal or friendly, casual or urgent. For instance, 'We were very interested to learn through Dr Andrews of your support for our proposed national staff exchange scheme and wonder if you would consider joining our panel of speakers'.

Develop a recent relationship

Have you only recently started communicating, either personally or by letter? Use the opening to develop the relationship: 'We are always happy to welcome a new client, so your request for a credit account will be processed as quickly as possible'.

Refer to the main topic or purpose of the letter

Word this reference in such a way that it emphasises the reader's needs or wants rather than your own. Refer to a common goal. 'We need some more information to finalise the opening of your account . . .'.

Switch the reader on

There are many ways to increase reader interest.

Answer a question or support a request

Yes, we can supply the books you require, and because you are a student we can offer you a special discount on most titles . . .'.

Pay a sincere compliment

Agree with a proposal or a decision which the reader has already made: 'Your new training program on Client Service appears to be very close to what we are looking for. We agree with your suggestion that we should encourage staff to attend voluntarily rather than having management select trainees'.

Share useful information

'I think you may be interested in the attached sales figures . . .'.

Make an original or unusual statement

Ask a question; create curiosity, so that the reader will want to see what follows.

Refer to a common interest

Mention a mutual friend or an activity in which both you and the reader have an interest.

Express appreciation and acknowledgment

Acknowledge a previous message

Rather than 'thank you', make an acknowledgment specific to the content of the message. When a friend brings you a cup of coffee you say 'Thanks for the coffee', not 'Thanks for the cup and saucer'. Instead of 'Thank you for your *letter*', say for instance, 'Thank you for the *advice*' or 'Thank you for *confirming the order*'. This acknowledgment should, however, be at the end of the opening paragraph (see page 166).

Acknowledge your contact

When no previous contact has existed, explain how you obtained the reader's name and address (from an advertisement, a friend, a satisfied customer or a professional adviser). This technique is called 'bridge-building'.

Use an appreciative tone

Bridge-building works best if you pay a compliment. Combine this idea with others in the opening: 'Your firm has been recommended to me by Peter Green of Brighton. He says the brochures you designed for him have given better results than any previous form of advertising. I would be interested to know whether you could produce something similar to meet our needs, and if so, what the cost would be'.

Be specific in describing your source

Name the paper in which you saw an advertisement and the date it appeared, the person or firm that gave you the recommendation. Vague wording such as 'I have been told . . .' or 'In your recent advertisement . . .' is not enough.

Although you have these four points to cover in the opening paragraph, a single sentence can deal with one, two or all of them together. This is where subject lines help. If you identify the topic and acknowledge previous communication in the preceding subject lines, there is no need to repeat any of this in the first paragraph. This leaves the opening free for you to concentrate on building the relationship and developing reader interest.

Subject lines

Most readers prefer subject lines. Like newspaper headlines, they act as an eye-catching leader for the first paragraph. They should also

- identify the *topic* and the *type* of letter;
- identify the message to which you are replying;
- list reference codes from the previous message.

Writing subject lines – guidelines

Depending on your preference, subject lines can be 'you'-oriented or 'action'-oriented. 'Action'-oriented lines start by referring directly to action that has been taken or will be taken as a result of this correspondence. The first words might be

'Approval of', 'Information on', 'Second request', 'Final notice' and so on, as in the example at the base of the page.

'You'-oriented lines begin by referring to the reader's communication: 'Your request for', 'Your enquiry on', 'Your advertisement for' and so on. (There is no need for 'Re:' or 'Ref:' at the start.)

It's a matter of choice whether subject lines are written in capitals or upper and lower case, underlined or plain, double- or single-spaced. What matters is that you present important but routine data about the letter in as few words as possible, leaving the opening paragraph free for more appealing thoughts.

- Use positive terms: 'Your request for action' instead of 'Your complaint about delay', or 'Final request for payment' instead of 'Delinquent account (legal action pending)'.
- Outline the topic or topics in as few words as possible.
- End with relevant file codes or numbers and the date of the original message. If acknowledging a phone call or a fax or computer message, include both the identification number and the time received (see the example below).

Remember that your letter may be handled by many different people. Write subject lines that will identify the letter either for action or for filing in both the reader's organisation and your own.

Openings to avoid

Letters have been a form of communication for thousands of years and some of the conventions developed over the centuries are hard to shake off. For example, as explained previously, the traditional 'Thank you for your letter' is of little value. As an opening, it's so routine that the value of the acknowledgment is lost. If you want to include a sincere thank you, there are two possible locations:

- At the end of the opening paragraph — that is, *after* you have the reader's attention: 'We are always happy to welcome new clients. *Thank you for your enquiry*'.

- In the middle or towards the end of the letter. If the main reason for writing a letter is to express appreciation, a 'thank you' in the middle helps to distinguish it from an ordinary acknowledgment.

Here are some other traditional openings that turn readers off.

'We are sorry' or 'We regret'
Apologies signal bad news to follow. Don't indicate that the letter contains a refusal. The body of the letter is the only place for bad news (see p. 164).

'We need a firm to help with our delivery problems'
Don't open with a discussion of *your* problems; talk about solutions that will meet the needs of both you and your reader. Say 'Would your firm be interested in handling our deliveries on a regular basis?'.

'With reference to' or 'Your letter has come to my attention'
Any kind of impersonal, bureaucratic opening gets a letter off to a bad start.

'We are pleased'
The only time you should begin with 'pleased' or 'happy' is in giving information that involves equal pleasure for the reader, as in 'We are happy to welcome you'.

'You *will be* pleased'
Leave it to readers to decide how they will feel about your letter.

'I am interested in . . .'
This is not as effective as 'I was interested to learn that *you* have . . .'. Talk about yourself *only* if you mention the reader in the same sentence.

'My name is Justen Franz. I am writing this letter to advise that . . .'
Tell readers what they need to know, not what they can see for themselves. Your name at the end of the letter is sufficient identification.

REQUEST FOR INFORMATION — NATIONAL SALES REPORT
Your Fax — 11.00 am, Friday 15 May — Ref: BV65−88-NSR

Your Advertisement — Computer Programmer — Grade 3
The Australian — Sat 22 July — Page 34 — Ref: 34M/87

Confirmation of Fax — Approval for Contract
21 Pan Rd Norgate TxCode 4021/K Recd: 12 May 4:26 pm

The body of the letter

Thanks to your opening paragraph and subject lines, readers now know what your letter is about and where they stand in terms of the relationship. This makes it easier to concentrate on exchanging information and developing agreement. Depending on which persuasive appeal is most appropriate for the topic (see Chapter 13), you will need sound facts and logical reasoning (based on those facts), plus other supporting material.

Don't 'beat about the bush'

The body of a letter can be very brief. Today's readers prefer short letters that keep to the point. If this style seems a little too direct when you first try it, persevere. How would you react to a letter that said 'We wonder if you might assist us in regard to certain problems'? A hundred years ago that kind of wording was supposed to present the writer as well-educated and genteel. Today, it's neither polite nor helpful. As readers compliment you on your letters, you will soon get used to the advantages of direct style.

Creating agreement — guidelines

1. Keep different ideas apart, but group similar ones together.
If you are discussing more than one topic, use separate paragraphs; if you need to list specific points, number each one. If it helps to clarify your reasoning, use short subheadings.

2. Build on facts already presented to proceed to a logical conclusion.
Give examples to help readers visualise the advantages of co-operating.

3. If you are making an offer, describe the benefits point by point.
Paint a picture of just what readers can expect if they say 'yes'. For example: 'As soon as the contract is lodged with the Registrar of Titles, the house is yours. If you sign and return the papers before 9 December, you can move in before Christmas'.

4. Add a personal touch.
Readers will be more inclined to agree with you if your letter sounds as though you were talking face to face. Be friendly rather than formal.

5. Give accurate information.
Quote the source of your data and say how it can be checked. The more precise the information, the better. Use the seven C's to add clarity, and credibility, while maintaining a concise writing style.

The seven C's

1. Count and measure — when giving information state facts in precise (countable) units: dollars, metres, grams or other standard measures. Non-measurable words such as 'cheap', 'expensive', 'heavy', 'light', 'far' or 'close' are unclear and less persuasive.

2. Calendar — state the precise dates. Do not say 'rather lengthy delays' — be specific. Instead of 'as soon as possible', say 'by 30 March'. Avoid 'next week', 'recently', or jargon such as 'inst' or 'ult'.

3. Clock — state exact times rather than 'after lunch' or 'later on'.

4. Country — when describing locations, give the exact position or address; don't rely on terms like 'nearby' or 'centrally located'.

5. Character — name the people who produced the facts. Include the names of experts or authorities, and if necessary list their professional qualifications.

6. Copies — instead of describing a problem document, enclose a photocopy so that the reader can see exactly what is causing the trouble.

7. Camera — there is no reason you should not enclose a photograph with a letter if it helps to increase clarity or reinforce the truth.

Say 'No' as softly as possible

The body of a letter is the only place in which to include negative messages, bad news, or other unpleasant information. The effect on the reader will be less disturbing there than in the opening or closing stages.

Dealing with negative messages requires care and thought, but this is part of the reality of business. There are times when you have to mention price increases and delivery hold-ups. You may have to advise a manager that staff are to be transferred. There are times when you have to give a direct 'no', and others when you must make it clear that you are tired of asking politely about overdue accounts, and intend to take stronger action.

Handling this kind of letter is one of the real tests of your ability, and how well you deal with the task can directly influence your reputation as a business writer. Take care; you place your communication and your business at risk each time you express

- negative thoughts, criticisms, doubts, suggestions that would disturb your reader;
- negative feelings, anger, sorrow, regret;
- threats that will cause readers to lose dignity if they succumb to your show of force;
- overuse of negative words such as 'unfortunately', 'regret', 'refuse', 'disappointed', 'sorry', 'cannot'.

The more you have to say about bad news, and the more you express doubt, criticism or anger, the greater will be the chance of a negative reply.

Look to the positive side

Many of the more common negative statements used in business letters are not even necessary! Look at this example. Is it really about bad news, or good news?

We cannot open a credit account for you at this point of time. Although your firm is well-known and reputable, it is the policy of our Accounts department that applicants for credit shall advise the name of their bank and list at least three firms with whom the applicant has similar accounts. Unfortunately you have neglected to do this, so I regret that I have no alternative but to reject your application until same are supplied on the attached form.

Avoid 'pressure' tactics

This example illustrates the common but risky strategy described as 'pressure persuasion', in which the writer loads letters with extra negative words ('cannot', 'unfortunately', 'neglected', 'refuse') in an attempt to speed up agreement.

In so many cases, as in the example above, the real message is positive. The account will almost certainly be approved, with only a short delay. Compare the above example with Figure 15.1,

p. 166. Notice the latter's positive tone. It would have been easy to make a negative comment about the reader's initial failure to provide the references, but this writer concentrates on getting the account opened rather than worrying about what is past.

Borrowed words are sad words

Why didn't the first writer take this kind of positive approach? People who are not sure how to express bad news tend to borrow phrases from other letters. What is worse, they often turn to the acknowledged experts in conveying bad news and using pressure persuasion — solicitors and debt collectors — and borrow *their* words. Unless a letter refers to debts or legal issues, do not write as if it does.

If you want to encourage a new customer and convey the idea of a positive relationship based on agreement and goodwill (as illustrated in Fig. 15.1), legal language and negative style are totally out of place.

Presenting bad-news messages — guidelines *clearly*

There are occasions when it is necessary to state bad news explicitly — situations in which readers might otherwise deny they were given specific information; for instance, giving an eviction notice, or having to say 'no' forcefully, to show that you are not avoiding an issue.

1. First state the facts clearly.
Precise, relevant information and logical arguments, presented first, help the reader to accept the bad news which follows.

2. Concentrate on being positive.
When giving an actual refusal, be as brief as you can. Let the main theme of your letter centre on other issues, perhaps on maintaining a good working relationship despite the present trouble. Make this appear to be your main reason for writing, and be sure that the closing paragraph stresses this positively, as part of the action ending.

3. Use the KKK formula.
This old formula is still one of the best: Kiss first (positive opening), then Kick (the bad news in the body) and finally Kiss again (positive action ending). If you feel that a negative message is the best way to

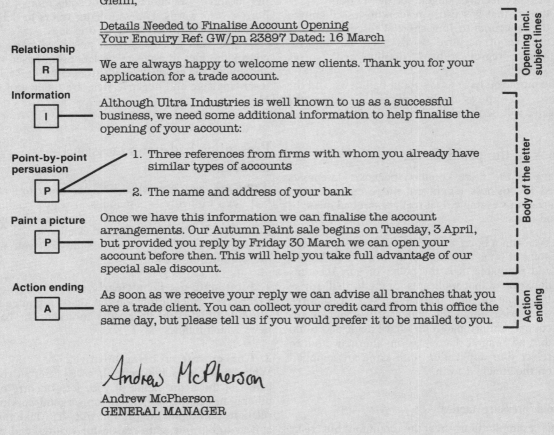

Mc Pherson's Paints Pty Ltd
CREDIT DEPARTMENT

21 March 1990

Glenn Wilde
Manager
Ultra Industries
PO Box 8576
Sydney NSW 2001

Glenn,

Details Needed to Finalise Account Opening
Your Enquiry Ref: GW/pn 23897 Dated: 16 March

Relationship

R — We are always happy to welcome new clients. Thank you for your application for a trade account.

Information

I — Although Ultra Industries is well known to us as a successful business, we need some additional information to help finalise the opening of your account:

Point-by-point persuasion

P —
1. Three references from firms with whom you already have similar types of accounts

2. The name and address of your bank

Paint a picture

P — Once we have this information we can finalise the account arrangements. Our Autumn Paint sale begins on Tuesday, 3 April, but provided you reply by Friday 30 March we can open your account before then. This will help you take full advantage of our special sale discount.

Body of the letter

Action ending

A — As soon as we receive your reply we can advise all branches that you are a trade client. You can collect your credit card from this office the same day, but please tell us if you would prefer it to be mailed to you.

Action ending

Andrew McPherson

Andrew McPherson
GENERAL MANAGER

Fig. 15.1 *Format of a well-written letter. Notice the positive tone used throughout the letter. It would have been easy to make a negative comment about Glenn Wilde's initial failure to provide the information, but the writer's idea is to get the account opened rather than worry about what is past*

gain agreement, or if you have genuinely bad news to convey, the only place to present it is in the letter body. Keep the first and last paragraphs of the letter free of any reference to the bad news.

There are occasions (for instance, payment-overdue letters) when the action ending cannot be entirely positive. The solution then is to use a conditional ending (see p. 168).

Avoid direct negatives

Where possible, make a negative statement indirectly or implicitly instead of spelling it out. Talk about alternatives; describe the solution rather than the problem. Explain the situation more clearly. There may then be no need to state the bad news in detail. In the letter below, the writer explains clearly why a request was not granted and suggests a positive alternative.

'Our firm recognises the excellent work that you are doing in helping unemployed youth, and I have been asked by the Board to convey their congratulations to you. We make annual donations to community groups in May each year and we would be very happy to receive an application from you next year when we are making this distribution. As long as your submission reaches us before 1 May, you can be confident that it will receive full consideration.'

It was not necessary to give an actual refusal anywhere in the letter; the absence of a cheque in the envelope made it clear enough. Also, the reader can see that part of the problem was the lateness of the application, but nowhere in the message does the writer mention the word 'late'.

Don't labour the apologies

An apology in a business letter will seldom sound really sincere. Using the words 'sorry' or 'regret' only serves to emphasise bad news and add to the reader's sense of loss. Compare the letter above with the following one, which puts so much emphasis on the negative aspects that the apology is wasted. The writer gives a direct refusal, stresses the problem instead of the reason, and dwells on the 'unfortunate' results for the reader.

'We are sorry to advise you that we cannot make a donation to your group as you failed to apply for same before the closing date, namely 1 May.

Unfortunately, we do not consider late applications. Please ensure that any future applications are not submitted after 30 April each year.'

Express empathy

Saying 'sorry' on behalf of a firm is rather pointless, anyway. Businesses do not have feelings of this kind; the people in the firm do. Instead of wasting words on a business apology, say something more personal. Letters carrying bad news are more acceptable if you talk *with* the readers, and express empathy: 'I can appreciate your feelings about the delay', 'We recognise your position and the effect this change will have on your plans', or 'I can understand your concern about the present arrangement'.

When legal action is next

If legal action is likely, do not say so in *your* letters. Once matters reach that point, hand them over to legal or debt-collection experts because it is they, not you, who will be responsible for carrying the action through.

The action ending

Use the last two or three sentences in the letter to help readers see exactly what you are asking of them. The best endings use direct, active language, and the theme should be one of action or activity. Styles will vary according to how strongly you wish to stress the desired outcome. You may
- make a direct request for reader action;
- list a series of actions needed;
- suggest special advantages for the reader if or when the action takes place;
- state a condition, related to the action;
- describe action you will take if reader agrees;
- summarise action already detailed;
- propose action sometime in the future.

1. Make a direct request.
If the letter is about a straightforward business matter, such as an order or an unpaid bill, first explain what you want and why, then ask for action: 'I need the disk before Monday 2 May. Please send it by express mail'.

If you know the reader well you can be more personal, yet still direct: 'It's a good idea, Gil. Send me full details'.

If you do not want to sound too demanding (when asking a favour), add 'can', 'could' or 'would' at the start: 'Could you phone and advise what date would suit you for next month's meeting?' or 'Can you please book two seats for Friday 2 May?'.

2. List a series of actions.

List all steps, explaining how they are to be carried out and in what order: 'Please send the package Air Express. Charge the cost to our account, No. QV32618. Please phone Adelaide 08 543 6021 advising the flight number and departure time so we can meet the plane'.

3. Describe benefits 'if and when . . .'.

Remind readers of additional benefits they will share *when* they act: 'We will phone you as soon as we receive the documents and your name has been registered'. Tell them *why* they will benefit by acting quickly: 'As soon as you submit your report, I will make an appointment for you to see the manager'.

4. Use a conditional ending.

Propose a bargain, using the 'If you do X, we will do Y' form of persuasion (see Chapter 13). This ending retains a positive tone while reminding the reader firmly but tactfully of the risk in failing to act: 'Your meter is due to be disconnected next Monday, but if you finalise your account by 4.00 pm this Friday, 25 May, we will guarantee continuity of your supply'. Threats like 'Unless you pay by Friday . . .' create resentment and ill feeling. People pay, but they appear to 'lose face' acting under duress.

5. State the action you are ready to take.

If you are fairly confident of acceptance, you can show this by ending with a description of what you will do (unless the reader disagrees): 'Would you please phone and confirm the plan? I will then book a seat on Flight 884 leaving at 5.00 pm on Monday 20 May'.

6. Summarise action already detailed.

Even if you covered all the important points in the body of the letter, you can close with a quick recap: 'It would help if you could arrange a meeting with the buyer to discuss the changes, as outlined above'.

7. Describe future action.

If your letter is about action in the future, acknowledge your agreement: 'I was very interested in your application. Please contact me personally in June, when I hope to have a position available that will suit your abilities'. A question about the future also makes a good ending: 'Would it help if we extended the lease until 1996?'.

The 'complimentary closing line'

Decide whether you want to end with a personal or a formal closing line.

Formal

'Yours sincerely' is now the most used formal ending in Australian business correspondence. Once-strict rules linking the close with the opening, such as 'Yours faithfully' with 'Dear Sir' and 'Yours sincerely' with 'Dear —— (reader's name)' are now largely ignored. Prime ministers and other national leaders close most letters to individuals with 'sincerely', whether or not the recipient's name appears at the top. 'Yours faithfully' is still preferred for legal and corporate letters.

Personal

The best personal ending is one that refers to a specific item or event and so could apply only to the one reader: 'Good luck for the opening on the 21st' or 'Meet you at the airport 8.00 am Monday'. More general ending lines such as 'regards' or 'best wishes' are useful only if they sound sincere. Slogan-lines like 'Yours in conservation' or 'Keep on making those sales' reduce the personal tone; they sound more like a recorded message than a letter ending.

No complimentary closing line

Writers who end letters without any closing line say that the omission is seldom noticed. Their letters are usually concise, very direct and often also omit the 'dear' line at the start, so that leaving the 'yours' line out maintains the tone.

Your signature

Sign your letters personally. A rubber stamp or facsimile signature suggests a 'don't care' attitude.

- Show your full first name (not just your initials) and your surname underneath the signature. If your first name could belong to either sex (as with Terry, Andre or Phil), and if it matters to you, add Mrs, Miss, Ms or Mr in brackets.
- On the line below, give brief details of your position — Sales Manager or Accounts Officer, for example.

Many writers add the date of signing below the name and position.

How *not* to end a letter

Introducing new ideas

New ideas in the last paragraph get in the way of the real purpose of the letter.

With uncertainty

Expressing your doubts at the end of a letter reduces reader confidence. Don't end with 'If you require further explanation, please contact . . .'. If you want to make this offer, put it in the letter body.

Hoping and trusting

Many writers feel a need to add a softer concluding sentence after a strong action ending. However, the examples previously given of action endings are meant to be final — *not* second last — sentences. To add 'Hoping you will be able to . . .' or 'Looking forward to . . .' takes the emphasis away from the main action and hints at a lack of confidence.

By all means tell readers in the *body* of the letter that you trust them to attend to your request or that you are hoping for an early reply, but 'hoping', 'trusting', 'awaiting' and similar '—ing' words are not used in speech as writers use them to end letters. Unless you write 'I remain, hoping to hear from you . . .', the sentence is incomplete and the action disconnected.

Assuming reader goodwill

'Thanking you in advance for your co-operation' sounds overconfident. You can't really be *that* certain, and if the reader does co-operate you will owe them a separate thank-you letter anyway.

Gloomy, pessimistic endings

It only annoys the reader to be told that 'Unfortunately we must again emphasise that without the proper qualifications there is little chance of your gaining promotion in this department . . .'.

Editing and revising

Reread your letter several times. Work out the you:us ratio (see p. 156). Check grammar, spelling and punctuation (see 'Proofreading', p. 153).

Chapter 14 included an example of how rewriting can improve a letter (p. 152) and listed the main steps in the editing and proofreading process. As well as a general edit, check your letter at this point for specific letter faults.

Common letter faults

Scaffolding words

Although some phrases help to build the letter at the draft stage, like any other kind of scaffolding they need to be taken away once the job is finished. In the following sentence, the words in italics are of no further use and should be deleted: '*We are writing to you to advise that* as soon as you send *the missing* Form B *to this office* we can process your claim'. Just say: 'As soon as you send Form B we can process your claim'.

Unfamiliar words

Unless you use a word regularly, there is a strong chance you will use it incorrectly. If you are doubtful about the spelling, this also suggests the word is unfamiliar.

Saying you are sure

If you feel uncomfortable about something in your letter, don't make it obvious. Saying 'I am sure that . . .' sounds as though you are not quite sure.

Using 'kindly' instead of 'please'

'Kindly', as in 'Kindly advise any change of address', was originally used by legal writers as a dominating word implying 'Don't make trouble, just do it'. It is not a suitable substitute for 'please'.

Using double negatives

The phrase 'in the *not un*-foreseeable future' means 'soon'. 'I am *not un*-happy with the decision' may be a roundabout, bureaucratic way of saying 'I am happy'. This vague and impersonal style leaves readers wondering if you *are* unhappy but don't want to admit it.

Unoriginal phrases

Many writers believe there are standard phrases that must be used in business letters. One example is 'Please do not hesitate to contact the writer', but words or phrases that you don't use when you speak are out of place in a business letter. Replace it with, 'If you need further advice, please phone me on 382 8952.'

Using old, worn-out letter language suggests that you are either unable or unwilling to think of new words. 'At your convenience' may once have meant 'as soon as possible'; today it sounds more as though you don't care when. The longer these old phrases have been in use, the less sincere they sound.

Telling readers what they already know

'Your business is at risk if you don't insure', 'A new firm needs to advertise' — is the reader so far out of touch that you have to explain such obvious facts? If it is important to mention something the reader might already know, make it sound like a reminder.

Talking down

Let readers make up their own minds about how they feel. Do not say 'After reading my application you must agree ...'. Even if you hold a superior position, take care if sending signals to this effect either through words used or the non-verbal tone.

Jargon

There are a number of kinds of jargon. Some have their place, but do any of them add quality to a letter?

Technical jargon

Use technical terms, but only when they add clarity or express meaning more accurately *and* you are sure the reader is familiar with them.

Intellectual (fog-word) jargon

Writing 'negative monetary expansion' instead of 'loss' *might* make people think you have a deep understanding of finance. But apart from the fact that it sounds terrible, it also causes fogging (see 'Reducing the fog level' in Chapter 18). Intellectual language makes you sound 'educated' but will only impress other intellectuals. Keep it out of business letters.

Bureaucratic jargon

In conversation, do you say 'My family consists of five persons, currently domiciled in a brick residence' or 'There are five people in my family, and we live in a brick house'? The former style has lost its power to impress people. It is cold and unfriendly, so it won't help create agreement. It is, however, the language comedians use in doing impressions of people they want to 'send up' as out of touch, stuffy, or old-fashioned. Use it in your letter and it could end up as the butt of a joke.

Bureaucratic jargon	Replace with ...
at your disposal	for your use
upon receipt of	when we receive
in reference to	about
expedite	hurry, speed up
conducive (to)	helpful
facilitate	help, assist
obviate	reduce, lessen
at this point in time	now, at present
your favour	your letter
consequently we have	so we have
please find enclosed for your information	enclosed
assuring you of our best attention at all times	we hope we can help you again in the future

Legal jargon

Even if you are writing about legal matters, do phrases like those in the chart below have any value in business letters? If the topic has nothing to do with the law they are even less appropriate, since they send the wrong kind of background signals.

Legal jargon	Clear and straightforward
persons	people, staff, clients
authorised persons	authorised staff/officers
parties	people involved
monies	money, funds
pertaining to	related to, associated with
nevertheless	however
peruse	read, examine
ultimo	last month
hereafter	from now on
enclosed herewith	included, attached
documentation	forms, contracts, files
above-mentioned items	items listed above
speed is of the essence	this is urgent

Rewriting

If you are not happy with the way a letter sounds, and there is enough time, set it aside for a day. Then go over it and rewrite any parts that are not fitting in comfortably or are too long (see the section 'Rewriting letters', in Chapter 14). Keep asking yourself if you would be happy to receive a letter like the one you have in front of you.

Word processors and business letters

There are many advantages in using a word processor to draft business letters. The freedom of being able to view different wording and try different combinations of ideas encourages rewriting, which in turn adds more polish to your final version.

Reusing your best phrases and paragraphs

You can copy a single paragraph from one letter and adapt it to fit another one. A really good paragraph can be reused with variations over and over again. This works well as long as you

- use only your own words, which means that even if you recycle the same words and phrases regularly, they must still sound as though you are talking personally to each reader;
- never recycle paragraphs you did not write yourself;
- check the finished letter before you sign it — recycling paragraphs has a built-in risk in that while the main wording fits the new situation, one or two words may not.

Never allow your name to appear at the end of a letter produced by combining extracts from other letters unless you have double-checked every word and are convinced that the end result sounds natural rather than machine-made.

Tailoring 'master' letters

Of course, entire letters can be stored on disk and reused with only minor changes to fit new situations. Whenever you find yourself writing the same kind of letter once or twice a month, you have a strong case for adding it to your bank of master letters so that you can adapt all (or part) of it each time the topic comes up in your correspondence.

A typical example is a letter of reference. Some paragraphs will need tailoring to make particular reference to an individual's skills and abilities; the rest can remain much the same.

Recycling or tailoring with a word processor is *not* the same as using a standard form-letter (see 'Standard format and multicopy letters', in Chapter 17), where only the name, address and minor details are inserted. Recycling takes a standard framework of ideas, and some common phrases, and develops them into a personalised letter that fits the individual reader. Recycling letters can be a real time-saver, provided you take a few precautions.

- Take the time to rewrite at least some parts of each letter to give an individual touch, even if most of the wording remains unaltered.
- Use different masters for different types of client. The opening paragraph of letters to long-term

customers might recognise their standing and mention the number of years they have been trading with you. Letters to short-term customers should *not* use the same opening, even if the remainder of both masters is quite similar.

- Make sure that no-one receives two similar letters within a short space of time.
- Be sure that the master does not convey a non-verbal message that could be out of context in some cases. For example, the master for accounts overdue may express, non-verbally, a sense of disappointment. Is this appropriate for the current letter?
- Take care that you (and not the computer) are in charge of the tailoring process. Always check the final wording to make sure the personal touch has been maintained.
- Avoid 'model letters' presented as ready-to-use text, whether in books or on computer diskettes, particularly those supplied free with commercial word-processor packages.

Letter layout

The way a letter is set out is determined by the person who types it. Some word-processor operators become comfortable with a particular layout, and may claim that what is familiar to them is in fact 'standard'. If you are not happy with the appearance of a finished letter, find out whom you need to see to have the 'standard' layout changed. Figure 15.2 illustrates some common layout styles.

Justification of text

Word processors and printers have the capacity to print letters in a number of different typefaces, and with lines which on the right are either uneven (unjustified) or even (justified). Be careful how you use these features. Job-application letters, for instance, should be unjustified, so that they avoid the appearance of being mass-produced. Many readers regard any letter with justified text as impersonal.

Draft-mode dot matrix typefaces should not be used for any letters; neither should fancy or off-standard typefaces. High quality, bold or near-letter quality (NLQ) faces are more acceptable.

Standard business letters

Many letters require a number of standard points to be covered, regardless of who the reader may be. Keep a list of these as a standard format, so that you remember to mention each point.

Order letters

1. Give complete details about the goods wanted (style, brand, size, price, colour, quality, etc.).
2. Quote catalogue numbers and date of advertisement as a double check.
3. State quantity required (and quality, if applicable).
4. Advise method of payment.
5. State alternative action if goods are not available or if delay is expected: for example, substitute order, cancel order or put on back-order.
6. Give full instructions for delivery, including delivery address and date required.

Enquiry letters

If writing to a stranger, build a bridge at the start by describing a common goal or interest or mentioning a mutual contact.

1. Describe the information or assistance you need in exact terms. Be specific.
2. Say why you need the information.
3. Say when you need it.
4. Offer to meet any costs involved.
5. If you wish to make the requested information public, ask for permission and advice on how it should be acknowledged.

Please-pay letters

1. Focus on the positive aspects of payment, such as maintaining a sound credit rating and the value of uninterrupted service. Avoid threats.
2. Remember that the more valuable the customer, the more important it is to write a special letter.
3. If the matter has reached the stage where legal action is likely, take legal advice on the correct wording.

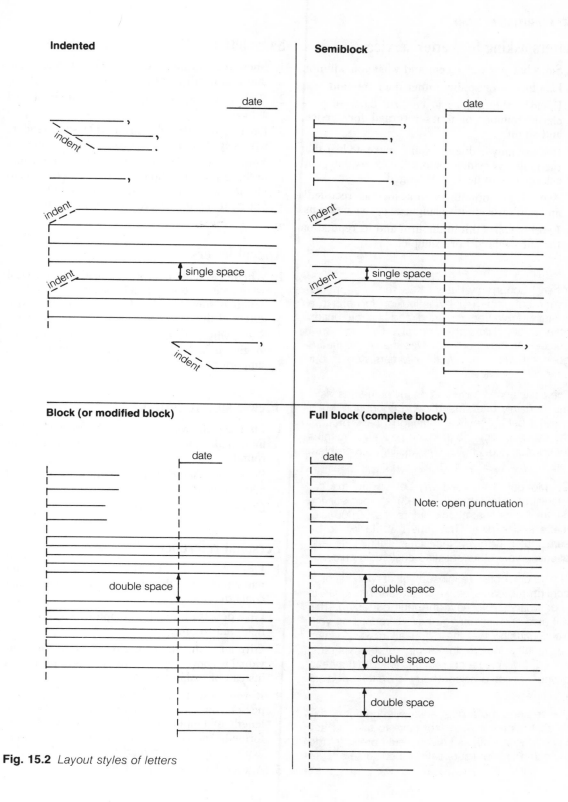

Fig. 15.2 *Layout styles of letters*

Letters asking for better service

1. Say what you will accept and what you will not.
2. Use logical reasoning rather than emotion.
3. Enclose photocopies to confirm dates of purchase, number of times returned for service, and so on.
4. If a warranty is due to expire, make it clear that the fault was evident before the expiry date, and ask for this to be acknowledged.
5. Avoid legal-sounding words, such as 'rectified', and don't use emotive language or make threats.
6. Express your faith in the firm and its reputation for fair dealing. For example:

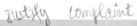

When I bought my Falstar K33 sedan from your firm in July last year I was looking forward to a year's trouble-free motoring and the protection of a 30 000 kilometre warranty. One reason I decided to buy from you was that I had heard good reports from other customers about your after-sales service.

The assistance I have had on my numerous visits has certainly been friendly and courteous, but it has not been effective. Although I have brought the car in six times during the past eight months for correction of engine overheating, the problem has still not been solved.

On Monday 19 June I will be leaving the car (Registration number JBN 793) at your service centre for its final check before the 30 000 kilometre limit expires. This time I would like to be sure that it is given the same skilful care and attention your other satisfied customers enjoy.

The photocopies (enclosed) of service records confirm the dates on which the car has been in your workshop to have the fault corrected. This will also ensure that you have a record on your file confirming that the overheating was evident six months before the expiry of the warranty period. I will give a copy of this letter to the head of your service division when I leave the car there on Monday.

Please send me a brief acknowledgment of this letter. I hope that I will not have to take up any more of your time, as I much would prefer to add my name to your list of satisfied customers.

Sales letters

1. Show readers that they need your product and that it is worth its price.
2. Base your claims on fact, but add emotional appeal as well.
3. Do not ignore the relationship side; show readers why they should buy from you, and you alone.
4. Your action ending should not be about 'buying' or 'ordering', but about why the reader needs to phone you to arrange a demonstration or to find out more about the deal you are offering.

Appeal letters

1. Whether asking for a vote, a donation or physical assistance in doing a job, offer a reward or benefit of some kind (see Chapter 13). Otherwise letters of this kind are usually a waste of time.
2. Show why it is in readers' interests not only to give help but also to become identified as supporters.

'Please stop it' letters

1. First explain why you want the matter ended, then make the request — not the other way round.
2. Spell out exactly what steps are needed. Avoid negative words.
3. Close with a strong action ending.

Personal references

1. Use a subject line that includes the individual's name instead of the outdated 'To whom it may concern'.
2. Give details of length of employment, positions held and so on.
3. Give an evaluation of performance; if the individual is above average, add details to prove this instead of making a general statement.
4. If you cannot say anything special about the person concerned, just give the plain facts about length of employment and type of work performed, and leave it at that. Do not include negative or critical remarks.
5. Always date a reference letter.

Credit references

1. Limit the message to the facts.
2. Write objectively. If a person has a weak credit record, say so, and leave it at that.

Quotation letters

1. Base the wording on fact, not opinion.
2. If the details are complex, attach them separately; mention only the total cost in the letter.
3. Never combine a quotation with a sales pitch. There is, however, nothing wrong with including two letters in the one envelope: the quotation and a sales letter.

'Good news' letters

1. Take the opportunity to promote good client relations — to lay the foundation for future communication (and sales): 'Although your motor was outside the normal warranty cover, we have repaired it free of charge. Customer satisfaction is very important to us and we hope you will let us know if we can help in any other way'.
2. Emphasise the reader's needs, not your own.

Letters of thanks, congratulations and best wishes

Letters that express thanks or appreciation are still too infrequent in Australian business.

1. Your words must be warm, sincere and original. Formal wording is useless.
2. Write letters of welcome to new employees (and to their families) shortly before they start work.
3. Letters of congratulation from a manager to individual employees build morale and need not be restricted to work activities; any employee appreciates being recognised in this way for a special achievement in sport, study or community service.

Summary

1. When planning, begin with a clear aim. Know exactly what it is you want the reader to do.

2. Do not try to compose a letter in your head. Draft ideas as rough notes first.
3. Letters are made up of three parts: the opening, the body and the action ending.
4. A good opening tells readers where they stand, refers to the main topic or aim of the letter and switches the reader on. It then either acknowledges the source of contact (how you heard about the reader), or acknowledges and appreciates previous messages.
5. Use subject lines to list acknowledgments, reference codes and any other routine information that would clog up the opening paragraph.
6. Today the central part of a letter is shorter than it was in the past. It should include facts, logical reasoning and whatever persuasive appeal is appropriate to the topic.
7. Use the seven C's to add clarity and credibility while maintaining a concise writing style.
8. The KKK formula is a reminder to Kiss first, (positive opening), Kick (the bad news in the body), then Kiss again (positive action ending).
9. Negative ideas should not be included in opening or closing paragraphs. Use a negative ending only if you want to avoid further communication with the reader.
10. Try to convey negative ideas indirectly or implicitly instead of spelling them out.
11. If you feel doubt about a letter, let your instinct guide you. Usually this is a sign that it needs rewriting.
12. Using a word processor to draft business letters increases your writing power and develops your style as well as your editing skills.
13. Although wording may differ, many letters require the same points to be covered. Make a list of these for use as a standard reference.

Exercises

1. Using the writing plan on page 142, draft a complete letter to Calshop ordering a suitable calculator.
2. You are the person responsible for writing to customers whose accounts are more than three months overdue. A customer of some twelve years' standing is shown on your computer print-out as not having made any payments at all for four months. The overdue amount shown

on the print-out is $4699.87. You know that this customer has always paid regularly in the past, and that she spends over $20 000 a year with your firm.

Write a suitable letter requesting payment. Close with a conditional action ending.

Case study 1: Woodside Homes

Your name is Terry Paulson and you are the manager of Woodside Home Improvements. Recently you quoted a fixed price of $4200 to carry out a home-improvement job for B. and C. Fellini of 17 Love Street, Woodside. The work was scheduled to start next week and to be completed in three or four days. (You can decide for yourself the particular type of job — possibly repair, installation, extension or removal — but whatever it is, specify it when you reply to the Fellinis.)

Woodside is a small firm, but one of the reasons it can offer competitive prices without reducing quality is its cash-payment policy. This is explained fully in the written quotes given to every customer. Under the terms of the quote the Fellinis were to pay half the amount ($2100) one week before the job started, and the balance of $2100 on the day the job was completed.

Both the Fellinis signed your official order for the job. This confirmed their acceptance of the quoted price and terms of payment, which included a clear statement of your 'no credit' policy. The first payment has been made as scheduled, but you have now received a letter from the Fellinis in which they say that they cannot make the final payment until the end of next month. They ask if you can finish the job as planned, while allowing an extension of time for payment. In effect, they are asking for five weeks' credit.

Draft a letter to the Fellinis
- indicating that although you appreciate their position, you cannot change the terms of the agreement, nor can you grant their request for credit;
- explaining why your firm does not give credit;
- suggesting at least one alternative arrangement that might solve the problem;
- explaining that you do not want them to cancel their order;
- closing with an appropriate action ending.

Case study 2: Bayview Real Estate

You are the owner-manager of Bayview Real Estate. In today's mail is a priority-paid letter (dated yesterday) from Lesly Chang of Kunnanurra, WA. The letter asks you to arrange for the immediate purchase of a house at 55 Glen Street, Bayview, which your agency advertised for sale at $98 000 in last Saturday's *Australian* newspaper. However, because Lesly has not sent any money as deposit or signed any purchase contract, you cannot finalise the sale. Telecom advise you that Lesly is not on the phone.

Reply to Lesly in a business letter of approximately one page (or no more than 1¼ pages). Start with a subject line (or lines). Cover the following points in the opening, body or ending:
- Until you have $5000 deposit and a signed contract in your office there is no legal sale. This means that if another buyer for the same house appears, and if that buyer lodges a signed contract and a deposit first, then Lesly will lose the right to purchase the house. As the law stands, you cannot change this. (Lesly would not be happy to miss out on the house, so you need to mention this for your own protection.)
- Offer at least one helpful suggestion as to how Lesly might arrange quick payment of a $5000 deposit to confirm the purchase.
- Offer similar help to get the purchase contract signed and returned to you quickly.
- Explain that you are enclosing the sale documents for Lesly's signature.
- Try to persuade Lesly that the decision to buy this house is sound. Offer any incentives that you think will help gain agreement.

Case study 3: The Surfers unit

Peta Joyce, who lives in Melbourne, owns a luxury unit in Surfers Paradise. About five months ago she agreed to lease the unit for $1000 a week. Peta decided that instead of having an agent collect the rent, the tenant could pay it directly into a bank account opened for the purpose.

A month ago Peta was advised by the bank that a cheque she had written for $930 to pay council rates could not be honoured because the account was already overdrawn by $2000. The bank also advised that no deposits had been made to the account for the past four weeks.

Peta phoned a Gold Coast real estate agency and asked them to visit the unit on her behalf. The tenant, when reminded, promptly paid the outstanding $4000 and the money — less a $400 collection fee deducted by the real estate agent — was banked in Peta's account. To follow up, the agent decided to write Peta the following letter:

Dear Sir/Madam,

I have to acknowledge your phone call of recent date and I am pleased to advise that the matter that you referred to therein has already received attention.

I regret that it should have become necessary for you to seek our assistance in regard to the failure of the tenant to pay the rent directly to your account. However, as a result of a personal visit to the unit concerned, certain undertakings were given and outstanding rental monies were duly collected. These in turn were deposited in the account as requested, after deduction of the agency commission of $400.

We look forward to your continued custom and remain,

Yours faithfully,

Stradbroke Sun Real Estate Ltd
per E. Summers Manager

(a) Make a list of the ways in which the letter fails as a form of clear communication, and any other faults in it.
(b) As the manager of the agency, write a more appropriate letter that would build a business relationship with Peta Joyce.

Case study 4: The Dryfast warranty

You are the Manager of Rocklex Appliances. Today (8 June) you received a letter from Kerry and Pat Finch, who live in Dantree, a nearby suburb. They ask you to arrange a free service call on a new Dryfast Model K44 clothes dryer, which they bought from your store on 27 May this year. The dryer will not run when set on the fast-dry position. This model is normally covered by a full 60-day after-sales warranty, but — as explained clearly in the instruction book supplied with it — there is no warranty if a dryer is installed by anyone except an authorised Dryfast agent.

While checking the sales book to confirm the purchase, you notice that the Finches did not pay the usual $20 installation fee. This suggests that they may have installed the dryer themselves (in which case there is no warranty) or arranged for another Dryfast agent to install it, which is quite in order. If this is so, the Finches need to send you a copy of the installation certificate to let you know that the warranty is still valid.

Dryfast's head office in Sydney say they have had no reports of similar problems from customers who had dryers properly installed.

(a) List very briefly, in the form of an outline or plan, the main points you will mention in the letter.
(b) Write a letter to the Finches in which you
- use a separate subject line (or lines) at the start;
- ask for details of the installation;
- suggest one or more ways of getting the dryer repaired;
- close with a positive and assertive action ending.

Case study 5: A computer complaint

Read the following letter of complaint from a dissatisfied purchaser of a well-known brand of computer.

Dear Sirs,

I am writing to you to lodge the strongest possible complaint concerning your continued failure to provide a satisfactory after-sales service for my computer purchased from you 11½ months ago.

If you would kindly refer to your service files, you will observe that I have now been forced to return same to you on no less than four occasions, seeking rectification of certain faults. I find it most disappointing that a firm should treat a valued customer in such an inconsiderate manner.

I hereby advise that I shall deliver my computer to your establishment on the 17th, while it is still under warranty, and I trust that on this occasion your staff will be able to provide a more satisfactory service. If this is not done I shall immediately place the whole matter in the hands of my solicitor.

(a) Make a list of the ways in which the letter fails to meet the guidelines for an effective complaint letter.
(b) Write a more appropriate letter that will create the action you want.

CHAPTER 16

Business reports

Learning to write effective reports can pay enormous dividends because reports are used to share important ideas at the middle and higher levels of management. As well as explaining how to *write* a business report, this chapter presents formats you can use to *set out* the document so that it will attract positive attention and hold the reader's interest. This include the use of an open layout, numbered headings and illustrations. Examples are given to show how an effective report should look and sound.

Topics

Making reports easy to read

Planning your strategy

Organising shape, structure and layout

Numbering headings

A model report

Writing parts of a report

The final edit

Presenting the report

Making reports easy to read

Easy-to-read reports are the ones most often read. The first barrier facing every report writer is reader resistance: reports are 'looked at', 'considered' and 'discussed', but not always read. Keep yours short, and make them attractive, and they will be read by the people you want to read them.

The world's best-selling reports are newspapers, and the techniques that make for successful business reports are very similar to those used in newspapers.

Reports should be easy to write

If you follow the advice given in this chapter and use the skills already developed from working through the previous chapters, you will find that writing reports is a straightforward procedure and surprisingly easy to master. While you may not be qualified to produce a technical report on, say, laser printers, you will be able to write a highly professional one about which brand of printer is best for your firm's needs.

Reports can be presented in writing or orally, or as a combination of the two, but they are made up of more than words. Today's reports usually include graphs, pictures and other non-verbal material. Video-tapes and on-screen computer graphics — in fact, anything that helps get meanings through — are often used as well, in the form of appendixes. Most report writing today involves the use of computers and word processors, which make the task easier now than it was in the past. Take every opportunity to use them.

The four stages

The four-stage approach to business writing (see Chapter 14) is ideal for reports:
- Thinking and planning
- Capturing ideas
- Organising the shape, structure and layout
- Editing, proofreading and rewriting

Writing should not be rushed. The more hurried it is, the less chance there is of success. There is no way you can write an effective report at a sitting.

Planning your strategy

Decide what you expect to be the outcome. Know why you are writing the report and what you want people to do after they read it. Develop a strategy, a 'plan of attack' on the best way of handling the topic. Once you have a definite goal, you're ready to begin.

Planning the investigation

Decide how far to go in your search for data. Business reports must be based on objective information; they usually include expert opinions, logical argument and informed predictions, but these too need to be drawn from objective sources. Collecting information can involve many different kinds of research and observation, so for a start, determine

- the scope of your investigation;
- what resources you have to carry out your research;
- what kind of research you are best at and what you should leave to others;
- what funds you have to carry out your study;
- whether you need to conduct interviews, run experimental trials or hand out questionnaires.

Plan a timetable

When should you stop collecting information and start analysing it? How much time can you then spend writing? Timing is a vital part of your plan. Table 16.1 gives a timetable that will allow you to produce a first-class report.

Choose strategies that build agreement

Plan a strategy to persuade your readers to agree with you. Ask yourself

- How much can I rely on straightforward logic and the weight of evidence to influence readers?
- Will I have to make use of more complex methods of persuasion such as quoting statistics, computer-based analysis and expert opinions?
- Will I need to include a broader appeal, describing the benefits gained from agreement and listing reasons why no other course of action is available?

Consider how much of the material you are gathering is objective and how much will be subjective

Table 16.1 *A well-planned report timetable*

Stage	Activity	Expected completion date
Investigation and research	Study history of problem	10.03.92
	Begin interviews	17.03.92
	Draw up questionnaire	04.04.92
	Distribute questionnaire	14.04.92
Analysing results	Collect answers	26.04.92
	Run computer analysis	10.05.92
Thinking and planning	Write ideas down first	
	Write first draft	21.05.92
Writing	Write second draft	
Organising	Complete all sections	1.06.92
Improving	Rewrite (final draft)	19.06.92
	Type	23.06.92
Editing	Edit, proofread	29.06.92
	Prepare index, contents page, etc.	4.07.92
	Safety margin (two weeks to go to annual meeting)	
	Printing, binding, etc.	11.07.92
Presentation	Board's annual meeting	19.07.92

(see 'Fact or opinion?', in Chapter 11). The answer will determine how the report is put together, the type of recommendations you make and, of course, its length.

Highly objective information

If you have access to facts, figures and photographs, the report should be easier to write and have a better chance of gaining agreement. Data based on actual tests or measurements — or on personal observations that you know are reliable — will enable you to write more directly and concisely.

Other objective information

Information not directly observed also has an important place in a report. This kind of information is usually more easily obtained, but will sometimes raise doubts about how accurately it reflects the real situation. In that case you'll need to spend time asking questions, sifting the relevant from the irrelevant, applying the seven tests for objectivity (see Chapter 11) and collecting extra evidence, so researching and writing will take longer.

Opinions and predictions (subjective information)

While objective data can stand on its own, opinions and predictions have to be supported by logic, reasoning and analytical discussion. This too means a longer report.

Establish the scope of the report

Whatever you decide about timing, level of credibility, length, research strategies and so on becomes the scope of your report and the basis of your planning. A report on a proposed new shopping centre would have a very broad scope; one on a faulty computer would be much narrower.

Capture ideas

The writing techniques explained in Chapter 14 — random writing, for instance — are useful at this stage. If you have trouble getting started, concentrate on ideas rather than on words. Don't try to write the whole report at the one time. Write a rough draft, look over it, consider the main ideas, and *then* decide how they need to be organised.

Organising shape, structure and layout

You'll find yourself using different writing techniques and thinking in different ways as you deal with various kinds of material, so it makes sense to divide the material into sections that recognise these distinctions. There are four main divisions (often more), and the names for them vary. Those given below are among the most common and will be used as standard headings throughout this chapter.

1. INTRODUCTION
   This establishes a credible relationship between writer and reader; it explains the purpose and scope of the report.

2. FINDINGS OR RESULTS
   This is objective information; it gives the facts, as a basis for later discussion.

3. ANALYSIS OR DISCUSSION
   This section builds agreement through logical reasoning and rational argument. It points the reader towards the action that will be proposed at the end of the report, explains what recommendations will be made and why they are necessary, and 'paints a picture' of the expected outcome.

4. RECOMMENDATIONS — the action ending
   These set out exactly what has to be done, and the report ends with a request for approval or a *proposed* specific course of action.

There will of course be more sections than this in many reports. A twelve-page document might need eight or nine such divisions, each of which needs a heading; you will then have many different headings in addition to the original four, as shown in the contents tables for Reports A and B at the top of page 181. There may also be extra units, outside the main report, perhaps including a synopsis and a series of appendixes.

The longer your report, the more organisation and the more sections it needs. By the time all the divisions and subdivisions have been set up and numbered, your table of contents (list of headings) may need a full page (see 'A model report', p. 183).

Report A	Report B
1. INTRODUCTION	Title page
2. PRESENT SITUATION	Synopsis
3. DELAYS IN DELIVERY	Table of contents
4. REDUCTIONS IN STOCK LEVELS	1. INTRODUCTION
5. LOSS OF SALES	2. METHOD OF INVESTIGATION
6. CONSULTANT'S REVIEW	3. TECHNICAL SPECIFICATIONS FOR TESTS
7. DISADVANTAGES OF OLD SYSTEM	4. DATA OBTAINED FROM TESTS
8. PROPOSED CHANGE IN DELIVERY SCHEDULES	5. CAUSES OF BREAKDOWN IN SWITCH GEAR
9. COST-EFFECTIVENESS OF NEW SYSTEM	6. DISCUSSION AND ANALYSIS OF EXPERT OPINIONS
10. PROPOSED CHANGES	7. PROPOSED CHANGES IN SWITCH SYSTEM
11. RECOMMENDATIONS	8. ADVANTAGES OF NEW SYSTEM
Appendix A	9. PROPOSALS FOR CHANGEOVER
Appendix B	10. RECOMMENDATIONS
	Appendix A
	Alphabetical index

Subsections

The major sections are further divided as writing progresses. Each subsection should be identified with its own numbered subheading.

Introduction divided into four subsections
1. INTRODUCTION
    1.1 Aim
    1.2 Authorisation
    1.3 Sources of information
    1.4 Overview and historical background

Findings divided into three subsections
2. FINDINGS
    2.1 Initial investigation
    2.2 Major findings
    2.3 Other findings

Advantages of subdividing

Dividing a report into smaller units breaks the content into more easily understood packages. As long as they flow smoothly from one to the next, the overall effect is to create a sense of logic and clear thinking which encourages agreement.

Some subsections may need to be split even further. This is no problem as long as you arrange them so that one part complements the next and together they give a balanced picture of the topic.

Create a logical sequence

Aim for a step-by-step sequence of ideas that will have meaning for the reader as well as for yourself.

Follow the rules for establishing this flow of ideas described in Chapter 14 — grouping similar topics together. In reports it is also essential to separate material with differing levels of objectivity.

Keep facts and opinions apart

It makes sense to use the findings section for facts and the analysis section for opinions and proposals. Readers need to know which are which — to distinguish proposed future action from description of past events. Use plenty of headings and sub-headings to indicate each change of direction.

Organising report topics

Table 16.2 will help you to organise topics into appropriate sections, according to their type (objective or subjective) and content.
■ Column 1 lists the different aims for each set of headings, using the RIPPA formula as a key.
■ Column 2 lists 'sample' (not standard) headings suggested for a typical business report on a problem situation.
■ The questions in column 3 help you to decide where each topic or type of information can best be used.
■ Column 4 presents an analogy; if you are still in doubt about where an item should go, compare it with the process involved when you visit a medical specialist.

Table 16.2 *Organising report topics*

Sequence	Report headings	Questions	Analogy
R Helps to establish a good business-like relationship	1. INTRODUCTION 1.1 Aim 1.2 Authorisation 1.3 Sources of information	What's this all about? What is the aim of the report? Who told you to write this? Where did you get these facts? How did you find this out?	 You explain why you want to see a specialist. You need a letter from your local doctor to introduce you to the specialist.
I Information, facts, data What did you 'find'?	2. FINDINGS 2.1 Problem 2.2 Causes 2.3 Effect	 Could anyone else 'find out' this information as you have done? If so, is this the kind of material that should go in the findings?	Results of the specialist's investigation. Actual facts as observed during the physical examination or results of latest tests.
P Opinions, explanation, logical reasoning Point-by-point persuasion P Paint picture of solution	3. ANALYSIS 3.1 Reasons a change is needed 3.2 Need to train all staff 3.3 Advantages of new system	Is this material part of a reasoned argument that is intended to persuade the reader or support the aim of the report? Is it a proposal for a specific course of action? Do sentences include words such as 'should' or 'if'?	Specialist analyses the findings: 'You appear to have a case of .... Some X tablets should soon fix you. Take two after each meal'. 'You should keep on taking them until you finish the pack. If you have no more symptoms you won't need to see me again.'
A A step-by-step set of proposals for action	4. RECOMMENDATIONS 4.1 That all new staff have ... 4.2 That the change-over date ...	Has each recommendation already been explained in the analysis? Is this a real 'action ending'? Does it say exactly what action needs to be taken and when? Do *not* include any reasons or explanations in this section.	The prescription lists a recommended action. It states conditions such as taking pills after meals, but does not say why. The doctor has already given you the reasons during your discussion.
	Writer's signature	The name and the signature of whoever makes the recommendations should appear at the end of the report.	The doctor's prescription will have no credibility unless it is signed.

Numbering the headings

The numbers to the left of the heading work in much the same way as the distance marks on a road map, telling readers where they are in the report or indicating the location of important items. Numbering needs to follow a clear, straightforward system.

Why decimal numbering?

The metric or decimal style uses numbers separated by decimal points. It is much clearer and easier to use than traditional letter-number systems, particularly if you want to renumber paragraphs. An example of decimal numbering in a report is given below.

---

1. DECIMAL NUMBERING

  1.1 *Advantages of the Decimal System*

     Decimal numbering follows a simple and very logical sequence, so paragraphs numbered this way are easy to locate. Alphabetical systems are more complicated.

  1.2 *Disadvantages of Other Systems*

     Avoid systems that use numbers and capital and lower-case letters mixed together. These create a number of difficulties, including

     1.2.1 Loss of continuity of ideas

     1.2.2 Difficulty in editing

     1.2.3 Reduction in clarity

Alphabetical and Roman numbers

Alphabetical 'numbering' (A-B-C-D) is useful for items outside the central numbering system, such as the cover pages, chapter divisions and appendixes, and for identifying figures or tables. Keep the lettering simple; use single letters and preferably only capitals. Unless you are sure that Roman numerals (I, II, XXI) will make the sequence of ideas clearer, why use them? Often items identified with lower-case Roman numbers (iii, iv) really don't need numbering at all. A series of asterisks (*) or dashes (−) work just as effectively.

Mixed numbering such as 1−(A)−b, (A) II.2, B.(c).3 or III−(i)−(f) is the most confusing of all. Regardless of the system you choose, don't place brackets around numbers or letters unless they are essential for clarity.

A model report

The sample on pages 185−91 shows how a typical business report should look and sound, and how the topics should be organised. Notice the following points.

- The structure is developed from the original rough draft with objective items in the findings and subjective opinions and proposals in the analysis.
- The pages are set out to look attractive, and are easy to follow. Notice the amount of 'white space', an essential requirement in a high-quality business report.
- The numbered headings support the structure. See how easily you can follow the hierarchy of ideas, and can locate major sections, subsections and minor units by following the system of numbering, indention and underlining.
- The language is concise, direct and businesslike. Some information appears in the form of listed facts instead of as complete sentences. There is no use of 'I', 'me', 'we' or 'you', and no personal comment.

Advice on how to write and edit particular sections of a report, including title page, synopsis, findings, analysis, recommendations and appendixes, is given in the sections following the model.

Case study: Kinland Pty Ltd

Kinland Pty Ltd is a medium-sized metropolitan company. The writer of this report is Kinland's personnel manager, Sandy Hollins, who has just completed a study of the methods currently in use by the company to motivate staff and has been asked by Terry Cavill, the managing director, to write a short report on the study.

The report will be presented at a meeting of the Kinland board of directors on 25 November.

Assume that Sandy has already completed the investigation stage, which included a series of interviews with various staff members and committees, reference to similar reports from interstate, and other reading. Sandy now has some draft notes (see below). They will give you a general idea of the topic and the context in which the report is being written. You'll notice that the language and style in the draft are *not* appropriate for a report, but you will see that they can be easily converted into report format.

Rough notes for report

1. Kinland Pty Ltd uses the following methods to motivate employees. First we use a salary-increment scheme. After the first twelve months' service, an employee receives yearly increases in salary. But payment of the increase is subject to the employee showing an improvement in a number of areas. These include punctuality, diligence, general efficiency and communication skills.

2. Secondly, we offer promotion opportunities to all employees. But promotion is not automatic. It depends on factors including proven ability to handle responsibility, above-average performance of duties and ability to work with others on a team basis. It also depends on what efforts the employee is making to improve work skills, as shown by additional study at a community college, university, or other recognised educational institution.

3. We have a staff training program too. For all staff, courses are run regularly on report writing, letter writing and public speaking. Supervisory staff are offered regular courses on basic supervision skills such as problem solving, decision making, negotiating skills and principles of management.

4. All the present schemes are operating well, and in my opinion should continue. The most obvious indicator is the extremely low turnover of younger (16–22) staff, (less than 2.5 per cent last year), which compares well with the industry average of over 10 per cent.

5. Morale is high, and when I interviewed them most employees expressed general satisfaction with the present program. (I wonder how reliable that sort of response really is. Would they tell me if they were not satisfied?)

6. We should now start introducing some additional training programs. Staff are enthusiastic about possible schemes, such as award restructuring. This should be tried next year. Morale and production could rise as a result if it works for us as it has in a couple of other local firms like ours. (I've got some data on this, too bulky for the report but could go in the Appendix along with my detailed plan for the new scheme.)

7. Planning should begin immediately so that we can start a trial award restructure program in January. If this happens, there should be a visible indication of increase in both morale and production by mid-April.

8. My one worry is that if we do not move quickly, the present level of staff support for the idea may slacken off. There is a risk that opposition companies may introduce a similar plan in an effort to attract top staff away from Kinland. I don't feel we should try any other schemes until the award restructure is working.

(End of rough draft)

Writing parts of a report

Cover page and title

Any report of five or more pages in length is worth presenting in the most professional way possible. As well as a separate contents page and synopsis, it should also have an outer cover, which should show

- the full title in large lettering;
- the name of the person or group for whom the report was prepared;
- the name of the writer or writers and the group they represent, if any (in smaller lettering).

Fix the whole document inside a plastic binder with a clear front sheet, so that the cover page is visible. A cardboard cover is inferior, and gives a negative first impression.

In the case of a short (two- to four-page) report, a plastic cover and separate cover page are optional, since the title also appears at the top of the first page (above the introduction).

Writing the title

An effective title may have to be two or three lines long if it is to include the following items (each of which performs an important function):

REPORT ON INVESTIGATION INTO THE CURRENT USE

OF MOTIVATION AND INCENTIVE SCHEMES —

KINLAND PTY LTD — BRIGHTON

1991–1992

Prepared for the Board of

Directors Meeting

25 November 1991

by

S. B. Hollins

Personnel Manager

and the staff of the

Personnel Section — Kinland Pty Ltd

SYNOPSIS

Kinland's motivational schemes are an important feature of the firm's overall corporate strategy.

Kinland uses several methods to motivate employees, starting with a salary increment scheme, subject to the employee showing an improvement in a number of areas. As the firm expands promotion opportunities are opening constantly, but promotion depends on a number of factors listed in the findings. A staff training program offers courses on many topics. Details are included in this report.

All the present schemes are operating well. This report considers which ones should continue and whether new ones should be added. Unless some new schemes are approved for an early start next year, however, the firm may start to lose staff.

This problem is discussed and recommendations are made on how to deal with it effectively.

[Note the way the synopsis is centred in the page with wide margins top and bottom, and much wider margins on both left and right sides.]

CONTENTS

REPORT ON INVESTIGATION INTO THE CURRENT USE OF MOTIVATION AND INCENTIVE SCHEMES — KINLAND PTY LTD — BRIGHTON 1991–1992

1. INTRODUCTION

1.1 Aim
To investigate the present systems of employee motivation and to suggest possible changes, where necessary.

1.2 Authorisation
As requested by T. G. Cavill, the Managing Director, on 5 September 1991, for presentation to the Board of Directors meeting on 25 November 1991.

1.3 Sources of Information
1.3.1 Discussions with supervisors
1.3.2 Discussions with staff committees
1.3.3 Reports on incentive schemes in other states
1.3.4 Personnel section records
1.3.5 Other sources: Management of People at Work, Donald S. Bauth, Penpress (1989)

2. FINDINGS

The company currently uses three different types of motivation and incentive programs:
* An annual salary increment scheme, commencing after the first 12 months.
* Promotional opportunities, based on the undertaking of further part-time studies, plus development of other abilities (teamwork and responsibility).
* A staff development program intended to provide training in specific skills required by staff who are seeking promotion.
These are explained more fully below.

2.1 Annual Salary Increment Scheme
This commences at the end of the first 12 months with the firm. The employee is eligible for further increases in salary at the end of each 12 months from then on.
However, rises are not paid automatically. Each employee is required to maintain a satisfactory level of performance during the year. This is assessed according to the following criteria:
* punctuality
* general efficiency
* communication skills
* general conduct

Assessment is carried out by the employee's immediate supervisor, at least twice during the year.

2.2 Promotional Opportunities

As Kinland is continuing to expand its operations, there are numerous opportunities for staff to apply for promotion. Employees are regularly advised that the factors that will increase their chance of gaining promotion include:

2.2.1 Demonstration of sound performance and working ability, including:
* proven ability to handle responsibility
* satisfactory performance in present position
* ability to work with others on a team basis

2.2.2 Additional study undertaken at any of the following:
* universities
* community colleges
* TAFE colleges

2.3 Staff Development Program

2.3.1 The staff development program for supervisors includes training courses on each of the following:
* team building
* problem solving
* negotiation skills
* principles of management

2.3.2 Other staff development programs, available to all employees, include courses on:
* report writing
* letter writing
* public speaking

2.4 Other Training, Motivation and Incentive Schemes

The following schemes have been used by similar firms in this area and could be introduced in the future:
* award restructuring including job rotation
* participative decision making
* delegation of responsibility (to lower levels)
* profit sharing

3. ANALYSIS

3.1 The Present Situation

Overall the firm's motivation and incentive schemes appear to be working soundly. The most obvious indicator of this is the extremely low loss of younger (16–22 years old) staff, which was less than 2.5% over the last year. This compares favourably with the industry average loss for younger staff, which at present is over 10%.

Morale is high, and most employees expressed general satisfaction with the program. (Although expressions of satisfaction are not always reliable indicators of true feelings.)

3.2 Proposal to Introduce New Schemes

Staff are enthusiastic about the possibility of additional incentive schemes, including those mentioned in paragraph 2.4, and in particular the proposal to offer award restructuring on a trial basis next year. To take advantage of this attitude, moves should begin immediately to introduce a trial award restructure program starting in January next year. See recommendations 4.1 and 4.2.

3.3 Expected Results

If award restructuring can be introduced next January, both morale and production should show a noticeable rise by mid-April. This prediction is consistent with similar experiences in other states where even the most simple restructuring programs have resulted in increased output and efficiency. (See Appendix B.)

3.4 The Need for Immediate Action

If the firm does not move quickly, the present support for the idea may lessen. There is also a risk that opposition companies may introduce a similar plan in an effort to attract top staff away from Kinland. A detailed plan for the introduction of the scheme is attached in Appendix A.

3.5 Introduction of Other Schemes

Evidence from other states (see Appendix B) suggests that introduction of other schemes would also be beneficial. It is preferable, however, for changes of this kind to be introduced one by one. No consideration should therefore be given (at present) to any other schemes. (See recommendation 4.4.)

4. RECOMMENDATIONS

4.1 That the award restructure program, as proposed in Appendix A, be approved.

4.2 That the scheme commence on 10 January 1992. (See Analysis Par 3.2.)

4.3 That all other schemes operating at present continue in 1992. (See Par 3.1.)

4.4 That no other new schemes be introduced until the award restructure scheme has been running successfully for at least six months. (Refer to Par 3.5.)

Sandy Hollins

Sandy Hollins
PERSONNEL MANAGER — KINLAND PTY LTD
27.11.91

APPENDIX A — Detailed proposal for introduction of trial award restructure scheme in January 1992.

APPENDIX B — University research findings on job-rotation schemes and increased employee morale in NSW (1981–1990).

- an opening phrase: 'Report on', 'Investigation into', 'Study of', or similar words;
- a 'time word' relevant to the subject of the report — for example, a *recent* event, one that is *current*, or a *proposed* activity.
- the main topic, and any subtopics;
- the name of the group, firm or organisation who will use the report (in a formal document this should appear as part of the title even if it is intended only for readers in the firm);
- the location (address, district or region) of the group referred to or of the activity dealt with in the text;
- the period covered by the report (usually just the year, or year and month — this avoids confusion with other reports having similar titles but referring to different periods.

Titles look best printed entirely in capital letters and underlined from start to finish.

REPORT ON PROPOSED PURCHASE OF NEW
VEHICLE — MANUFACTURING DIVISION,
CLEARVIEW HOLDINGS LTD —
WINDSOR — 1991

INVESTIGATION INTO RECENT CHANGES IN
EDP SYSTEM AND RESULTING VARIATION IN
POLICY — NORTHERN BRANCH, CLEARVIEW
HOLDINGS LTD — MANLY — DECEMBER 1990

Synopsis

A synopsis at the start of a long report helps to catch the reader's attention and arouses interest, encouraging people to look further.

A good synopsis describes the content and explains why the report is important and what can be gained by reading it. It should not give any findings or recommendations, nor should it attempt to summarise the whole report. Like the synopsis on the back of a video cassette, it should arouse interest but should not say how the report ends.

Even for a very long report, a synopsis of 200–300 words is sufficient. Some people prefer to write a shorter one as part of the introduction, but as a summary, a synopsis has most impact immediately after the cover page. Notice that in the Kinland report the writer uses extra white space and wider margins than in the rest of the document.

Table of contents

Presentation of even a short report is lifted by having a table of contents listing headings (with page numbers). This provides a quick summary of the whole text as well as a means of finding specific topics.

Even in a short (four- or five-page) report, a contents list will show that the material has been organised clearly and logically. This increases reader confidence in the report and in you.

If you used an outline (your collection of draft headings) as part of the early writing stage, you will already have your table of contents almost completed. Many word-processor programs have an 'outline' function that lists a draft contents table without your having to retype any headings.

Introduction

The introduction also helps to establish a positive, professional reader–writer relationship, which encourages trust and confidence when the report is read by executives of higher rank than the author. Readers need to know *why* it is important for them to share the information you have. Some may not even know you, since reports will be passed from the first reader (who does) to higher levels in the organisation, and two strangers cannot communicate effectively without some kind of introduction. The following story may help to explain this.

It is after 10 o'clock at night. You are alone in the house. You answer a knock at the front door and find an attractive and very well-spoken man asking for you by name. 'Excuse me, but are you ——?' The man, a complete stranger to you, is impeccably dressed in a style very much like that worn by legal executives in Great Britain.

What is this all about? (*Aim*)

That's a quite natural reaction and it's much the same as you can expect from a reader facing a strange document by an unknown writer. So the first thing to do in the introduction is to describe the aim of the report.

Suppose the stranger answers your question by explaining that he represents a British legal firm called Jones, Jones & Smith and is acting on behalf of your late Uncle Henry, who has named you as sole beneficiary in his will! Your visitor tells you that the plane was late arriving, and he has to be on the early flight out of town tomorrow. So, late though it is, tonight is the only time available for you to sign the necessary papers. 'Now,' says the stranger, 'if you will just allow me to step inside and get your signature on certain legal documents, Uncle Henry's fortune will be yours!'

Not until I see it in writing! (*Authorisation*)

There are almost certainly some questions you'd like answered before you accept this suggestion. Most people in your position would like some proof (on paper) that the stranger is authorised to handle legal matters. A report authorisation should play the same role as a letter of authority, telling readers on whose instructions you wrote the report and what those instructions were.

Writing the introduction – guidelines

Help the reader; anticipate questions like those above and answer them as part of your introduction.

1. Explain the purpose of the report in one short sentence (*aim*).

2. State who asked you to write the report, the date you were asked, and any conditions or terms of reference. If the request is on record as a memo or a letter, mention this (*authorisation*).

3. Identify your main sources of information — meetings, interviews, personal observations, and particularly the methods used to obtain figures or accounting data. Reassure readers that the report is genuine, and the result of thorough investigation. Executives like to know
   - what kind of facts will be presented and how reliable they are;
   - how they were obtained (careful research, detailed interviews or guesswork);
   - whether the views expressed are expert opinions or just the writer's ideas.

This may require a fourth heading in the introduction: 'Method of investigation'. If so, just give a brief summary. The details belong with the facts in the body of the report.

Findings — results of investigation

The findings are the factual part of the report. A good test to decide whether an item belongs in this section is to ask whether the reader could have 'found' exactly the same information. If the answer is 'yes', the information belongs in the findings.

Presenting the findings

Clear, specific information helps readers to agree with what you say. Use examples to illustrate important points.
- Important data should be stated in kilometres, kilograms or similar measures rather than words that mean different things to different people.
- If you cannot produce figures, use precise descriptive words. Use the seven C's (see p. 164).
- If lengthy statistical data, complex specifications and so on threaten to overfill the findings (or if any numerical tables run to more than half a page), summarise the data in that section and include the full item as an appendix.
- Give sources of important findings. If experts supplied factual information, don't just say 'experts suggest . . .' — identify them; give names, technical qualifications, and where they can be contacted. If quoting from audited accounts, name the auditor and the audit date (see 'Quotes, references and acknowledgments' in Chapter 18).
- If your information was obtained by personal observation, say so. If test equipment was used, describe it. List statistical tests used to verify data.
- If you can, it is better to *show* than to *tell*. Use photographs. Illustrations make a page more interesting and facts more credible. Use graphs, tables and diagrams (see 'Visual and graphic illustrations', in Chapter 19). If important evidence is contained in specific documents, certified photocopies are more reassuring than quoted contents.
- Set the information out in a clear and logical sequence. For instance, your main findings could be in either chronological or geographical order, according to the topic. Chapter 31 includes many more examples of recognised ways to order information.

Do not include *ANY* findings in the introduction; this suggests lack of organisation.

Analysis or discussion

This section should explain why action should be taken, what decisions are proposed and why readers should support specific actions (recommendations). In formal or academic reports it is often titled 'Conclusions'; in business reports 'analysis' or 'discussion' is a more appropriate heading.

Writing the analysis – guidelines

1. Begin with a 'Where we are now' statement.
Summarise important points from the findings and highlight the present position.

> 3.1 Reasons for Current Fall in Sales
> Events leading up to the present fall in sales have been explained fully in paragraphs 2.3 to 2.6 of the findings section. Of these the most serious are:
> 3.1.1 Failure by the previous Board to change the advertising program from that used in the 1980s. (See Par 2.3.)
> 3.1.2 Lack of training for sales staff on basic service procedures. (See Pars 2.4.1 and 2.4.2.)

2. Make a logical analysis of the facts.
Discuss how facts and findings and expert opinions should be interpreted. This requires a mixture of both logical and persuasive writing.

3. Discuss proposed recommendations.
Use sound logical argument to steer readers towards a specific action. Explain the reasons behind each recommendation. If the findings show that worker A is better qualified than worker B and that machine X will run faster than machine Y, develop a plan to make the necessary changes.

4. Give predicted results.
Include details such as the estimated cost of implementing the recommended action.

5. State recommendations in full or summarise them.
Do this with *each* proposal; it is far easier for readers to assess a recommendation if they know *exactly* what it is.

6. Have confidence in your position as an 'expert'.
Your own opinions are important. The more time you spent investigating, collecting evidence and talking to people, the more qualified you are to offer specialist views.

7. Argue your case.
Although a report should be written objectively, there is no reason against putting the case for action as a powerful argument that 'steers' the reader towards agreement, as the following example illustrates:

> 3.5 Need for Immediate Approval
> If the new system can be installed and fully operative before the end of the financial year, it is predicted that savings in the annual stock-take alone should pay for the cost of installation. (See Par 2.3.2, page 4.)
> This will not be possible, however, unless installation commences this month. (See Par 2.3.7.) If it does not, it will have to be delayed until after the annual stocktake is completed, and apart from the failure to take advantage of the savings outlined in paragraph 2.2.3, this will mean the loss of any taxation benefit for the current year.

Notice that rather than repeating what has already been said, the writer simply refers to relevant paragraphs.

Language and style in the analysis
Although the style is clearly aimed at encouraging specific action, words such as 'if' and 'should' are included to leave the way open for the reader to make the final judgment. Compare the language and writing styles of the Findings and the Analysis in the Kinland report.

Recommendations

Recommendations are like a recipe for action. Tell readers exactly what, when and how action needs to be taken. The less room for doubt, the more confident busy executives will feel about accepting your proposals.

Setting out recommendations

Provided each proposal appears as a numbered item, there is no need for headings. However, if recommendations can be grouped according to topics, list them under appropriate subheadings.

Opening lines

There are two ways of starting a recommendation. The example below illustrates the usual concise style. To save repetition, start with a single line: 'It is recommended that ...' (in practice, this line is often omitted). Sentences are often incomplete, leaving out all but the most essential words, as in this example.

Concise recommendations — incomplete sentences

4. RECOMMENDATIONS

It is recommended that approval be given for:
- 4.1 Allocation of $80 000 for planning and implementation ...
- 4.2 Setting aside $1000 from this amount for purchase of ...
- 4.3 Expenditure of up to $2000 as initial deposit on ...

For formal reports just add the phrase 'That approval be given for ...' at the start of *every* recommendation. Sentences are complete (no missing words) to ensure a more 'legal' tone. This style is preferable if approval is being recorded in minutes or formal documents.

Writing recommendations – guidelines

1. List recommendations in a logical sequence.

Notice that in the above example the first recommendation is for allocation of money. Until this is approved, other proposals cannot be considered. End with low-priority items needed just to tie up loose ends.

2. Give only one item per recommendation.

Each one needs to be discussed and approved individually. Combining items increases the chance of rejection.

3. Number recommendations individually.

In meetings, people can then refer to them easily: 'Recommendation 4.5 cannot be considered until we discuss 4.4'.

4. Be specific.

If equipment is needed, give the technical name, the model number and the supplier's name and address. State exact dates and amounts. Ask that '... the current travel fund ($2000) for the financial year commencing 1 July be increased to $2250', not that '... the travel allowance for next year be increased'.

5. Use direct, active language.

Don't be apologetic, or beat about the bush.

6. Don't make a recommendation that cannot be referred to the analysis.

If you think of an extra proposal, be sure to add the topic concerned to the analysis.

7. Keep explanations and reasons *out*.

Keep recommendations free of any discussion for or against the ideas. Some writers feel the need to support each one by including reasons for acceptance, as the next example shows. The words in italics should have been left out. They contain important arguments in favour of the proposals that should have been included in the analysis.

---

4. RECOMMENDATIONS

- 4.1 *There is a risk in accepting an unwritten guarantee from a used car dealer because it can be denied later.* Insist on a full written warranty that covers labour as well as parts.
- 4.3 *You cannot sign a sale agreement first then tear it up afterwards if the car is found to be mechanically unsound.* Always have a car checked by an independent expert before you sign any agreement. *A dealer who will not agree to this may be trying to hide something.*

When you are in doubt ...

Sometimes you just cannot get the facts you need to help you make clear recommendations. It is better in such cases to suggest further investigation than to make recommendations based on insufficient data. Saying 'I don't know' about one item makes your other proposals appear more reliable.

Safeguard recommendations

Some decision makers may reject a recommendation unless they are sure the request does not 'exceed the guidelines'. For this kind of reader, recommendations 4.2 and 4.3 in the example below add assurance that it is safe for them to say 'yes'.

---

4. RECOMMENDATIONS
It is recommended that:

4.1 Approval be given for an increase of $60 000 a year in the equipment allowance for the Perth and Hobart branches.

4.2 Authorisation for use of this additional allowance be restricted to the State Managers in each branch.

4.3 All officers be advised that the restrictions applying to equipment allowances as listed on pages 34 and 35 of the Administrative Handbook, and in Par 2.4 of this report, are to be adhered to.

'Either-or' recommendations

These leave decision makers free to choose a number of different 'cut-off' points. Notice, in the case below, how recommendation 4.2 suggests two alternatives, allowing the reader to select the one that best fits the current situation. This speeds up decision making and saves having to reject the report, as might have been the case if recommendation 4.1 had been submitted on its own.

It is recommended:

4.1 That approval be given for an increase in the equipment allowance for the Perth and Hobart branches.

4.2 That this increase be either $5000 for the present half-year or $2500 for the present and $2500 for the following half-year. [The 'either-or' recommendation]

4.3 That if approval is not available for any

---

increase in equipment, branches should not take any new clients for the coming year.

Negative recommendations

Executives who like room to make their own decisions may prefer less precise wording. Recommendation 4.3 in the example above is worded in the 'negative'; this is a tactful way of allowing the reader freedom to choose what to approve.

Ending the report

Some people like to include a very short summary as a way of tidying up the ending, but it is not essential.

Signature and position

A signature emphasises the writer's confidence in the reliability of the report. An unsigned document suggests (non-verbally) some doubt or uncertainty. If several people worked together to produce it, either all can sign or one can sign as team leader.

- Signatures can be hard to read; print the names below them. If appropriate, add technical or academic qualifications; they give more credibility to the report.
- Under the name, give the position held; for example:

    Leader — Investigating team
    Manager — New Zealand Export Division
    Chief Safety Officer

- If the report is going to many different readers, or if it was prepared by a committee, it is useful to include the name of the branch, committee or group responsible for producing it.
- Beneath the signature, add the date of signing to indicate exactly when the report was completed — an important piece of information.

Lyn McKay

Lyn McKay, B.Bus, RANM
Senior Marketing Manager
ALPHA HOLDINGS PTY LTD
15 August 1992

Conclusions — a quiet alternative

There are occasions when you cannot close your report with actual recommendations:

- when it has to be presented on a fixed date and vital data is still not available;
- when a superior (who asked you to write it) wants to read it before deciding on the form of recommendations;
- when you are personally involved in the outcome and your recommendations could appear to be biased;
- in an investigative report, which presents only a set of findings without any detailed analysis.

In these circumstances you can still make suggestions, but call this softer ending 'Conclusions' instead of 'Recommendations', as in the following example.

4. CONCLUSIONS

Studies so far (as outlined above) show no clear evidence that a change in pricing policy would have a positive effect on sales.

It would be wise, however, for research into market trends to continue, and if the firm's own research team is available, they may well be the group best equipped to carry out this study.

If this is not possible there are a number of other groups, including Le Grande Systems, who are already familiar with the work and could be called on to continue investigations.

Notice that conclusions like these could easily be rewritten as recommendations.

The appendix

There may be several appendixes to one report, identified as A, B, C and so on. Some may even be larger than the report itself. Typical items in an appendix include

- items that are too long or too bulky (maps, blueprints, computer print-outs) or objects other than paper (video tapes, models, samples);
- items that are only supplementary to the main findings — a mechanical report, a witness's statement — but cannot be left out altogether;
- raw data — unedited or original material from which the figures in the report have been condensed;
- supporting evidence — material that only a few readers need, but which (because those people are experts) could be vital for the report to get their backing;
- other items to back up your results — photographs, affidavits, or calculations that prove your figures to be correct or add credibility to the findings;
- background information — a course syllabus, another report, a technical manual — items that help readers put the report into perspective.

If they are quite short (two or three pages each), all the appendixes are included with the report in one cover, after the close (and signature). Bulky items are better in separate covers.

Note that the term 'annex', or 'annexure', is also used to describe the same type of attachment.

The final edit

Remember the table at the start of this chapter showing a typical time plan? It allowed two full weeks for the final edit stage, and that's a realistic estimate. Editing, rewriting and polishing takes time, but it's rewarding to watch the report improving and know that its chances of success are increasing with each day's work. Chapter 18, 'The final polish', explains the steps involved, which include

- checking for cohesion and unity;
- increasing readability (reducing 'fog');
- building credibility;
- checking for errors (proofreading);
- condensing.

Of these steps, condensing is the most difficult. Chapter 20 explains the techniques in detail and includes a worked example, showing you how to write a shorter report (and a synopsis at the same time).

How long should the report be?

Most reports are far too long and — as mentioned earlier in the chapter — reports that are too long are not read. The ideal length depends on the reader's 'page limit' — that is, the maximum number

Report on the Length
of Reports

Findings:
Most reports are too
long.

of pages he or she will read before losing interest or running out of time. Often that is as little as five to eight pages (not counting the table of contents, cover, illustrations and appendices).

If you cannot condense a long report to the required limit, an alternative is to write a special version known as an 'executive summary' (see Fig. 16.1), using the techniques explained in Chapter 20 to select key points from the main sections (Introduction, Findings, Analysis); recommendations are usually listed in full. This version looks just like a full report, with a cover, synopsis and contents page, but other parts of the original document (or the complete report itself) are presented separately as appendixes, as illustrated in Figure 16.1.

Presenting the report

Each of the following, added to a report, can lift the overall standard of presentation.

- Glossary: Similar to an index, this is an alphabetical list restricted to special terms or phrases used in the report. A brief explanation is given for each item. Include the page numbers where the terms are found.

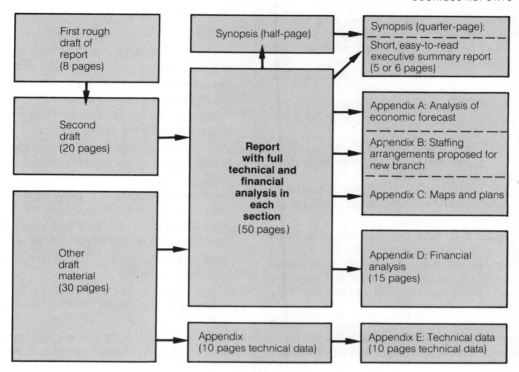

Fig. 16.1 *Condensing a report to meet a reader's needs*

- Alphabetical index: This lists important subjects and other key words used in the document (and relevant page numbers).
- Letter of transmittal: A short but formal letter accompanying a report or submission, this can be used to express views that could not be included in the report.
- Professional binding: First impressions always count, and the outside appearance of a report is important. Professional binding adds a strong visual appeal.

Private views

Keep your private opinions out of the report. Words such as 'I' or 'me' reduce the impersonal quality that conveys a sense of objectivity. If you need to offer a personal (and subjective) opinion, do so in either of the following ways.

Positive — a personal letter
A personal letter accompanying a report can mention a wide range of feelings (such as satisfaction, appreciation disagreement, hopes, fears or doubts) that cannot be included in the report.

Negative — a statement of dissent
If the report has been written by a team and you as a member are not happy with the end product or with some particular recommendation, it is in order for you to advise the group that you are writing a statement to this effect. Make your own position clear, and give reasons for your views.

Summary

1. Easy-to-read reports are the ones most often read. The first barrier facing the report writer is reader resistance. Keep your report short and make each page attractive to the eye.

2. Writing and setting out a report is a straight-forward task and surprisingly easy to master.

3. Reports are made up of more than words. They can include graphs, pictures and symbols.

4. There are four main divisions in a report. Names vary, but the most common include
   - INTRODUCTION, which establishes the reader–writer relationship, outlines the purpose and scope of the report and states the aim in one short sentence;
   - FINDINGS, which presents objective information — gives the facts as a basis for discussion;
   - ANALYSIS, which tells readers what action is proposed and why, and builds support for the recommendations;
   - RECOMMENDATIONS which makes up the action ending, listing steps needed to get results.

5. In addition to these four sections, other items in even a short report include a synopsis and (often) an appendix. A contents table shows that the report has been organised logically, with a clear division of ideas into sections. This increases reader confidence.

6. When setting out the report page, number all major headings. Metric or decimal style numbering has many advantages over letter-number systems.

7. State important data in kilometres, kilograms or similar measures that have the same meaning for every reader.

8. Give a source reference for important findings. If experts supplied factual information for the report, identify them by name.

9. Sign every report personally. An unsigned report suggests that the writer is lacking in confidence and commitment.

10. If you cannot condense a long report to the required number of pages, an alternative is to write a special version known as an executive summary.

11. Keep personal views out of the report. Words such as 'I' or 'me' reduce the impersonal quality that conveys a sense of objectivity.

Exercises

1. List four different items that should be included in a report title.

2. List some reasons for having a separate introduction section in a business report.

3. What items should be included in the introduction? What items should not?

4. Why is it important to keep the material in the findings separate from other sections?

5. Give two guidelines a writer should follow in choosing and classifying material for use in an analysis section.

6. What kind of material or wording should *not* be included in the recommendations? Why?

7. What type of material should go in an appendix to a business report?

8. Explain four page-layout techniques that writers can use to make a report more attractive to the reader.

9. Write a short (four to six pages) business report on a topic of your own choice. Include the following:
   - cover page;
   - synopsis page (100–120 words only);
   - contents page (including page numbers);
   - introduction with standard format — half to three-quarters of a page;
   - findings set out in business style with numbered headings and including objective information on the topic;
   - an analysis which discusses the findings, makes proposals or predictions, and explains and supports the recommendations that will follow;
   - recommendations — each item numbered, with *no* discussion or reasons;
   - at least one diagram, photograph or other form of non-verbal, graphic or visual data;
   - an appendix (optional).

CHAPTER 17

Memos, short reports and electronic mail

Apart from memos, this chapter deals with a number of variations of the standard report and business letter — some familiar, some new. Using a computer system to produce multicopy or standard form 'letters' requires special care.

Benefits of electronic data transfer (including electronic mail and fax systems) are considered in brief.

Topics

Writing memos

Memo reports and memoranda

Short business reports

Electronic mail systems

Standard format and multicopy letters

Writing memos

Memos are a vital part of the formal communication systems in most business organisations. Some are like letters, others more like reports, but the essential requirement is that they should be kept *short*. Use them for official messages and for matters of importance.

Memos should

- deal with information and action rather than with business relationships;
- be based on objective data rather than on subjective opinions.

If an ordinary note or a phone call will produce the same result, choose it in preference to a memo. You can sound petty, even ridiculous, if you use a memo to deal with issues such as the purchase of a new teapot.

Personal (one-to-one) memos

Personal memos are useful to make sure that personal messages are received clearly, but even these should be reserved for matters of some depth. They can, however, still be friendly. Writing in memo style gives you the chance to draft and redraft your message to make sure that it will not be taken the wrong way. This you cannot do when speaking face to face or on the phone. And of course with a personal memo, both parties have a record of the message to serve as a reminder.

- Use a light tone, keep to the subject and be concise.
- Include the receiver's first name in the memo address, and use it in the body of the text if the relationship warrants this.
- Personal memos that include official information or requests should be recorded and filed as with any other official correspondence.

Memo format

A complex format wastes the time memos are intended to save: avoid all unnecessary detail. Use different colours to distinguish urgent messages from standard ones. The sample message on page 202 includes all you need in the way of headings.

Date: 18 March 1990   Reference No. TRAN-873

To: Alex Petersen, Sales Manager

From: Sandy Jensen, Personnel Training Officer

Subject: Sales staff to attend letter-writing course
          May 17–18 (Reply to your memo TRAN
          763–12 March)

Yes, Alex, we have budgeted for three staff from your
section to attend the Advanced Letter-Writing course.
Because this is an advanced program it is essential
that all participants have completed at least one basic
letter-writing program in the past year. It does not
matter whether the course was one of ours or one run
by another organisation, such as TAFE.
Please let me know by April 20:

  1. the name of each person who will be attending;

  2. what courses on letter writing the individual has
     attended previously;

  3. the date and duration of each course attended;

  4. where the course was held.

Thanks, Alex. As soon as I have the three names, I will
contact each participant personally and pass on full
details.
          Sandy

If this format needs to include any more details, such as the sender's position, department or section, have them preprinted on memo blanks for each user.

Memo tone

Memos are not as personal as letters, so there is little need to develop or define the two-way relationship; the background signals still make it clear. Notice that Sandy, in the example above, starts with 'Yes, Alex' and in the action ending says 'Thanks, Alex'. That's all that is needed to set the tone — to establish the relationship as friendly. Always close with an action ending, as in any other message, and always sign a memo personally.

Formal memos

These have a more official tone, but should still use 'I', 'we' and 'our' to refer to the writer and 'you' or 'your' to the reader. They are in many ways the same as letters as far as their role in communication is concerned, but because they use a simpler and more standard wording they are easier to write.

A formal memo might, for instance, confirm your appointment to a higher position and list your duties and the conditions of the appointment.

Multiperson memos

These are not necessarily addressed to people by name; they might, for example, use a general address — 'To: All Section Heads'. The name and position of the writer goes at the end, and it is preferable that all copies are signed personally.

Guidelines for writing memos

The four-stage writing method described in Chapter 14 and the letter-writing techniques in Chapter 15 apply in general to memo writing, with some variations.

1. Keep memos short.

Use short words and short sentences. Deal with only one idea in any one paragraph. Complete sentences are not essential. If you list points one under the other you use fewer words. Long memos do not work.

2. Avoid bureaucratic jargon.

Some writers fill memos with standard phrases like 'in reference to the above matter'. Why? Perhaps it saves having to think of shorter but less familiar phrases. Some (misguided) writers believe that long words are necessary to make a memo sound — well — 'like a memo ought to sound'. This may not be entirely their fault. If they have seen many memos written in this way it will be easy enough to think that long words are part of memo style, but this is not so. In the 1990s they don't create a good impression, nor do they help communication work.

3. Use face-to-face language.

Use the active tense. Be direct and personal. Let your memos be more like an extension of conversation. Avoid the third-person style ('It has come to the writer's attention that . . .'). This may save putting a personal emphasis on a message conveying bad news, but it is better even in those cases if the memo takes a direct approach and uses face-to-face language.

I notice that

4. Monitor background signals and tone.

Memos contain non-verbal messages (whether you want them to or not!). Read a memo aloud (before you send it) to yourself or to a colleague. If it sounds artificial, or like a parent chastising a child, rewrite it.

5. If the matter is urgent, do not use a memo.

Senior managers tend to forget that if a memo arrives after 11.00 am the reader may have already made plans for the day or be busy with an urgent task. If a topic involves anything that needs action in under three or four days, other communication methods are safer (see 'Electronic mail systems', p. 206).

6. Allow sufficient time for replies.

In your organisation, how long does it take for a multiperson memo to move from the writer's desk, through the administration system and onto readers' desks? Often it's a day and a half — sometimes longer, depending on how the memo is typed, printed and distributed. When asking for a reply by a certain date, take this delay into consideration.

7. Give each memo a headline and a number.

One memo tends to look very much like another. Use a prominent headline or subject line, and make the date clear, too. Use a numbering system, so that if necessary you can refer specifically to the number, rather than saying 'My memo of the 28th'.

8. One subject — one memo.

If you need to communicate about several quite different topics, then use separate memos. A single memo that reads like a mini-newsletter is confusing.

When to use memos

Memos work best for conveying good news or simple requests for action that require no special persuasion and which will be easy to agree to. If an issue is complicated or controversial, face-to-face communication may be called for.

When *not* to use memos

When giving bad news

In these circumstances, write a letter. This applies in particular to any kind of reprimand or withdrawal of privileges: a memo is not a good channel if you have to assert your authority. Never use one to say things you are not prepared to say to a person's face.

make feel better

For 'pep up' messages

Morale-boosting is a skill that requires personal leadership in a face-to-face situation. You cannot lead people or change attitudes by writing memos; in fact, the opposite effect is more likely. If you try to lead in this way you will be seen as weak and ineffectual.

To convey personal news

Use a letter to advise people of promotion or to welcome someone to a new job. Similarly, use a letter to offer congratulations on personal success.

Memo reports and memoranda

A memo-style report is brief (one to three pages). The heading follows a memo format but the rest, while concise, is similar in style and layout to other reports. It usually ends with recommendations

relating specifically to direct action. The following is a sample opening.

> FROM: Deputy Director, National Training Council
> TO: Chairman, National Conference Committee
> Subject: Venue for national conference — Confirmation of bookings
>
> 1. INTRODUCTION
>   1.1 <u>Aim</u>
>   This report presents the results of the recent investigation into booking problems experienced with the National Conference at . . .

From that point the text follows standard report form (see Chapter 16).

Departmental memoranda — public service format

A similar but more formal message called a 'memorandum' is often used in public-service communication. This also uses a report format except in the opening stages, but the language is more formal and recommendations are stated in an impersonal manner, using parliamentary or semi-legal wording.

> Memorandum to: THE HONOURABLE THE MINISTER FOR INDUSTRY AND COMMUNICATION
>
> Subject: INVESTIGATIONS INTO RECENT CHANGES IN THE *AUSTRALIAN BUSINESS WRITING ACT 1982–1989* AND THEIR EFFECT ON REGISTRATIONS IN THE CAPITAL TERRITORY – 1990
>
> [*Sender's name and position may be shown here, but often appears only at the end of the document.*]
>
> 1. INTRODUCTION
>   1.1 <u>Aim</u>
>   This memorandum presents the results of recent departmental investigations

into changes in the Australian Business Writing Act

[*The body of the memorandum is set out in much the same way as a report.*]

4. RECOMMENDATIONS

   4.1 That the Minister proceed with proposals as set out above to appoint a committee to consider the implications on Australian communication of recent amendments to the Act.

   4.2 That membership of the committee be restricted to those persons whose names are listed in the attached (confidential) appendix.

[*Signature here*]
James Boldwin
Secretary to the Commission for
Australian Business Writing
   29.05.91

Short business reports

Executive or summary report

A report of fifty or 100 pages might be read by a few specially interested individuals. Many others — particularly busy executives — need a report they can go through in a few minutes. An executive or summary report follows the same sequence as the model report, highlighting key points from each section. Chapter 20, 'Summarising and condensing', explains how to produce such a short version quickly and easily, using business condensation methods.

Variation report

Some short reports deal with aspects of an earlier report that have been previously approved. If a variation from the original recommendations is needed, a variation report can be more effective than a series of memos or letters. This document deals only with those sections of the original material in which variation is needed, explaining why it is necessary, what extra cost will be involved and so on. It should, however close with new recommendations concerning the variation.

Implementation report

Like a variation report, this involves a follow-up on recommendations or actions already approved. The implementation report considers only such details as the way in which the original recommendations should be carried out, but may close with additional recommendations about them.

Investigative report

This contains mainly findings; it may include a short analysis, or may have none at all. No recommendations are made. It may become the basis for a full report.

Report as attachment to a letter

It is a mistake to include more than one or two paragraphs of detailed information in the body of a business letter, yet often when you write a letter there is much more information you need to share with the reader. If the information is very detailed, particularly if it contains figures and statistics (for instance, a quotation for supply of goods or services), it should be attached as a separate document set out in business format. It may only be half a page long, it may be many pages, but in a report that uses numbered headings and white space the material will be more acceptable, more easily understood and more likely to gain agreement than it would if it had been in the middle of your letter.

The best example of this is a 'report' about yourself, (your personal résumé). A résumé should never be included within a letter (see 'Your personal details', in Chapter 21). Other types of information that should be presented in similar attachments include facts and figures on a firm's financial position, a statement presenting a series of problems, or complex technical data. Each is in effect a report in that it contains collected and collated information arranged according to type, so it makes sense to present it in a way that will make it clear and easy to follow.

Proposals and submissions

A submission, like a report, offers a way of communicating with people who might otherwise be hard to contact. Submissions may meet considerable resistance, or may have to compete against many others for limited resources, so setting out and presentation are vital. Chapter 31, 'Presentations, projects and submissions', explains how you can achieve this.

Routine or seasonal reports

Most organisations require regular reports — say, once a month — from branch managers or travelling representatives. This type of report will often contain little new material and no analysis or recommendations. In many cases it follows a standard format, with only figures, times and places changed to reflect the operations for the period covered. The main characteristics of this kind of report are as follows:

1. Any change or variation from normal procedures is highlighted. If sales in the region have fallen sharply, the report format must be such that the drop cannot be hidden among other data.
2. Reasons are given for the change. The writer should be encouraged to discuss the problem, so that others can understand what is happening.
3. Solutions or suggestions are included.
4. Anything that has not changed is either left out altogether or is recorded for statistical purposes, the record requiring a minimum of effort from both writer and readers.
5. The writer should be able to express expert opinions on local matters, predict future trends and offer suggestions.
6. The report format should allow for explanation in the event of a problem being caused by failure on the part of others (including head office).

Preprinted forms, even if designed to cover every possible situation by having the writer tick boxes or cross out items that do not apply, are not suitable for these reports. In fact, they can serve to hide most of the items listed above while highlighting routine data.

A well-designed form with the initial section devoted to variations and problems and the last page used for routine items such as stock on hand will serve both purposes and still save time. A recent variation is to supply the 'blank form' on a computer disk. The writer types in the figures, and the report (on disk) is submitted by mail or modem.

This allows collating of facts and figures (without retyping) into a state report.

Standard report forms

Sometimes people find themselves in a position where they must make a report involving a special field in which they lack experience. A common example is the report you write when making an insurance claim. Imagine the work if you had to draft your own report without any guidelines! In this kind of situation, a standard report form with every question printed and spaces left for the answers is the only way to make sure the claimant does not leave out essential details.

Electronic mail systems

At the time this second edition was being written there was still considerable resistance in the Australian business community to the concept of electronic mail as a method for exchanging messages other than within a single organisation. The idea appears sound: instead of sending a letter, fax or memo, the writer keys the message into a computer; it is then transmitted by wire, satellite or optical fibre to the receiver's computer. The obvious advantages are speed and the ease with which one message can be directed to a large number of receivers without extra copying.

Why call it 'mail'?

The distinction between 'live' computer transmission (where both parties are watching the computer screen *during* transmission) and electronic mail is that for the latter the receiver does not have to be present. The message is held in an electronic version of a mailbox until the receiver makes contact at that end of the system.

It is therefore like ordinary mail in that it has to wait until the receiver wants to read it. This is one inherent weakness. Other disadvantages include
- computer breakdowns during which the message (or the entire file with all the messages in it) may be lost;
- the need for the receiver to switch on his or her computer and load the communications program before the message can be received;

CLAIM FORM   X2430

Please read the conditions of your policy before completing the form.

Policy No _____

Name of insured _____

Address _____

_____ Postcode _____

Telephone number (where you can be reached between 9 am and 5 pm) _____

Situation where loss, damage or injury occurred _____

_____

_____

_____

Date of loss, damage or injury _____

Explain fully how the loss, damage or injury occurred _____

_____

_____

_____

_____

Details of article for which claim is made	Date purchased	Present replacement cost	Amount claimed

Signature of insured _____

Date _____

- inability to tell *whether* a message has been received and read, or *when* it was read;
- risk of a message reaching the wrong person;
- cost, if long-distance transmissions are involved or if an intermediary 'holding' service is used to retain the message until the receiver dials in (subscriptions to such services are not cheap, and some of the people you want to contact may not subscribe to your service).

On this analysis it would be very easy to predict that electronic mail systems using keyboard input and screen output still have a limited future. Similar predictions were made in the past about the telephone, the typewriter and air travel. By the time you read this page, electronic mail may have overcome its initial problems; there may even be a message waiting for you in your mailbox at this very moment.

In-house networks

One kind of electronic mail system that has been successful is the internal form operating on a single mainframe computer or network, since it avoids the problems of the external kind. It speeds up the distribution of memos and avoids the problems described at the start of this chapter. The system also provides a very effective electronic notice-board, operating in the same way to advise of social events, meetings and so on.

Club bulletin boards

Another success is the bulletin-board system operated by clubs and societies, using a computer with enough disk drives to cope with the relatively small amount of mail exchanged by its members. Some of the more sophisticated clubs have extended this service to link with other clubs in Australia and overseas in a co-operative system that uses honorary operators to deliver family messages worldwide for a very small cost.

Other electronic data transfer

On-line banking, using personal computers to transfer funds and check accounts, is already familiar and popular. Tax returns in most states can now be submitted on disk or by modem. Other successful systems include the one described above in which reports, text and files are exchanged 'on disk', the method used by the authors, typists and editors of this book to transfer manuscript interstate. The most successful of all, however, is the facsimile transmission, or fax.

Fax systems

The advent of cheap and efficient fax machines is one of the reasons that there is less demand for an electronic mail system. You don't have to type a fax message to get it into the system, and fax machines transmit illustrations, handwritten notes, signatures and the firm's logo as well as words. Fax messages are received automatically, and delivery is confirmed immediately. One other result of this has been the almost total demise of telex as a means of business communication. Telegrams, too, have joined the list of defunct systems.

Standard format and multicopy letters

Standard format (multicopy) messages sent out in their thousands by a business organisation are 'cold'. They must be, because shops, business firms and government departments are 'cold' communicators. They can communicate in the sense of being able to exchange ideas and information, but the firm itself cannot send human messages about feelings or emotions, nor can it say anything believable about caring for people or trusting someone. A business cannot have a warm 'relationship' with people, but its staff can.

Warm, personal messages from one human to another — as distinct from the cold kind — are the ones that determine the success of a business. They are the best messages, through which individual, personal (warm) contact strengthens positive working relationships.

When to use standard format messages

There is a place for mass-produced business messages as long as they are not dressed up as personal letters, and there is no need to do this. Many day-to-day business messages can be quite impersonal without doing any harm as long as the information they contain is appropriate for mass production.

■ Routine notices such as the first reminder of an overdue account can safely be left to a computer, and no one is upset by a rate notice that is not in the form of a nice, warm letter from the Mayor or County Council.

Multicopy-message problems

What does upset people is the mass-produced message dressed up to look like a letter from a human being — the so-called mail-merge letter, in which personal data for thousands of clients are merged with standard paragraphs to produce what at first appears to be a 'letter'. People are inclined to mistrust a message that claims to be what it is not. The mail-merge letter was effective for a while when computers were first used in business, but as a technique it is now rapidly becoming out of date;

be aware of this whenever anyone suggests using a computer to produce fake letters.

Most people can spot a mail-merge letter without opening it, which makes sending it largely a waste of time. Sometimes the data does not even match correctly. In a well-known case, a car-sales letter was supposed to read 'All your friends and neighbours in [insert second line of address here] will envy you when they see you driving a new car from XYZ Motors'. Clients who had something other than a street name as the second line of the address (PO Box 234, perhaps) received some very funny letters!

Making multicopy messages work

Since there is no chance of a 'form' letter ever sounding like a personal one, make it clear from the style and layout of your master that it is *not meant* to be personal. Use a style more like that of a memo. People today appreciate the need for computer-generated reminders; there is no necessity to camouflage them. Adding a signature won't make a multicopy message look like a personal one.

Revise multicopy masters regularly

Take the typical example of a standard account-overdue reminder in which the individual name, address and amount owing are inserted from the computer's data bank. If your firm is spending large amounts of money sending these reminders and your records show that on average it takes four of them to get a reader to settle an account, think of the cost benefit if an improved version could produce a response even 10 per cent better! It would certainly be worthwhile taking several hours to devise even minor improvements, using the guidelines in this chapter and in Chapters 14 and 15.

You do not have to use the same words month after month. Write several different masters and change them around regularly. Spend a few hours every six months checking them all to make sure that the wording is up to date and reflects the current situation. In particular, be careful to remove wording that could appear sexist and any form of persuasion based on negative appeals. Make sure the masters are kept free of jargon and old-fashioned phrasing.

Decide what kind of message will work best

Before you write or transmit any routine or multi-copy message (especially through a computer), make quite sure it does not *need* a personal touch. If it does, forget the mail-merge — write a letter or use the phone. A computer-printed follow-up may, however, be in order.

Consider alternatives

If a personal touch is not needed, there are a number of alternatives that may work better than a computer-typed 'letter'.

- A colourful, preprinted form with only the personal details inserted by the computer is quite satisfactory for many things, from insurance notices to dog licences. It looks far more professional than a plain computer print-out.
- If your intention is to sell something, do it properly. A colour brochure with high-quality illustrations will present a better picture than a computerised letter.
- Use a letter format, but not standard computer type. Have the words printed by a high-quality laser printer, or employ a commercial printing firm. This is appropriate for letters written, for instance, by public figures. No one expects an original, 'one-off' letter from the prime minister — a mass-produced version is understandable and acceptable as long as the quality is top class.

Summary

1. Memos are a vital part of the business communication system, but to be effective they must be short.

2. Use face-to-face language when you write a memo. Long words create neither a good memo nor a good impression. Avoid bureaucratic jargon and the third-person style.

3. Memo-style reports are short (one to three pages). The heading uses a memo format but the remainder, while concise, is similar to an ordinary report.

4. An executive or summary report is a four-to six-page condensation of a much longer document. It is designed to be read by busy executives.

5. Other short reports include variation, implementation, investigative, and routine or seasonal reports.

6. Facsimile systems are so efficient that they have largely superseded earlier forms of electronic mail.

7. External electronic mail systems that require keyboard input and special computer programs appear to be gaining only limited acceptance in Australia. Internal electronic mail, operating on a single computer network, is more popular.

8. There is a place in business for multicopy messages, but do not try to dress them up as personal letters.

9. Consider alternatives to the multicopy, computer-typed 'letter'. A preprinted form or a coloured brochure may be much more satisfactory.

Exercises

1. Collect examples of 'fake' computerised letters. How could they be improved?
   Suggest some more suitable alternatives.

2. Collect and analyse some bureaucratic-sounding memos. Rewrite them so that they are warmer and more personal.

CHAPTER 18

The final polish

Chapters 14 to 17 covered the everyday aspects of writing letters, memos and reports using the four-stage writing method. At the end of the fourth stage, however, you can add 'polish'; this includes developing continuity and cohesion, two factors that readers look for in high-quality writing. Reducing the fog level increases readability. Polishing can also include adapting your own or others' writing to fit the needs of special readers.

Polishing your writing can be enjoyable, and it is only in taking this extra step that you discover your full potential as a writer. Professional writers often spend as much time re-editing and polishing as on any of the other stages.

Topics

Get in the mood

Continuity and cohesion

Reducing the fog level

Tailor writing to fit

Adapting other writers' text

Quotes, references and acknowledgments

Get in the mood

A constructive but critical approach puts you in the right mood for making improvements. Avoid the (natural) tendency to justify your work as it stands.

- Work quickly. Don't spend too much time considering each change.
- Experiment. You still have your previous version if the trial doesn't work out.
- Be self-critical. Every writer has weak points he or she is not aware of. If you can discover yours, you can learn to overcome them.

- Let others read your draft, and welcome their reactions. The faults you miss are the ones only they can tell you about.
- Work with one aspect in mind at a time (for instance, continuity). If you try to cover everything from grammar to discrimination at one sitting, you'll lose concentration.

If you have the time, put the work aside for a day, a week, or longer. This makes it easier to notice the rough spots. They won't have been evident before because you were so closely involved with the writing process. People who leave writing until the last minute miss the opportunity to take this step, and the quality of their work suffers.

'Sleep on it' overnight if you don't have more time. You will still find you can make improvements, almost automatically. Although you haven't given any conscious thought to the topic, your mind will have been working on it.

Continuity and cohesion

Continuity

A paragraph is a cluster of related ideas, but it has no fixed length. It can contain one or many sentences, provided they all deal with the same topic. In a well-written paragraph, ideas follow one another smoothly and sequentially, without gaps or sudden jumps, so that the paragraph communicates a sense of wholeness to the reader. That's what is meant by 'continuity'.

Topic sentences

Start a paragraph with a key idea or a 'topic' sentence. The best opening sentences are usually positive, and deal with actions rather than reasons. This helps the reader focus on your thoughts and see where your ideas are heading.

Alternative openings

The opening statement does not always have to be about action; it really depends on how you want to involve the reader. Start with a direct or active statement if you are providing information or giving advice. Finish with an active sentence if you want to be more persuasive; your reader will have had more time to become involved in the fabric of your thoughts.

Example A: Active 'topic' sentence
Adopt a positive attitude before you begin to write. For many people, negative thoughts are distracting and reduce their ability to think cre-atively. This makes the task more difficult.

Example B: Action at end of paragraph
For some people writing is seen as a difficult task. This negative attitude is distracting and reduces their ability to think creatively. Before you begin to write, always adopt a positive attitude.

Body of the paragraph

Follow the opening with associated ideas, but position points carefully — like a set of building blocks, each one maintaining a logical relation to the next. Each of the body sentences should support (or relate to) your opening statement; the paragraph structure will then reflect order and unity. If you need to make a negative comment it's best placed here (in the middle) rather than at either end. The final sentence should add a sense of completion.

Ending a paragraph

In deciding *when* to end a paragraph, ask yourself 'Does the next sentence relate to this topic or to a new one?' If it's a new topic, start a new paragraph.

Paragraph structure

1. **Heading** — label or signpost pointing to contents of paragraph
2. **Topic sentence** — main idea (active and positive)
3. Secondary topics, associated with main idea
4. Evidence or argument to support main idea
5. Any negative aspect related to the main idea
6. **Last sentence** — closing thought, a sense of finality
7. Blank line before new paragraph

Keep paragraphs apart

For business readers a document with pages of unbroken text, without divisions and subheadings, will fail to hold their attention. Concentration is harder, their eyes wander, they may lose the place. Each of the following methods helps to avoid this.

Blank lines

Give readers time to relax. A blank line following a paragraph invites the reader to rest. It's a non-verbal signal that the topic has been dealt with and it's time to move to a fresh one — either related to the last paragraph or in contrast to it, but in any case something new or different.

Numbered headings

Headings point the way to better organisation. Numbering adds to the sense of structure. As the heading separates one paragraph from the next, it also helps summarise the contents.

Unity (cohesion)

To achieve unity is to tie all parts of a work together as a complete package — to arrange each section so that it links up with the next. This gives your writing direction and emphasis.

Well-organised writing increases clarity and understanding; disjointed writing can be boring, confusing or irritating. Here's an example of an assignment that lacks unity — the ideas jump around too much. There is obviously a broad link-up, but the writer's thoughts need to be rearranged.

Double agents forced to choose sides

Many buyers forget that changing homes every few years can be a costly exercise. Instead, an expert buying agent could have made sure that the home chosen would have been suitable for many years ahead. Australians are not used to paying commission when they purchase a property as well as when they sell. But all that is set to change.

The real estate industry has always had problems with agencies which act for both buyer and seller. It's like the same lawyer acting for the defendant and the plaintiff. But agents are now finding that buyers are refusing to deal with them at all unless they can guarantee that they are acting exclusively and not for the seller as well.

European buyers normally leave the work of bargaining to a paid agent. In Australia the practice is becoming much more popular. The cost of exclusive buying agency services is about 1 per cent of the purchase cost, but if you can get the agent to negotiate a matching reduction in the price then the service costs nothing.

A vendor in New South Wales recently advertised a commercial building for rent and received over twenty offers from agents of this kind. Large companies facing a move often have a special team that looks after locating and finding the best accommodation deals.

When people read something like this, the author as well as the article may be downgraded. 'If the writer's thinking is so disorganised, he or she obviously doesn't understand the subject.' This is a natural reaction, but not necessarily correct. The problem may be a lack of cohesion that could be solved by a few minutes' work getting the ideas in the right order.

Improving unity and cohesion — guidelines

1. Arrange ideas in an obvious pattern (past, present, future or A, B, C, D).

2. Keep similar or related topics together.

3. Different or unrelated topics must be separated.

4. Use numbered headings.
In the assignment on real estate, one or two headings would have shown up the lack of continuity. Writing out a list of headings like a table of contents or outline (see Chapter 14, page 145) also helps show if topics are in the best sequence.

5. Use a title that reflects the main theme.
The title in the example refers to double agents. It sounds colourful, but the double-agent issue has little to do with the central topic.

6. If an item is irrelevant, remove it altogether.
The last point, 'Large companies facing a move often ...' really has little to do with the topic. It distracts the reader.

7. Ask others to read your work.
They can tell you if the sequence is clear to them. If it is not, rearrange the work.

8. Give strong points priority over weak ones.
The point about agents having to act only for buyer or seller could be a good one to end with, but at the beginning of the main paragraph it draws attention away from the central topic.

9. Use connecting links.
Connections may be obvious to you, but may not be as clear to others who are seeing your message for the first time. Outline the purpose of moving from A to B and then to C.

10. Explain the relationship between topics.
Use connecting words like 'however', 'therefore', 'on the other hand', 'in contrast' and so on to connect ideas in one paragraph with those that follow. If necessary, add a short linking sentence to emphasise the connection. See how the paragraph

in italics connects the two in the example below (taken from 'Double agents forced to choose sides').

> ... unless they can guarantee that they are acting exclusively and not for the seller as well. *A more practical solution already well established overseas is to employ a separate agency that handles buying only and is paid on a commission basis.*
>
> European buyers normally leave the work of bargaining to a paid agent. In Australia the practice is becoming much more popular. A vendor ...

Reducing the fog level

Shakespeare, Churchill and Einstein expressed their most important ideas very clearly in short words and simple sentences. So can you, if you follow the old KISS formula:

'Keep It Simple for Success'

Aim for the 'ordinary reader', your average customer, client or employee rather than the specialist. If your only reason for using 'intellectual' language is to sound intellectual, you are wasting the reader's time. The best business writing is crisp and precise, and uses the same kind of language as one would use in a face-to-face conversation.

How many of your readers are experts in English? How many speak it only as a second language? No matter how much you want to use that long technical word, no matter how much you feel that a few intellectual-sounding phrases would help emphasise your point, *remove* them as part of your final polish.

Readability and 'fogging'

Business people are busy people. Writers who use too much complex grammar, overlong sentences and multisyllable words are in danger of leading their readers into a situation known as 'fogging', a dulling of the reader's senses caused by excessive use of

- long sentences
- long words
- negative words
- abstract or 'hard to picture' words

When all four occur together, the combination overloads the reader's thinking processes, as the following example demonstrates.

> It is not *impossible* that a *relatively* danger free *nuclear* power *generator* can be *developed* in the not *unforeseeable* future. (20 words) *However* as a *consequence* of the 1986 Chernobyl *disaster*, even the most *enthusiastic* and *dedicated* supporters of the *concept* of *nuclear energy production* find *themselves* unable to deny that at the present time there remains the *continued probability* of *accidental radioactive contamination*. (42 words)
> It is therefore *understandable* that a *considerable proportion* of Australia's *population* remains *antagonistic* towards the *excavation* of our *national uranium* reserves. (21 words) It is claimed by such persons that *minimising* the mining of *uranium* provides the only *possible* way to *negate* the danger of *nuclear pollution* and *ensure* our future *survival*. (29 words)

Measuring fog levels

Check your own fog-levels regularly, but don't rely on reading by itself. You may not notice fog in your own writing as easily as in other people's. Some word processors have a program to measure fog levels as part of their utilities package, but it is quite easy to work it out on paper using the Australian Fog Index (AFI) formula, as explained below.

The AFI is based on an original test developed by an American, Robert Gunning; his 'Gunning Fog Index' is probably the best known in the English-speaking world. The Australian version varies in recognising the fogging power of short, abstract words such as 'enhance' and 'negate', whereas Gunning's test did not count words of less than three syllables.

Reading levels and the AFI

The figure you obtain from the AFI test is at best only a rough guide and is not supposed to be precise. It represents the *approximate* number of years of study or regular reading needed before a person could handle the sample text without becoming 'fogged' or at least losing some degree of understanding. If a text has a fog 'index' of 10, it should be understandable to most readers who completed Year 10 at secondary school.

Testing for fog

To use the AFI test to find the fog level of your writing, take a sample of 200 to 300 words and follow the steps below.

To simplify the explanation, the following symbols are used:

A — total number of words in the extract
B — number of sentences
C — number of fog words
X — average sentence length (words)
Y — percentage of fog words

Step 1
Count the total number of words in the sample (A), and the number of sentences (B). Then count the number of fog words (C).

Fog words include
- any abstract word (see p. 31), regardless of length — for example, 'imply', 'ensure', 'concept', 'improvement';
- negative words of any length, such as 'neglect', 'unfortunate', 'misunderstanding', 'unforeseeable';
- other words, whether concrete or abstract, of three or more syllables — for example, 'del-e-gate', 'com-pos-it-ion', 'co-ord-in-ating'.

Most long words are also abstract, but multi-syllable words built up from short ones — such as 'rapidly', 'reducing' or 'deleted' — are easy to decode, so don't count them. Actual names, in this case 'Chernobyl' and 'Australia', are not fog words for the same reason.

The following figures refer to the passage above about uranium mining.
A = 112 (words in passage)

B = 4 (sentences)
C = 37 (fog words, in italics)

Step 2

To calculate X, divide A by B:
112 ÷ 4 = 28 (X)

Step 3

To calculate Y, divide C by A and multiply the answer by 100.
37 ÷ 112 × 100 = 33% (Y)

Step 4

Add X and Y
28 + 33 = 61

Step 5

Divide the sum in step 4 by the conversion figure, which is always the same (3), to give the fog index.
61 ÷ 3 = 20.33
The fog index for this extract is therefore 20.33.

occasional long words, but as long as you follow the guidelines they will not cause fogging. The paragraph in the next example conveys the same meaning as the previous one on uranium mining: notice that some fog words (those in italics) are still used, but they represent only five words out of sixty-eight, (7.3 per cent), and sentence length is down to an average of seventeen words. Also, there is less emphasis on the negative. As a result, the fog level has been reduced to around 8 AFI. Anyone who spent eight years or more at school (and completed primary school) should be able to read it without feeling 'fogged'.

Safe *atomic* power stations may be built in the future but right now the danger of *accidental* leakage remains. After the 1986 Chernobyl *disaster*, even the strongest supporter of *nuclear* power must admit there are still risks. It is easy to see why so many Australians are still against the mining of our *uranium*. They feel it is safest for everyone if it is left under the ground.

Reducing fog

- Use more full stops. Shortening sentences can cut fog by two, three or four levels. If a sentence contains two ideas, divide them.
- If you need to use a long sentence (thirty or more words), follow it with a short one.
- Use shorter words.
- Use direct, specific (concrete) words, the kind that readers find easy to picture.
- When using long words (three or more syllables), put them in short sentences or surround them with short words.
- If you use an abstract (hard to picture) word, add a short example or explanation to clarify the meaning, as this paragraph does to explain 'abstract'.
- Use direct, positive statements in place of abstract and/or negative ones.
- Use shorter paragraphs.

Using long words effectively

It would be impossible to write about most business topics without using some abstract terms and the

Tailoring writing to fit

Tailoring writing can add significantly to its power and its ability to overcome reader resistance.

Increase the 'you' attitude

Make sure you have maintained the approach known as the 'you' attitude, particularly when polishing business letters. This conveys a sense of partnership; it reflects a special interest in the person you are writing to and recognises that person as an individual.

- Describe the situation as the reader would see it: 'Repair of your toaster' rather than 'Customer complaint No. 765432'.
- Tell readers all they need to know. Leaving out essential details suggests a lack of 'you' attitude. When writing a repeat order, for instance, restate the details of item type and quantities required rather than 'Send a further shipment as previously'.
- Use an adult-to-adult style rather than a critical or parent tone.

- Use words and sentences that match the reader's level of understanding.
- Maintain a balanced you:us ratio as explained in Chapter 14. A good ratio is at least one positive 'you' word for each 'me' word, but with practice it is quite easy to do even better.
- Avoid talking too much about yourself.

Notice that strengthening the 'you' attitude requires more than simply using the word 'you' a few extra times, or sounding polite and courteous.

Build credibility

To gain credibility as a writer, your ideas must appear believable to the people whose support you seek. To test credibility, examine what you have written from the point of view of someone who may question your argument.

- Is there enough supporting evidence to back up key points? If so, is it fully referenced? Failure to acknowledge the source of important facts suggests doubt on your part.
- Have you used enough pictures, graphs, tables and diagrams to make the essential data not only clear and convincing, but interesting?
- Would any information be more believable if presented numerically rather than in words?
- Will the non-verbal parts of your message support what you have written? Readers love to put their own interpretation on hidden meanings, so check non-verbal content just as carefully as words and grammar.
- Are there any emotional claims that suggest bias? Are there negative statements that would sound more acceptable rephrased in positive terms, as explained in Chapter 15 (p. 165)?

Is your reader visual, aural or tactile?

Have you used words that tie in with this particular reader's way of looking at the world? Chapter 4 explained how you and your readers can differ in this regard.

- Have your words painted the picture clearly enough for the visual reader? Are your pages set out attractively, with headings and subheadings to help guide both visual and tactile readers?
- Aural readers understand more when you write as though you were talking to them. Do your words have this face-to-face sound?

- Relationships are critical for the tactile reader. Have you referred positively to the two-way relationship between you? Tactile readers also react favourably to writing that talks about getting things done, or 'delivering the goods'. Does your action ending reflect this?

When you need to cater for a number of different readers, include a mixture of visual, aural and tactile appeals. Watch for a tendency to overuse your own style, which naturally you prefer, but which — just as naturally — your readers may not.

Use the RIPPA formula

The RIPPA formula lists five essential topics that you need to cover in most business communication. Use it as a further check in polishing your message.

The relationship

Will this letter (or report or memo) have a positive effect on your business relationship? If the reason you are writing about an overdue account is to maintain a sound business relationship with a valued client, is that the point you have emphasised? Or have you ignored the relationship and mentioned only the outstanding debt?

Exchanging information

Have you included the right kinds of information? Have you given too much or too little?

Point-by-point persuasion

If you are writing in order to gain agreement, have you highlighted points that will appeal to the specific reader?

Paint a clear picture

Will the reader be able to see clearly what you want? Have you used white space, graphics and illustrations to ensure visual appeal?

Getting action

Have you described the action you want in clear, straightforward terms? Have you asked for feedback in the form of a reply or confirmation? Have you told the reader how to let you know that the action has been carried through?

Adapting other writers' text

If you can polish your own writing, you can also improve material written by others. There are many occasions when writers need to take this approach.

- The language may be too dull or long-winded.
- An overseas writer's use of technical terms may need 'translating' into a form familiar to Australian readers.
- You may not agree with the original but want to discuss it, or to contrast its ideas with new and different ones of your own.
- You may want to add your own explanations and examples to increase its value for your particular group of readers.

Whatever the reason, adaptations along these lines are valid and professional forms of writing, provided you acknowledge the original. Here's an example of rewriting. The original is an extract from an academic paper.

Industrial Relations — The Scope for Reform

Any reform of the industrial relations system will need to address the traditional relationship of manager to employee with the expectation that this will lead to the development of a more participative environment directed at improving competitiveness as well as a more rational balance of power between these two groups and at the same time moving the system closer to a point where it has the flexibility to meet specific employee needs at an industry or enterprise level.

After rewriting to reduce the fog and improve the continuity, your version might read like this:

Industrial Relations — the Future

Reforming Australia's industrial relations system must consider three important changes in the traditional relationship between manager and employee:

1. developing a more participative, shared relationship that will help the firm to compete successfully in business;

2. developing a sensible balance of power between the two groups;

3. at the same time increasing the flexibility of the industrial relations system so that it can meet individual employee needs at every level.

When you adapt someone else's work in this way, make it clear that your ideas were based in part on the original work, or influenced by it. You can do this either in your introduction, in a list of acknowledgments at the end, or by using the original title as part of your own: 'A Program for Reforming Australian Industrial Relations' [original title]: Notes on Dr S. Graves' talk to the ASM Conference, Hobart, 1991, by [your name].

If you quote extracts word-for-word from the original, put them in inverted commas to indicate this and acknowledge them.

If rewording a specialist's opinion, use indirect language. The original writer might have said, 'As an expert, I believe that . . .'. In your revision, say 'Dr Graves, an expert on the topic, believes that . . .'.

Although there is no copyright on ideas as such (only on the method and the specific words used to express them), if you plan to rewrite and change someone's material it's good manners to contact the author and ask permission.

Quotes, references and acknowledgments

Referencing information

If you want people to support your reasoning, it is important to tell them where you obtained your information. In particular, numeric data such as statistics or accounting figures need a source reference. Even if you don't have a well-known 'name' to quote as your source — for instance, if the data were obtained through personal observation by your own team — identify the people involved and state their qualifications. Helping readers who doubt your data (or your quotes) to locate the primary source increases their confidence in what you are saying. If they need reassurance that your facts or figures are correct, they can check for themselves.

Quotes and acknowledgments

Whenever you quote from any source, include a clear and obvious acknowledgment. Give readers all the information they need to locate the original. You can do this in one of three ways:

- full reference in body text;
- reference to title and year of publication only;
- footnote references.

Direct reference in text

Giving the full reference in the body of the text is the simplest and fastest form of acknowledgment. Use this method for ordinary business reports and submissions in which you are using few quotes or want to maintain an informal tone.

> Peters and Waterman (*In Search of Excellence*, Harper & Row, NY, 1984) say that in the USA participative management schemes offer the best means of encouraging employees to strive towards higher standards in client service (Aust. edn, Ch. 5, p. 87).

Note that as well as the author and title, the reference includes the year and the country in which the book was published. The chapter number and page references are optional, but helpful. If you know a particular reader needs only a basic reference, just give the author and title, without publication details, as in this example:

> Ron and Dianne Baldwin, in *The Export Credits Plan*, take a more positive view. They say that once Australia's trade ratio comes into balance, the nation will have one of the most open economies in the world.

Reference to author and year only

In academic writing people tend to use far more references per page. Direct referencing as used above would break the flow of ideas, and would waste space if you quoted from the same source several times on each page. So only the author's surname and year of publication are given in the text body and the reader is expected to refer to the bibliography or book list at the end of the document for full details of the source. In the text, all the reader sees is this:

> Peters and Waterman (1984) say that in the USA positive rewards motivate employees more than threats or punishments. Nutting (1985) agrees that the best way of encouraging Australians to take part in the 'pursuit of excellence' is by praise rather than criticism.

A quote from a well-known authority adds a professional touch to any business writing, particularly where you need to persuade or build agreement. You also strengthen both the quality of your findings and the power of your argument if you quote other books or journals that support your view. A lesser but important reason for acknowledgment is to show that you are not trying to claim the ideas as your own.

The bibliography

A bibliography is a separate unit, at the end of the document. Regardless of the acknowledgment method used, it adds strength to the overall message. All references (including texts from which direct quotes were *not* used) are listed together with authors' surnames in alphabetical order. The author's surname is followed by the title and details about the publisher, and the place and year of publication.

> BIBLIOGRAPHY
> Baldwin, R., *The Export Credits Plan: Let's Tilt the Scales in Australia's Favour*, Leutenegger, Brisbane, 1990.
> Davies, M., Kreis, K., Nutting, J. & Tronc, K., *The Business of Communicating*, 1st edn, McGraw-Hill, Sydney, 1981.
> Himstreet W. & Baty, M., *Business Communications*, Wadsworth, Belmont, 1973.
> Nutting, R.E., *Skills for Positive Living*, Pitman, Sydney, 1985.
> Peters, T.J. & Waterman, R.H., *In Search of Excellence*, Harper & Row (Aust. edn), Sydney, 1984.

There are special rules that apply to setting out bibliography material in academic or high-level reports, but for ordinary business purposes clarity and ease of understanding are the main criteria.

Footnote references

Footnotes are a less effective way of referencing, but some organisations prefer the method in formal documents. The quotation or information referred to is numbered in the body of the report, and the full reference is listed under a matching number at the foot of the same page. The reader has to locate the matching number to obtain full reference details.

Other acknowledgments

It is in order to make a formal acknowledgment of special assistance given to you in writing a report or submission, particularly help in obtaining information or data. The acknowledgment, however, should be low-key and formal. Unlike a reference, it usually goes at the end of the document unless the people named are important public figures, in which case acknowledgment might be better at the beginning (usually after the contents page).

Make sure that you spell the names of people correctly. In business writing it is usually not appropriate to acknowledge the help of your own family, but do thank team-mates, fellow workers and supervisors if they gave valuable assistance. If family members gave professional help, acknowledge them by name, but not as 'my husband' or 'my children'.

Summary

1. The more critical an approach you take to your written work, the more your writing improves.

2. Continuity and cohesion are a sign of high-quality writing. Make sure ideas follow one another in order without gaps or jumps.

3. Your most important ideas can be expressed clearly in short, simple words.

4. The fewer abstract words you use (and the shorter they are), the better your writing will be.

5. If you must use long words (three or more syllables), put them in short sentences or surround them with short words.

6. When referencing or acknowledging, give readers all the information they need in order to find the original. As well as author, title and publisher, it helps to include year of publication and edition (Australian or overseas). Chapter numbers and page numbers are a help, too.

7. For business reports and submissions, a direct reference in the body of the text is more help than footnotes or a reading list separated from the item being quoted.

Exercises

1. What are 'abstract' words and why do they cause reading problems?

2. What are the causes of 'fogging'? What are some guidelines for reducing 'fog' levels?

3. Take a sample of 300 to 350 words of your own writing. Use the AFI fog test to measure the fog level.

4. Rewrite the example on page 213 about real estate agents. In particular, aim to develop continuity and cohesion. Use headings and other techniques suggested in this chapter, and give the extract a new title.

5. When polishing your writing, how can you use the RIPPA formula to make sure you have covered all important points?

6. List some guidelines for tailoring writing to fit the needs of a special reader.

7. List some guidelines for adapting another writer's text so that you can include it in your own.

8. Reword the following paragraphs to improve style and clarity, and to remove errors. You can change any or all of the original words as long as your version conveys the same meaning. It must be positive, active, free of jargon and shorter than the original.

(a) We beg to acknowledge your favour of the 15th of this month confirming your order. We are pleased to advice that same will be processed by us immediately and dispatched to you this day by rail transport.

(b) We are sorry to advise that unless you pay your long overdue account by next Friday we will be forced to withdraw your operating privileges.

(c) To avoid delays, please note that payment should not be made other than in cash since certain alternative methods can result in hold-ups.

(d) In reference to your recent telephonic request to the writer concerning your Austudy application, we are pleased to confirm that you was a full time employee of this establishment from 1 June to 30 December 1988. This is hereby confirmed in writing.

Pls settle other pay your long overdue by next Friday

CHAPTER 19

Technical writing

This chapter is about keeping things simple in an area noted for complexity and confusion; it explains how to make your technical writing clear, concise and helpful so that people can look forward to reading it. Instruction books and employee manuals, for example, need *not* be hard to follow.

Round holes — or circular orifices?

Some people who write on mechanical and scientific topics love jargon. They would prefer to describe a round hole as 'a circular orifice'. Certainly the term 'circular orifice' is accurate and precise, but is it any more so than 'round hole'?

If there is no gain in understanding or accuracy, who do technical writers use complex terms in place of simple ones? Probably because they are following the style used by the technical writers who taught *them*. However, breaking this copy-the-leader cycle is important if your technical writing is to help people rather than impress them with your vocabulary.

Guidelines for technical writing

1. Who are your readers?

What kind of people need to read (and understand) technical writing? Suppose you are writing an instruction manual to accompany a dishwasher. All kinds of people use dishwashers. Give a thought to the variety of individuals your instructions need to cater to: some are young, others old; some are skilled, some awkward with their hands, some good at plumbing and electronics but poor readers, others brilliant at English but hopeless with anything mechanical. In most cases the user is unlikely to be an expert on dishwashers and will know little (if any) dishwasher jargon. To be effective, your instruction manual has to be written to suit people like these.

Suppose, on the other hand, you are writing an academic paper to be presented at the International Teaching Conference of Highly Experienced Experts (ITCHEE). In this case technical language is perhaps appropriate, yet even here it may be out of place. Your highly technical paper may earn you great respect, but if many of the international delegates speak only limited English the content will remain a mystery.

2. Write *for* people rather than *at* them.

A general rule is to imagine a group of your friends, relatives and associates and to pretend that you are writing not a technical article, but some helpful notes for *all* members of this group. Think in their terms rather than in yours. What you put on paper may not be a technical masterpiece, but many people will be able to read it and use its helpful advice.

3. Describe the process step by step, using clear, simple language.

Writing about each step in the correct sequence is harder than you think, so check this carefully. Are you sure you have not left any steps out?

4. If a short, non-technical explanation will do, *don't* go on.

Give enough detail to allow full understanding, but do not include unnecessary technical data. If a

short, non-technical word will do, use it. Instead of writing 'AEU' (air exchanger unit), call it a 'fan'. Ask yourself whether readers need to know the name, purpose and function of each internal part. If a machine will work just as well without users knowing its internal units intimately, why mention them? If you feel some people might need extra details, attach a technical appendix.

5. Identify control items clearly.

Do tell people about controls. But instead of 'Speed may be varied by adjusting the oscillator control', say 'If you want it to go faster or slower, turn the red knob in the front left-hand corner'. If you have to use a technical name, follow it with a non-technical description of what the object looks like and where it is.

6. Stick to one term for each part.

If you do use a technical term, make sure you use the *same* word next time you talk about the object concerned.

7. Use visual explanations as well as words.

Many of your readers will be visual or tactile thinkers (see Chapter 6); for them, words alone are unclear. Add a diagram or a sketch showing the whole unit, with an arrow pointing, for instance, to the red control knob. Label other parts clearly, using the terms you use in the text. Plenty of drawings, photographs and diagrams will make your writing a success where plenty of words alone cannot.

8. Keep visual items and their verbal descriptions together.

Readers need to refer from words to pictures and back again. Keep both on the same page, or on facing pages. If you have to separate them, give page numbers as cross references both in the text and under the picture.

9. Put yourself in the position of the inexperienced user.

Recognise that some features will be so familiar to you that you may forget to include them in your instructions. People new to computers find this a common problem: the manual explains all the complicated procedures, but doesn't cover things such as how to tell which side of an unlabelled disk is 'up'.

Employee handbooks

Take the same helpful approach when writing employee handbooks or instructions. Make sure that the language and terms used are at a level that *all* readers can understand. Write in a direct, conversational style, as though you were sharing useful advice with a colleague. Use the word 'you' regularly; for example: 'If you have any difficulties fitting into the new job, you will find our branch training officer (Debbie Miles) ready and waiting to help'. Compare this with 'The branch training office provides facilities for dealing with those persons who might experience on-the-job problems only'.

Remember that

- the reader is probably a newcomer and will be unfamiliar with many routine procedures, so explain these first;
- beginners need reassurance as well as advice (a good employee manual gives both).

Make sure that words familiar to you can be understood just as easily by an inexperienced reader. If a term is important, explain it carefully.

Using fear or threats as a means of encouraging obedience is counterproductive.

- Limit your use of the directions 'Do not' and 'Never . . .'. If you do use them, explain exactly why the advice is given in such strong terms.

Exaggerating possible risks for the same reason is similarly unwise. If a handbook sounds like a legal manual it will turn people off; in fact, they probably won't read it at all.

Fig. 19.1 *Graphic illustration to suggest, for example, that the number of Australians owning their homes has decreased*

Try your draft manual out on a range of readers, both inexperienced and experienced; a thorough 'road test' is the only realistic guide to how well it will work. Experienced readers may feel you have gone into unnecessary detail, but let the *least* experienced tell you if this is so. The experienced ones can best help you by pointing out technical errors.

Visual and graphic illustrations

Any visual item or any non-verbal material that helps understanding can be termed 'graphic'. Graphs and drawings add appeal to any written or printed page: people not only will understand more, but also will be motivated to keep on reading. Ten thousand years or so in the past people were using pictures on cave walls to record information. Until this century, however, the cost of producing and copying pictures was so high that words and figures were the standard form for storing and exchanging most information. Today it's almost as easy to produce a picture as a page of printed words.

Apart from specific terms describing units of measurement, such as 'dollar' and 'kilogram', words can never create as accurate an understanding as a drawing, a map or a photograph. While they are essential for activities such as selling and negotiating, when it comes to technical details verbal messages are at best a substitute for or an addition to drawings and pictures.

Photographs

Almost any picture lifts the quality of your page, adds eye appeal and attracts attention, but a striking photo (such as in Fig. 19.2) can achieve far more. How much power does this photo add to verbal claims about the strength of these cars? People find it hard to disagree with evidence in front of them. There is no more convincing way to back up an otherwise sound argument.

Place your photo as near as possible to the text it refers to, preferably on the same page, and beside it put a short, descriptive caption, mentioning also the paragraph to which it relates. In the text, mention the photograph as a cross reference.

The best pictures of all are those that move. A video recording gives a report additional credibility

Fig. 19.2 *The Volvo car stack* COMPLIMENTS OF VOLVO AUSTRALIA PTY LTD

that words (or even still photographs) could not convey.

Using graphics

There are many different kinds of graphics and all add to the quality of whatever you are communicating. There is no reason why graphics need to be static, or restricted to the printed page. A series of moving, computer-generated graphs on a screen can add striking and influential meaning to figures you are presenting to a meeting. However, the most common graphics in business are those that appear on paper.

Computer-generated graphics

Most computers can turn tables of figures such as those on page 229 into colourful graphs with minimal effort from the operator. Many programs are available which combine the computer's capacity for converting figures into shapes with the printer's ability to transfer the graph onto paper. This is an important breakthrough, because people with no artistic ability can now turn out highly professional artwork literally overnight.

Graphs

While less detailed than numeric tables, graphs offer a more visible, more interesting and therefore more meaningful comparison of data. There are plenty of different types of graph to choose from, depending on the topic. The best are those — regardless of type — that create their own visual appeal.

Bar graphs

Bar graphs are easy to draw, either by hand or using computer graphics programs. They are useful when you want to compare a number of totals, but little else. Bars can be of the same or of varying widths, or three-dimensional (see Fig. 19.3).

Line graphs

Simple line graphs are nothing more than the result of joining a series of points representing different positions (see Fig. 19.4) or changing situations, such as the rise and fall of the Australian dollar.

Pictorial graphs

When scarce resources (for instance, money) are being shared among a number of groups, a pie graph shows how much of the total 'pie' each one receives. While the round pie with slices radiating from the centre is the most common, the same idea can be used with any shape or object that relates to the topic.

A third kind of pictorial graph uses simple shapes (representing people, cars, ships or similar objects) to illustrate expanding or contracting relationships over a period. For each year, for example, a different-sized symbol is used to illustrate growth or shrinkage. These are among the easiest of all graphics to produce: just select a shape and use a reduction photocopier to make smaller versions until you get all the sizes you need.

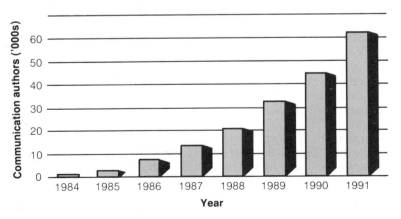

Fig. 19.3 *A bar chart*

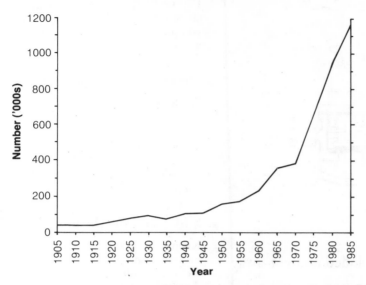

Enrolments in technical education, Australia

Note: The figures from 1965 onwards reflect a major reorganisation of technical education. Prior to 1981 the data relate to gross enrolments. From 1981 the data relate to net students.

Source: Australian Bureau of Statistics, *Year Book Australia 1988*, p. 413

Fig. 19.4 *A simple line graph*

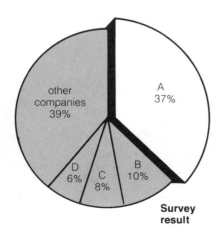

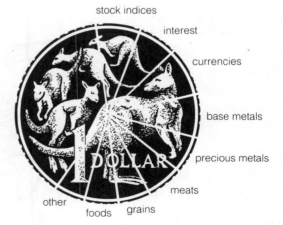

Fig. 19.5 *Two examples of a pie chart*

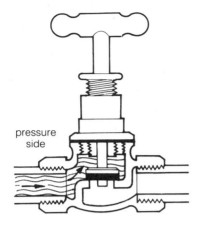

pressure
side

Fig. 19.6 *A cut-away drawing*

Cross-sectional, exploded and cut-away drawings

Cross-section and cut-away diagrams (Fig. 19.6) help readers to see what happens inside a complex object, such as a valve — or the human body. However, they may need to be drawn by an artist, which makes them slower and costlier to produce than other graphics.

Exploded drawings, such as the illustration in Figure 19.7, serve a similar purpose; they help to show how various parts are put together to make a complete unit (and conversely, how to take one apart).

Other graphics and illustrations

While the types described above are the most common, you will find many other ways of illustrating whatever ideas or information you need to share with others. Keep a scrapbook of examples.

Remember that items such as the company logo or trade mark are also an important form of graphic communication.

Slides and overhead transparencies

Keep these in mind when making any kind of visual presentation. Overhead projectors require less technical skill to use than any other projection device. You know the power the projected slide has in helping students to remember important points; there is no reason why you should not use the same power in sales presentations or other face-to-face communication. Computer programs that print lettering in large, bold letters are better than hand-drawing for producing overhead transparencies.

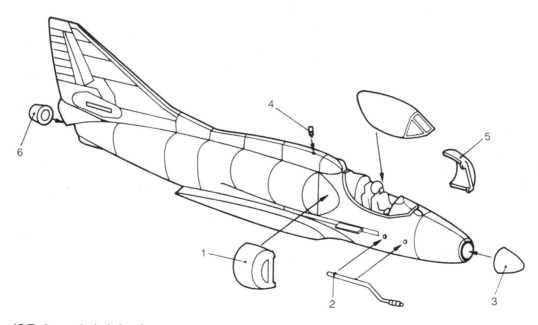

Fig. 19.7 *An exploded drawing*

Table 19.1 *Student enrolments, Roweskamp Community College, autumn semester (Feb.–June) 1992 (classified by age and course)*

Course of study	Under 17	17–21	Over 21	Total enrolment for each course
Degree				
Business	——	219	327	546
Computing	45	326	459	830
Engineering	10	223	351	584
Other courses	——	21	47	68
Subtotal	*55*	*789*	*1184*	*2028*
Diploma				
Accounting	10	119	124	253
Small business	5	24	59	88
Subtotal	*15*	*143*	*183*	*341*
Other courses				
Certificate in office management	1	23	54	78
Introduction to computers	190	727	690	1607
Subtotal	*191*	*750*	*744*	*1685*
Total (all courses)	**261**	**1782**	**2111**	**4154**

Numeric tables

Figures in sentences are hard to follow. Figures in columns are easier to comprehend, and therefore more believable. Numeric tables also make comparisons easier, which aids agreement.

- Use clear labels for each unit in the table and include a title (above the table) or a caption (underneath the table). Choose a title or caption that identifies the content and distinguishes the table from others containing similar data.
- If the content relates to a particular location or period, say so in the title. For example, 'Sales of new vehicles, Darwin, Jan.–June 1991'.
- Even if it means using more space, do not make a table too cramped or figures too small.
- Use headings and subheadings to identify separate units of data.

If you use a computer and spreadsheet or database program to create numeric tables, you can recalculate figures and amend data as new information comes to hand without retyping the whole table. Include all headings and lines as part of the layout on the screen, then print the table as it stands. It is quite acceptable for numeric tables printed in this way to be pasted into the body of a report just as you would add a photograph. Table 19.1 is an example.

A thin, ruled line around the outside of any list of tables or figures can add a professional appearance to a business report. Vertical lines and horizontal lines inside the box help to identify main divisions, but don't overdo them. A useful trick to get every line to run square with the text is to type horizontal lines initially as a set of hyphens:

To keep vertical lines square, just place a ruler beside two vertically aligned hyphens. Then rule over the hyphens to complete the horizontal lines. Use white-out to cover excess lines at the corners.

Summary

1. When writing on technical topics, write *for* people rather than *at* them.

2. Give enough detail to allow full understanding, but if possible avoid technical names for parts or processes.

3. If you do use a technical term, make sure you use the *same* one next time you refer to the object concerned.

4. Technical topics need a visual key to connect words and ideas. Use visual material to support your verbal message.

5. Some features of a topic will be so familiar to you that you may forget to include them in your instructions. Check with a reader inexperienced in the topic to make sure you don't leave out simple yet vital material.

6. Limit use of the instructions 'Do not . . .' and 'Never . . .'. If you do use them, explain exactly why the advice is given in such strong terms.

7. Place photos as near as possible to the text they refer to, preferably on the same page.

8. Though less detailed than figures, graphs offer more interesting and therefore more meaningful comparisons. They also add eye appeal to a page.

9. Choose whatever style of graph best illustrates the ideas or information you want to share. Keep a scrapbook of sample styles as part of your technical writing kit.

10. Figures in a table are easy to keep track of, easier to understand and more believable than figures in sentences. They also make comparisons easier, which aids agreement.

11. Just a thin ruled line (a box) around the outside of any list of tables or figures can add a professional touch. Vertical and horizontal lines inside the box help too.

Exercises

1. Think of an everyday object — a torch, can-opener, trouser belt, fishing rod, mirror, razor or weighing machine. Write a short set of instructions for a person who has never seen or used the object and who speaks only limited English.

2. Imagine the same person asking for written instructions on how to use *one* of the following: a personal computer (not yet plugged into the power system); the disk format program in that computer; an adjustable office-chair; a fishing rod with casting reel. Write suitable instructions for operating it.

3. Explain (orally or in writing) the steps involved in locating this book in a library and borrowing it.

4. Take an instruction manual on operating any familiar unit of equipment. List (from a communication point of view) its good and bad points.

5. Write a shorter and improved version of the manual.

6. Select a technical article from a newspaper or magazine that you feel fails to communicate its message clearly. Rewrite it in a more suitable form.

7. Prepare a collection of graphs from current newspapers and magazines to illustrate the variety of styles used to communicate information.

8. Find one or more graphs that appear to use intentional distortion to present a biased view of information.

9. List some of the guidelines for clear technical writing.

CHAPTER 20

Summarising and condensing

A summary takes less time to read than the original, so more people read it. As well as highlighting important ideas, it helps to create interest in the book, report or article that it summarises. An effective summary should arouse interest to the point at which a reader will want to find out more about the topic and may even want to read the full-length version from which your summary was condensed.

Topics

Different kinds of summaries

Summarise ideas — not words

Executive or summary reports

Different kinds of summaries

The topic, the type of material, the target reader and the amount of time that reader will have available all help to determine what kind of summary will be most effective.

- **Synopsis**
  This is a short outline of a quarter to half a page at the beginning of a much longer document such as a report, a submission or a book. It provides an overview (and sometimes one or two samples of the most interesting points) to create interest in the main document.

- **Abstract**
  A very short summary of fifty to 150 words for use in a reading list or database, this contains little information but identifies the type of material in the original document.

- **Executive summary or executive report**
  This is a condensation of two to six pages that is meant to be read *instead of* a longer document, such as a full report. The aim is to make vital information accessible to busy executives who haven't time to read the full version. Some data is missed, but the important ideas get through to key people.

- **Non-technical summary**
  This condensed version provides an easy-to-read outline of a technical document.

- **Summary extract**
  A precis of bulky information, this is useful when only parts of the original document are relevant.

- **Condensation**
  In this less drastic form of reduction, far more of the original material is retained. Condensing or shortening written material to fit a time limit or a set number of words might require a 15 or 20 per cent reduction.

- **Business summary**
  This is a more drastic reduction than a condensation. In business you often find that a summary of a 10 000-word document is expected not to exceed 200 words.

Summarise ideas — not words

Writing a business summary requires techniques quite different from those used in condensing. They are based on one simple principle: 'Summarise *ideas* instead of *words*'. This allows you to make a summary as long or as short as you need to. The worked example (pp. 233−5) shows how a news article of 860 words is reduced first to 150 words, then to a synopsis of forty-five words. Summarising is easier if you follow a sequence of six steps.

Summarising — step by step

1. Read and comprehend.

If you need to summarise another person's work, then thorough reading — and comprehension — is the starting point from which to determine the writer's purpose. (See Chapter 9 for detailed guidelines on reading comprehension.) If you are summarising your own material, skip this step (unless you are unclear about your own purpose!).

2. Ignore or discard sections not worth summarising.

If any part of the text displays the following characteristics, there is no point in summarising it.

- Low credibility: if you are condensing another writer's material, this may get rid of a large proportion of it immediately. If you are summarising your own work, you should have edited it to remove any such material already.
- Overly emotional or dramatic wording: the more emotional the tone of any item, the less it warrants any place in a summary.
- Unimportant, unnecessary or irrelevant items: ask 'Will this idea seem at all important to the reader?'. If it will not, don't summarise it.
- Generalisations and exaggerations: ideas that are vague, non-specific or overstated are not important enough to summarise.
- Examples and explanations: examples help to explain and reinforce important ideas but seldom need to be included in a summary, although the 'ideas' they illustrate may be important (see step 3).
- Topics of no interest to summary readers: be firm and critical. Throwing out ideas or information of interest to *you* may be hard, but you cannot create an effective summary until you do it.

3. Make a 'rough' list of significant or key ideas.

This is the heart of successful summarising. Do not use complete sentences; just note each point as

briefly as possible in the shortest words you can think of. Try not to use words or phrases from the original text. The order of ideas is not important at this stage; just get them on paper. Identifying key ideas is largely a matter of common sense, but there are signposts that point to them.

- Can the idea be expressed in a few short words? The *more words* taken to describe it, the *less chance* there is that it is really important!
- Is an idea mentioned several times? The more often a topic appears, the stronger is the chance that it should be recorded. To save words, try to combine the different references into one short point.
- A key idea is often compared or contrasted with opposing ideas: management/workers, low cost/ high quality, negative/positive, fast/slow, recent/out of date, and so on. The points being compared may be side by side, but may just as often be in different parts of the text.
- Ideas illustrated by examples are usually key ideas. If you see an example being given, look for the key idea behind it.
- Numbers are often used to express key ideas. Usually you need to summarise the numbers too, giving only totals. (Some numerical data may represent only examples or illustrations.)
- Often the final paragraph is itself a summary.

Discard any material that fails to qualify as a key idea. You'll notice how quickly this cuts down the length when you read the worked example on page 235.

Valuable data that *some* people may want to read need not be totally discarded. Sections from a lengthy report (or the whole report) can be retained in separate folders or as appendixes so that specialist and technical readers can refer to the details if they hold special interest.

4. Begin with a rough draft.

No one can write the best summary straight off. Arrange the most significant ideas at the top, but don't worry about getting the lesser ones in order. The least important will be discarded in the final trimming, anyhow.

5. Calculate how many ideas will fit into the final version.

Assume that it takes thirty-five to forty words (two or three sentences) to describe each idea. Divide the required word length of the summary (for example, 200) by forty to find out how many ideas you can include. Then calculate the number of words in your draft. To do this, count the words in five average lines and divide the result by five to get an average number of words per line. Then multiply that number by the total number of lines in the draft. This will tell you how many ideas you still have to discard (or combine) to get down to the limit.

6. Prepare the final summary.

The following points are all helpful in reducing the length and completing the summary.

- If a word can replace a phrase, use it. If a phrase can replace a sentence, let it.
- If you have to discard more ideas, it is easier to decide what must be left out than to choose what must stay in.
- At this point, start writing full sentences. Aim for

a style that is smooth-flowing and concise, but not too abrupt.

- If summarising someone else's writing, make sure the original purpose (as well as the meaning) is still reflected in your summary.

In a summary of more than half a page, do use some headings. (They take up extra lines, but add few extra words.) If it is intended for business readers, headings are vital to prevent your 250-word summary from looking like a 250-word essay.

Using sentences from original text

Whole sentences 'lifted' (without summarising) out of the original text won't fit the short, sharp style of the summary. Sometimes a special phrase or technical description must be copied word for word, but only as a last resort.

Case study: Writing a summary and a synopsis

Aim

1. To illustrate the process of selecting key ideas and the way in which these are used to write a summary of 140–150 words of an article of some 860 words.

2. To write a synopsis of forty-five words of the same article.

Step 1: Read and comprehend the original.

This article is the one you read previously in Chapter 9. Read it again, using the steps for comprehension listed in that chapter. You cannot summarise a passage until you are sure that you understand it.

Youth and Unemployment in Australia

A generation of young Australians is growing up with many of its age-group unable to find work. The total number of 15- to 18-year-old school-leavers looking for full-time work represents 18.7 per cent of that age bracket. They make up more than a third of the total number of unemployed and face an average wait of five months after leaving school before they find some form of part-time employment. Many have yet to work in any kind of full-time job and a percentage have been out of work for longer than a year.

Some stay at school until a job comes along, even though they would rather be in work. Some have given up looking for work altogether and adjusted their lifestyles to the point where they seem able to exist for ever on unemployment benefits. Some become involved in voluntary community work in return for meals and hand-outs. Even those who study and gain qualifications are not immune. There are cases where young graduate scientists are

working as gardeners, while qualified accountants sell ice-cream.

As the average length of time out of work increases (along with the number looking for jobs), it becomes progressively harder to motivate the young unemployed to keep on looking for work. Today, thousands of young Australians seek apprenticeships unsuccessfully; that means there will be a chronic shortage of trade technicians during the 1990s and beyond.

Experts cite many causes of unemployment. Inflation and economic recession have reduced the opportunity of industrial expansion in areas which would have absorbed large numbers of workers. Some blame increased unemployment on the high birth rate of the 1960s and the consequent spill into the workforce of larger numbers of young people. Many see technology, particularly computerisation, intruding into a widening area, particularly in offices and retailing. As the school leaving age increases, many employers argue that this actually reduces the employability of school-leavers when they enter the workforce at a later age but with no work experience.

Speaking at a Youth Employment seminar in Sydney last week, Australian Consolidated Credit's National Manager (Dr Lyn Baldwin) told participants that the problem of youth unemployment had two important contributing factors.

'Current wage scales for juniors act against school-leavers gaining employment', Dr Baldwin said. 'The pattern of most awards was established many years ago when most young people left school at the age of 14 or 15 and had some years of work experience by the time they turned 18 or 19. Juniors at that time received a low rate of pay for a start, but by the time they reached 19 the gap between their pay and the adult wage was quite small. Their work experience made them worth their increased pay rate. Today young people enter the workforce at 18 with no experience, yet expect to start on high rates of pay.'

But the main cause of youth unemployment, according to Dr Baldwin, is the increased participation of mature-age women in the workforce. 'This', said Dr Baldwin, 'is the most significant change in employment patterns in the last thirty years'. Dr Baldwin quoted Australian Bureau of Statistics figures to show that mature-age women now occupy 27 per cent of jobs which at one time would have been reserved for juniors. Women are often preferred to juniors because of their training and work experience. They are also more stable as long-term employees. 'Remedies are not easy', Dr Baldwin said. 'It is naive to think of reducing the wage levels of juniors to give them an economic advantage in the job market. This ignores the realities of the industrial relations system. It is illegal to discriminate against women in terms of employment and it would be against Australia's best interests socially and economically to discourage women from maintaining their present role in the workforce.'

National TAFE Research Officer Pat McPhee, who also spoke at the seminar, said planning was going on continuously to find new ways to ease youth unemployment. Additional emphasis was being placed on the problems experienced by students in handling the transition from school to work. Schemes that enabled students to gain work experience while they were still at school had been partly successful, but by far the best results had come from TAFE programs that focused on giving school-leavers the practical skills they needed to get jobs.

Other suggested solutions include government- and industry-funded traineeships, and a modernised apprenticeship system for the skilled trades. Greater emphasis is now being placed on compulsory community service for those on unemployment benefits or not undertaking full-time study, to help them maintain their working skills and avoid the negative stigma (often associated with unemployed youth) of having no useful role in the community.

Adapted with permission from an article originally published in the *Courier Mail*, Brisbane.

Step 2: Discard all unnecessary material.

Delete as much as possible, including all items with the following qualities:

- low credibility — '... able to exist for ever on unemployment benefits';
- dramatic, emotional or exaggerated claims — 'A whole generation of young Australians ...'.
- irrelevant or unnecessary illustrations — 'graduate scientists work as gardeners ... accountants sell ice-cream' (the article is about 15- to 19-year-olds, not university graduates);
- stating the obvious — 'Remedies are not easy', 'planning goes on continuously ...';
- descriptions of no special interest — 'at a Youth Employment seminar in Sydney last week'.

Step 3: Make a 'rough' list of significant or key ideas.

Read through what is left of the article and select the key ideas.

- Combine similar ideas from different parts of the article.
- Make brief notes of long, wordy sections.
- If you notice repetition or duplication of key ideas, record each once only — for example, *women in workforce* and *lack of work experience as an employment barrier* are mentioned in several places.
- Condense detailed examples. Paragraph 1 is full of statistical data on youth unemployment. All your draft note need say is 'One-fifth of 15 to 18-year-olds out of work, one-third of all Aust. unemployed'.

When you have finished, your rough notes should look something like those below. Notice how sentences have been shortened and words changed from the original.

1. Many young Australians unable to find work.
2. Some take jobs below their qualifications, some stay at school.
3. Fewer jobs now for apprentices means future shortages in skilled trades.
4. Causes include economic problems (inflation and recession), increased number of births in the 1960–70 period, more computers, mechanisation and technology replacing manual labour, high wage-scales for juniors, increasing number of women in jobs.
5. One-fifth of the 15–18 age group out of work, that is one-third of all unemployed.
6. Some have never had full-time jobs.
7. Longer the time out of work the less motivation to look for it.
8. Solutions: combination of programs including work experience schemes for high-school students, government- and industry-funded traineeships, modernised courses for skilled apprentices, special TAFE short courses to build work skills, compulsory community service for those on dole.
9. Voluntary groups try to help, but not much success.

Step 4: Count words.

What is the maximum length of your final summary to be? If it takes between thirty and fifty words to summarise each idea selected you know you have room for only three or four ideas, so keep on discarding and combining ideas until you have the right number.

Step 5: Write a rough draft.
Rearrange the ideas in a rough order of importance. If the length is over the limit, discard less important ones. If any ideas are of limited importance and you are not sure whether to keep them, put them in a separate paragraph headed 'Other points'. These may fit in at the end; if (as in this case) they do not, they will be dropped when you write the final summary.
- Group similar ideas together, keeping each of the (combined) items down to approximately thirty-five or forty words.
- Save words by listing certain items (such as causes of unemployment) one under another rather than in sentences.

Step 6: Write the final version.
Start converting main points to full sentences, but continue to list the shorter points one under the other. In the final version given below, note that the draft notes have been further shortened and that headings have been added to highlight the main theme. A title has been added, too, to reflect this theme and give information about the source of the original material.

Australia's Unemployed Youth — Causes and Solutions
Summary of an article published in the Brisbane *Courier Mail*, 7 May 1986
The problem
Many of today's young Australians are out of work. One-third of all unemployed are aged 15–18. The causes include:
- economic changes

- increased births in the 1960–70 period
- computers and other modern technology
- high wage-scales for juniors
- more employment opportunities for women

The effect
The longer the time without work, the less the motivation to look for jobs. Fewer people trained now means a future shortage of workers in the skilled trades.

Solutions
Answers to the problem include a combination of programs:
- work-experience schemes for students
- government-funded traineeships
- improved apprenticeship system
- special TAFE courses to build work skills
- compulsory community service for those out of work

[140 words]

If the result is still too long, rewrite until you produce a shorter version. If this won't cut it sufficiently, discard more ideas.

Writing a synopsis
An even shorter summary, the synopsis, can be achieved by dropping the least important of the four remaining ideas (the one about future effects), and then condensing the remainder. The title and headings are also deleted.

Many of today's young Australians (15–18 years old) are unemployed. Causes include inflation, modern technology, high wages and more employment opportunities for women. Effective solutions include work-experience schemes, government traineeships, a modernised apprenticeship system and TAFE work-skills courses.

[43 words]

Condensing versus summarising
Condensing is a less drastic process than summarising. Even so, aim for the shortest possible article that will meet the reader's needs. The less time it takes to read, the more time people have left to appreciate the important points.

Condensing is also a way of ensuring high-quality writing. Many writers start with a draft manuscript 50 per cent longer than they need with the expectation that they will discard any lower quality material at the condensation stage. The original manuscript of this book was nearly twice as long as the version you are reading.

Executive or summary reports
Executives who feel happy about reading a report (because it does not take too much time) are more

likely to agree with it. The ideal length depends on the reader's page limit — the maximum number of pages he or she will read before losing interest, running out of time or handing the document to someone else to be summarised. Often that limit is as little as five to eight pages (apart from the table of contents, title page, illustrations and so on), depending on the purpose of the report. If you cannot condense a report to this length, an alternative is to write a version known as an executive report that is within the page limit.

The executive version looks just like a full report; it has a cover, synopsis and table of contents, but contains only the main points in each section (main findings, and key arguments from the analysis; however, it usually lists all recommendations).

Each section keeps its numbered heading, and there are usually some subheadings. This type of report may be incorrectly referred to as a 'synopsis', but it is far too long to qualify as such.

Summary

1. A summary takes less time to read than the original, so more people read it.

2. The best length for a summary is that which is right for its readers rather than the length you would like it to be.

3. Summarise ideas, not words. In this way you can produce a short business summary of a few hundred words from an article many thousands of words long, or from a whole book.

4. A synopsis is a very short summary of a quarter to half a page.

5. An abstract is even shorter — no more than 50 to 150 words.

Exercises

1. Choose a chapter from any text, magazine or journal on business communication. Write a list of ten points covered in the chapter, as the summaries in this book cover the points in each chapter.

2. Write a short executive summary (one and a half pages) of the Kinland report in Chapter 16 (pp. 185–91).

PART 4

Communicating
on the job

◄ CHAPTER 21 ►

Getting the job you want

Getting a job involves much more than just writing applications and going to interviews. Successful job hunters 'sell' themselves just as they would any other worthwhile product. If you have a good product (yourself) people will be interested, but first you have to get their attention and then you have to tell them why the product (you) is what they need in their organisation. This chapter shows you how.

Topics

Marketing yourself

Writing your application letter

Your personal details (résumé)

Before the interview

The job interview

After the interview

Marketing yourself

Whether you are looking for a first job, a promotion or a change in career, the marketing approach is a sound basis for getting a job. As with any marketing, you need to consider several things.

1. Your personal attitude

The more you want one particular job and know why you want it, the better will be your chances. Believe in yourself and your ability to do that job better than any other person. This will give you an immediate advantage over others who might apply for the position because they just want to do 'any job'.

2. What you are offering

What are your best features? What kind of work can

you do really well? What kind do you dislike? Be honest: there is no point in marketing a product if you cannot deliver it or if you do not believe in it.

3. Market research

Which of your abilities are those that employers are looking for at the moment? Where are the jobs you want likely to be found? What kind of opposition is there? Which are the best months in which to apply?

4. Promotion and advertising

How can you tell the world about you, your abilities, your special talents? The more people who know about you and what you are looking for, the more offers you will get. Tell everyone you know what kind of work you are looking for and ask them to tell their friends and associates too.

5. Price

Know what rate of pay you really are worth. Consider whether there are certain benefits (a car, free air travel) you would find more attractive than money. How much less would you take if these conditions were part of the package?

6. Presentation

How you dress and stand and talk at an interview is obviously part of your presentation; so is the way you write your application and set out your résumé.

Writing your application

If you apply for a job through the mail, when your letter is opened it will be put with a large pile of other applications, each one in direct competition with yours. To save time, most employers start by going through this pile just glancing at each letter and making a quick decision.

If your letter is well written and mentions abilities that the employer is looking for, he or she will then turn to your personal details (résumé), which should be attached but separate from the letter.

If the details in the résumé confirm the positive first impression, your application will go into a pile of ten to twelve (the 'short list') from which people to be interviewed will be selected.

If a letter is poorly written, too long, or opens with the wrong kind of information, it will be discarded. You could have the skills necessary for the job, but the employer may not even look at the résumé to discover them.

Notice that while it is the letter that is responsible initially for persuading an employer to turn to your résumé, it is the résumé that gives proof of your ability (see pp. 242–9).

Planning your application letter — guidelines

1. Have a clear purpose.
Are you sure what you are aiming for? Your letter should explain why your name should be on the interview list rather than why you ought to be given a job.

2. Create interest in your application.
If readers are to be interested in *your* letter, you have to create the interest yourself. There will be no reason that anyone will want to read your particular application unless you supply one.

3. Make your letter stand out from the crowd.
Think about the reader's problems: a vacancy to fill, a busy day ahead and a hundred applications to read. Write an application individual enough to get special attention. It must not look like a standard form letter or a recorded message. Show that you can think for yourself and have the initiative to write your own letter. The more sincere and personal it sounds, the stronger its chances. Avoid 'standard' wording or phrases copied straight from 'model' application letters.

4. Explain why you want *this* job.
Applicants are taken more seriously if they express real interest in the particular job. Say why you want this one rather than any other.

Typed or handwritten?
Most employers are quite happy with a typed or word-processed letter as long as it is the original. Never send a photocopy. If your writing is good, it is worth handwriting important applications. If it's bad, type everything.

The opening paragraph
First impressions are important. To write an opening that sounds different from most is not as hard as you might think, because so many of your competitors will have begun theirs with familiar openings: 'I am writing to apply for', 'I wish to apply for', 'In reply to your advertisement for' and similar lines. You gain an advantage immediately if you begin with a 'relationship' message instead.

Identify a common interest
Begin by talking about yourself and the reader together. Express a mutual interest or describe a common goal that unites you (the 'you and us together' technique described on page 156, Chapter 14).

> 'I was interested to learn that Corbond Ltd is opening a new branch in this area next month, because I am a fully trained word-processing operator with three years' experience in the kind of office you describe in your advertisement.'

Give one good reason why ...
Notice how that opening gives a specific reason for being interested in the advertised job. You can *say* you are interested, but unless you back this up by stating at least one reason for your interest, the words carry little weight. If you like the type of work, explain that *this* particular position has a special appeal for you — avoid giving the impression that you care little about the kind of work you get or who you work for as long as you get 'a job'.

Identify the actual advertisement
Whether you saw an advertisement in a newspaper, heard it on the radio or read about it on a noticeboard, name the source and give the date it appeared.

The body of the application letter
Summarise your skills, experience and abilities. It is better to be brief than to say too much; up to three-quarters of a page is plenty. Think of this part of the application as something like the tasty samples that marketing people hand out at shopping centres.

Their aim is to arouse your interest so that you want to find out more, and a good application letter should work the same way. Give a brief outline only of your present employment and/or previous work. Highlight only the features (the extra tasty samples) that will sharpen the reader's appetite. Save the rest for your résumé.

Explain what you can do rather than who you are

Convince the reader that you are one of the few applicants who has something special to offer. Illustrate your understanding of the advertiser's needs — show how you could be the very person to meet them. Talk about what you can do for the reader, not what the job can do for you (this is demonstrated in the sample letters, pp. 243–4).

Summarise studies, training and qualifications

Highlight subjects or training courses *only* if they are particularly relevant. Again, refer your reader to the résumé.

Draw attention to personal qualities that fit you for the position. Employers are attracted by the winner image. If you are a high achiever, if you enjoy hard work or like taking responsibility, say so.

Mention referees

Although you can claim that your abilities match the needs of the organisation, it's more convincing if the reader can confirm this by checking with others — by 'referring' your claims to someone else. Name people who can be contacted, and who are prepared to verify what you say.

Avoid oversell

Some people think they ought to add persuasive comments that stress how strongly they feel they are right for the job. But be careful! It is easy to sound 'pushy' or overconfident if you say 'I am sure that after reading my letter you will agree that I am . . .'.

Close on a positive note

Close on a positive note that confirms your confidence in yourself. You could do this by
■ asking straight out when interviews will be held

(so showing that you believe you are worth interviewing): 'Please would you contact me and advise when you will be conducting interviews? My phone number is 223 0985';
■ saying how you can be contacted (if you prefer a less direct close): 'If you require further details, please contact me either at 16 Bindi Street, Avoca Beach or by telephone on (087) 359 2949. Could you also let me know when you will be holding interviews?';
■ asking for more information: 'My home phone number is 45 6237. Could you please advise me when I can call and see someone personally to find out more about the position?'

Stress your availability. As well as a postal address, always give a telephone number. After the closing 'action' paragraph, say 'Yours faithfully' or 'Yours sincerely' (either is now considered correct). Always sign a letter, and type or print your name clearly underneath. Avoid closing phrases such as 'I would appreciate it if you might consider interviewing me at your convenience'. They sound false and insincere.

The complete letter

Two typical letters of application are shown on pages 243 and 244. Note how they follow the RIPPA format, as explained in Chapters 14 and 15. The first is a short application. The second example is a longer letter, and the application is for a higher position.

Your personal details (résumé)

A well-written and professional-looking résumé is as essential as your letter if your application is to place you on the interview list. As with the letter, it needs to stand out from the rest.

While the letter was intended to arouse interest, the résumé is a straight, factual document. It should be between one and three pages long, typed, clearly set out and, above all, easy to read at a glance. Write in the third person (no 'I', 'my' or 'me'). Be objective and unemotional. Stick to facts that the employer is looking for, presented so that they are easily seen in scanning the pages.

The master copy of a résumé should always be typed; however, whereas your letter must be original, it is quite acceptable to use a photocopy of a résumé. Have it retyped, though, if it needs to be

R   Your advertisement for an Office Manager with word processing skills ('Positions Vacant', Saturday's 'Adelaide Mail', 29.6.89) was of special interest to me because I am keen to gain more experience in this area.

I   I am currently completing a full-time Business Computer course at Kerong College and over the past year I have had a number of part-time jobs using different word processors. My typing speed ranges from 60 to 70 words a minute.

P   At school I won the Dean prize for Accounting three years in a row. Since I completed my secondary education at the end of 1990 I have had a number of other office jobs in which I also handled all banking and the office accounts system. I am enrolled in the part-time TAFE Associate Diploma in Management starting in July, and hope to complete this over the next five years.

P   I am twenty and have a current driver's licence, and I have worked part-time in a variety of jobs since I was 14. Your advertisement mentioned travelling as part of the job. I would enjoy this as I am friendly and outgoing, with lots of energy, and I'm willing to do most kinds of work. My personal résumé, school results, references and a recent photograph are attached.

A   I am available at any time for an interview. You can contact me by telephone on Kerong (054) 373 4813 or at my home address, 34 Dean Street, Westlake.

Yours sincerely,

---

varied to suit a special position. If you use a word processor, make sure your print-out is of a high quality, not draft mode.

Writing a résumé — guidelines

Personal details

Be brief. Give only those details the employer needs. State the date of your birth rather than your age. Do not include your marital status or family details, and give only highlights of your education and your highest qualifications. (Family information is low priority; list it later on.)

Current employment

Describe your present job first. Name the position and the firm. Say how long you have been in the job, the type of work you are doing and the location.

• Emphasise positive features, such as your level of responsibility, technical skills and so on.

Previous full-time employment

Give the actual title of each position held, the full name of each firm or employer, and the location. Describe the type of work, and (if there is room) add a few details to give a better picture of your work experience. State the year *and* month each position started and ended. (The earlier the position, the lower it will be in the list and the less detail is needed.)

Special activities associated with work

If you have acted in more senior positions, mention this. List special duties you have performed or any special project team or committee you have worked on. If you have been responsible for controlling, leading or supervising other staff, emphasise this even if it was only on a temporary basis.

Your advertisement for the position of Regional Marketing Manager with your company on page 23 of The Australian (Saturday, 23 September) was of special interest to me because of my experience in this type of work. I have just enrolled in a part-time degree course in Marketing Studies with the aim of gaining full qualifications as a Registered Marketing Consultant, a goal I have been working towards for the past five years.

The position, as you describe it, involves a number of special skills that I have in this area, so I would be very interested to learn more about it and exactly what the work would involve. I am now 25, and I have been involved in marketing since I started work in 1988. I am currently employed as Regional Manager at Greendale with the Drew Marketing Group.

A full list of positions held previously is included in my personal résumé (attached). However, I would like to mention in particular my two years as Assistant Sales Manager (1989–1990) at Longville, with the Bond Marketing Group. I also spent a year (1991) as Branch Sales Manager.

During my three years of study for the Associate Diploma in Marketing at Clearview Community College (1986–1988), I concentrated on the following subject areas. These would, I feel, be particularly suited to the duties and responsibilities listed in your advertisement:

SUBJECT	PASS LEVEL
MTS 548 Business Communication	Honours
TMB 758 Marketing A	Credit
TMB 579 Advanced Marketing	Honours
TMB 658 Marketing Project	Honours

The last two subjects included practical and field research as well as theoretical study. This has given me first-hand experience in many of the technical areas that you mention.

One of my first part-time jobs was as a market research interviewer for Palmer & Ross during 1982 and 1983. I have also worked for a number of community organisations, carrying out the same kind of work. This has given me further experience in the same area (see résumé). In 1988 I was Honorary Secretary of the Greendale Retailers' Association. In addition, I worked for twelve months in a part-time position on the Greendale Development Association, as Honorary Public Relations Officer (see résumé, letter of reference from the Association, and press cuttings from Greendale Courier).

I would be particularly interested in the opportunity to take over management of the North West region because I see this as one Australia's fastest developing areas. As the references (attached) point out, I am the kind of person who will give my best in any job as long as I am allowed to share the responsibility for making decisions that go with that position.

Please could you contact me by telephone at Lilydale (032) 373 4813 or at my home address, 15 Baker Street, Lilydale, and advise me when I could call and talk to you to find out more about the position?

Part-time work experience

Mention jobs held while at school or before obtaining your first full-time job. If self-employed at any time, give the relevant dates.

Membership of professional or statutory bodies

Playing an active role in professional bodies, trade associations or similar groups shows another positive side of your activities.

Schooling

Give only the briefest outline of your primary and early secondary subjects; few employers need these details before the interview. But do list the names of schools or colleges, the years spent at each and the levels of education achieved. If you feel a course outline or subject list would help, attach it, but keep it apart from the résumé. Photocopies of certificates and results are better kept in your portfolio for inspection at the interview.

Studies since leaving school

People who undertake regular part-time study when they are working are seen as being energetic and ready to take responsibility. Name the course and college, but do not include excessive subject details.

Other activities

List awards, scholarships or other outstanding achievements. Make special mention of any community work you have done and of positions held in community or service organisations, particularly positions such as branch president or secretary. It may be better not to include party political activities.

Sporting or recreational activities

Employers are attracted by the 'winner' image. No matter what it is you play or where you compete, mention prizes, trophies or competitions that you have won.

Travel

Highlight work, study or business experience overseas or interstate. The fact that you have travelled appeals to employers and must be mentioned; otherwise there will be a gap in your history, and that worries them. Working-holiday jobs such as waiting or bar work show that you get on well with people, so list these.

Family background, health, travel restrictions, other constraints

If you have good health, say so. Give details of your marital status and immediate family. If the employer has read as far as this, he or she is definitely interested and will now want to know these details. If there are any conditions that prevent you from doing some types of work or from travelling, mention them now.

Other information

Hobbies are of interest. If you enjoy working with computers or have special computing skills (even at the hobby level), mention them. If you have had any experience speaking in public, running meetings or debating, this is a strong feature. If you have a particular or unusual skill with, say, machines, animals, plants, art, photography, designing or fashion, mention this at the end of the résumé. List any program undertaken that involves personal development, such as the Duke of Edinburgh Award.

Your photograph

Many successful applicants say that including a photograph helps to get interviews, as long as the picture is of high quality, clear, and shows you to good advantage.

Referees

Give names, titles, positions (business), addresses and phone numbers.

How easy to read is your résumé? — check-list

1. Can it be scanned rapidly?
The employer needs to scan quickly, looking for the particular skills or abilities needed. Make it easy for readers to find details they want without having to read everything else.

Divide the page vertically into thirds. Major headings and key data (dates and positions held) should appear on the left-hand third; notes and details go in the remaining two columns. Use a headline to identify each section. Use wider than normal margins.

2. Is it credible?

Credibility requires the use of specific, accurate language, free of overstatement or generalisation ('I am skilled at every kind of work'). The record must be complete, with no periods unaccounted for, and must be up to date. A cramped document

---

PERSONAL RESUME

Full Name: Kelly Patrick JONSON

1. Personal Details

Born Brisbane, 21 March 1965
Present Address: 12 Raven St, Northvale, SA 5431

Qualifications

Diploma of Business, North Adelaide TAFE — 1988
Currently studying Bachelor of Communication, University of NA

2. Current Employment

May 1991 to present date   ASSISTANT MANAGER — Myall and Co. — Computer Sales
Responsible for all day-to-day activities, particularly sales and stock control. Conduct staff training in client service and public relations. Other duties include:
— Financial control other than routine bookkeeping
— Recruit and select new sales staff

3. Previous Full-Time Employment

1989—1991   SENIOR TRAINING OFFICER
Responsible for organising and conducting training programs for all levels of staff (list attached). In charge of a staff of seven trainers and two clerical workers. Introduced a new training incentive plan which has now been adopted statewide. (June 1989—May 1991)
1988—1989   TRAINING OFFICER — AEC Computers
Responsible for organising and conducting a wide range of training programs for all levels of staff (list attached). (April 1988—June 1989)
1986—1988   ASSISTANT TRAINING OFFICER — AEC Computers
Responsible for conducting training programs for junior staff. (January 1986—April 1988)

4. Special Activities Associated with Work

ACTING MANAGER — Myall and Co — Computer Sales
Managing firm for three weeks during Christmas sale period while owner overseas. (December 1989)

1

lowers credibility, so allow plenty of white space to give an impression of openness, even if this makes it a little longer.

3. Is it well organised?
Collate information to combine similar types of data.

The first example (pp. 246−7) is of a full résumé (2−4 pages, business format).

Some employers prefer a very short résumé, as in the example on pages 248−9, set out in formal style. This type can also be used as a summary sheet — a contents page at the front of a longer

---

5. Part-time Work Experience

　　SALES ASSISTANT — BRD Computers
　　　　Part-time during school holidays. (1983−1986)

6. Studies Since Leaving School

　　1988−1990 — Diploma of Business, North Adelaide TAFE
　　1991−present — Degree Course — Bachelor of Communication, University of NA (Student No: 133378/441). Details of subjects attached.

7. Membership of Professional Bodies

　　Registered Member, Association of Computer Management
　　Associate Member, Australian Institute of Programmers
　　Justice of the Peace

8. Schools Attended

　　1986−1987 — State High School, Northacre, NSW
　　1987 — Leaving Level Senior Grade 12 Examination, State High School T.E. Score 912. (Details of subjects attached separately.)

9. Sport and Recreation

　　Golf and tennis.

10. Travel

　　Twelve weeks touring Europe and SE Asia, May-July 1989. Attended International Conference, Institute of Marketing, Berne, Switzerland.

11. Family Background

　　Married — two sons (Peter, 5, and Jason, 7).

12. Health

　　Excellent — no restrictions on travel.

Referees

　　[Names of people who may be contacted by the employer to verify information in résumé]

2

PERSONAL RESUME

KYM NATHAN BLACKGROVE B.C., Dip.Bus.Mgmt (TAFE), J.P.

Born: Brisbane, Queensland, 21 Sept. 1966

EDUCATION

1989–1994 — Degree Course — Bachelor of Communication — University of
            NA (Details attached)
1985–1988 — Diploma of Business, North Adelaide TAFE
1984–   Senior Grade 12 Examination, Avery High School
            Score 912 (Details of subjects and grades attached)
1980–1983 — State High School, Northacre

CAREER SUMMARY

1989   SENIOR TRAINING OFFICER — Australian Banking Systems
(to present   Ltd
date)
              Responsible for organising and conducting training pro-
              grams for all levels of staff (list attached). In charge of a
              staff of seven trainers, and four clerical workers (see details
              attached).

1988–1989   TRAINING OFFICER — AEC Computers
              Responsible for organising and conducting a wide range
              of training programs for all levels of staff (list attached).
              Introduced a new training incentive plan which has now
              been adopted statewide.

1987–1988   TECHNICAL TEACHER — Technical and Further Education,
              State Education Dept
              Taught at Prescott and South Bank Community Colleges.
              Taught subjects in the Certificate (Associate Diploma level)
              in Business Communication, Management, Business Psy-
              chology, Business Computer Software and Word Processing.

1986–1987   TEACHER TRAINEE
              Joined State Education Dept as TAFE Trainee Teacher.

1985–1986   SELF-EMPLOYED
              Milk-run, Tully, N. Qld, until October 1986.

document. You can list work history either in de-scending or ascending order.

Personal history listing

The more important a position, the more an em-ployer may want to look into your background. This is particularly so if the job involves security, finance, or a high level of trust. A brief history attached to the résumé is all that is needed, but it must be complete *and* it must cover every year from the time you finished high school: gaps suggest the possibility of activities you do not want to talk about.

MEMBERSHIP OF PROFESSIONAL BODIES

Association of Computer Management
        District President 1990–1991
Australian Institute of Programmers
        Member since 1989
Justice of the Peace — Registered 1990

OTHER ACTIVITIES

1986–1987   PUBLIC SPEAKING — Aust Inst. of Debating
        Member National Debating Team. Winner of R. G. Menzies
        Trophy for best speaker, 1986
        Leader Champion National Debating Team, 1987
        Winner of R. G. Menzies Trophy for best speaker 1987

[Names of referees on separate sheet, attached.]

Details of specific subjects studied

Many subject names with no explanation mean little to an employer. While it is best to keep this information in your portfolio folder and show it at the interview, in some cases it is worth adding a summary as an appendix to the résumé. Mention only the relevant ones, not every subject ever studied.

Before the interview

If your letters and résumés present a clear picture of your skills and abilities, plenty of employers will invite you to attend various kinds of interviews, as described below.

Whenever you are offered an interview, accept. The experience is too valuable to miss. You are a player in a tough game (one of the toughest), and the best practice you can get is to keep on taking part in interviews. There is no need to feel embarrassed if you don't perform brilliantly every time.

Know as much as possible about your potential job

As soon as you are advised of the time and date for the interview, start planning. Find out as much as possible about the job, the organisation and its policies. Remember how important first impressions are. You must be on time for your appointment, so work out transport and parking details.

Ask if there is any way you can visit the organisation before the interview to find out more about the firm itself. Even if the employer seems uninterested, you can still decide to drop in if you 'happen to be in the area'. Talk to as many people as you can. Some people do this even before applications close, so that they can use what they learn in their letters.

Be prepared

Think about all the different questions that might be asked. Imagine yourself answering them. Better still, get a friend, a relative or a teacher (or all three) to interview you not once but several times. (Ask immediate family members to do this only if no one else is available. You know each other too well for such an interview to seem real.) Get used to being asked — and answering — questions on all the following topics.

- Background: 'We've read your application, of course, but it would be useful if you could tell us more about yourself and your background.'
- Qualifications: 'What are your strengths?' 'Why do you believe you are particularly qualified for this position?'
- Experience: 'What previous jobs or training have you had that would be useful in this position?'
- Reasons for applying: 'Why are you seeking this position?' 'Why do you want to leave your present position?'
- Career goals: 'What are your long-term ambitions?' 'Where do you expect to be working (what kind of job will you be doing) in eight years' time?'
- Permanency: 'Do you see this position as a long-term one?'
- Initiative: 'What would you do if . . .?' The

interviewer here is checking to see if you can think quickly and for yourself, rather than having to be told what to do. Show that you can think clearly and logically under pressure.

Have questions of your own

Have two or three questions ready to ask the interviewer. It is very likely that you will be invited to do this, so having nothing to ask suggests lack of preparation. Ask first about opportunities for advancement, or support given to employees who study or gain extra skills. Then ask about hours and conditions, such as annual leave. Mention payment last.

Organise your papers

Employers like talking to someone who is organised. Get all your papers fixed in a folder, and practise until you can make it fall open at the right pages. Have your questions organised, too.

The job interview

Initially you may be phoned by the employer, to talk about your application. This is actually an 'interview', so do your best to give a good initial impression. You will then be invited to a personal meeting, which may be

- a single interview — face-to-face communication with a single selector who has been given the task of meeting with all applicants and forming an opinion before making a recommendation;
- a series interview — in which you are questioned in turn by a number of interviewers, each of whom is responsible for checking a particular aspect of your job competence;
- a panel interview — in which you are subjected to examination by a group who will individually ask questions relevant to their own particular backgrounds, but will also work together (one panel member may pick up and investigate further a response you gave to another).

In the interview

The aim of the interview is to exchange information. If you have prepared yourself, you'll have answers to most of the commonly asked questions as listed in the previous section. Competition for jobs is strong and the questions asked in today's interviews are frank, direct, probing, and often rather blunt. The words used may not be important — there is another kind of information that the employer is seeking and you'll probably convey many of the answers non-verbally. However, the points the employer is checking happen to be the ones that usually win or lose the interview.

Are you positive about the type of job you want?

Never go for an interview just because you 'need a job'. Go because you want *that job*, and that one alone. Proving you will enjoy it is largely a matter of non-verbal communication. You can say 'I enjoy working in a laboratory', 'I like using spreadsheets' or 'I've always wanted to be a parking inspector', but no statement will mean much unless you show enthusiasm in your face and with body language.

Do you have the ability and drive to *win*?

Show that you are a winner in some field. It does not even have to be in a competitive sense. If you have triumphed over some major obstacle in life, if you have stuck at something difficult until you mastered it — that too is the mark of the winner, and the employee with potential.

How hard will you work?

Showing a readiness to work hard has probably won more interviews than brains and technical qualifications combined. Every firm needs people who are not afraid of putting in a special effort when the going gets tough. However, claiming that you have the quality is not enough. Have written references that describe you in these terms. Perhaps you can tie this in with your sporting history — people who play hard are likely to work hard, too.

Are you prepared to show initiative and accept responsibility?

The same comments apply to these qualities. If you can show you possess them, you'll be successful in interviews.

How persistent are you?

Persistence is highly prized by employers. If you've stayed with a difficult study program while holding down a demanding job and raising a family, describe your determination not to fail. You'll find that evidence of determination and persistence (your diploma or degree) is more convincing than your words. Employers appreciate that night or weekend classes may take a little of your energy, but your part-time study record is convincing evidence that you have a strong sense of responsibility, are a good worker, and have many of the other qualities mentioned above.

How much do you really believe in yourself?

When you believe in yourself and your ability to do the job, it will show in everything you say and do. Stress your conviction that what you have to offer makes you a special person, not just an average applicant.

Stress interviews

Some interviewers may seem rude and some questions may border on an invasion of your private life. Don't overreact. You may be experiencing a common selection technique called the 'stress interview'. The interviewer (or one member of the interview team) will be deliberately antagonistic — acting in an unpleasant way or expressing anger about you or your answers. In this case the firm is looking for someone who can keep cool under pressure.

Other circumstances deliberately set up to cause stress include
- very long interviews (two to three hours or more), designed to weed out candidates who can keep up a false appearance for thirty minutes, but not much longer;
- pressure interviews, subjecting the candidate to a barrage of questions, interrupting answers with more questions and not permitting the candidate to relax for a moment.

Negative questions

Some interviewers ask negative questions such as 'What would you say are your main weaknesses (or your main faults)?' Prepare an answer that stresses the positive side of any 'weaknesses' you are prepared to discuss. 'I tend to overorganise.' 'I sometimes neglect my family because of job commitments.'

Fix it quick!

In this case the interviewer, without warning, gives you a series of problems to solve. 'How would you go about opening up a new branch?' 'How would you handle a factory breakdown?' 'How would you cope with two employees having a fight?' Don't panic. The interview is not an exam, and you are not required to know the 'right' answer. What is expected is that you will be able to think of *something* to do. A candidate some years ago when asked about two employees fighting said, 'I'd chuck a bucket of water over them'. He got the job because he showed that he had enough self-confidence to remain calm and maintain a sense of humour in a difficult situation. This was exactly what the employer was looking for.

At the end

A good interviewer will summarise the important aspects of the meeting, indicate what happens next, thank you for your interest and inform you when or how you are likely to hear the results.

After the interview

1. Take time to think back.

What was the best feature of the interview? What aspects could you improve with additional practice?

2. Keep on trying.

If a particular job is important to you, keep applying for it. Be persistent, as long as you do not make a nuisance of yourself. Many people get the best jobs because they go out looking for them, and employers are impressed by this kind of initiative. Instead of waiting for the next vacancy to be advertised, phone firms in which you are interested and ask about jobs. Accept a temporary position, because once you are on the 'inside' you have a better chance when the next 'good' job comes up.

Not winning your first or second or tenth interview does not prove you lack the qualities of a good employee. There may just have been someone equally good who wanted that job. (Now they have it, they can't compete with you for the next one!)

3. Enrol in a night or weekend course.

Enrol in a course of study of some kind. This will keep your mind active and boost your chances next time you apply for a job.

Summary

1. The more you want one particular job and know why you want it, the better your chances.

2. If your letter and résumé are well written, your application will go onto the 'short list'. As long as this happens regularly, you will have plenty of job interviews.

3. The letter initially persuades readers to turn to your résumé, but the résumé is just as important. It must, like your letter, stand out from the rest.

4. Give specific reasons for your interest in *this* job. Back them up by offering evidence or a reference that confirms your special interest.

5. In your letter, explain what you can do rather than who you are. Convince the reader that you are one of the few applicants who has something special to offer.

6. A credible résumé requires specific, accurate language free of overstatement or generalisation. It must be complete, with no periods unaccounted for, and *absolutely* up to date.

7. A cramped document lowers credibility; allow plenty of white space.

8. Accept every interview you are offered. The practical experience is too valuable to miss.

9. Employers know that people who study part time usually have a stronger sense of responsibility than others, and make good employees.

10. Believe in yourself and your ability to do the job you are applying for; let this show in everything you say and do during the interview. Stress the things that you think make you special, and better than any other applicant.

Acknowledgment: Sections of this chapter on application letters and résumés were originally published by Downs Holdings in *Australian Business Letters* (1986). Reproduced with permission.

CHAPTER 22

The telephone at work

For an invention now well over 100 years old, the telephone is a remarkable machine. It seldom requires maintenance and uses very little energy. Compared with other electronic communication the phone is still a low-cost system, and this makes it efficient. However, for the phone to be effective the results of your calls must be positive and practical.

This chapter explains how to make the telephone work for you efficiently and effectively, and how to overcome the commonest communication problems associated with it, particularly the four telephone barriers.

Topics

Effective phone calls

The introduction barrier

The credibility gap

The misunderstanding barrier

The positive message barrier

Persuasion over the phone

Managing your telephone system

Mobile phones

Effective phone calls

There is no doubt about the phone's *efficiency* when you need to communicate for a short time over a long distance. However, whether or not it is *effective* depends on how well the call works — whether it really helps to get a job done or reach an important objective. Two significant factors can undermine telephone effectiveness.

■ You can't see the other person. In ordinary conversation your spoken words are reinforced by non-verbal signals such as body movement. Over the phone the only non-verbal support comes from the tone of your voice, and that can be distorted.

■ Both sender and receiver have difficulties remembering details of the conversation. People tend to hear what they want to hear. Over time, details of the call become distorted, and unless both parties record the call in writing, memories about what was said will vary.

These two factors are responsible for the 'telephone barriers':
1. the introduction barrier
2. the credibility gap
3. the misunderstanding barrier
4. the positive message barrier

Once you know about the barriers and how to deal with them, your phone calls will be far more effective.

The introduction barrier

It's understandable that a phone conversation between two strangers works more effectively after they have been 'introduced'. If both make a little extra effort at the start, the introduction barrier soon disappears. A good introduction helps each to find out the other's name and whether that person is feeling relaxed and happy or formal and distant, and to form an impression of the other in terms of power and status. Whether you are calling or answering, first impressions are important.

If you are making the call — guidelines

1. Introduce yourself in a polite yet friendly way.
This encourages the other person to respond the same way.

2. If calling a stranger, identify yourself immediately.

'Hello. Paul Martin here. I'm trying to get in touch with . . .'. Failure to identify yourself at the start is a non-verbal signal that worries many people.

3. If the listener does not know you, explain how you obtained the number.

Was it advertised? Did you get it through a personal contact? If the contact is a mutual friend or colleague, mention that person's name: 'This is Dominique Valez from Stafford. I'm president of the Stafford P. and C. committee. Sue Salimon, our treasurer, gave me your number and suggested . . .'.

4. Put the listener at ease.

Add a further remark in a friendly, personal tone to show you are relaxed and looking forward to communicating. Your introduction should say (verbally and non-verbally), 'I'm happy to meet you'. If appropriate, it should also signal your preference for the conversation to continue on a first-name basis: 'Kerry Hudson speaking. I'm Gil Jackson's personal assistant at MIL. [*pause*] Jerry Lang from your sales division has given your name as a reference . . .'.

Most people respond positively to this type of approach, particularly when your non-verbal tone matches your words.

5. Add to the listener's picture.
After your name, add other details to help the listener develop a clear mental picture; for example, the name of your firm, your department or your location and your reason for calling: 'Hello. I'm Wendy Greenup from Phillips Motors in Bairnsdale. I phoned to ask about your . . .'. Refer to the topic you are calling to discuss, particularly if the listener is someone who does not know you well: 'Misha Wellings from Tamworth here. Do you remember talking to me about your new book at the Communication Conference at Katoomba last month?'

6. Refer to previous discussions or activities.
Fill in possible gaps in your listener's memory: 'Is that Kel Blakie? It's Angela Stevens. I'm the graduate who flew over from Perth last week to see you about a job as a project officer'.

Even if talking to someone you know, indicate clearly what you are calling about. Make the opening sound as much like '*you*' as possible. Develop a variety of different openings rather than a fixed formula.

Answering the phone

A positive opening provides the basis for a successful call. A poor *first* impression can become a potential customer's *last* impression.

Confirm the connection

Give your telephone number or the name of your firm or organisation, or both. It helps if you also mention your section or unit. Then give your first name and surname and assure callers that they have the right number (unless you know that the switchboard operator does this before the call reaches you): '356 261, Cairns Holdings, John Anthony speaking'; '732 628, Galway Rental Service, Pat Joyce here. Can I help you?'.

Even on a call transferred from a switchboard it pays to open with a similar identification, to assure callers they have reached the correct extension: 'Furnishing section. This is Shalini Khan. Can I help you?'. If you prefer, you can give your name first: 'Peta Grey speaking. This is the electrical repair section. How can we help you?'.

At home, many people prefer to wait for callers to identify themselves first. This option is *not* good for business. If employees are worried about giving their names, arrange training to overcome the barrier. In the meantime, they should not take outside calls.

Unsuitable answers

Avoid using opening words such as those in the following examples. They project non-verbal signals suggesting a distant and superior attitude or a lack of interest in anyone as an individual.

- 'Accounts Payable' suggests that the speaker is part of a system where nobody cares about names.
- 'Seven Seas Restaurant' projects a similar image of a restaurant where customers and staff are not expected to be friendly.
- 'Hello' followed by silence suggests a closed attitude (you do the talking, I'll do the listening), a poor way to start any business relationship.
- 'MacMillan!' — using a surname by itself to open a conversation is outdated and impersonal.

After the introductions

Having started with a friendly introduction, wait for a cue from the person on the other end. The response will tell you whether to continue your open, personal style or to switch to a more formal tone; whether the listener wants to match your first-name approach or use surnames. However, no matter how formal the tone, you should know the name and the business of the person you are talking to. If after your introduction this is not given, ask for it. You have a right to know.

- 'Could I please have your name?'
- 'Who am I talking to, please?'
- 'Can I ask who's calling (speaking)?', or 'May I *say* who's calling?' if you are going to transfer the call.

If an unidentified caller asks for information, particularly for personal details about *anyone*, explain that you cannot help until you know who the person represents and why he or she cannot make a written request. Even if the answer sounds satisfactory, be careful: give information only if you are authorised to do so.

Keep the connection

If you are transferred to another section during a call, complete the picture for the new listener. Introduce yourself again, refer to your location and so on, and mention the names of the people you have talked to already.

The credibility gap

Phone calls are far more effective *after* trust is established, and even if you and the other person are strangers when you meet on the phone you can reduce the credibility gap in about 70 to 90 per cent of calls.

Reducing the credibility gap — guidelines

Because callers cannot see each other, trust-building can't be left to itself. The less people know about each other, the less they trust each other. Throughout any call, keep working on ways to increase trust between you and the listener.

1. Describe yourself rather than your position.
Choose words that help the listener to 'see' you. Once two people have an image of each other, they are more prepared to listen to different points of view and to help each other.

2. Make information more believable.
Most information conveyed by phone sounds less believable than written or face-to-face communication. (If someone wants to tell a lie, the phone is well known as the channel that offers the best chance of success.)

Suppose you advertise your 'faithfully restored' vintage MG sports coupé for sale. A caller from interstate suggests that if the car is in really good condition he will pay substantially more than local buyers; however, he still seems doubtful about the car's condition. Offer extra evidence. Ask if someone known to the caller could check the car. You know you are telling the truth; it's in your interests to help listeners confirm this.

3. Paint word pictures.
Assuming that your MG is in top condition, use words that help the listener to visualise it clearly. Describe the shine on paintwork, the softness of the upholstery, the sound of the engine, and what it feels like when you get behind the wheel.

4. If you are receiving information, take the opposite position.
Treat what you are told with more doubt than you would in face-to-face conversation. Be careful not to agree with something because it *sounds* true or you'd like it to be true. Seek extra clarification.

5. Ask for confirmation in writing.
Either you or your firm could be at risk if what is claimed to be true (over the phone) proves false. Do not be embarrassed about insisting on written confirmation. In business, it shows good sense. If people object, you have reason to be suspicious.

The misunderstanding barrier

Meanings are easily either misinterpreted or missed altogether over the phone. It may seem strange that your words, so clear to you, fail to have the same meaning for others, but some listeners seem to think they know better than you what you really meant to say. Misunderstanding adds to the credibility gap but there are ways in which to avoid it.

Avoiding misunderstanding

'Visualising' your meaning

If you are giving directions on how to find a particular address, ask the listener to get a street directory and follow your instructions with eyes as well as ears.

Offering additional information

Instead of 'I'll meet you outside the station at about eight', say 'I'll be waiting in front of the King Street Station at the top of the stairs at 8.00 pm'.

Asking for feedback

You cannot always ask a person straight out to repeat what you have just said (unless you know each other well enough), but you can say 'I'm not sure I explained that very well the first time. Can you play it back to me to make sure I outlined all the details?'.

Do not ask directly whether you have been understood; the telephone barriers discourage admission of failure to understand. People say 'yes', when they mean 'I'm not sure', but when they put in their own words what you have said, you soon find out what they have in fact understood.

Sharing decisions

The more complicated the instruction or the action to be agreed on, the more it pays to use shared decision making. If you ask, 'Which stairs do you normally use when you come out of the station?', this involves the listener more and clarifies the picture for both of you. If your listener then says, 'Well, there's only one stairway; the other exit is an escalator', you've identified a possible point of confusion.

Offering feedback

Make a point of stating your understanding in your own words. 'You'll be parked in King Street, outside the south entrance of the station at 8.00 pm tonight. Have I got it right?' Note the wording of the feedback request, 'Have I got it right?'. This makes it easier for the listener to acknowledge the possibility of a misunderstanding.

Using notes or sketches

If you are receiving directions, take notes or draw a sketch *while* the steps are being explained. Then read your notes or describe your drawing by way of feedback. If you cannot take notes, at least repeat the directions as you understood them. 'So I need to go to the very end of Bligh Road before I can see your house. Then I look for the red-tiled roof and the tall pine tree.'

Listening to your own message

Check your words for possible double meanings, lack of clarity or ambiguity. There is an old saying that if your message can be misunderstood in several different ways, it will be misunderstood in the way that does most harm. As explained in Chapter 7, a sender is not likely to be aware of any double meaning in his or her words. Imagine someone saying, 'I NEED A TALL POLE FOR A SPECIAL ROLE/ROLL'. On the phone there are no visual clues such as the spelling of 'roll' or 'role' or a capital P for 'Pole' to give the correct meaning. It could be a request for a long wooden pole for rolling, or someone from Poland, who is 210 centimetres tall, to play a special role in a TV series.

Expect misunderstandings

On the telephone, as in any kind of communication, things go wrong more often if people become over-confident. If anyone is unwilling to admit that his or her phone call might be misunderstood, they increase the chances that it will be! Chapter 4, 'Understanding — what do you mean?', explained the dangers of your overlooking the other person's point of view or of believing that yours is the only possible meaning, and this can also apply to the listener. If you are assured by a caller that 'you can't miss it', you need to use extra caution. If you feel quite sure that you understand a message, that you 'got it straight the first time', use feedback and questioning to double-check. When you arrive at the wrong place or at the wrong time, it is too late to discover that you could 'miss it' after all!

The positive-message barrier

It takes extra effort and empathy to share positive feelings (liking, trust, respect, enthusiasm) over the phone, yet when you express negative feelings (dislike, distrust, boredom, anger), the message seems to travel very easily. Take extra care about what you say and how you say it. Despite the barrier, it is possible to send positive messages about your feelings.

- Learn to 'smile' over the phone. You will *sound* as though you are smiling if your face muscles are formed into a smile as you speak, and like any other kind of smile, this makes the listener feel like smiling too. You can also project other kinds of body language over the phone. If your body is positioned in a friendly and relaxed manner, your listener will picture you this way.
- Monitor your tone of voice and non-verbal expression. Learn how to tell the difference between a positive tone and others that make you

sound negative when perhaps you are just un-happy or tired.

- Practise using sharp, distinct speech (a 'micro-phone' voice). Emphasise the first word of each sentence or the first word after any pause. Speak a little more loudly than in normal conversation: unclear speaking can suggest negative feelings.
- Put yourself in the receiver's position. Be friendly; show that you care. People who are happy and relaxed on the phone will also be feeling co-operative. Try to create this atmos-phere for both of you. Use active listening (see Chapter 8).
- Repeat the other person's first name during the call — in fact, you can use the person's name a little more often than you would in normal conversation.
- Plan phone calls in advance. This saves time and helps you clarify your ideas before you ring. Choose a time to ring that you know will suit the other person as well as yourself.
- Keep business calls as short as possible. There may be other callers waiting to get through to both of you.
- Listen for clues. A sudden pause or change in the conversation may be a signal that the other person is upset by something in your vocal tone, or that you might have used a phrase that gave the wrong impression. The positive message barrier makes it harder to offer an apology, or to sound sincere when you say 'I'm sorry' or 'I didn't mean it that way', but give it a try, anyhow.
- Treat listeners as adults. You may be annoyed by a caller's attitude, but try not to 'talk down' to anyone. If you become angry or adopt a tone of voice signalling a superior (parent to child) atti-tude, you'll send negative signals that reduce *your* chance of gaining agreement over the phone.

What not to say on the phone

The following familiar phrases make you sound impersonal and uncaring. They are used far too often already — a further reason to cross them off your list.

'I haven't got a clue'

This sounds as though you are saying 'I don't know and I don't care' — not the impression you want to give to customers or clients. Say 'I'm sorry, but I don't know' or 'I haven't heard anything about it, but I'll find out and let you know'.

'Hang on a sec' or 'Half a mo'

If you are going to check details and want the caller to wait, say how long you expect to be (a minute or five minutes, but not 'a sec', a 'couple of ticks' or 'a mo'). Ask if the caller minds waiting. (If it is an STD call, he or she would probably prefer to phone again.) Better still, suggest that you call back. If the caller wants someone else, explain if you do not know where the individual is and then ask how best you can help: 'If you don't mind waiting. I'll see if I can find her', or 'Can I get him to phone you?'.

'You'll have to ...'

An example of this is 'No, he's not in this depart-ment any more. You'll have to phone 658 3298'. Telling listeners they 'have to' do anything sounds uncaring and unhelpful. The first thing to say in a case like this is that you are sorry you cannot help. Then offer a suggestion: 'You could try to get him on 658 3298', or 'Can I contact him and ask him to call you back?'.

'Have a nice day'

Compliments and good wishes used on the phone in other countries do not 'transplant' well into Australian soil. They sound too artificial. The most successful way to wish someone a good day is to use your own words, not imported or 'prepackaged' ones.

'That's all right' or 'Oh, that's OK'

A response like this is no way to acknowledge personal thanks. If a caller says 'Thank you for helping', respond by saying 'I'm pleased I could help you', 'Happy to help', or 'It was no trouble; I'm glad we could share in your success'.

'No, we don't have any'

If a caller asks whether you have a particular item in stock, never just say 'No', and leave it at that. Explain *why* it is unavailable. If it has been ordered, say when stocks are expected to arrive and ask for a number so that you can call the customer when they do. Alternatively, ask if the caller will wait while you see if anyone knows where the item can be obtained.

'IRC Finance. Best people when you need cash in a hurry. Good morning'

Using a slogan in this way gives the impression that the firm is more interested in making a sales pitch than in listening.

'Let me know if it's not all right'

This is probably the most dangerous phrase you can use on the phone. Why? Because it is primed to fail. The speaker is saying that if *nothing* is heard from you, he or she will assume that everything *is* all right! Is this logical? The more difficult the problem, the more chance there is that you will be unable to call back to say it's *not* all right. The opposite approach is the only safe one. Say 'Let me know when it's ready', or 'I'll wait for your confirmation before I do anything'.

Persuasion over the phone

Make a list of the benefits that will appeal to the listener if he or she agrees to what you suggest. To do this (as explained in Chapter 13, 'The power of persuasion') will make it easier to get across an already convincing argument.

Talking to front-line employees

When you telephone people at the front line of the organisation — mechanics, drivers, store and dispatch clerks — talk to them in a friendly way, using first names. Don't use impersonal labels such as 'Dispatch', 'Typing' or 'Transport'.

If you know the name of the person you are talking to (even if it is not the person you are really calling), it pays to use it. This simple telephone technique is so useful that it deserves a special mention. A switchboard operator, for example, appreciates it when you say, 'Hello, Denise, how are you today?'. When you want help with a delayed call, Denise will be happy to help. She may not be as willing to assist people who call her 'Switch'.

Don't attack an innocent party

No matter how badly treated you feel, do not attack a front-line employee (for instance, a secretary or a switchboard operator) because someone higher in the system has let you down. It's unfair, it won't solve the problem, and it may lose you the support of someone who could have helped you.

Managing your telephone system

The telephone is your organisation's 'front line'. It provides potential customers with their first image of your business and how it is run. A well-managed system should meet the needs of people at the other end of the phone as well as your own.

Choose the right switchboard operator

A cheerful, outgoing switch operator — someone who enjoys talking to people and likes solving problems — can be worth thousands of dollars in terms of your group's public image. People who are shy or who become tense and irritable when things go wrong should not operate a switchboard, even temporarily. They may *say* the right words, but a poor attitude can be transmitted non-verbally and this may do irreparable damage to goodwill and public relations.

Don't let a phone ring for more than 20 seconds

As a general rule, all business calls should be answered within 15–20 seconds. You may be tied up on important matters, but it's neither fair nor good for business to expect a caller to wait until you have time to answer.

Today's telephone systems can be programmed to allow a call unanswered within a certain time to be automatically redirected to someone who will answer it. Reorganise your system so that there will always be at least one phone available within the 20-second deadline. If you leave your personal phone even for a short time, ask someone to take your calls. Train all staff to make firm arrangements for calls to be redirected in the event of long absences.

Don't let the phone take over

If you are planning a meeting, a discussion or an interview, arrange for all calls to be diverted. Stopping a face-to-face discussion to answer the phone sends negative non-verbal signals about you, your communication style and your attitude towards others in the room.

When to avoid the phone

There are situations in which using the phone is risky because too many things can go wrong. Try to use written or face-to-face communication in the following circumstances.

Explaining technical details

If you have to order things such as spare parts by phone, use numbers rather than words. Be very specific, and use the correct technical terms. Use the phone to see if the parts are available, then ask the firm to hold them while you arrange for a written order to be sent by mail or fax. The person taking your order may claim written confirmation is not necessary. Send it, anyway.

Expressing personal appreciation

A telephone call cannot convey a message like the one you extend when you go down to the factory or shop floor yourself. If you want to thank a group of employees who worked over a weekend to help the firm meet an important contract on time, your appreciation will seem far less real if it reaches them through a bit of thin wire.

Discussing confidential or private matters

The phone is not a private channel, as many public figures learn when the contents of their 'secret' phone calls are published in the media. You cannot tell whether anyone is listening to your phone calls, but it's wise to regard it as a real possibility.

Exerting power and authority

If you have to tell an employee to do a job that you know he or she does not want to do, the phone is an unreliable channel. Ask the individual to see you personally or send the instruction in writing, or do both.

Difficult situations

You can't avoid difficult phone calls completely. If you must use the phone to solve a problem because time is critical, concentrate on the solution rather than on getting rid of your frustration. Angry words on the phone are easily misinterpreted, and trying to persuade people to co-operate when they are angry doesn't work anywhere, especially not on the phone. Sometimes you receive difficult calls without warning. If possible, however, prepare for them beforehand. Work out what you want to say and what responses you might expect. A modified version of the RIPPA formula helps.

1. Relate to the caller. If the call is about an overdue account, do not launch straight into money matters without some relationship-building first.

2. Get information. First find out as much as you can about the problem, concentrating on facts rather than feelings. If the other person involved is angry, try to find out why. For instance, use open-ended questions, with the key words 'how', 'why', 'when', 'where', 'who', 'what', 'would you'.

3. Exchange information. It is easier for both parties to remain logical and unemotional if you centre the discussion on cold, hard facts.

4. Paint the picture as clearly as you can. Discuss what action is to be taken, where and when it will be taken, and who will take it.

5. Persuade, point by point. Deal with one thing at a time. Once agreement is reached on one point, make a note, read it back, get it confirmed. Recap and summarise regularly.

6. Agree on an acceptable solution. Ask for (or give) a specific commitment. Advise the other person that you'll be sending a written message confirming the agreement.

Keep a record

Keep a written record of important discussions, noting the time of day, date, length of call and number or extension called (if you were the caller). Memories of what was said and what was (or was not) agreed to will alter as time goes by. There are some situations in particular in which it pays to take notes.

Saying 'yes' or 'no'

To the caller who *wants* you to say 'yes' you may sound as though you are in agreement, even if you are not. If you have to say 'yes' or 'no', send written confirmation to the listener and to anyone else involved in the decision.

Media interviews

The telephone barriers place you at risk if you are talking to a media reporter; media assurances about confidentiality are not always reliable. Take notes as you talk (see 'Meeting the media — press conferences' in Chapter 26).

Recording phone calls

In Australia it is not permissible to tape-record a telephone conversation without the agreement of everyone concerned. If you are taping a conference call, begin by asking for this approval to be given orally (on the same tape and by each individual speaker, identified by name). Even if you are having a call monitored on a second phone and recorded in shorthand, first obtain the listener's agreement.

Mobile phones

Overseas experience points to the possibility that many such units are used more as status symbols than as a means of saving time or money. Mobile phones are costly, and if a pager will do the job there may be little reason for the more expensive alternative. Portable units do have their place, but before buying one check the cost against the advantages. Overseas surveys suggest that, apart from high-level executives, the groups who gain most from car-phones and other mobile systems are

- problem solvers: a mobile phone is essential in any emergency situation, and portable units help a team of problem solvers keep in touch with each other;
- very small (or single-person) businesses; the lone operator can handle calls while on the job or travelling from one to the next, saving the cost of full-time office staff or a two-way radio system;
- people who sell products in highly competitive market areas, such as real estate, and who need to know immediately of anything that affects buying or selling.

Summary

1. Introduce yourself in a polite yet friendly way. This encourages the other person to respond in a similar fashion.

2. If you are making the call, and particularly if calling a total stranger, identify yourself immediately the other person answers.

3. If answering the phone, give your telephone number or the name of your organisation, unit or section.

4. If a caller asks for information, particularly for personal details about *any* person, be careful. Give information only if you are authorised to do so.

5. Help listeners to 'visualise' your meaning. Offer additional information that will clarify the picture.

6. Expect misunderstandings when using the telephone.

7. Learn to 'smile' over the phone. You will sound as though you are smiling.

8. Use a sharp, distinct style of speaking (a 'microphone' voice).

9. Give positive feedback throughout the conversation. Treat listeners as adults.

10. Prepare for difficult calls. Plan what you have to say and what response you may expect.

11. Keep a written record of important telephone discussions, noting time of day, date, length of call and (if you were the caller) number or extension called.

Exercises

1. You are making a phone call to someone who does not know you. Using your own name, suggest three different ways in which you could introduce yourself.

2. Using your own name and position, suggest three different ways you could answer the phone at work.

3. At times you have had to communicate with switch operators who did not enjoy their work. Describe the effect these experiences had on you and on others involved.

4. How would you select switch operators? How are they selected where you work?

5. Paul is giving you directions over the phone. 'Just go right down the end of Grey Street; it's the last house on the far side. You can't miss it.' What questions would you ask Paul to clarify his directions?

6. You are working late and are alone. An officer from a police station in another state phones at 8.30 pm wanting the home address of Debbie, one of your advertising executives. Debbie's parents have been seriously injured in an accident. The police found Debbie's work number in her mother's bag and phoned, hoping someone could help them contact her urgently. (Debbie doesn't have the phone on at home.) How would you handle this problem?

CHAPTER 23

Decision making and problem solving in a group

This chapter is about groups. While the emphasis is on the typical work group of five to fifteen people, groups of any size are inclined to follow similar patterns when deciding what to do about a problem. Decision-making bodies can, however, be of any size, from two people up to hundreds.

'Group dynamics' (the technical term for these patterns and the pressures that go with them) is an enormously complicated field of study and this chapter covers only a few of the most significant features. Chapter 25, 'Corporate communication' and Chapter 30, 'Making meetings work', continue the study.

Topics

What is a group?

Making decisions in a group

Choosing a problem-solving strategy

Alternative problem-solving methods

Dealing with disagreement and conflict

Groupthink

Group conflict

Groups and leaders

What is a group?

Any number of people who work or play together as a sales team, a board of directors or a lunchtime darts game can be called a group. Groups form because

- each member shares a common goal or purpose;

- each member finds it more worthwhile, more productive and more enjoyable to work with others.

For any group to exist it also needs a common communication channel, one that every member can use. The better the communication, the more successful the group will be.

Communication and group morale

Good communication and high morale go hand in hand. Probably the most important of all group communication concerns the way people deal (or fail to deal) with problems: 'problem solving' and 'decision making' are joint activities. Groups that solve their problems effectively have high morale and work better. Problems that members talk about are problems that are on the way to being solved. It is the ones they don't talk about that cause the most trouble.

Making decisions in a group

A group decision involves a number of choices about how to fix something, whether to change something, how to go somewhere or how to get something moving. There may be supplementary choices about when and where the solution will be implemented. A sound decision means making a sensible choice or, more often, a series of choices.

Fast or slow decisions?

In a group there is never just *one* solution, nor a *best* solution, so there needs to be sufficient time to consider alternative views before making any choice. Rushed decisions are rarely good ones: people who want a 'quick vote', or hurry to adopt the 'obvious solution' five minutes after a problem is presented, are not helping the group. It may be that they are impatient or the problem may make them feel uncomfortable, but a hurried choice without proper examination of the issue is not good problem solving. On the other hand, some people enjoy discussion (or the sound of their own voices) so much that they seem to prefer talking to deciding.

Balancing decision-making styles

It takes skill to balance the conflicting methods that individuals will want to use. Those who use a decisive thinking style (see Chapter 6) will be confident they already know the 'right' solution, while those who prefer a more flexible approach will want time to consider each aspect carefully. Specific-fact and logical-linear thinkers who prefer a step-by-step sequence and creative-intuitive and feeling-style members may each want to follow their preferred methods. This is one example of the challenges facing the person in charge of a group discussion.

Reducing stress

People can be worried by the problem itself, by public discussion or by all sorts of other things that cause stress. An initial step, even before decision making begins, is to lower stress levels. There is nothing abnormal about feelings of stress, anxiety, or nervousness at this stage, but if they are present people cannot make effective decisions.

> What are some other reasons why people can feel stressed at the start of a problem-solving discussion?

Reduce personal stress levels, before you begin *any* problem solving. If you are a leader, this means calming yourself as well as the group. A cup of tea or coffee or a meal together is a good tranquilliser, but it may also take some strong yet quiet talking by

leaders to remind people of the advantages of calm consideration and teamwork.

Help members to distinguish between the group problem and their personal and immediate 'problem' — their stress level. Distinguish also between real solutions and those that appear more attractive, but only because they reduce everyone's stress.

Deciding how decisions will be made

It's wise if the group starts by agreeing on some kind of formula or 'meeting procedure', preferably one that allows for balanced discussion among members. Unfortunately, the more stressed a group is the more everybody is inclined to skip this step and settle for the alternative 'let's just talk about it' method. There are several reasons why this approach to decision making (though terribly inefficient) is so popular.

- It's easy to use — there are no rules. However, this means that anyone with experience can use the 'let's just talk about it' period to promote their views ahead of others with less confidence.
- It allows the group leaders greater control because they can influence the final choice more easily.
- It's familiar — it's the most commonly used method in Australia, so everyone 'knows how it works'. (In fact, it's questionable whether as a decision-making method it 'works' at all.)

A little informal talk at first helps people to relax (and reduces stress), but too much is a waste of time. If you are leading a discussion, call a halt and get the group to determine which decision-making method will work best. Do this *before* the process of problem solving begins, otherwise too much time is wasted 'just talking'. If the group cannot agree quickly on a method it may be necessary for its leaders to choose one

If you are studying this chapter with a group, here's a test. Finish the chapter, then split into smaller groups (of five or six). Start the exercise, 'Lost in Antarctica' (p. 274). Five minutes later, see how many of the small groups have chosen a decision-making procedure and how many are either still 'just talking about the problem' or have moved on to 'talking about the decision' without any problem-solving strategy.

Choosing a problem-solving strategy

Some of the ways of dealing with problems suggested here are well-recognised and much used; others are less well-known but are specially suited to particular kinds of problems.

The step-by-step formula

This traditional formula uses a step-by-step, analytical format to keep the group on track. It works well provided that

- there is plenty of reliable information available on the problem being discussed;
- group members are happy to use a logical, analytical approach;
- stress levels remain low at all times.

Step 1: Define the present situation

Step 1 is often called the 'where we are now' stage. Ask the group these questions.

- Who and what are being affected by the problem?
- How are they being affected?
- How reliable is the data on the problem?
- Is what is being considered the whole problem or is it only part of a group of connected problems?
- What is the central cause of the problem?
- What are only the symptoms?

Often when a group starts talking about 'the problem', they are really only talking about the visible signs that show it is there. The statement 'Production is behind schedule' describes a symptom, but it is not the main problem. Find out *why* production is down.

Are people using colourful labels to hide a problem? Saying 'It's a personality clash' to explain conflict sounds dramatic, but it's only another symptom. Don't let it stop you getting to the real issue.

Step 2: Define the end goal

What do you want to achieve in making this decision? A useful question at this stage is: 'How will we know when the problem has been solved?'. An answer such as 'When production is back on target' is too vague. Specify and quantify. 'How many units a day is "on target"?'

There is a risk if the group moves on to any of the next steps until at least a majority are in general agreement about 'where they want to be'.

Step 3: Define limits (constraints) or restrictions on solutions

Step 3 helps to keep decisions closer to reality. Constraints the group needs to keep in mind include

- limits on expenditure — budget restrictions;
- limits on the group's legal power;
- limits on information (data on the problem is restricted);
- time limits (how soon is a solution needed?);
- limit of personal commitment: people may talk loudly about the need to act, but the question is how much practical effort each speaker is willing to contribute.

Of course, there may be ways around constraints. Don't accept a limit without being sure it is real. 'Who says the problem has to be fixed today?' 'Why can't we spend more than $7000?'

Step 4: Make a menu of possible choices (options)

Talking about options rather than solutions helps members to be more open-minded about different ways of dealing with the problem.

Collect as many options as possible

Write each one on a board, card or screen. Let everyone see what is on the menu. The best solutions are often 'synthesised' — built up from a mixture of several options, so the more possibilities, the better. Two special methods for generating a greater range of options are force field analysis and brainstorming (see p. 267).

Do not reject random ideas out of hand

Some people will put forward well-thought-out ideas; some will suggest ideas at random. While logical, reasoned suggestions have a strong appeal, a random one may be just as useful.

Discourage competitiveness

Put a hold on discussion or criticism of options when they are first presented. Some members treat problem solving as a contest in which they try to be the first to come up with the 'winning solution'. They criticise everyone else's ideas, especially any that might be superior. Apart from the effect this has on clear thinking, such a spate of negative comments makes others wary of offering any suggestions at all.

Step 5: Select the option you'll try first

A problem may have many solutions, and there is often no way of predicting the 'best' one. Selecting one option to try *first* is more practical, keeps thinking open, and focuses on practical issues, such as these.

- How well might any one option help you reach your goal?
- What are the chances of success for any one option?
- How long will it take to get any one option going? (Would a slightly less popular solution produce a quicker result?)
- What is the 'marketability' of each option? Will people give an idea the support needed to make it work?
- What is the risk factor? (Is there a chance that implementing a solution will in turn create a new problem?)
- Will there be external effects — on the environment, for instance, and the quality of life?

Don't rush the decision. The following pages warn of such dangers as 'groupthink', the false belief that a unanimous vote proves the decision is a good one. Be careful also of overly emotional judgments, but recognise that some people's creative-intuitive feelings may be pointing to something others have overlooked.

Step 6: Who? How? When? Where?

Decisions made at a group meeting do not in themselves fix the problem. What has been achieved is agreement on a common approach.

Supplementary matters to be considered include who will be responsible for implementing the option, preparation of a timetable and a budget, and other practical steps needed to transform the decision into reality.

Step 7: Make sure it really happens

Even the best decisions need people to turn them into actions. Groups often find this step the hardest of all. Gerard Egan (see reading list) estimates that up to 80 per cent of group decisions are never implemented: key supporters may be promoted or transferred; people who originally opposed the decision cannot now be relied on to support it fully. Therefore, without allowing the group to become too negative, look ahead. The time to consider what might happen to block your solution is *now*, not when trouble strikes.

Select an alternative solution (plan B)
Any solution, no matter how well planned, can also create new problems. It helps if you can forecast and be prepared for them. Look at alternatives — either an entirely new option (plan B) or a way of getting the first one (plan A) back on the rails again.

Follow up every decision
It is your job — and the job of all supporters of the decision — to keep a regular check on the progress and effect of the decision. If necessary, make adjustments or modifications when difficulties are encountered. Follow-ups should be comprehensive at first, but can tail off with time as new procedure becomes familiar.

As you become familiar with the step-by-step procedure, you will find it is not essential for the seven steps to be in sequence. Sometimes you define the goal *before* you define the problem. For example, you might decide that you want to buy a new car (the goal) then make a list of the mechanical faults in your old car (defining the present situation).

Alternative problem-solving methods

There are many other ways of finding solutions to problems at work. They can either replace the entire process explained above or can be used within its framework. For instance, several other alternatives can be used at step 5 to help select options.

Experiment — trial and error

If time and the type of problem permit, an experimental 'try the option and see if it works' approach may be better than making a firm decision. Keep in mind that there is no such thing as a failed experiment — every result, whether positive or negative, adds to your understanding. The section

'Experiments' in Chapter 31 explains how to use a similar method.

Consultation

Often the problem is one that requires special expertise. In this case, why try to tackle the task alone? Ask people who have dealt with similar issues in the past to join the meeting.

Lateral, creative and intuitive (gut-feeling) thinking

Lateral thinking (see Chapter 11) and creative-intuitive thinking ('I know I'm right but I don't know how I know', see Chapter 6) are methods used by some of the world's most successful decision makers — not all the time, but when appropriate. The only way to find out if these methods work for you is to try them and see. Be careful, however; intuitive decisions are based on a special 'feeling' that you learn to recognise in time. Just because a choice feels like a good one, it is not necessarily either intuitive or correct.

Weighing up

A table with a 'points score' for each desired factor is useful if the group only has to choose which make and model of computer or which investment fund will fit a particular need. Weighing up is easier if you have comparative figures on each point, but as Table 23.1 shows, there are other ways of projecting comparisons. Weighing-up methods are not reliable if you need to evaluate human factors — for instance, if you have to select the best candidate for a job.

Force field analysis and brainstorming

These two activities do not 'make' decisions, but they do help to develop creative and lateral thinking.

Brainstorming involves getting everyone to 'throw in' as many random ideas or solutions as possible. These are written on a board without *any* discussion until all ideas are in.

Force field analysis is a more structured system in which ideas are again 'thrown in' but are sorted into two groups before being written down.

Group A: Where we are now ⟶ *Where we want to be*

List every positive idea, force, value or other feature, large or small, that ⟶ could help the group get closer to where it wants to be (*solution*) ⟶ or further away from where it is now (*problem*).

Group B: Where we are now ⟵ *Where we want to be*

List every negative idea, force or other factor, large or small, that ⟵ might stop or slow the group's move from where it is now (*problem*) to where it ⟵ wants to be (*solution*).

Sometimes the process works so well that a solution is found, but more often force field analysis provides a starting point for further discussion. It is

Table 23.1 *Weighing-up method*

Item brand	Price ($)	Production rate (units/hr)	Product quality	Error rate (%)	Service life (yrs)
A	5000	3.0	***	5.5	4
B	4500	4.0	****	3.1	5
C	6000	5.5	******	0.5	10
D	2000	2.0	**	8.2	3

particularly useful for identifying hidden factors not observed in ordinary discussions.

Doing nothing for the moment

It is surprising how many problems, if left alone, will solve themselves. In some instances a 'wait and see' approach is a valid option, but only if it is agreed on *after* step-by-step analysis, not instead of it (see 'Denying there is a problem', p. 271).

Dealing with disagreement and conflict

The methods described above work best in a climate in which decisions can be reached amicably, but if there is a division or conflict that none of them can resolve, there are many other ways by which a group can reach a decision. The most productive methods include

- compromise
- consensus
- referral to a committee

Other methods, which have disadvantages but may have to be used to resolve serious disagreement, are

- majority rule
- leader-influenced decision

Compromise

This involves members making concessions so that a decision may be reached based on those points on which all can agree, while playing down aspects on which they cannot, a method often associated with political issues. Persuasion, bargaining and negotiating skills (see Chapters 13 and 24) are needed here.

Compromise decisions are not always sound. Some are achieved because individuals feel that agreement at any price is better than spending more time in a boring meeting. Often long-term benefits are conceded in return for short-term appeals. In an industrial dispute the real problem may be dull and unrewarding work, but rather than face the difficulty of changing the way tasks are organised, a compromise is reached under which workers are paid a few more dollars each week.

To achieve a more lasting solution, the group needs to spend more time analysing, discussing and debating the issue.

Consensus

Provided people have the motivation (and the time) to debate a problem, it can be a highly productive activity and the result is one of the best of all forms of decision making — consensus. Such debate, while it is hard work, is noted for its dynamic and positive atmosphere. It's generally a high-pressure process, but this helps to generate ideas faster and makes far more use of the human potential (and the pool of ideas) in the group.

Everyone has the opportunity to put views forward. There must be time for positive and negative feedback and constructive argument in a climate that allows people to criticise other views and accept criticism in return. The debate continues until the group hammers out a mutually acceptable decision. Everyone may not be completely satisfied, but decisions reached by consensus have significant advantages.

- Hammering ideas out (combining the best of all the original proposals into a 'master solution') produces high-quality decisions, their value proved by their having survived debate.
- Faults in reasoning that might not be detected in an ordinary discussion are more likely to be identified in consensus debate. The decision can be modified on the spot to overcome these.
- Consensus, if not unanimous, at least gives every person present a sense of having contributed to the outcome. Members are therefore more committed to supporting the decision and seeing it successfully implemented.
- As a result of the debate, people originally against an idea may be persuaded that it really is sound, and so become supporters.

Referral to a committee

A committee may be given power only to 'look into the problem' and report on it. (This is more effective than having a large group all trying to find out 'where we are now'.) If it also has the power to take direct action and to implement decisions, the committee can work through the remaining decision-making process faster than a larger group could;

however, the smaller the committee, the smaller will be the pool of ideas. (Chapter 30 looks at other advantages and disadvantages of the committee system.)

Voting

Voting is a quick means of making a choice, but has serious disadvantages. It offers a rough way of finding the most popular choice, but since many of the more effective solutions are *not* popular, voting is not an effective way to make a choice between alternative solutions. On occasion it has to be used to resolve a deadlock, but this should take place *after* full discussion and *after* other methods have failed — not *instead of* more effective methods, and especially not if the only reason for using it is to save time. Voting does not 'make' a decision, but by indicating numbers for and against a particular position it can help groups reach a compromise.

Methods not recommended

Majority rule

If you do take a vote, what happens if the result is 51 per cent in favour to 49 per cent against? If the group regards this as a 'decision' and tries to implement it, they need to be aware that almost half of their number have not been in agreement with the choice and therefore may not feel at all committed to its implementation. It's better to treat such a result as 'no decision' and to continue discussions until at least a 75 per cent majority is achieved.

Leader domination

A meeting is called — supposedly to make a group decision, but the choice has in fact already been made. People are told why the decision is good, then asked to vote in favour of it. The group *accepts* rather than *makes* the choice. Members comply with what the leaders want, regardless of what they personally think. This makes for good decisions only when the leaders have obvious expertise and the rest have no idea of what to do.

Groupthink

At times it seems as though a group has reached a unanimous decision (or even consensus) when what you really have is a leader-dominated decision of a

Majority rule

special kind, called 'groupthink' — a serious problem identified by Irving Janis in his book *Victims of Groupthink* (1973). Janis describes the familiar situation in which a highly cohesive, decision-making group can delude itself into making what seem like sound, rational choices when in fact their decisions are illogical, insufficiently thought out and often totally wrong.

Indicators of groupthink

Groupthink is happening, says Janis, when all or most of the following attitudes are in evidence when decisions are made.

The illusion of invulnerability

Groups that have worked well together for some time and have already made a number of good decisions start to imagine that their decision-making skills are far above those of others. They believe that if they vote unanimously on any issue, it must prove that the decision is sound. This illusion creates a situation in which a group loses the vital ability to question its own decisions, which in turn makes it easier for the other groupthink illusions to develop.

Stereotyping

It may be agreed, for instance, that 'all New Zealanders are hard to do business with', which blinds the group to the possibility of rational decisions that New Zealanders as well as everyone else would find acceptable.

Rationalisation

Groupthink decisions, because they are not logical, need some way to block out obvious criticism from outsiders. For example, Company X owes the group money, but hundreds of employees — and other firms — are relying on Company X to trade out of its troubles. It has a very good chance of doing this, but the group decides to force the company into immediate bankruptcy. They rationalise this decision by saying, 'It was going to fold, anyway; we were only doing what someone else would have done'.

The illusion of morality

Similarly, members in a groupthink environment typically tell each other (and their leader may confirm it as correct) that what they decide is morally good even when it involves illegal activities such as insider trading, collusion, prejudice towards employees, or the destruction of a competitor's business.

The illusion of unanimity

Members who do have doubts keep quiet for fear of upsetting the smooth functioning of the group. This creates the illusion that a decision is unanimous when in reality those members would have liked to criticise it or to suggest other choices.

Closing of the group to outsiders

Meetings become restricted to certain individuals. Outsiders are not allowed to take part even when expert advice is needed. Members typically come to think of themselves as more expert than 'technical boffins' (stereotyping again) when it comes to making important decisions. Reports of proceedings are treated as confidential documents, making it harder for anyone outside to discover that serious mistakes are being made by the group's top decision makers.

Direct pressure

Those who do express doubts may be directly pressured by other group members to conform, being told, 'Don't rock the boat'. Sticking together becomes more important than making a sound decision — loyalty and mateship are placed ahead of logic.

Groupthink is common in Australian business and government circles, though of course if you tell people they are suffering from it they will only see you as another uninformed outsider. This is an extremely dangerous situation for the group: in the short run it will continue to make small but wrong decisions that will pass unnoticed, but when things go badly wrong, mistakes grow bigger and bigger and decisions worse and worse until they result in financial ruin or legal action.

Defences against groupthink

- Bring outsiders into group discussions. Do not allow the group to become closed to new or different ideas (see 'Consultants and technical experts', in Chapter 31).
- Encourage group members to stick to the kind of problem-solving strategies suggested in this chapter. Do not develop the habit of deciding on a majority vote.
- When looking for options, explore every possible alternative and make sure that all members are encouraged to question information they are not satisfied with or do not fully understand.
- Everyone involved — especially group leaders — should keep personal choices to themselves until all aspects of the issue have been explored.
- Encourage senior group members to act as devil's advocates (see p. 272) to ensure that opposing views are promoted as strongly as those favoured by the majority.
- Be on the lookout for any signs of groupthink. The best defence of all is to know that it exists and to tell people about it before the 'illusion' stage sets in and it becomes harder for members to see what is going on.

Avoiding group decisions

The following ways of 'making' decisions are very common. This does not mean they are successful. They offer an easy way out, and avoid the hard work associated with real problem solving.

Fairy-tale solutions

These are quick and pleasant-sounding suggestions that are either unrealistic or rely on some future event which (*if* it happens) will solve everything with a minimum of effort (. . . and we'll all live happily ever after). For instance: 'Let's borrow the money and buy it now. Interest rates must come down soon, but if they don't we'll just advertise more and increase sales'.

Solving problems means finding a *practical* route from where you are now to where you want to be, not an imaginary one. Solutions that avoid hard thinking are pleasant to dream about, but seldom successful.

Making the problem illegal

Making suicide illegal will discourage some individuals from attempting to kill themselves. However, it can also make it harder for someone who is suicidal to discuss his or her 'illegal' objectives with others. Think of some examples of someone at work or in your study area trying to solve a problem by making a rule that something should not happen — for instance, putting up a notice saying 'Wasting photocopy paper is forbidden. By order'.

Ordering someone to fix the problem

Telling other people that it is 'their job' to fix problems does not give them any options to work with. It will raise their stress level, though. What effect will that have?

Ignoring the problem

People who are uncomfortable about facing a problem may accept that it exists and then put it out of their minds. Or they may say it is of too little importance to require any attention — a solution that is valid only after full examination of the issue, not as an escape from it.

Denying that there is a problem

This is common when people are put on the spot, such as in a current affairs program on television or radio. They simply either deny that the problem exists or say that it is no concern of theirs (see 'Denial barriers', p. 66).

Other faulty approaches to decision making

- Look at only one aspect of an issue in great detail.
- Look only at the broad issue, and ignore details.
- Be overconfident: 'No worries! She'll be right, mate'.
- Sidetrack — talk about easy topics to avoid working on difficult decisions.
- Believe that there is only 'one' solution and that all the meeting has to do is find where it's hidden.

People who propose these solutions are more often not so much naive or foolish as expressing discomfort with having to be involved in problem solving and a desire to avoid the problem in any way possible.

Group conflict

A competitive spirit can encourage members to strive hard to come up with better ideas. This doesn't mean challenging individuals to see who can come up with the 'best' solution; there are other ways to use controlled conflict — for instance, by forcing people to come out in the open and discuss real issues instead of fairy-tale ones.

The devil's advocate (positive conflict)

If one particular point of view is being accepted too readily or without thorough consideration, a senior member of the group may deliberately oppose it. This individual is playing the role of 'devil's advocate' — the label is a complimentary one (borrowed from the church).

What the 'devil's advocate' does is in effect to challenge others to make a more critical appraisal of their views before making a decision. Watching someone play this role provides an illustration of just how well the process of well-managed, positive conflict can help a group make better decisions.

Destructive debate (negative conflict)

Destructive conflict arises when personalities rather than ideas become the focal point of the debate. If group members are being manipulative or trying to force decisions that will benefit them personally, the group suffers. It is the task of leaders to watch for any sign of destructive conflict and to contain it as quickly as possible.

The 'invisible solution'

Some choices will prove effective *if* they can be put into practice. However, unless people know enough about the reasons behind a decision, it may become a source of so much conflict and group resistance that it is not given a chance to work. In line with the saying that 'Justice should not only be done, but manifestly and undoubtedly be seen to be done', to avoid conflict a decision must be *seen* to be a good one. Conflict may result if, for instance, a decision

- is announced without sufficient warning;
- is not explained in sufficient detail;
- is rushed through so quickly that people are not even aware there was a problem;
- involves new technology which no one is able to explain clearly;
- is preceded by comments such as 'Trust us, we know what is best', or 'It's too late, the decision has already been made';
- is made without consultation with the 'front-line' users, the people who will actually put it into practice.

A decision that has been discussed fully and negotiated — or at least explained fully to those involved — has a much better chance of success. It has the quality of 'visibility'. Some managers and leaders avoid making their decisions known in advance on the basis that opponents will attack them for political or selfish reasons. This may be so, but the more visible the solution, the less ammunition people have to manipulate the situation. It is the hard-to-see solution that provides the best chance for manipulation, because people react to it emotionally rather than rationally. A good solution will survive the debate, and its visibility will be enhanced as a result.

Groups and leaders

Leaders communicate with the group about group issues. They also help members communicate within the group about:

- tasks and goals
- raising morale
- managing conflict
- protecting or increasing group resources
- concerns and needs of individual members

Certainly, the type of person who can do these things will be likely to possess well-developed communication skills and be interested in people, but such qualities alone do not make a leader. Neither does simply holding a position of authority over a group make a leader.

Group leadership requires a special relationship between the individual who holds the position and the group that accepts that person as leader. The real leaders are those who can communicate two things to a group:

- the special power or ability they have;
- the way in which this can be used to help the *group* to achieve its goals.

Members of a group follow a leader who they see as helping them to achieve their goals. Political party members, for instance, will follow their leader *only* for as long as he or she is seen as helping them win the next election.

Informal leadership

Good leadership can add to the success of a group, but the existence of a single leader is not the prime condition for its formation, nor for its continued existence. Several people can act as joint leaders, particularly if they each play a role to help improve group communication. Leadership positions obviously are dependent on ability to 'deliver' whatever assistance the group is looking for: Chapter 13 lists some of the different kinds of power available to a leader or potential leader. Some of these, such as authority, are more closely allied with formal positions than with leadership. By contrast, if you have personal power as an expert, or a 'referent' figure, you will almost certainly find yourself in a position of leadership even if it is not formally recognised.

Informal leaders can be very effective; they will influence almost every group decision and may help a group resist the control of an unpopular authority figure. It is important, especially in meetings, to identify such people and either work with them or gain their co-operation in other ways.

Summary

1. Good communication and high morale go hand in hand. Groups that solve problems have high morale and work more effectively.

2. Sound discussion and consideration are needed before any decision is made.

3. Agree on a formula or 'meeting procedure' that will encourage a balanced discussion and keep it on track.

4. There is never just *one* solution, or a 'best' solution.

5. Alternative ways of finding solutions include lateral thinking and creative-intuitive methods, used by some of the world's most successful decision makers.

6. If conflict in the group is affecting decisions, try to reach a compromise or consensus.

7. Voting does not 'make' decisions. At best, it is a way of finding out which choices are the more popular.

8. Groupthink occurs when a highly cohesive group deludes itself into making illogical and poor decisions.

9. The role of 'devil's advocate' is a responsible one in which positive conflict is promoted to encourage discussion.

10. Solutions — and the reasons for them — must be 'visible' if all group members are to support them and help to put them into practice.

11. Leaders need to be able to show members that they have the power to help the group achieve its goals.

12. Leaders must communicate with members about group issues and also help members to communicate within the group.

Exercises

1. If eleven out of twenty-one people vote 'yes' in a meeting, does this make the decision a 'good' choice? If two of the eleven had been sick and unable to attend, would the resulting 'no' vote then prove the better decision? What does this tell you about decisions based on voting and about close votes in particular?

2. List some examples of group decisions you know of that appear to have been the result of groupthink. Describe some of the symptoms in your example that match the indicators given on page 270. (An example would be the 1987 'Joh for Canberra' campaign.)

3. You and two friends are at home on Monday afternoon at 4.50 pm, when a stone from a motor mower next door hits your front picture window, smashing the glass into fragments! The three of you have to go out at 5.30 to attend an evening class that you cannot miss — but there are reports of a thief being active in the area. How would you deal with this problem?

4. Suggest some ways of dealing with stress at the start of a group meeting.

5. Your student council has been given an old shop, one block away from the campus area. The only conditions are that the shop must be used to raise at least $10 000 a year (after expenses) and that this money must be used to benefit students. Working in a group, make a decision on how the building will be used.

6. 'Lost in Antarctica'.
This all-Australian version of the NASA problem, 'Lost on the Moon', is based, with grateful acknowledgment, on an earlier model devised by a group of valued friends and professional colleagues: John Wellings (New South Wales Board of Adult Education), Ian Pedersen (Royal Agricultural Society, Victoria) and Keith Topfer (Tasmanian Department of Agriculture).

The situation
You and a small group of friends are the survivors of a plane crash on an icy mountain very close to the South Pole. You are all uninjured and in excellent physical condition. The group has agreed that the best chance of rescue is to walk from the crash site to the Australian Antarctic Base on the coast. Estimated time for this is six to seven weeks. However, the closer you get to the Australian base, the better are the chances that a search plane will see you. It is Christmas Eve.

Resources
In your personal backpack you have sufficient dehydrated food (in special lightweight packs) for at least two months and plenty of highly efficient thermal clothing. The group has a light 2-metre sled, tents and eight weeks' supply of fuel for lighting and heating, in the form of self-igniting heat blocks.

The problem
Before the plane burst into flames you had time to save the items listed below. You now have to decide which of them (if any) are worth taking with you. All are in good working condition at the moment. You are able to take up to five of them (no more) in addition to the resources listed above. However, you must be able to explain your reasons for taking each one of the extra items. If you can manage with less than five, do so. You can discard parts of any item and take only what will be useful, but that part will still count as *one* of your five.

1. A 20 litre metal drum of distilled water
2. A 2 litre bottle of Bundaberg Rum
3. A 20 metre length of Nylex plastic garden hose
4. A magnetic compass
5. A portable gas cooking-stove with 20 kilogram gas cylinder (full)
6. An AWA battery-powered FM radio receiver
7. A high-powered rifle, with twenty rounds of ammunition
8. A shaving mirror
9. A five-cell battery-powered Eveready torch (batteries included)
10. A small snakebite kit, including bandages and splints
11. A gas-type disposable cigarette lighter
12. A large plastic Australian flag (8 metres × 5 metres)
13. Six large (850 millilitre) cans of pineapple juice and a can-opener
14. A large meat cleaver
15. Twenty copies of the *Australian* newspaper
16. A 1 kilogram jar of Vegemite
17. A packet of Jaffas
18. A copy of the New Testament translated into an Aboriginal dialect
19. A tin of Kiwi boot polish (black)
20. A pair of pliers

Note:
- *All* decisions must be reached by consensus, *not* by voting.
- The force field method can be used with this problem. List all the qualities each object has that could help you get 'where you want to be'. Then list all the qualities (for instance, weight or size) that could slow you down or keep you 'where you are now'.

CHAPTER 24

High-power communication

Much high-level business communication, including selling and negotiating, involves methods used to influence people or convince them that they need to move towards a goal or to take action, both of which are vitally important to you or your enterprise. This chapter shows how you can create movement, co-operation or action even when others (initially) say they don't want to move.

To do so increases your power as leader, manager or organiser and extends your control to cover almost any situation. For this reason the chapter considers the nature of 'control' and also of its companion functions, including power, command and influence.

Topics

Getting people to move

Negotiating power

Testing power

Negotiating techniques

Getting people to move

Negotiation and bargaining are ways of getting people to move from a position they find comfortable and from which they often do not want to move. Your task as a negotiator is to show

- why they need to move;
- how moving can benefit them;
- why a move in the direction you require will be more worthwhile for them than any other.

Of course, there are many other ways of achieving these results. You can motivate people, you can use positive persuasion, or you can use negative methods such as threats, force and manipulation. However, negotiation and bargaining are superior methods that gain results when simpler techniques fail.

Find the middle ground

You can negotiate more successfully if you are prepared to give and take — that is, to compromise on some aspects of a deal. Your willingness to compromise puts pressure on the other person to do the same for you until the stage is reached where you both agree. An important aspect of bargaining and negotiating is therefore to find where this middle ground (the area of common agreement) lies (see Fig. 24.1).

Not all negotiation is about buying and selling — well, certainly not in monetary terms. You can easily find yourself negotiating about anything of value, particularly power and status in your job, time, working conditions, or the standards that you believe in. In every case, if you want others to move from their position, or they want you to move from yours, start by using simple persuasion or motivation techniques (see Chapters 5, 6, 12 and 13). Try assertion (see Chapter 12). If none of these work, it's time to start moving into the negotiating mode.

Negotiating power

One of the negotiator's basic tools is power, so review the kinds of persuasive power explained in detail in Chapter 13. The more you understand about power the more effective you will be at communicating about it and therefore at negotiating and bargaining. And the less power you will give away unnecessarily. But what do people really mean by 'power'? Ask people what the word means and you get a variety of definitions. 'Power is authority' is a common response, but that does not explain

really what it is or what it does. Neither does it explain the relationship between power and control.

Control

Control is the means by which you make something happen or ensure that something takes place according to plan. Full control means that the event takes place how, when and where it was supposed to, despite any forces that may be working against it. When a problem is solved in the way you planned,

you say 'It's under control'. If a strike or a breakdown prevents a task being finished on time, you say 'Sorry, matters beyond our control ...'. Controlling is, of course, one of the basic functions of management.

Power

Like power stored in a battery, human power is not always visible, but waits quietly until needed. People

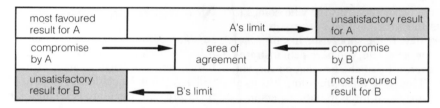

most favoured result for A		A's limit ⟶	unsatisfactory result for A
compromise by A ⟶	area of agreement	⟵ compromise by B
unsatisfactory result for B	⟵ B's limit		most favoured result for B

Fig. 24.1 *Negotiate to find the middle ground*

with power do not use it all the time, or make it obvious. Just the knowledge that they have power is often sufficient to persuade others to co-operate, to create movement, to get a job done on time.

Power is the *ability* or *potential* one has to exercise *control*. Like control, however, power is only effective if you can apply it despite opposing forces or influences (such as weather, strikes, personal opposition or breakdowns). If you fail to deal with these problems, your power as well as your control suffers.

Characteristics of negotiating power

The different kinds of power, as explained in Chapter 13, include
- reward-penalty power
- authority or position power
- expert power
- affiliate power
- other kinds of power
    special information
    seniority or referent power
    contracted or shared power
    force and pressure
    charismatic and manipulative power (twin forms of power)

When faced with power, you need to identify the various kinds, and their effect on you and your position as a negotiator. With reference to each one, consider the following points.

Is it personal or impersonal?

Some kinds of power, such as expertise, rest very much with the individual. Others — for instance, authority — attach to a position and can move from one individual to another according to who is 'sitting in the chair'.

How easy is it to gain (or lose)?

Know which kinds are the easiest for you to attain. Expert power, for example, can be built up by study and so is available to almost anyone, but it takes much time and effort to develop. Authority power is harder to attain. Manipulative power is readily available and gets results, but you lose rather than gain by using it.

How easily can you match the power?

Power based on rewards (such as money) is easy to match in negotiations. Expert power is much harder to match, or to resist.

How well does one kind of power combine with others?

All can be strengthened by combination with others, but the more personal the power, the less this combination is possible.

Testing power

Wise negotiators need to know what kind and what degree of power they are up against. The more visible the power (the degree to which it can be observed, tested or measured), the easier it is to deal with. Two tests are possible to help identify it and determine its level of legitimacy (see Chapter 13).

The 'Finger in the socket' test

You can test power by calling a person's bluff, or walking away. This is a challenge: if the person is bluffing, it becomes obvious. For instance, suppose that the new supervisor says 'Anyone who comes to work late gets the sack' and you start coming to work late every day. If the supervisor has no *power* to sack people for being late, you have demonstrated that fact. However, if he or she has that power, you lose your job. This test must therefore be used with caution. It may also force the other person to exercise far more power against you than was at first intended.

The verbal 'What will happen if . . .?' test

A better way to find out what kind and what strength of power you are up against is to ask people 'What will happen if . . .?'. Here are three ways of doing this.

Making a polite enquiry

Your lecturer might say, 'Your low marks are a direct result of the time you waste watching television. Give it up immediately'. This is either a joke or an excessive use of power, so to test the strength of the lecturer, you ask 'What will happen if I just watch educational documentaries and nothing else?'.

Note that you may not even need to ask the other party to the negotiation. Asking other students 'What will happen if I keep on watching television?' will also give you useful data on your bargaining position.

Finding out how close you are to agreement

Sometimes the 'What if . . .?' question is a more direct part of negotiation strategy as discussions reach the compromise stage. '*What if* we pay you $1000 more and you handle the registration? Then will you agree?' A 'yes' answer tells you that the opposition either wants agreement and is ready to co-operate or has not much strength left to bargain with and is close to compliance. A 'no' tells you that discussions still have a way to go.

As a warning to the other negotiator

In a tough negotiating situation — say between unions and management — the question might be '*What* [will you lose] *if* you go on strike now instead of waiting for the new award to come into use?'.

Negotiating techniques

In some cultures there is no such thing as a fixed price — or even a marked price. If you go to a bazaar and ask what an item costs, the merchant will say, 'How much do you want to pay?' or 'Name me a price'. Bargaining is second nature to people of these cultures, whereas Australians tend to reserve it for important financial matters: buying a house, getting a divorce, merging a company.

Not knowing how to negotiate means that you are probably paying too much for a lot of things and will eventually pay too much for something significant. What's more, even if you possess it negotiation is a skill that needs to be developed and kept *active*, otherwise it will let you down when you need it most.

There are plenty of opportunities to learn to negotiate, if you look for them.

Practise your negotiating skills

Where can you practise? Start with small businesses and independent service firms. Use the phone. Ring six different carpet-cleaners and ask how much they charge to clean every room in an average house. Explain to each one that you find that particular price high in comparison with others you have contacted, then ask how much the firm *really* wants. Finally, ask how much it would be if paid in cash. If you have to buy two or more items at one time from one shop, ask how much less you need pay for 'the two together'. This may or may not get results straight off (though you may be surprised); the real value is that it gets you into the habit of regarding price as a flexible amount, not a fixed one. If you don't develop the experience and self-confidence to negotiate for small things, you will have no hope when it comes to the big ones.

Most of the first set of guidelines below apply whether you are dealing with money, power, time, status or anything else that people value and therefore need to bargain about. Others, listed separately, refer more to buying-and-selling situations.

General negotiations — guidelines

1. Work out in advance exactly what you are willing to negotiate.
What are you prepared to exchange, give up, trade or pay in order to create movement? To decide this

you need to know exactly what your position is now and why you prefer not to move, but to persuade the other party to move instead. Know exactly how any move that person makes will benefit or harm you and your position.

2. Find out why an individual wants to negotiate with you.

This will give you a better idea of how far he or she might be prepared to move if you stand firm, or whether in fact you are the one in the weaker position.

3. Find out about the other party's background.

Research this person's length of experience as a negotiator, type of training, level of bargaining skill, and any particular negotiating tricks likely to be used. If you find out personal details as well, it pays to drop them casually into the opening conversation. It gives you an advantage if you can convince the other person that you are better informed in this respect than he or she is about you.

4. Find a blemish.

If, for instance, the other person has made a mistake in addressing a letter to you and it is late reaching you, make the point. This, too, detracts from the other party's opening position.

5. There is no such thing in negotiation as a fixed position.

If people really intend to take a fixed position they signal this by refusing even to consider negotiating with you. The fact that you are discussing possible negotiations is evidence that there is at least some willingness to move.

6. Don't move too soon.

The one who makes the most offers — or shows too early a willingness to move — loses negotiating points. Try to get the other side to state its position first and to propose more moves than you do.

7. Never be in a hurry!

You can't negotiate as effectively if you're pressed for time. Apart from money, time is one of the most common negotiating points; the more you have, the greater your negotiating power will be.

8. Patience helps you to win points.

If you have developed the self-confidence to hold a

position without moving, you have the makings of a powerful negotiator. One of the main skills in negotiating is to give the impression that you are ready to forget about the whole thing if the other person does not start moving in the direction you want (but *never* put this idea into words!).

9. Find out what concessions appeal most to the other person.

Negotiations, as stated, can be about money, power, status, time, and many more things, including personal desires. Include them all in your bag of concessions that you can offer in return for other concessions that you want. People often value peace of mind far more than dollars. A longer warranty, a free trial to prove that an item is sound, or good after-sales support will make more sales than 'off the shelf' or 'take it as is' items costing far less.

10. When making a concession always ask for a matching one in return.

If you can, trade a concession that has little value for you, but will have strong appeal to the other party. For instance, if someone has no way of transporting a bulky item and you have an empty truck and a driver who is short of work, offer free delivery as your concession; if time is vital for you, ask for extra time to pay in return for your offer to handle delivery. Don't give anything away because it has no value to *you*.

11. Question every fact presented by the opposition.

Ask for proof and specific evidence or verification. Don't rely on words alone. Some of the opposition's so-called 'facts' may be bluff. Some that they believe to be true may in fact collapse when you test them. Use the tests for objectivity (Chapter 11) and the 7 C's (Chapter 15).

Negotiating to buy or sell — guidelines

1. Every price is negotiable.

Very few people put things on the market unless they want to sell them, and since they *want* to sell, they will usually take less than they're asking. People who want to *buy* will usually pay more than originally intended, but may have a fixed limit in money terms. That need not stop you getting a better price in terms of time to pay or other conditions.

2. If you are selling, know exactly *why* you are selling.

How much would you like to get? How much do you expect? What is the lowest you'll accept? (This may involve more than just money.)

3. The person who quotes a price first loses some strength.

Whether seller or buyer, once a person names a price, the other party can begin to negotiate for something lower or higher, according to which side of the deal applies.

4. Tailor your opening offers.

Most people *under*-estimate the market value of whatever they are selling and *over*-value the amount they will have to pay for something they want. Take this into account.

5. State your position firmly.

Make it clear that if you don't buy or sell an item at once it will not be a problem, and that you have other alternatives already in mind. Unless you can walk away from any deal that is not fair and beneficial to you, you are in no position to start dealing.

6. Be prepared to take your time.

You can't deal effectively if you're pressed for time, which is exactly why so many purchases in our time-conscious society can't be negotiated. If you're in a hurry to buy a car or a washing machine, expect to pay a higher price than necessary. Put the purchase off until you are on holidays. Patience is the key.

7. Find out what the other person really wants.

For sellers, this may not always be money. People who sell things of personal attachment — old houses, antiques or pets — usually want the item to go 'to the right person', and will sometimes take a lower price if you show that you will value it as much as they did.

8. Don't let anyone impress you by naming a figure.

Some people are overwhelmed when a seller says 'I'm looking for $100 000 for this'. They feel it will somehow be insulting to offer less than $80 000, but to do this defies every rule of bargaining. If somebody quotes an opening price of $200 000, look surprised and say, 'Oh dear, I was thinking of $75 000'. Then see what happens. Maybe you'll go up to $100 000 or maybe you'll be shown the door, but there are plenty of cases in which the buyer asks for $200 000 and ends up taking $75 000. Don't be ashamed of starting low.

There's a story of an agent asking for $1 million for one of his client's books. 'A million!' gasped a prospective publisher. 'I wouldn't pay you a cent more than $20 000!' 'Great', said the agent. 'That's the best offer I've had so far. Here, sign the contract!'

9. Cash may be more valuable than a cheque or credit.

If the quoted price for a piece of furniture being sold privately is $500, it never hurts to ask 'How about $350 cash, right now?' and pull out the money. The sight of cash is quite often sufficient to close a deal on the spot.

Opening negotiations

There is a large gap between total domination at one end of the negotiation scale and total submission at the other end. A good negotiator avoids confrontation, and tries instead to find a middle-ground

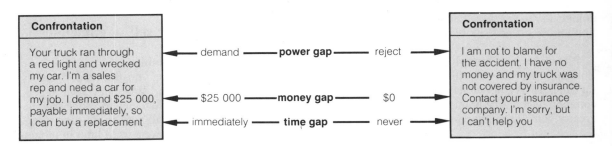

Fig. 24.2 *A confrontation opening reduces the chance of successful negotiation*

(compromise) position in which both parties reap the benefit. How successful you are may depend on the way you begin.

Compromise or confrontation?

Figure 24.2 illustrates a confrontation approach. If both parties take an extreme opening position like this, it is difficult for either to move. Negotiation cannot begin. The gap between each is too wide and there is no point on which to open discussions.

Ambit opening

In Figure 24.3, both parties have taken positions that again give the impression that negotiation is not being considered, but this is not so. Each party is in fact setting up an extreme position or 'ambit' as an indication to the other that he or she will not move beyond that point. Reread the words; notice that party A uses the phrase 'I am prepared to accept . . .', while party B says 'It's a matter for my legal advisers'. The ambit opening is a form of bluff; it focuses on the width of the gap rather than either party's position, but sometimes this kind of opening is necessary.

Negotiation for agreement

In Figure 24.4 (p. 282), the gap between agreement is enough to show that each party feels in a strong position. The openings by each party contain arguments about why the *other* should move, but this in itself is a signal that his or her position is not fixed either.

Notice how, through a series of shifts, the time, power and money gaps are all reduced until quite suddenly the possibility of agreement is obvious. Note that in the final step (8) the owner of the truck arranges for the agreement to be recorded on paper — a very sensible move. It should be signed and witnessed, with a copy going to each party before the negotiation is considered finalised. Depending on the type of negotiation, it may be wise to have the agreement checked by solicitors for each party.

Closing negotiations

There are a number of ways in which negotiations can end. Of these, compliance and submission are to be avoided. A checkmate situation is risky, and is best defused so that negotiations can continue. The ideal is a compromise.

Compliance

In negotiation, to comply is what you do when you run out of power. When a police officer signals a driver to stop most people comply rather than keep driving, because they have no room to negotiate. If a union organiser demands that you stop at a picket line, you might consider whether you must comply with the request or try negotiating a compromise.

Compliance is the less-than-willing acceptance by one person that another has more power on a particular issue. Do not make the mistake of seeing all compliance as a 'backdown'; it is a matter of choosing 'second best', so that you make the most of the situation.

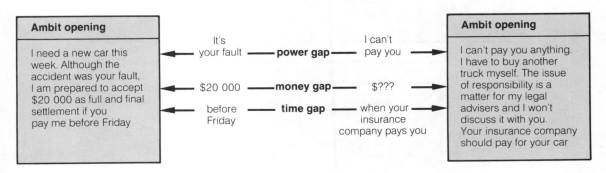

Fig. 24.3 *An ambit opening is still extreme, but allows room to move and to negotiate*

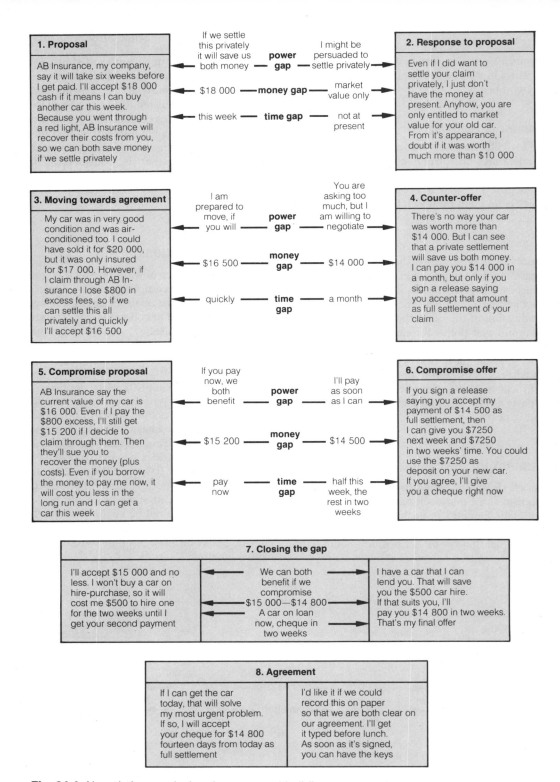

Fig. 24.4 *Negotiating — closing the gaps and building agreement*

Submission

Submission, on the other hand, is the complete surrender of one party to another, with no compromise. The loser is denied the right to negotiate or even to choose a stage at which to comply. Total submission is seldom a satisfactory result for either party. Often the victory is only a short-term one, and meanwhile the dominator earns a reputation for inflexibility that reduces his or her effectiveness in future negotiations.

Checkmate

In some situations you may be confident that you cannot be beaten no matter what moves other parties make. You could move to secure their compliance or submission, but why do this? A skilled negotiator avoids a situation where others lose face.

- Help them to see the position more clearly. They may not be able to see, as you can, that they have run out of negotiating power.
- Try to set up a strategy that lets them back out gracefully, without being left with a losing image.
- Offer a minor concession to help sweeten the situation. Often the only thing preventing agreement is the fear of 'losing face' or backing down, or of being seen as a total loser. A small win can ease acceptance of a bigger loss.

Summary

1. Negotiation is a way of getting people to move from a position which they prefer to a position that suits both parties.

2. Show the other party the reason for and the benefit of moving.

3. You negotiate more successfully if you are prepared to give and take — to compromise on aspects of the deal. This approach is more likely to persuade the other person to do the same for you.

4. Not all negotiation is about buying and selling. You can negotiate about anything of value, particularly power and status in your job, free time, working conditions and standards.

5. It's a help if you can identify the kind of power you are up against, and its level of legitimacy. Two useful tests of power are the 'Finger in the socket' test and the verbal 'What will happen if . . .?' test.

6. Work out in advance exactly what you are willing to exchange, to pay or to give up.

7. Find out why the other individual concerned wants to negotiate with you.

8. The party that makes the most offers or shows too early a willingness to concede loses negotiating power.

9. If you've got the other person in a corner, offer a minor concession to sweeten the situation and help the other to avoid losing face. A small win softens a bigger loss.

Exercises

1. How much and what kind of negotiating power does a manager or leader have over other people at work?

2. What kind of power does a lecturer have over students? If the students are adult and studying part time, does this increase or decrease their level of negotiating power?

3. Negotiate with your lecturer about some concession that will benefit the whole class — an outing, an earlier finishing time or an alternative method of assessment in place of a proposed test.

4. You and a 'partner' are setting up a small business. With your partner, discuss the following points. Make as many decisions as you can.

   (a) The office must be open every weekday from 8.00 am to 5.00 pm.

   (b) The office must also be open on Thursday nights from 5.00 pm to 8.00 pm and on Saturdays from 8.30 am to 1.30 pm.

   (c) At present you have no other staff and no company vehicle. If you are to purchase any item or employ anyone, the cost will have to be carried by you equally, as partners, or taken out of your profits.

For the moment, decide which one of you will take charge of

  (i) Saturday morning trading;
 (ii) Thursday night trading;
(iii) handling the money, including daily banking (normally between 2.30 and 3.30 pm);
(iv) buying stock from visiting representatives (who often take clients to lunch);
 (v) buying stock from large firms who take orders over the phone;
(vi) selling stock to over-the-counter customers;
(vii) selling to large clients;
(viii) cleaning the office;
(ix) keeping the yard tidy;
 (x) hiring typists;
(xi) hiring truck drivers;
(xii) negotiating with your bank manager for a loan.

CHAPTER 25

Corporate communication

Communication systems are similar in most organisations, large or small, public, private or community-based. This chapter looks particularly at communication as it takes place in a commercial environment. In particular, it draws attention to

- the ways in which organisation communication differs from personal communication;
- official systems that organisations use to convey messages;
- unofficial or 'shadow' systems that carry messages within the organisation;
- communication problems in organisations;
- options for creating more effective communication in organisations;
- communication with overseas organisations.

Topics

Organisation systems and communication

Corporate communication systems

Corporate communication problems

Changing the system

International communication

Organisation systems and communication

To understand why an organisation communicates in ways that often seem inefficient and unwieldy, stand back a little and look at it from the outside. Try to see it as 'a system', rather than as 'XYZ International' or 'Greenberg City Council'. Powerful forces operate within any system; some help to hold it together and some (if they get out of hand) tend to break it apart. Naturally these forces have a

profound effect on everything that the organisation does, particularly on the way it communicates.

An organisation's communication network operates within the larger system, but it is the communication network that shapes and controls all the other systems. This means that understanding the network is the key to managing and controlling most aspects of the organisation. That is why this chapter begins by looking at four factors related to communication networks:

- the cold communication factor
- the trust factor
- the screening factor
- goal conflict (the 'iron triangle')

The cold communication factor

'Warm' messages are people-oriented. They consider the receiver's feelings and reactions. They help build relationships between receiver and sender. 'Cold' messages are more often task-oriented, expressing concern about 'getting the job done' irrespective of the effect on people's needs and interests.

Organisations naturally use cold communication. Most routine, mass-produced messages they send are impersonal, lacking the ability to communicate on important issues such as enthusiasm, loyalty and trust. It's hard to gain people's support and understanding if you rely only on cold messages.

Leadership and corporate communication

Companies need leaders who can translate cold, corporate ideas into warm, human messages; those who use too much cold communication may succeed as 'managers', but not as leaders.

When you want to send a message requiring the human touch, personalise it; let it seem like *you* talking, not like a recorded message. If it is written, sign it. If you transmit a personal memo electronically, add some individual 'signing off' comment to emphasise that it is not part of a bulk distribution (see Chapter 17).

The trust factor

The colder the communication level in an organisation, the lower will be the level of trust. In turn, a low level of trust can freeze up communication, leading to misunderstanding and conflict. The level of trust affects most other aspects of company management as well as communication, so the trust factor is a common issue in most organisations.

The screening factor

Sorting machines use grids — or screens with holes of a set diameter — to separate products of different sizes. In organisations, people are sorted according to how well they conform to a predetermined style. This applies as much to communication style as any other. Those who fit most comfortably into the firm's corporate style do well, are promoted and in their turn help to maintain that style. Those who do not fit are gradually screened out, because they are 'different'. The effect is to apply a powerful though unwritten form of control over communication styles in the organisation.

- There is a tendency to communicate through the organisation in standard ways, which become well recognised. People who try something different are often told that they are using the 'wrong' style, whether or not it is an improvement.
- Those who question standard styles tend to be trusted less by the established majority. An old communication system may be breaking down, but those who point this out often find they are threatened with 'screening'. This is particularly common in political groups (which happen to be very prone to screening problems).
- Since those who communicate in the favoured style tend to be promoted more quickly than those who want to change, conformity of opinion at the top is reinforced in its communication style, management style, corporate goals and resistance to change.

Are there any people in your own company who are good workers but regularly miss out on promotion? Might this be because they do not measure up to the standard communication pattern? Are there people you know who had no success in your firm but have since done tremendously well in a different company? If so, perhaps the screening factor is at work in your organisation.

In larger companies the screening factor can operate in different parts of the same firm, people tending to be grouped in departments according to preferred styles of communication. Note the similarity between this and the causes of groupthink (see Chapter 23).

Goal conflict

Communication is essential for resolving goal conflict. Companies need clear corporate goals. If group or individual goals conflict, the company suffers. Usually there are three specific goals, triangularly opposed (the 'iron triangle'), and companies tend to organise their work around these three despite the fact that they oppose one another.

Goal 1: Getting the work done on time (the task goal)
Groups such as manufacturing, sales and transport have goals related to getting products made, sold or delivered.

Goal 2: Getting the job done economically and efficiently (resource goals)
The accounting division, for instance, and middle management are less directly concerned with getting the job done but very interested in doing it as cheaply as possible, and in minimising waste.

Goal 3: Getting people to do the job willingly (motivation and 'people' goals)
The third side of the organisation triangle (sections like personnel, training, and often senior management) tends to concentrate more on motivational (people) goals, with issues such as morale and profit-sharing incentive schemes.

Naturally, goals that are so different in nature tend to compete against each other.

- The sales group want more money for expenses, but they are competing with the transport unit, who want bigger trucks.
- The accounts section resists both requests, because the added costs would reduce profits. Administration resists, too, because the extra

expenses would mean additional paper work.

- The people in sales and transport have motivational goals — part of the reason they come to work each day. If they don't get their extra expenses or their new trucks, they may lose some of their motivation. This is more likely if they see themselves as losing out in the competition with other sections.

The iron triangle

Imagine three people holding a large metal triangle. It is rigid: it will not bend or stretch. If each person pulls on one corner (towards a chosen goal), what happens? A lot of energy is used up, but no one gets anywhere unless one of the three is strong enough to pull the others away from their goals. Much energy is wasted, without any real progress. This is why the goal-conflict issue is described as an 'iron triangle'. It's a case of goals that don't match.

This kind of conflict exists in every organisation. If a company has problems getting different sections to communicate effectively, it is likely that part of the cause can be traced to goal conflict.

Reducing goal conflict

There is no magic cure for this, but the first step in reducing its effect is simply to bring it out into the open by communicating about it. Try to obtain open recognition by everyone in every group that there is at least one point on which they all agree: the need for a *common goal*. Point out the benefit of everyone pulling in the same direction compared with the wasted energy when hundreds pull against each other!

Try to get more people pulling in the one direction.

- First you'll need to get agreement about what the 'right' direction really is. (Let everyone have a say in choosing corporate goals.)
- Try to achieve common agreement that goal conflict is wasteful, reduces the effectiveness of the group, and blocks communication.
- Help people to accept that goal differences are a natural part of an organisation, not the result of personal differences.
- Finally, help them to see that when all are in agreement and working together for a joint goal they achieve a higher standard of work (task), use up fewer resources and are more highly motivated. So each corner of the triangle wins!

Corporate communication systems

Communication systems in an organisation can be classified as external or internal; vertical, horizontal or diagonal; and formal, semi-formal or informal.

External communication systems

External systems are used to exchange messages with customers and/or clients, an important function in any company. How well the organisation handles external communication — such as its letters, invoices and press releases — will have a major bearing on its profitability and survival.

Internal communication systems

Messages that travel within a company are just as important, but play a very different role. Internal messages can move from top-level managers down to the operations level, and are exchanged constantly between groups; they will be concerned with how, why and what resources are being used, how well people are carrying out their jobs, what is being done and what is not.

Internal channels can be subdivided into

- the formal or official system
- the semi-formal or consultative system
- informal systems

The formal or official communication system

This is easily identified, because it uses official channels. If you look at a chart of the organisation structure you'll see the lines of communication that link everyone together, officially. (You'll notice that they cross some lines and bypass others.) Most important messages are supposed to travel on these channels, which include

- official memos, internal letters, electronic mail;
- internal reports and submissions;
- balance sheets, files and records;
- instruction manuals and rule books;
- official announcements (on a noticeboard or in a staff newsletter).

Formal messages can just as easily be conveyed face to face or on the phone. However, most formal messages are in print or handwritten, since they need to be sighted by those in authority and so copies can be kept. Some aural communications (such as after-dinner speeches and reprimand interviews) fall into the formal area, but even these are usually recorded in writing.

The role of the computer

Today internal and impersonal messages can be processed, distributed and stored by computer if they contain only formal company data. This means there is less need for the traditional hierarchical (pyramid-shaped) organisation — created over two thousand years ago — to monitor data passing through official channels and so minimise human error. Figures still need to be checked, but not as often nor in as much detail, so there is not the same requirement for close supervision of routine communication. This leaves more time for managers to spend in face-to-face communication with company staff about 'people' issues.

A second effect is a reduction in the number of middle managers needed. The pyramid-shaped organisation may still have its place, but its use as a channel for internal messages is declining rapidly. This, in turn, is leading to the creation of successful organisations with as few as four levels between front-line workers and top management. In addition to improved communication, other results include higher morale, higher production, faster problem solving and higher profits.

The semi-formal communication system

This system allows for greater personal contact and communication. The basis of semi-formal communication is the meeting system (see Chapter 30, 'Making meetings work'). Messages exchanged during meetings are not very formal, and are not controlled as formal messages are. If a manager is trying to develop new ideas or to solve a dispute, a semi-formal meeting is ideal. If people can see each other when consulting and being consulted about a topic, verbal and non-verbal feedback adds to their confidence and speeds up agreement.

Decisions reached in the meeting may then be written up and fed into the formal system as minutes or instructions, so that messages which start informally become formal statements — which is why the system is seen as semi-formal.

Deep slice committees

In setting up systems to avoid communication overload, most managers unfortunately also set barriers against messages that *should* be heard. One way of filtering out unnecessary messages while helping important information to travel more freely between top-level management and front-line workers is to establish a 'deep slice' committee, whose members are drawn from all levels so that they represent a cross-section of the organisation. As a group they are in an ideal position to share and clarify data from all levels. Each member can take the latest information back to his or her own section the same day. (How long might it have taken through the regular systems?)

Committees like these also help people-oriented communication to flow from the top to the lower levels of the organisation. Managers and supervisors can give more personal recognition, and praise for jobs well done.

Informal communication systems

Horizontal communication

Horizontal messages are those shared by people at the same level. They help to co-ordinate operations and to build team spirit. They tie one person's work in with another's, deal with shared problems and so on. If the channels followed match the horizontal lines on the organisation chart the exchange may in fact be part of the formal system, but most horizontal exchanges are oral, informal, and more personal than official exchanges.

Diagonal communication

People in one department often communicate directly with individuals at other levels and in other departments. The communication path is diagonal, moving across section boundaries and up or down to reach a particular person at a different level. Time is saved by avoiding the slower official pathways. For example, a production supervisor who needs to know what time pay cheques will be distributed can ring the pay office or — in a computer-linked system — send a request directly through the network. An immediate answer enables the supervisor to plan the afternoon's schedule more efficiently.

Person-to-person communication systems

Messages about how people feel at work, about their attitudes, beliefs and values, about morale and motivation, are worker-oriented. They are very important to the individuals who share them and should not be ignored by the company.

Social functions allow employees to mix with others not normally met on a daily basis. Communication at this intergroup level contributes to a sense of corporate identity and cohesion among employees and helps managers tune in to important 'people' issues.

The grapevine

The grapevine (or 'bush telegraph') has no definite structure; you cannot draw a diagram of it as you can of official message systems. Yet every organisation has its grapevine system. A chance meeting in a corridor or a phone call is all it takes to exchange grapevine messages, but there are three typical problems.

Communication chain effect

Although the grapevine can convey some kinds of information with reasonable accuracy, the effect of passing the message through a lengthy communication chain is bound to cause distortion.

Personal bias

Messages about other people's motives, attitudes and feelings are particularly open to misinterpretation. People view situations from their own standpoints. For instance, it's true (and the grapevine is correct on this) that Robin is to be the new manager. What's not correct is the rest of the grapevine version about *how* Robin won the promotion.

Filling in the gaps

Although incorrect, grapevine messages often seem very believable. People talk about what is 'really happening' even when there is uncertainty. They fill in the gaps (as explained in Chapter 4) with whatever makes most sense or with what they would like to hear. They pass on what they believe or hope to be right, and as the message goes along the chain, it grows and changes. Before long myth, wishful thinking and fabrication are being taken as the truth.

True or false, most of the messages on the grapevine are given credibility by most receivers, and since the grapevine reaches every corner of the organisation, they cannot be ignored. No one can stamp out the system, or block it. On the contrary, managers who support poor communication practices create the right conditions for excessive use and abuse of the grapevine. This is likely to happen when an organisation

- fails to give people enough information through other channels;
- gives official information that is unclear, ambiguous, too late, or contrary to what seems to be the real position;
- tries to stop people communicating by any means other than through official channels.

None of these conditions are good for the company, anyway, so removing them is beneficial in every way.

Corporate communication problems

Message chains that change the message

Suppose top management makes a decision to encourage front-counter staff to spend more time talking and listening to customers. The message starts out as a statement of policy. As it is passed down the line, middle management is supposed to add details of how the new policy is to be put into effect. By the time the message gets to the people in the front line, it should have been developed into a specific set of instructions to guide staff on how they should implement the policy.

However, as the message must pass along a chain of communicators there is a risk that the original idea will be altered — part may be lost, detail may be added. The result? Front-counter staff, who were supposed to spend more time talking and listening to customers, may be issued with a set of rules for 'dealing with customer complaints'. In large organisations there is a tendency for many messages filtered from the top to reach the lower levels either so changed that they are unrecognisable, or not at all.

Communication overload

Too many messages at one time — particularly written ones — overwhelm people. Does everyone

Communication overload

need to get every memo? Do you need to read every memo you get? Information overload is reached when you get so tied up with responding to routine incoming messages that you forget to send important ones to members of your own team. This is demonstrated brilliantly in the group simulation game on message overload, *Up and Down the Organisation*, created by Tom Plazier (1982, see 'Other resources' on p. 361). Cutting down on the number of messages is the best way to reduce overload.

Message filtering

Formal systems are very suitable for conveying orders or instructions *down* the line to subordinates, but not nearly so suitable for the reverse procedure. Most are designed to intercept and filter upward messages.

When a subordinate communicates with a superior there is a tendency to give only good news and prevent management from finding out, for instance, about unsuccessful performance or breakdowns in production. Unless the communication climate is such that staff can discuss mistakes and problems openly with superiors, people will naturally filter out as much of this kind of information as they can. If, however, subordinates know that delivering bad news will not lead to abuse or unfair penalties, superiors will find out about problems while there is still time to fix them.

Distortion

Alternatively, bad news may be passed on in such a way that the blame is attached to the wrong people. The message, which was supposed to *convey* facts, will be distorted to *hide* facts. This is most likely to happen when management puts too much emphasis on blame and punishment instead of looking at ways of fixing the problem.

To overcome the problems of distortion and filtering, a company needs to

- create a communication climate that emphasises trust and openness;
- encourage accurate feedback from staff on all issues, regardless of whether the news is good or bad (see 'Negative or error feedback', in Chapter 3).

Many top managers take regular 'walks' through every section of the company, stopping to talk to rank-and-file staff. Others make a point of having morning tea with a different front-line group each day. Some go further, and actually spend time each week working alongside front-line staff. Is this a waste of valuable management time? Not according to managers who use the system, and who happen to be some of the most successful in Australia. They know that their success depends on keeping in touch with exactly what is going on and reducing the chances of filtering and distortion.

Gatekeeping

A person who selectively controls the flow of messages is a 'gatekeeper'. A technical expert who presents all the data in favour of plan A (but all the data against plan B) is gatekeeping. A discussion leader who chooses the 'best person' to speak on each item of business is doing the same. So is a secretary who decides who will or will not be given an appointment to talk to the manager. This last case can be based on a genuine need to protect senior staff from communication overload, but often people who start out using gatekeeping for legitimate reasons also tend to use it as a source of personal power or influence.

Changing the system

Organisations that cannot change have little hope of surviving in the 1990s. However, changing a corporation that has communication problems is never easy. If an individual makes the attempt it is likely that he or she will be confronted with a maze of screens, filters and other barriers. Often such a person fails in the attempt, and leaves, thereby reinforcing the old system. There are, however, ways of making changes possible.

- Arrange for an outside consultant rather than a member of the organisation to identify communication problems.
- Gain acceptance through meetings and discussions that the problems pose a real and serious threat to the future of the organisation.
- Create a climate in which debate and constructive criticism is seen as healthy and productive (see Chapter 23, 'Decision making and problem solving in a group').
- Encourage individuals with different points of view to join decision-making groups. Recognise that while they may create discomfort in the short term, in the long term they represent the basis for survival.

By opening up discussion of the communication issue you make people more aware of it, and because they want their communication to be effective, once they have identified a problem — and if they are encouraged to discuss it regularly in meetings — they will find a solution.

International communication

More and more Australians are finding that they need to communicate with business organisations in South-east Asia, Japan, China, the Middle East, and many other nations where English is not universally understood. Many overseas corporations have executives and translators who can read, write and speak excellent English, but is it sensible to leave your presentation entirely in their hands? It is in these cases that the following guidelines are worth noting.

1. Use professional interpreters.

There is a risk that an inexperienced interpreter may guess at a meaning sooner than admit to a difficulty in translation. A language teacher may speak excellent Chinese but have little knowledge of Chinese business customs or negotiation techniques. A professional interpreter will cost more, but could save you thousands of dollars if your communication involves negotiations.

2. Don't accept a word-for-word interpretation.

Ask the translator to explain important ideas in detail. For instance, in some languages the translation of 'cannot consider at this time' (refusal) and 'will need time to consider this' (undecided) could be almost identical. What if the interpreter did not make this clear?

3. Do not rely on a single interpreter.

If the matter is important have at least two interpreters, working independently. If members of your own staff are sufficiently familiar with the language and its idiom, have them make further translations.

4. Remember that a trained interpreter will include non-verbal signals in translation.

Make it clear that you need help with customs of both writing and speaking, and also with the use of correct non-verbal tone.

5. If meaning is doubtful, ask for clarification.

Most overseas writers would far sooner give an additional explanation than risk a misunderstanding that would affect their business as well as yours. If an initial translation does not seem correct or logical, make contact again to confirm (by expressing it in your own words) that you have correctly understood the message.

6. Recognise your limitations.

Remember that the firms and the people you are writing to may be far more experienced than you are in dealing with international business. If you are a newcomer to the field, don't try to act like an expert. Ask for guidance from your overseas counterpart.

7. Recognise foreign business customs.

Find out something of the customs that business people in other countries like to observe. In what ways do their traditional ways of negotiating differ from ours? The Japanese, for instance, prefer a formal and polite tone, and may be uncomfortable if you follow a 'true blue' Australian style. Many nations consider it impolite to discuss business during a meal; others will only do so *after* food and drink have been shared. You can obtain advice on what is considered good manners from the local embassy or consulate for the country concerned.

8. Remember that people who do not 'speak' your language can often 'listen' with considerable skill.

Monitor your facial expression and tone of voice as well as your words. Do not assume that anything you say in English will not be overheard and understood!

9. Most dual-language dictionaries do not include a full coverage of business jargon.

If you say 'Please ship the stocks via air', the word 'ship' may be translated as having to do with sea transport, 'via air' may not translate as air *freight*, and 'stocks' can have a variety of meanings. Say instead: 'Please send the goods we ordered on Invoice 459 by Cathay Pacific air freight, Flight 769 (Thursday 29 March)'.

10. Use short sentences.

The longer the sentence, the harder it will be to translate. If you have several points to make, put them in separate sentences. In a written message, list them one under the other.

Summary

1. Four powerful factors affecting company communication are (a) the cold communication factor, (b) the trust factor, (c) the screening factor and (d) goal conflict (the iron triangle).

2. People are often less influenced by cold, official messages than by warm, personal messages from respected leaders.

3. Some companies tend to 'screen out' people who try to make changes. This has the effect of ensuring that the existing style of communication is maintained.

4. Companies usually have three diverse goals (forming the 'iron triangle'):
   - getting the job done;
   - getting the job done as economically as possible;
   - getting people to do the job.

   The resulting conflict and competition between the three goals affects communication.

5. A step that helps to reduce communication problems arising from goal clashes is to bring them out into the open.

6. External systems are used to exchange messages with customers and/or clients, an important function in any company. They include letters, annual reports, telephone calls, public communication, advertisements, press conferences, press releases, promotions and public relations.

7. Internal communication systems include (a) the formal or official communication system, (b) the semi-formal communication system (meetings) and (c) informal, hidden or 'shadow' systems. There are also subsystems.

8. Messages about how people feel at work; about attitudes, beliefs and values; and about morale and motivation are worker-oriented. They are very important. Encourage this type of communication.

9. The grapevine (or 'bush telegraph') has no definite structure, yet every organisation has one. Grapevine messages are likely to be distorted by factors such as the communication-chain effect, personal bias or expectations, and the desire to hear what one wants to hear.

10. If a message travels through a chain of communicators in an organisation, typical 'chain' problems can be expected.

11. Message overload results when a person is overwhelmed by too many messages — particularly written ones — at the one time.

12. Filtering is used in most formal communication systems to intercept upward messages including news about unsuccessful performance or breakdowns.

13. A person who selectively controls the flow of information is a 'gatekeeper'.

Exercises

1. Are there any points of conflict or disagreement at your work or college that you would like to see settled? Identify the task and the main goals involved. Is part of the trouble conflict between goals, particularly in different sections? For instance, is upper management more interested in getting a task finished on time than in saving money or looking after people? Are there individuals who want to use up too many resources and so leave fewer for everyone else? Is part of the trouble a lack of communication? What other points of conflict can you identify? Suggest some solutions.

2. Think back to Chapter 6, 'Style and fashion in communication'. What will be the likely effect on an organisation or profession that screens people according to their thinking styles? For example:
   - Do linear-logical or specific-detail thinkers tend to group together in the accounting profession while lateral-creative, intuitive types group themselves in marketing or advertising?
   - Are communication teachers the same kind of people as other teachers?
   - If a mixture of aural (spoken word) thinkers and tactile (hands-on) thinkers get together for a meeting, what kind of format will each find most comfortable?
   - What kind of format might visual thinkers prefer?
   - How effective in an organisation will a person be who uses parent-style communication? In your own organisation, what would be the chances of such a person gaining promotion?

3. Think of some examples of the screening factor in your own organisation. What type of individual do you find in selling, maintenance, staff training, clerical, personnel and transport departments? What effect does this have on communication at (a) the formal level, (b) in meetings, (c) in informal communication?

CHAPTER 26

Public communication, publicity and advertising

By its very nature, public communication offers you and your organisation a chance to reach out and put yourself in touch with thousands of people. Public communication makes up an important part of your overall communication program, but it needs careful management.

Topics

Different kinds of public communication

Public relations

Client service

Advertising

Writing a media release

Meeting the media — press conferences

Designing forms

Public communication and the law

Different kinds of public communication

Public communication can be described as any form of transmission which is available to people without restriction — or at least which is published with the intention of making it freely available. The many forms include

- public relations;
- publicity;
- client-service programs that focus on excellence in service and on ways of communicating this to the public;

- media advertising (TV, radio or the press);
- advertising using letter drops, brochures and so on;
- indirect advertising — promotions, displays, sponsorships;
- media releases and conferences;
- forms, invoices, receipts and similar documents used to exchange information with your 'public'.

Other ways in which businesses make contact with clients, customers and the community — for example, sales presentations, telephone conversations, after-dinner speeches or board meetings — can also be classed as public communication. If you produce computer programs or staff training guides and offer them for sale, you are communicating publicly. From a legal point of view, a poster on a tree, a painting in a gallery or a photo in a shop window are all public messages, too!

The risks

When you transmit a message to a large number of people outside your organisation, you have no guarantee that the reception will be friendly. Some members of the public hold views that differ widely from yours. Some will suspect your motives, no matter how honest you are. Some may be directly opposed to your goals. So public communication requires a cautious approach and careful planning.

While expecting that whatever your message, it will probably draw criticism from some source, with care you can avoid hostile reactions when you speak, write or appear in public. Learn to recognise danger points, and how to overcome them. Watch for possible risks in an apparently harmless media message. Take the most care with messages that contain negative information, criticism or blame.

This is not public relations

(Note the section at the end of this chapter on legal aspects of public communication.)

Public relations

Public relations (or 'PR', as it is often called) is concerned with the relationship between your enterprise and its clients, customers and the community, although it can also form part of a successful marketing or publicity program.

Making public relations work

To be effective, a PR program must communicate specifically about such issues as
- your group's corporate goals, its philosophy, and the reasons behind its policies;
- the way you want people to see your organisation, and how you want this image to develop;
- where the enterprise is heading and how you plan to share its future with the community.

It must also look constantly for new ways to share your information with the public.

Good PR also considers relations with the media, and with all branches of government. If the future of a business depends on the support of these groups, its PR program may involve publicly recognising this dependence.

What is *not* public relations

Communication is the basis of *all* public relations, but all public communication is *not* PR.

What organisations actually do in their PR programs can vary widely. What one firm calls PR may be seen by another as marketing or advertising. A third group may describe exactly the same thing as a promotion. Handing out pens with the firm's name on them is promotion, not public relations. Getting a shot on television of the Lord Mayor opening your new shop is publicity, not PR. Putting the company logo on football uniforms is advertising. Bizarre stunts achieve publicity, but may have a negative effect on public relations. PR is not a matter of generating sophisticated publicity: cocktail parties may help to maintain good relationships, but they are not the basis of a PR program.

If you want to find out more about any aspect of public relations work, you can refer to some of the many excellent books now available. Because they are written by PR people, they make interesting and enjoyable reading (see 'Additional resources and bibliography').

Good PR is honest and open

If people feel they are being subjected to a PR campaign based on what the media call 'hype' they will have little respect for the firm responsible, nor will they feel positive about relations with it.

A program that is shallow or dishonest implies an equally shallow attitude towards the public. Conversely, a firm that treats clients in an unreasonable or unreliable manner will develop a matching PR image. This applies particularly when groups face difficult situations (see opposite page, 'Public relations emergencies').

Planning a PR program

Apart from the usual aspects of business planning (budgeting, goal-setting and so on), when you plan a PR program, consider the following points.

- **Purpose and objectives**
  How do you want to relate to the public? What are you really 'relating' for? What is your firm's 'mission'? What is its place in the community? Why does the public need you and your product?

- **Strong points and weak points**
  How does the public view your enterprise at present? Is it popular, unpopular, well-known, unknown? To discover the answers you'll need to be involved in two-way exchanges, when you will listen, as well as talk.

- **Timing**
  When are the best times to develop relationships? Should your program be seasonal or year long?

- **Choice of channels**
  Which channels will serve your purpose best? Will you choose mass media, trade journals, special events, displays, addresses to groups, or sponsorships?

- **Your target**
  Is there a special group you should concentrate on? How can you contact its members? How can you strengthen relationships with leading people in that group?

- **Communication barriers**
  What are the main communication barriers between you and the public? How can they be reduced? How can you promote a better understanding of the products, policies and problems of your enterprise?

Your program should provide the answers to these questions and influence public opinion so that it is more positive towards your group.

If you are facing public opposition, you'll need a program to explain (or defend) your position. For example, say a firm needs to demolish an old house as part of the development of a new shopping centre, and two 80-year-old pensioners who rent the house need a new home. Good PR in this case would include using the firm's resources to help them, perhaps using its trucks to move their belongings. This can result in the kind of news story that gets positive headlines in the local media and is worth thousands of dollars in goodwill.

What else might you do in this case to develop good PR?

If an organisation is making changes in its structure or ownership and these affect its service to the public, a special PR plan will be needed to handle community reactions to the changeover.

Public relations emergencies

Your organisation also needs to plan for emergencies. You can map out specific steps for dealing with accidents, strikes, attempted takeovers or attacks by disgruntled customers via the media, but the emergency might just as easily be something no one has thought of. In many cases the future of the organisation and its staff will depend on how well the PR team can handle unforeseen situations.

It's also good PR to thank the public for its support after a difficult period such as a strike, a breakdown or some other crisis.

Client service

An associated communication field involving your relationship with clients and customers is that of 'client service' (also called 'service management' or 'process management'). This is a policy which involves every person in the corporation in the development of a philosophy that ties the firm's very reason for existing to the customer or client.

- The customer is seen not as someone on the outside but as part of the enterprise, and every member is encouraged to communicate with customers rather than leave the job to front-line employees. This helps to weaken old attitudes such as 'It's not my responsibility — I don't make the decisions around here', and encourages everybody to look for better ways to serve the client.
- The total commitment that is so vital to the success of the policy is highlighted by a client-service motto: 'If you are not serving the customer yourself, then you should be serving (supporting) somebody who *is*'.
- There is less distinction between the external client (the customer) and the internal client

(organisation members who deal with the client). On organisation charts drawn (or shown) upside down the customer is often placed at the top of the structure.

- Customers are consulted regularly about ways in which the organisation can best serve them. If client needs require a change in policy or an extra effort to meet an individual customer's needs, the service-oriented group will do this instead of (as in the past) rejecting requests if they fell outside 'standard guidelines'. Rule 1 in the client-oriented policy book is 'Serve the customer'. Rule 2 is 'Do it as quickly as you can'.

If anything gets in the way of serving the customer, the whole organisation works as a team to fix it. Scandinavian Airlines, one of the successful pioneers in the client-service area, have an arrangement providing direct telephone contact between the pilots of all planes in flight and the company's top management. If pilots need help to get a plane away on time, they are expected to use the phone to go 'straight to the top'.

Does client service work?

All this may seem a little unrealistic to Australians, who are used to something below this level of service from the average business or public service organisation. Two commonly asked questions are 'Does it really work?' and 'How much extra does it cost?'. The answers are quite clear. A series of studies of the fastest growing and most profitable firms in the USA, Japan and Europe suggest that a client-service approach is a major factor in almost every instance (Peters & Waterman, 1984). Many Australian companies — Myer, for example — have already shown that the idea will work in Australia. One area for developing client service in the 1990s could well be Australia's public service and local authority organisations, faced with a need to reorganise rapidly to keep pace with changing public attitudes.

Advertising

Advertising as compared with public relations is more concerned with informing buyers about products and services. Effective advertising is based on an analysis of the market, using research to find out what kind will serve you best. Different kinds work in different situations; you must decide whether you want to develop general awareness or knowledge of a product, to alter existing customer attitudes, or to achieve something stronger, such as an actual sale.

Planning your advertising

If you are planning an advertising program it pays to consider the following questions.

- Target audience: Most buying groups are only a small section of the public. For instance, if you were advertising a student bookshop, whom would you target?
- Choice of media: Will your advertising dollars be best served by using television, radio or the daily press? Do you need local, state or national coverage? Where would you advertise the bookshop?
- Time frames: When is the best time to advertise? For how long?
- Content: Is it better to repeat one message or use a series? Should you concentrate on words alone or add visual appeal? Should you give full details or just enough to get people interested?
- Your product: What are you selling? The best feature of the product may be something intangible — safety, respect or status. Promote the firm's name as well as the product and don't assume people already know what you sell.
- Results: How will you find out if your advertising worked? Some advertising leads directly to a sale, but *all* advertising should create interest, awareness or enquiry. Sales figures do not provide a fair idea of effectiveness; counting the number of enquiries may be more reliable.
- Expenses: How much should you spend? Comparing the number of enquiries with actual sales will tell you whether advertising pays. For example, the paper you used has a circulation of 350 000 and you had 350 enquiries (one per thousand readers) in response to your advertisement. If sales average one for each ten enquiries, how much can you afford to pay for each advertisement?
- Competition: Check what your competition is doing — the state of the market. Get as many facts as possible and research conditions thoroughly before making a decision.

Different advertising styles

You can create your own advertising program, but it is wiser to employ an agency to handle major media contracts. You only have to watch late night television to see what happens when people try to write their own scripts for commercials. However, anyone in business should know something of the way an advertising agency works and you should at least be able to compare the alternative forms used — sales-oriented, attitude-oriented, hard sell, soft sell, and creative styles. Each has its place, but there can be wide disagreement as to which is best for a particular product.

Sales-oriented advertising

This is used to
- inform customers of the benefits and best features of a product;
- support earlier advertising with new appeals (reduced price or improved quality);
- move potential buyers closer to the point at which a sales representative can approach them;
- persuade people to write, call or phone so that you can tell them more about a product;
- launch a new product;
- increase your share of the market.

Attitude-oriented advertising

Use this style to
- build long-term customer loyalty and potential for future sales;
- maintain after-sales confidence in products already purchased;
- tell people what is happening about a future product;
- promote your organisation's name without trying to sell any particular item.

The hard sell

You can spot a hard-sell advertisement by its use of low-cost production techniques and characteristics like these:
- scripts littered with words such as Now! Only! Special price! Just $9.99! This week ... At last! Hurry! Look at these ... Unbelievable! Amazing! Fantastic! and so on;
- loud voice, disco soundtrack, bright colours (or spot colour in a press advertisement) — high

sensory stimulus in order to attract attention;
- use of puns, wordplays and deliberate mis-spellings — 'Time to retyre at Kleen Karr Co.', 'Duck in for cheep prices at Merv's BBQ Chicken Shop';
- frequent repetition of retailer's name, product name and price.

This kind of advertising often attracts criticism.

The soft sell

In contrast to the previous style, this technique
- includes little or no mention of price, brand or retailer's name;
- maintains a low-key approach to 'buying';
- develops a desire or preference for the advertised product over others of a similar kind.

'Creative' advertising

Advertising agencies love to use the word 'creative', and in their jargon it refers to a style which is as much a work of popular art as a selling tool. The message is carried via a 'concept' that is highly original, outrageous, amusing or shocking, and beautifully produced. The creative advertisement, therefore (the advertiser hopes), conveys product benefits in a memorable way and this fixes a positive product image in the consumer's mind. This kind of advertisement
- presents a concept which, at first, seems totally unrelated to the product being advertised — you may not immediately be sure whether it is an advertisement or part of a program (or the editorial content if you are reading a magazine or newspaper);
- is pleasing to look at or listen to — has attractive pictures with not too much information and is more entertaining than a straight 'sell';
- often appears in the style of another item or culture, such as a popular movie or song.

You may find yourself unconsciously tuning in to this type of advertisement. You stop and think about it, or look more carefully the second and third time.

Part creative, part soft or hard sell

There are also advertisements that have elements of all three of these styles. Some productions are built around catchy jingles or famous personalities.

Some contain deliberate mistakes. A mixture of styles can work as effectively as any one on its own.

Which style is best?

The debate rages in advertising agencies and business houses everywhere. There are, however, some general guidelines.

1. The style should be appropriate to the product category.
Deciding factors include
- the needs and desires of target buyer group
- the price of the product
- how often people purchase it
- how your competition advertises
- your position in the market

You'd use hard sell to sell mousetraps. You'd use a creative TV commercial with gentle background music to advertise a luxury holiday tour.

2. The style should also match the purpose.
Do you want a long-term campaign, or just a short burst to promote a sale? While hard sell may be effective over a short time, it can annoy consumers to the point where they 'switch off' or develop a negative attitude towards the product. A creative style may have only slight impact over a short period but be very effective repeated over a longer time. You could, for example, use just one slogan as the focal point of a campaign over the next five years.

3. Consumers become more sophisticated.
As this happens, they develop the ability to 'switch off' or become cynical about hard-sell advertising. This suggests an increased place for soft-sell and creative styles.

4. High cost does not automatically mean high quality.
A creative advertisement can be an expensive exercise in self-indulgence (if an agency wants to set your mousetrap commercial on a yacht somewhere on the Great Barrier Reef, for example).

5. Combinations can be effective.
You don't have to go completely one way or the other. There is plenty of room for a mixture of styles.

Direct-drop mailing

Users of direct-drop mailing (insertion of 'letters' or printed sales material in thousands of letter boxes) report either tremendous success or virtual failure. This depends on several things.

Care in preparation

This is a special type of message — one that must try to attract the attention of people who did not ask for information and of whom only a small number will be at all interested. The right kind of wording and layout *can* achieve this (see Chapter 13, 'The power of persuasion').

The advertiser's expectations

In many cases a response rate of one enquiry for every 200 drops is regarded as excellent. Advertisers who do not understand this can mistakenly assume that a drop has failed when it has really produced a good response.

An appropriate choice of product

Is the product to be advertised likely to sell this way? A firm that used drop advertising to offer a '24 hours, seven days a week' plumbing service reported an overwhelming response. Why? Because the message in people's letter boxes was friendly and personal and contained something that people wanted to know. It said: 'We're happy for you to call us on weekends or in the middle of the night to fix your plumbing problems, and we really do have staff on duty all the time. Try us'. People tuned in to the assurance that their call would be welcomed, something other plumbers did not make clear. The 'personal letter' style was more effective than a media advertisement.

Telephone and fax 'cold' canvassing

This is not a popular form of advertising, since it begins with the use by a stranger of a private telephone or fax number. Firms that do this tend to be 'pushy' by nature, so their sales approach is usually too heavy as well. It may sell products, but it can also damage the selling group's image.

Classified advertisements

If you need to find just the right customer to match a special one-off item such as a house, a car or an original painting, classified advertisements offer an easy and inexpensive way to do it and to get a fair price.

Set yourself a clear goal. Keep in mind that your chief aim in classified advertising is to get people to call you so that you can raise their interest to the point where they decide to see the item for themselves. It is only *after* this that you actually start the selling process, so don't confuse the buyer by putting 'selling' messages in the classified wording.

Classified advertisements — guidelines

1. Put yourself in the reader's chair.
Think of what readers want to know, not what you feel they ought to be told. 'House for sale' describes the situation from *your* point of view. If the advertisement is correctly placed in the classified 'HOUSES FOR SALE' section, there's no need to say 'for sale' at all. Begin by naming the suburb, then say 'Modern house' or 'Architect-designed home'.

2. Explain why you think your house/car/computer is better value than others advertised.
This suggests to readers that they should see it before looking at any others. But present an accurate and honest description.

3. Give a definite price.
Classifieds without a price have far less chance of getting a response. It is often the advertisement without a price that gives least detail in other respects too, like this one: 'House for rent — good condition — three bedrooms — southside — ph. 333 8976'.

4. Give a clear idea of location.
In the advertisement above, 'southside' gives no idea of the real location. People tend to ignore such advertisements. Do not give the exact address, but name the suburb (and perhaps the street); this encourages people to phone for more details, including the full address.

5. Use descriptive phrases.
Paint a picture in the reader's mind. Instead of

'good position', say 'High on hill, bay views and breezes'. Words like these create an image that 'good position' does not.

6. Give the age of the item.

This is important. If it is a 40-year-old house, don't hide the fact. Sooner or later buyers are going to see it, and its age will be obvious. Mentioning the year of construction, as in 'Architect-designed, master-built (1954)', creates a sense of openness and honesty which inspires confidence both in you and in what you are selling.

7. Do not abbreviate important descriptions.

Ordinary words attract more enquiries than professional advertising jargon. Instead of 'as-new cond.', a description such as 'New paint inside and out' — while half a line longer and costing perhaps a few dollars more — can encourage many additional enquiries. Spelling out important features in full like this shows that you are confident you are describing a top-value item, and can afford to do so. Abbreviate less interesting items ('auto w/ mach.', for example).

8. Mention special features.

Include at least one or two words to show that the item is a special one. Describing a feature not usually mentioned in similar classifieds helps make yours stand out.

Compare the following examples. How well does the first one follow the guidelines above? Where does the second fail?

MOTOR VEHICLES FOR SALE

TOYOTA CELICA — 1985. Original owner needs to sell urgently. Genuine 90 000 km supported by log book and service receipts. Body, upholstery and paint all first class. Mechanical check by your expert will confirm 100% condition. $7500. Phone Lyn Ross 256 0962. East Stradcliffe (Private advertisement).

LATE MODEL CELICA — Retired banker going overseas needs to sell. Good cond., runs well. Log bks. RWD cert. $7500. Ph. 256 0962, Bus. hrs only.

Advertising a coming event

The section 'Posters and leaflets' in Chapter 27 gives a sample layout for a poster advertising a coming event such as a meeting, a training course or a community activity. The same format can be used to set out a small 'box'-type advertisement in a paper.

Indirect advertising

Sponsorship

Almost any community event, charity or contest can be sponsored. Supporting a football team or a race is good for business, but may prove a costly form of advertising. Take care that the activity you support matches the image you want to project. Recognise that if the yacht with your logo on it goes on the rocks, so does your advertising.

Displays

A static display in a window can bring an immediate response in sales; displays that show a product instead of telling about it are good advertising. And naturally, the more spectacular the display, the more people will notice it.

Promotions

Promotions have a definite use in terms of putting your name in the public eye, but they do not produce actual sales as effectively as does direct advertising; they serve more as a type of publicity. They can take many forms, including competitions, free give-aways, and events staged in shopping centres, on beaches, and anywhere else the targeted public can be found.

Writing a media release

A media release does not need to be a finished news article. Neither does it need to be written by an expert. Rather it is a short summary written in such a way that it can, if an editor wishes, be used as it stands. However, its main aim is to excite interest enough to ensure that news editors phone or send a reporter and a photographer to get the full story. Anyone can submit a media release.

There will be no payment for it, but as long as it produces good publicity, from a business point of view the result is more than worth the effort.

A requirement of a good media release is therefore that both you and the publisher share the benefit. It must be interesting enough to qualify as news or information of value. A news editor will not use it if it has no audience or reader appeal, or if it seems to be an attempt to gain some free advertising.

What attracts interest?

Items that attract editors, readers and listeners include

- news of real interest to the community, such as the opening of a new shop or service;
- a success or achievement that reflects well on the community;
- coming events open to the public: conferences, seminars, talks, training courses, camps, bus tours, fairs, fetes, sports days, field days and so on;
- reminders of deadlines such as closing dates for competition entries (many successful publicity campaigns are centred on competitions for just this reason — the contest has news value in its own right and so will be well-publicised even though tied in with commercial sponsorship);
- descriptions of useful services or products (so that people can share the benefits) or technical reviews of new products;
- news of prominent or colourful community characters.

Set clear goals

Work out first what you want to achieve. Many media releases fail at this point. If the goal is to get free publicity in lieu of paid advertising, this will usually be so obvious that the item will be rejected by most editors.

The opening paragraph — four W's and an H

If too much work is involved in sorting out the real news in the release, there is little chance that it will be used. Media editors prefer a particular style for the opening paragraph: one that states 'what-when-where-who-how' — and perhaps 'why' — in just one or two sentences. This content plan is illustrated below and is followed by a sample release.

What happened?	**When did it happen?**
(or what is going to happen?)	(or when is it going to happen?)
Who did it?	**Where did it happen?**
(or who will do it?)	(or where will it happen?)
How was it done?	
(or how will it be done?)	
Why?	
(not as important, but mention in opening paragraph if you can)	

The order of the answers is not important as long as the opening paragraph carries *all* this information. Note that in the sample release, sentences are quite long. A headline helps to draw attention to the main features but should be kept short.

MEDIA RELEASE
Date: Mon. 16 December 1991
(for immediate publication)

NOWRAL STUDENT WINS STUDY MEDAL
A 27-year-old Nowral accountant, Mr Michael Welton, was named today as the top student of the Greenfield Community College for 1991. Michael scored a total of five honours and two credits in his examinations for the Bankers' Institute of Australia course, conducted locally by the College. The Director of Community Education in NSW, Dr Peta Walker, who announced the names of graduates, said that Michael's pass was the highest in the state. Dr Walker will visit Nowral tomorrow (Tues. 17 Dec.) to present Michael with a silver medallion.

Michael is currently head accountant at the Nowral Branch of the Westpac Bank. Now that he has completed the final year of the course, he hopes to enrol in an economics degree program at the University of NSW. He is president of the Nowral West Branch of Rotary International. Last year he won the Rotary award for top public speaker for New South Wales.

He is a keen tennis player, and well-known as a local football referee.

He and his wife, Pam, are both prominent workers for the Nowral Conservation Association.

END

(Photo attached shows Michael Welton (left) and the principal of the Nowral Community College, Dr Helen Ford.)

For additional details contact:
Peter Argent, Nowral Public Relations, Phone (054) 345 378, or after 6.00 pm, (054) 454 982.

Avoid jargon and technical terms; use the language newsreaders use. Also avoid vague statements, such as 'Several students graduated recently from our local college'. Give exact dates, times, places and numbers.

Middle paragraphs — the 'body'

Notice how the middle paragraphs, the body of the release, give further details to maintain interest. However, stick to important items — do not go into detail. If the news service or paper wants to add to the story, the editor or reporter will phone you. Note also that body sentences are shorter than those in the opening paragraph.

The end paragraph — the 'tail'

Notice that the end of the release is made up of short items; these form the 'tail' of the article. Tail paragraphs, apart from being complete in themselves, are arranged in a descending order of importance and written in such a way that the sense of the release will not be changed if the editor decides to cut them altogether. Why do this? Because the editors of news publications (or TV news programs) are often faced with last-minute problems. An editor may need a news item urgently to fill a gap of a particular length, and the fastest way to get one is to take a release and remove parts of the tail until it fits the space. Your story will be chosen ahead of others if it has a tail that is easy to delete.

General advice

1. Date the release.
Some notices are sent out in advance of the release date. If you do not want your item published until a particular date, note this clearly at the top: 'EMBARGO – NOT TO BE PUBLISHED BEFORE 12.00 NOON FRIDAY 16TH DECEMBER'.

2. Do not duplicate a release.
Most editors will reject a story if they think the opposition has an identical copy, so it is a waste of time sending everyone a photocopy of the release. If you want it to be used by several different publishers, rewrite it to suit the language and style of the various media. For instance, local papers would use an informal style, with first names throughout, as in the example above. Compare the opening in that example with the one below, re-written for metropolitan news media.

The Director of Community Education in NSW, Dr Peta Walker, today announced the names of the graduates in the 1991 examinations conducted by NSW Community Colleges on behalf of the Bankers' Institute of Australia. A 27-year-old Nowral accountant, Mr Michael Welton, was the state's top student with a total of five honours and two credits.

3. Learn the style favoured by each publisher.
What kind of language is used? Are sentences short or of medium length? Does the typical article use quotes, or is it written in a less direct form? Is news presented in a sensational or a conservative form? The better you can match each style, the greater the chance that your release will be used in several different publications. Try to give a different — appropriate — point of view in each version, as well.

4. Use recordings as a guide.
If you are writing regularly for radio or TV, use recordings of similar stories as a guide to correct wording and style. Keep a scrapbook of your own past media releases (particularly the ones that were used), so that you can adapt to the same style and format for later stories.

Photographs

Media editors need high-quality photographs printed on glossy paper and measuring at least 15 by 20 centimetres. Black-and-white pictures reproduce better than colour. Type a short description on a strip of paper and tape it to the back of each photo; never write on the back of the photo itself. If the picture shows faces clearly, name everyone (reading from left to right) and say what each person is doing. At the end of the release, mention the photo (as in the sample above).

Meeting the media — press conferences

If your release is successful in attracting attention you soon find yourself in more direct communication with the media, either face to face or on the phone. This is generally a positive process, but there are several areas that require caution.

1. Do not say anything that you do not want published.

It is extremely hard to persuade a reporter to forget your comments if they happen to make more than usually interesting news, and saying 'That's off the record' has little or no effect. Once the TV camera or tape recorder has captured your words, they tend to be used no matter what you say (although you may be able to get a court injunction to stop this if the issue is important enough).

2. Some reporters will go to extreme lengths to get you to make outspoken comments.

Be careful if a reporter ends the interview, buys you a drink, and then says, 'Now, strictly off the record, what really happened?'. Similarly, some TV interviewers say, 'That's a wrap . . . Cut! OK, now that we're off-camera, what do you really think about the situation?'. Can you be certain that one recorder is still not running?

3. Beware of deliberate provocation.

A reporter may try to provoke you by quoting something uncomplimentary an opponent has said about you and asking how you feel about it. Do not be drawn by such tactics.

4. Keep written records.

Journalists have a reputation for changing facts around to make a story more interesting. If you are making an important statement, it is better to have the essential details typed and handed out rather than rely on the reporter to get it right. If you are being interviewed by phone, announce that you are recording what you say. Ask to have important sections read back to you for confirmation.

5. Check before publication.

If you feel it is essential, arrange to call at the media studio or office to check the story before it goes out. This is your right, but your visit may be resisted. If it is vitally important, get a media solicitor to assist you at this point.

6. Prepare for talk-back and chat shows.

Appearing on television and radio chat shows is great for publicity, but there are risks. If you know about it in advance, study the style used by the host and note any interview techniques that might catch you off your guard. Have someone from *your* side run you through several dummy interviews, serving up the type of awkward questions you might encounter. After several such rehearsals you will be much better prepared for the real thing.

Designing forms

Invoices, statements and all the other forms that go from you to the public — together with all the forms that you ask people to fill in — make up an important part of your public communication. A well-designed form provides an efficient way of exchanging information; a poorly designed one produces frustration and often fails to share the information it was meant to.

Designing forms — guidelines

1. Design forms to work in with your computer system.

Check with your system planners and operators to make sure the design is efficient and easy to read' when it comes to keying in information. Do they find dotted lines (for people to write on) easier to work with than blank spaces or ruled boxes?

Make sure that the position of blank areas for preprinting information matches A4 computer paper *exactly* in terms of length, width and space between lines. Information can then be entered on the form using any computer printer.

2. Place important information where it is most easily seen.
If the surname is the most important feature, put the name box close to the top of the form. Group least needed information at the end.

3. Give as well as request information.
If a form or account has to be returned by post, highlight your *postal* address in letters large enough to be easily read. Phone numbers and contact names often change, so rather than having these printed on the basic invoice, add them by computer printer. If a sales invoice is a computer print-out, add a personal touch by including on it the name of the person who actually dealt with the customer: 'You were served by ——'.

With multicopy items such as enrolment forms, of which the client retains one copy, allow some blank space for last-minute information to be added by computer printer — dates, times, venues, contact phone numbers, for instance.

4. Allow room to write.
Wherever people have to write anything, especially a signature, allow at least 10 (preferably 12) millimetres of vertical space, and plenty of width. Narrow spaces are hard to fill in and the writing is hard to read. Boxes that require ticking should be at least 5–6 millimetres square. A cramped form turns people off.

5. Leave as little as possible to be filled in by hand.
The advent of the computer printer and continuous-form paper makes it easy to preprint all kinds of standard details that apply to groups of users — names, addresses, and much more. When the client has to provide information, the latest systems provide for this to be typed into the computer records and printed with the form, leaving even less to be handwritten.

6. Ask only for essential information.
Do you really want to know how old everybody is? In how many business situations does anyone need to know whether people are male or female and what their marital arrangements are? Some data may *seem* important, but ask yourself, for example: Suppose a client says he or she is 36 years old and married, when in fact neither is correct. Would this bending of the truth affect the purpose of the form? If the answer is 'No', why ask the question?

7. List choices to show what you are looking for.
Marital status in itself may not matter, but if you need to know how people want mail addressed, label a box 'Mailing address' and in it list the most common alternatives — Mr, Ms, Miss, Mrs, Dr, Prof. — with a blank line for 'other titles'. A line just labelled 'Title' leaves room for misunderstanding.

8. Ask questions rather than give directions.
If a question is likely to produce the answer you want, ask it. A famous government questionnaire in the 1950s requested migrants to 'State length of residence in Australia'. Thousands of newcomers, unfamiliar with bureaucratic language, took tape measures and dutifully measured the 'length' of their residences. Asking 'How many years have you lived in Australia?' or 'In what year did you arrive in Australia?' would have been better. Make sure that your requests or statements are not ambiguous.

9. Ask one question at a time.
If you require several different items of data, ask each as a separate question and allow for a separate answer.

Field-test all new forms

One of the most important parts of designing any new form is thorough field-testing. A form may look perfect to the people who designed it, but it's still a good idea to put it through a series of trials, first with staff and then with clients. Before it is too late to change the form, arrange for dummy processing right through your system of about a hundred completed samples. This will reveal unsuspected problems and will also give lower level staff a feeling of pride at having shared in the process. Because they have to handle forms daily, lower level people often prove to be the real experts and contribute the best ideas on form design.

Public communication and the law

As explained at the start of this chapter, any form of communication that is available — or is intended to be available — to the public is a 'publication' in the legal sense. This includes signs, displays, after-dinner speeches and the message on your telephone answering machine. Letters of reference intended to be seen by many readers and identical letters printed and mailed to a number of people both are public communication. If a message is sold for public consumption, it is definitely public communication.

In the widest sense, the term 'public communication' can be extended to cover even a single statement if it is available for public viewing or expressed in a public place. However, unless what you say is highly inflammatory or contrary to the law, there is little to worry about in that regard. Remember, though, that even private letters can be collected and published after the writer has become a public figure. You never know who might be keeping yours in expectation of such a day.

When to take care

Certain types of communication require the use of caution.

Matters 'before the court' (sub judice)

You must not make public comments on matters that are subject to current legal action, or pending action (for instance, any matter over which a writ has been issued). Sometimes courts prohibit the publication of information such as the name, address or other identifying details about a person involved in the action. Making these facts public in defiance of a court order could involve a gaol sentence.

Confidential material

Do not reveal information about secret processes or special techniques used by your firm, or about any confidential data entrusted to you. If you are a public servant, these restrictions are even wider under the conditions of the various state and Commonwealth Public Service and Official Secrets Acts. If you are employed by a bank or an insurance company, remember that information such as a client's tax file number or whether an account is in credit is strictly confidential.

Discriminatory material

There are certain legal conditions governing the way in which published material can describe or classify people (see Chapter 28, 'Communication without discrimination'). One example prevents the advertising of job vacancies in such a way that certain individuals are either prevented from applying — or else singled out as the only suitable applicants — by reason of personal characteristics such as race, sex or marital status. Similar conditions apply to the advertising of accommodation.

'Truth in advertising'

Advertising that makes false claims or promises, or uses false data in an effort to influence buyers, is risky and probably illegal. Be sure that you can 'deliver' on any promise you make in an advertisement.

Warranties

There is a growing number of regulations concerning what must and what must not be included in a written warranty. As consumer education develops and awareness increases, you can expect that this area will become more complex. If you are doubtful about wording an advertisement, or if you are involved in publishing any kind of warranty or guarantee, it is a good idea to consult a legal expert. If you do not offer a warranty but are involved in the provision of goods or services for sale, it is wise to check to what extent you are still liable for action from dissatisfied clients. You may be better protected by a written warranty.

Prohibited products

Media advertising of products such as cigarettes and alcohol faces greater restriction each year. On the other hand, advertising by medical and legal professions, which in the past has been prohibited, is gradually being accepted.

Censored material

Censorship is a murky issue. Publication of some types of material poses considerable risks, and while — if a court action ensues — you may ultimately be cleared of legal wrongdoing, public knowledge of your involvement can be a disaster from a business point of view. It is better to keep well away from such areas.

Defamatory statements

Never make a statement — either oral or written — that a person is incompetent, or mentally or morally unstable. Do not accuse anyone of committing a criminal offence. You may be quite correct in what you say, but your part in publicising the knowledge may leave you open to legal action.

Corporate responsibility

It is possible that you could find yourself legally responsible for a statement made in public by an employee under your control. The fact that you were not aware that the statement was to be made, or were aware but could not stop publication, might not be sufficient justification. The best form of protection from this risk is for your firm to take out insurance cover against damages claims arising from such a situation.

Restrictions on copyright

Copyright protects not ideas, but the words and methods used to communicate them. Copyright restrictions are based on the principle that the original sender of any message retains ownership of it for at least fifty years, during which time it cannot be reproduced without the owner's permission. As well as text, pictures, graphics, artwork, songs, movies and computer programs, 'messages' such as trade names, trade marks, logos, business slogans, advertisements and the names of firms are all subject to copyright. The titles of books, films and plays, however, are not copyright. (Some years after the first edition of this book was published a British author also produced a book called *The Business of Communicating*.)

In theory you are breaking copyright laws each time you videotape a movie, copy a computer disk, tape a record or photocopy more than a few pages from a textbook. The chance of your ending up in gaol for this is slight, but it is not the criminal aspects that you should be most concerned about. The main issue is whether the original owners or publishers stand to lose money (or whether you or your firm stand to make a profit or save money) as a result of using the copied material. If this is so, you are wide open to a costly claim for damages.

If you want to reproduce a particular item, and especially if the copied material will be used commercially, contact the copyright owner. Usually a small fee will suffice to put the whole operation on a businesslike basis. You could well benefit from contact with authors, for example, who might provide you with more up-to-date material, or perhaps offer to make a personal appearance to help you promote your work.

Payment of a fee does not mean that you take over the copyright; for example, you cannot give permission to others to copy the work — you have simply paid for the use of it in your own publication. However, whether a fee is paid or permission is given without any payment, you must still acknowledge the source of copied material and identify the copyright owners (see 'Quotes, references and acknowledgments' in Chapter 18). Whatever the arrangement, make sure the approval is in writing.

If you cannot find an author or publisher and you particularly want to use extracts from someone else's material, you should at least acknowledge the source and print the author's name at the beginning or end of the item; this shows your recognition of copyright and invites the owner to claim the cost of such use from you. You cannot avoid copyright by making one or two changes or using only part of the original; the law covers 'substantial copying' as well as total copying.

Copyright offences

There is much misunderstanding about the criminal aspects of breaching copyright. Usually police action is taken only against people who set out deliberately to defraud the owners of a significant amount of income. Civil action is much more likely. Criminal charges are likely, however, if people

- make multiple copies of items to be used or sold in competition with the original ('pirate' publishing);
- deliberately avoid co-operation with legal authorities who are investigating possible breaches of the law (this can include destroying records of copying, or having not kept them at all).

Even in a civil case, failure to keep records can be more expensive than producing them. Owners of copyright will have little difficulty in showing that they have lost financially by unauthorised reproduction of their material. However, if there are no records, the claimants may be inclined to exaggerate the amount lost.

Summary

1. The term 'public communication' refers to any message made available to the public, but the words used to describe it vary widely. What one person calls 'publicity' may be 'promotion' to another. A third may call it 'advertising', 'marketing' or 'public relations'. Learn to tell the difference.

2. An effective PR program must tell people about your group's relationship with the community, its image, its long-term corporate goals and the reasons for its policies.

3. Good PR is honest and open. If people feel they are being subjected to PR hype, it will not work.

4. Client service or service management is similar to PR but involves an organisation-wide policy that puts people first.

5. When planning an advertising program, begin by deciding whether it is to develop (a) knowledge of a product, (b) a decision to buy or (c) a long-term attitude in potential customers.

6. Advertising can be (a) hard sell, (b) soft sell, (c) creative, (d) sales-oriented, (e) attitude-oriented or (f) a mixture.

7. When writing classified advertisements, your chief aim is to get people to call you so that you can persuade them to come and see the item for themselves. Don't expect the advertisement to make the sale for you.

8. A media release is a short summary, not a finished news article, but it must be interesting and contain news or information of some value.

9. At a media conference, say nothing that you do not want published! There is no such thing as an 'off the record' comment.

10. If you are making an important statement, present essential details as a typed document rather than an oral message. If you are interviewed by phone, take notes of everything you say.

11. The forms you ask people to fill in are an important part of your public communication. A well-designed form is also a very efficient way of gaining information.

12. Design forms to work in with your computer system. Check with users, system planners and operators to make sure the design is efficient. Ask only for essential information.

13. Public messages that require particular care include (a) statements that criticise others (whether justified or not) and (b) matters before the court (sub judice).

14. Corporations are legally responsible for most statements made in public by employees.

15. Copyright protects not ideas, but the words and methods used to communicate them. The original sender of any message retains copyright ownership for at least fifty years.

16. If you want to reproduce material, contact the copyright owners (authors and/or publishers).

Exercises

1. You have just completed a course. Write a classified advertisement offering your textbooks and other items for sale.

2. List some examples of (a) creative, (b) hard sell and (c) mixed styles of advertising. How effective was each in changing your feelings about the product?

3. Write a classified advertisement offering
   - your house for sale or rent;
   - accommodation in your house, with shared rent, for three people;
   - an old car for sale.

4. Write a media release announcing an introductory course in basic computer operation for senior citizens, to be held in a week's time, or some other coming event such as a sale, an official opening ceremony or a community activity.

5. Write and design a small 'box'-type advertisement for the same activity, for insertion in a local paper.

6. List the names of local firms that you have noticed practising some form of client service or service management. List others that do not. How did you tell the difference?

7. Suggest an improved layout and design for the enrolment form currently in use for a course you are studying.

8. A rival private business college has mounted an active campaign to entice students away from your college. The group is offering what claims to be a superior program, but at a higher cost. Plan an advertising and public relations program to counter this.

9. A credit-card group uses a statement form on which all details are printed out by computer. The entire top half, which shows your name and address and the date of the statement, is designed to be torn off and returned with your payment. Suggest some possible improvements in the design of this form.

10. A preprinted student enrolment form has a tear-off payment section. On it are the words 'It would assist greatly if you would write your course name and number on this slip when returning it with your payment'. Suggest a possible change of wording.

11. Design a questionnaire form for distribution to past students of the course you are studying. The purpose is to find out what they are now doing and how much they feel the course helped them with their careers.

12. Describe some instances of hard-sell advertising that you find particularly annoying. Would you, however, deliberately avoid buying the advertised product?

CHAPTER 27

Newsletters, notices and signs

Newsletters and house publications provide an excellent communication channel for all levels and all members of an organisation. They can raise morale and bring about a sense of unity. They can inform and educate. They can give everyone a sense of participation, and much more — provided they are read. The first part of this chapter suggests how to produce writing and publishing that will ensure maximum readability.

Signs can provide up-to-date information and help to avoid problems; they can also serve as a form of promotion and advertising.

> **Topics**
> Newsletters and company magazines
> Page design and layout
> Signs and notices
> Posters and leaflets

Newsletters and company magazines

In business you often become involved with the production of newsletters, organisation magazines or trade papers. For simplicity's sake, in this section the term 'newsletter' is used to refer to all three.

Focus on special interests

Divide a newsletter into sections, each clearly identified so that it attracts its regular readership.

In reality, most people skim through newsletters searching for items of interest to them and ignoring the rest, so the best way to plan and write one is to forget about cover-to-cover readers.

Lack of reader feedback can be taken very personally by some editors, although it does not mean that nobody has read the publication. However, the doctrine that newsletters are intended to be read from cover to cover — though understandable from an editor's point of view — is not a realistic one.

Why people don't contribute

The other complaint often heard from newsletter editors is that their readers fail to produce enough contributions. This results in editors writing the material themselves and including, more often than not, instructions that readers should write more items for the next edition. The idea that the readers of a newsletter have to contribute most of the material is a myth.

Writers for any publication are in a minority

Writers are usually greatly outnumbered by their readers. Professional journalists write their stories without being upset because readers don't write too. Teachers don't worry because the students fail to write worthwhile notes for class hand-outs. If you are part of a newsletter team, accept that the task of writing and production will rest largely on your shoulders, and be proud of your ability as a writer-editor.

By all means invite and encourage contributions, since somewhere in your organisation there might be a rising new contributor whose talents can lift the quality of your publication. (Henry Lawson and Banjo Paterson got started this way.) But do not be discouraged if contributions are fewer than you hoped for.

Writing newsletters — guidelines

1. Balance text and visual content.

Remember that some of your readers are visually oriented while others, the aurally oriented, are more concerned with words. Editors with too strong an aural background can produce a publication with too many words and little visual appeal. They tend towards small type and few pictures (to fit in as many words as possible), whereas visually oriented editors go the other way, producing pages with strong eye appeal but less material content. This draws criticism from aural readers. The solution is a balanced mix.

2. Choose the content carefully.

There must be an element of originality in the content of any internal publication — some special appeal, something that readers cannot get watching television or reading commercial magazines. Reproducing items that have already been used in a hundred other newsletters destroys this element. Include a mixture of

- useful facts that readers cannot get elsewhere;
- items giving recognition to organisation members who have succeeded at work or in sport or community activities;
- news of successes attained by the organisation as a whole — victories that everyone can share in;
- reminders of coming events, particularly of deadlines and closing dates;
- information on new technology for use at work and at home;
- ideas on management and company policies, which make your newsletter a forum where individuals can put these forward;
- high-quality, original humour — this is always popular, but also rare (it's better to have none than to lower your standards).

3. Know your reading public.

Print what people want to read, not what you or anyone else thinks they ought to read. Do experiment, however, with new features; test them for audience appeal. If a regular feature is no longer popular, drop it.

4. Don't rely on casual reader judgment.

People who have no experience in publishing or editing will offer critical advice on your performance as editor. Do not take this too seriously. If there are ten sections in your newsletter, you will find a group of readers who support one or two, tolerate a couple more and want you to cut out all the rest. As surely as you do this you will find that the deleted items were at the top of another group's list of favourites. If you do want to measure popularity ratings, conduct a full survey.

What *not* to include

An editor is legally responsible for what appears in any publication. With this responsibility, however, goes considerable power and authority to decide what will be printed and what will not. Sometimes people assume (mistakenly) that an editor must print anything submitted, and cannot alter it in any way. This is not correct. You have the right to reject, condense, and if necessary alter the content of any item before it goes to print. In such cases it is wise, however, to advise the contributor of the changes and seek approval. If you make major changes, the article should carry a note: 'Condensed from a report supplied by ——' or 'This article is an edited [or condensed] version of text supplied by ——'.

Committee reports or technical papers

Technical writers and committee leaders all seem to have a desperate desire to see their work in print and may contribute regularly, but the material seldom has mass audience appeal. Short extracts, heavily edited, may be worth including, but leave it at that.

Management 'pep talks'

Sincere and well-deserved praise from management deserves a place. However, if a paper contains what appears to be corporate propaganda, its credibility is reduced. A boss who feels that a newsletter is a personal mouthpiece should be discouraged.

Extreme or biased points of view

If the newsletter appears to be a platform for a few individuals wanting to air extreme views, it will lose the support of the majority of middle-ground readers. For the same reason, it is best to avoid political content.

Gossip

Rumours and gossip may guarantee readership, but will lower the standard of the publication beyond the point where it will be taken seriously.

Page design and layout

A two- or three-column layout adds to readability, because the short lines are easier to read. A three-column format is also easier to work with when you are fitting in artwork or photos alongside text. Text in columns must be fully justified (straight margins on both left and right edges).

- Use plenty of headings and subheadings to break up the text. Bold lettering and capital letters emphasise important points and look more professional than underlining.
- A right-hand page tends to attract more attention. Use it, rather than a left-hand one, for important items or to start an article that runs over several pages.
- The page centre and the top and bottom right-hand corners are strong attention spots, so use them for pictures or graphics.
- Photographs are important, provided that your printing system can reproduce them clearly. To put one or two on each page is better than making some pages all pictorial and some all text.
- Stick to a few standard typefaces, even if your printer can produce more. A mix of too many type styles marks you as an amateur.

Signs and notices

Stand in the reader's shoes when you are planning a sign. A common fault is to leave out important details because 'everybody already knows that'. If you have driven interstate you will have noticed that many highway signs appear to have been either written by local people or written for people who are familiar with the area and only need to know *when* to turn off for places with names like Greenfett and Wentworthston. Missing are directions on how to get out of Melbourne, go straight through Sydney or avoid the Newcastle city centre. Mostly this stems from the YCMI (you can't miss it) problem described in Chapter 7.

- Use signs to tell people what *they* need to know. When you plan and produce a sign, remember that the more familiar you are with any information, the harder it is to see just what others (who are not familiar with it) need to know. Keep this in mind.

Outdoor and road signs

Drivers in moving vehicles can spend only a fraction of a second reading your sign. Use plenty of white space and colour to give it eye appeal. Keep the message short. If it contains more than *five* or *six* words most drivers will not be able to read it all, nor will they remember its message.

Use very thick lettering

Make words large enough for people to read easily 50−100 metres away. What is clear at arm's length will not even be readable from a moving car.

Choose the best location

The position of a sign is as important as its appearance. Do trees, poles or other signs obscure it from certain angles? Should it be lit after dark? If it is to be read from the road, test these factors by driving past.

Create unusual signs

The best attention-getters are colour, light, movement and novelty. A large and unexpected object placed beside the sign (or as part of it) makes it stand out. A bush service station in north Queensland gained nationwide publicity by painting its advertisements on the bodies of old cars wedged high in the forks of trees along the highway. You can make a moving sign by pasting posters on each side of a large cardboard carton; hung by a string attached to the centre of the lid, it will turn slowly all day.

Indoor signs, posters and notices

Notices on a board where they must compete for attention with many others also need something special to grab attention. Pictures and drawings are effective. So are humorous cartoons, provided that they are appropriate to the topic. To emphasise key words, make them larger or underline them.

You have seen 'public notices' posted by building developers which seem to have been made as unattractive as possible. (Perhaps the developer does not want you to read the sign in case you discover what is happening on the construction site.) Make sure your notices are not like this; follow the guidelines for business writing (see Chapter 14).

- Use a separate paragraph for each idea.
- Surround each idea or item with plenty of white space.
- Use headlines and subheadings.

The headline for any indoor sign should be large enough to be read at 6–10 metres. Computer programs that can print lettering this size are freely available in a variety of typefaces. They are ideal for generating signs for noticeboards.

Use a computer to produce printed lettering rather than doing it by hand. If you need illustrations or symbols, they can be cut from other signs and reduced or enlarged on a copier. If you need different-sized typefaces, enlarge or reduce these to fit as well, then paste all together to produce a master. Make a final copy from this paste-up, so that the joins don't show.

Most indoor signs or notices deal with everyday matters. If you take your role as the writer too seriously, the result might sound dry and formal when it could have been positive and direct. Be polite, without being dull or impersonal. A notice is just another form of communication, and if being friendly or humorous will be more effective, why be dull and distant? Which will get the best results?

Compare the language in the examples in Table 27.1.

Writing signs and notices — guidelines

The examples above clearly illustrate many of the points made in these guidelines.

1. Be positive.

Notice that the right-hand signs explain what *should* be done rather than what should not. State good news in big letters; keep the bad news in the background. Instead of 'DANGER: Do NOT connect cable while switch is on', say 'SAFETY FIRST! Connect cable only when switch is OFF'. A notice that threatens or relies on fear to get results is a bad notice.

2. Emphasise the solution, not the problem.

The best notices also give helpful advice on how to deal with a situation.

3. Use plain language.

Many people who want to read your notice speak English only as a second or third language. Keep

Table 27.1

Dry and formal	Friendly and positive
Due to circumstances beyond our control, this lift is temporarily out of service. Kindly use alternative service.	This lift is not working today. Please use the lift in the main foyer.
We most sincerely regret any inconvenience to our valued customers while this store is undergoing renovations. Normal shopping will be resumed as soon as possible.	As you can see, we have started work on our new shop layout. When it is finished (in about four months) you will be able to enjoy the best shopping in town right here. Meanwhile, thank you for putting up with the noise.
Kindly retain the parking ticket on your person at all times to avoid theft.	To avoid theft, do not leave your parking ticket in the car.
WARNING:	PLEASE:
Students are forbidden to loiter or congregate in this hallway. Use the facilities provided. By order of the Principal	Do not block this area. If you need somewhere to talk, use the student recreation room three doors down. It has plenty of comfortable chairs. Kym Smyth (Principal)

words short. Bureaucratic language such as 'Kindly retain the key on your person' is not standard English and therefore harder for overseas readers to translate.

4. Avoid jargon.

Don't use cliches — 'by order', 'regret the inconvenience', 'earliest possible', 'situation outside our control', 'persons' and so on.

5. Watch for double meanings and errors.

Unintentional double meanings — 'Old people cross here at night', 'This door is alarmed!' and similar classics — turn a serious sign into a joke. Spelling errors such as 'Fashion Pavillion' and 'No dogs aloud' affect the credibility of both sign and sender, especially if they remain uncorrected.

6. Be honest.

Don't say 'Sorry' unless you mean it. Who really believes signs that say 'We sincerely regret any inconvenience' when the development that is causing the problem is going to make the sign's owners millions of dollars?

7. Remove out-of-date information.
A sign saying 'temporary delays' that stays on display week after week is a bad sign. Change it. Signs promoting coming events should be taken down as soon as the date has passed.

8. Avoid discrimination.
Signs that refer to 'workmen' should be replaced with something more appropriate to present-day usage, such as 'repair team'. (See Chapter 28 for other suggestions.)

9. Don't begin a request with 'Kindly'.
'Kindly' does not mean 'please'. It has too directive and dominating a tone and is not appropriate for signs or notices. If you mean 'please', say 'please'.

Advertising signs

Good signs are good for business. Bad signs turn people away. Have you ever gone into a shop after seeing a sign saying 'Computer Disks $5.00 a box' only to find that the disks are an odd size, that you only get two in a 'box', or that the sale finished last week? If you have had this type of experience, you will appreciate how people feel if they respond to an

Greenlands Community College	Name of organisation or company at top of form
One-day computer expo for the small-business operator	**Main heading** (in large, bold letters and set in a box)
A display of latest hardware and software for use by self-employed business owners and small-business managers	Subheading (in smaller type but still emphasised)
Wednesday, 25 June 9.00 am to 10.00 pm	Details of when, where, and time of day. Name the day as well as the date. Give both opening and closing times
■ Latest version of Austro Spreadsheet ■ New 48-pin printers ■ Design your own accounting system ■ Desktop editing and printing ■ Scanners and digitisers ■ This year's newest computers	List of major highlights (in point form)
With Prof. Rita Robbins from Stanfield University of Technology (NSW) as guest speaker	Guest of honour and other public figures who will be present
Official opening by the Mayor, Lyndsey Hibble, at 10.00 am	
Admission: $4.50 adults (cash or credit card) Student card holders $3.00; $2.00 under 14 years	Details of the exact cost (including any concessions), what it covers and how payment can be made
Includes morning tea only	
Lunch available on site	
Phone Ricky Cousins, Computer Dept, Greenlands College (073) 783 281 After hours (073) 785 945	Name, address and phone and/or fax numbers of person to contact for more information (including at least one after-hours number)
Sponsored by Greenlands Community College Council	Authorisation details if necessary (perhaps to confirm that the activity is officially sponsored)

advertising sign that is incorrect. Make sure your advertisement paints a true picture and tells an up-to-date story.

Posters and leaflets

Advertising a coming event can be costly if done by professionals. A well-planned poster or leaflet is easy to produce yourself and can produce just as good a result.

'Coming events' posters

A poster should give *all* the information an interested reader needs in order to know exactly what the event involves. The format illustrated at left manages to highlight all important points without cluttering the layout, but an added telephone number enables anyone with additional questions to get an immediate answer.

Use language that sounds enthusiastic, but don't exaggerate. Choose a catchy title.

Mass coverage is the secret of successful do-it-yourself publicity. Run off hundreds of posters rather than ten or twenty. Display them everywhere. Once you have established the wording and format you can use similar but smaller versions for local newspaper advertisements, signs in windows, and leaflets. In the case of a leaflet, it helps to include a short, tear-off section at the bottom which can be detached and posted with payment or as a form of enrolment. This saves people having to write a note to send with their money.

Summary

1. When writing newsletters, balance text and visual content. If pages have too strong an aural emphasis they will lose visual readers, and vice versa.

2. Originality is vital to the content of newsletters. Aim for a special appeal — something that people cannot read anywhere else.

3. A newsletter editor is legally responsible for what appears in the publication, but has the right to reject, condense or amend the content of any item before it goes to print.

4. Make sure that signs and posters paint a clear picture and contain the necessary information.

5. Keep messages short on signs and notices. If signs contain more than five or six words, they may not be read in full.

6. A notice among many others on a board needs eye appeal. Pictures and drawings attract attention. Humour and cartoons are powerful attractions.

7. Dry, formal notices don't work. Positive and direct ones do. If messages deal with every-day matters, *don't* take your role as writer too seriously.

8. Explain what *should* be done, rather than what should not. Emphasise solutions, not problems. Write good news in big letters, keep bad news in the background.

9. Use language that is friendly, personal and polite. Use plain words. Many people who read your notice speak English only as a second language.

10. Advertising a coming event can be costly if done by professionals. A do-it-yourself poster or leaflet is easy to produce and may produce as good a result.

Exercises

1. Design wording and layout for a poster advertising a coming event in your community or college.

2. A few people still smoke in your canteen, despite the standard 'Circle and bar' signs.

   Imagine that recent legislation in your community makes this illegal, and punishable with a fine of $250. Design some new signs to be displayed in the canteen. What supplementary publicity would you suggest to add to their impact?

3. You are conducting a 12-hour introductory computer course for retired people and senior citizens (all over fifty-five years old). The program includes basic computer operations, spreadsheets and word processing. The cost is $80 ($50 for pension-card holders), but participants must bring their own lunches.

Design a suitable poster to advertise the course. Where will it be displayed and how will you distribute it?

4. Collect examples of signs, posters or notices that are out of date, unclear or contain errors. Display these (or photographs of them) in your group, and give a prize for the worst example.

5. Collect examples of advertisements, posters or notices that have left out an important detail, such as the location of an event or a return mailing address. How could this have happened?

6. How could the following notice be improved?

```
NOTICE
THIS OFFICE IS
TEMPORARILY CLOSED
BACK IN 1 HOUR
```

7. Collect examples of house publications, newsletters and trade journals. Discuss how some of them might be improved.

8. Write an item for submission to the editor of one of these, for possible publication.

CHAPTER 28

Communication without discrimination

Discrimination is equally out of place whether you are on the phone or in a meeting, or whether your message is published in the media, in a report or in a private letter. This chapter suggests some ways to avoid discrimination when you communicate. Quite often the result is an overall improvement in style as well.

Topics

Defining discrimination

Different kinds of discrimination

Seven ways to avoid discrimination

Defining discrimination

When people express a preference for one item ahead of another, they're using discrimination. That's fine if the choice is only of something such as a new car or the best accounting system for a firm. Classifying or selecting *people* according to personal characteristics, such as the shape of their bodies or marital status, is another matter.

Not all discrimination is based on a person's sex. Referring to people as less — or more — worthwhile according to race, religion, colour or physical handicaps is discriminatory, too. To do this today is unacceptable, and may even be in breach of the law. A proven case of hardship or loss resulting from discrimination can cost a firm thousands of dollars in damages and fines, and might cost you your job as well.

Different kinds of discrimination

Personal discrimination

Any message that highlights characteristics such as sex, race, marital status or nationality suggests that these details are significant and that receivers need to know about them to judge the subject's worth. Look at these examples:

- John Anderson, a New Zealand psychologist, says that mankind's needs follow a clear pattern.
- Miss J. Grey, a 45-year-old woman, was recently named as the state's first female Police Commissioner.

Group discrimination

The writer discriminates between groups of people according to race, religion or sex when

- writing about a profession as if membership is exclusively male or female — 'switchgirls', 'repairmen', 'newsmen';
- using words such as 'manpower' or 'mankind' to describe people in general (this can include referring to a group as if all its members were of one sex) — 'Every manager dreams of the day when his firm's name is added to the prestigious membership list of the Australian Businessmen's Council';
- misplacing descriptive words like 'women' or 'Aborigine' in a sentence — instead of saying 'More Aborigines should be trained as computer operators' (correct), a discriminatory communicator might say, 'We should train more Aboriginal computer operators', which sounds as though

Aboriginal operators are different from other operators;

■ making unreasonable generalisations about a group — referring to 'womanly weakness', or 'oriental inscrutability'.

Mention of personal characteristics such as race or religion will not always discriminate. Such important details can help to support discussion of a topic. Consider the two examples below. Both statements emphasise, within a meaningful context, personal details about race, religion and nationality.

1. Charles Jackson, an Australian Aborigine, supports a continued policy of 'self-determination', saying it will help to raise the standard of living for all Aboriginal people in the next decade.

2. Abraham Groeter, a Jewish psychologist, said that Jews develop a positive self-concept by identifying with a cohesive, cultural group.

Personal details give weight to the subject being discussed. In the cases above acknowledgment of race and religion help to raise the writer's credibility, improve logic, and add strength to the overall argument.

Advertising in Australia in the past exhibited many examples of discrimination, particularly the use of male-associated terms to describe job vacancies or positions. With certain exceptions, the media can no longer accept advertisements for employment or accommodation if the wording suggests that

- applicants could be excluded on the basis of race, sex, marital status, family situation or physical handicap;
- one sex is considered to be more skilled or better equipped to fill a particular position at work.

Seven ways to avoid discrimination

Here are several different ways to make sure that your communication is free of discrimination.

- Personalise.
- Pluralise.
- Describe the occupation, not the operator (person).
- Refer to groups in terms of their common interests.
- Redraft expressions, using different words.
- Use first names rather than Mr or Ms.
- Describe the problem, not the people working on it.

As you'll notice in the examples below, when you make alterations you often improve the quality of your communication in other ways as well.

Personalise

All you do in this case is change 'he' to 'you', 'his' to 'yours' and so on. The more direct your words, the more readers will feel that your message is for them individually. You get a better you:us ratio as well. Compare these two examples.

- Impersonal and discriminatory: A leader must remember that he is nothing without the support of his team. They are the men who made him their leader, and they are the men who can destroy him.
- Personalised: As a leader, remember that you are nothing without the support of your team.

They are the people who made you their leader, and they are the ones who can destroy you.

Notice how the words 'you' and 'your' add a more positive tone to the message. Personalising is one of the best ways to avoid 'male only' terms in textbooks, rule books and instruction manuals.

Use the plural

Replace a singular term with a plural one.

- Discriminatory: Mothers! Protect your child. Have him immunised now!
- Non-discriminatory: Parents! Protect your children. Have them immunised now!
- Discriminatory: Today's businessman needs this product in his shop.
- Non-discriminatory: Business owners need this product (or: The business community needs this product).

Pluralising saves having to use the more awkward 'he or she' or 'she/he'.

- Complicated (singular): A solicitor may be asked if he/she will prepare a contract.
- Plural: Solicitors may be asked to prepare contracts.

Describe the person's occupation, not the person occupying the job

People object quite rightly to the exclusive use of 'man' in words referring to professions or occupations. A quick solution for some is to substitute the general word 'person' for 'man', 'woman' or any similar term; however, the result is a longer word and one which often sounds clumsy. The 'person' solution is too easy. Use it only as a last resort. Instead, try to replace 'man' terms with more descriptive words that explain exactly what kind of work the individual performs. 'Tradesman' says nothing about an individual's area of expertise: communication must be clearer if you describe the person as a carpenter, plumber, plasterer, bricklayer or home-renovator. Instead of saying 'man on the land', be more specific: grazier, farmer, beekeeper, orchardist, grain-grower, rural manager, for instance.

Many people are better described in this way, using terms that refer to their specific skills. Dividing a term into two words adds clarity as well.

Traditional word	One-word version	Two-word alternative
switchgirl	switchperson	switch operator
policeman	policeperson	police officer
garbage man	garbageperson	refuse collector
fireman	fireperson	fire fighter
cameraman	cameraperson	camera operator
housewife	houseperson	home manager
horseman	horseperson	rider
cowboy	cowperson	cattle hand or ringer
stockman	stockperson	stock worker
foreman	foreperson	team leader, supervisor
repairman	repairperson	repair technician
storeman	storesperson	store controller
seaman	seaperson	sailor, mariner
man of letters	person of letters	scholar, academic

Avoid attaching the word 'female' or 'male' to a stated position, and also discard words with endings such as 'ette' or 'ess'. Terms that previously applied only to one sex are now used for anyone doing the job.

Discriminatory term	Standard term, regardless of sex
lady mayor	mayor
female parliamentarian	member of parliament
cleaning lady	cleaner
girl Friday	administrative assistant
female reporter	reporter
women's welfare committee	welfare committee
tea lady	tea server
founding fathers	founders, ancestors
father figure	symbolic parent
lady chairman	convenor, president, head of committee discussion leader
male nurse	nurse
manageress	manager
actress	actor
authoress	author
air hostess	flight attendant
usherette	usher
millionairess	millionaire
wife	partner or spouse
husband	partner or spouse
manpower	workforce, human resources
man-made fibre	synthetic fibre
man in the street	average individual

Refer to a group's common interest

Replace terms that suggest that membership of a particular group is restricted to either males or females. Describe a group in terms of common interest, which after all is the real reason for the members getting together. Say 'concerned parents', not 'worried mothers'; say 'sporting groups' instead of 'sportsmen', and 'teams of three' instead of 'three-man teams'.

Do not typecast people

Do not label members of any group as characteristically weak, dominating, emotional, caring, uncaring or anything else. Avoid labels that project a stereotype or 'conventional' image of a group or which draw attention to imagined characteristics. All members of a particular race, sex or profession do not have similar personalities.

All accountants are not well-organised. All academics are not absent-minded. An Irish surname does not make a person illogical or anxious to start a fight. Avoid terms such as 'girls', 'men', 'ladies' and 'gentlemen', 'womenfolk', 'fathers' or 'sportswomen' when you are really describing 'members', 'supporters', 'families' or 'parents'. A particular sales team may be comprised solely of men, but since being male is not a requirement for membership, why call them 'salesmen' rather than a 'sales team' or a 'field marketing group'?

Redraft expressions

Rewording a sentence has many advantages. Instead of 'One man's pleasure is another man's pain', the idea can be conveyed, perhaps even more clearly, by saying 'One person's pleasure is someone else's pain'. It is discriminatory and unclear to say 'We need more women engineering students' when what you mean is 'More women should be studying engineering'. Sometimes it's only a matter of leaving words out. Instead of 'Ask your local bank manager for his advice', you can say 'Ask your local bank manager for advice' or just 'Ask at your local bank'.

The English language has always contained many non-sexist words and your thesaurus will help you find them. Use 'maturity' instead of 'manhood' and 'humanity' in place of 'mankind'. Would a word like 'parental' convey your meaning just as clearly as 'motherly' or 'fatherly'? If it's hard to find any one word to replace a term such as 'spokesman', as in 'A spokesman for the union said . . .', just redraft the sentence: 'A union representative said . . .' or 'Mila Konstantides, speaking on behalf of the union, said that . . .'.

It takes a little more rewording to deal with discriminatory terms that describe personal qualities.

statesman-like decision	wise political decision
workmanlike results	professional results
man-to-man talk	open and honest discussion

Reword personal descriptions that stress physical attractiveness, instead of personality — for instance, 'Landfield's personnel manager, auburn-haired Lucinda Powers, is an attractive 27-year-old female psychologist'.

Use first names

Identify individuals by their names rather than their occupation, sex or personal attributes. Write 'My friend, Numchai' rather than 'my Asian friend'; say 'Phone and leave a message with Melinda' rather than 'Leave a message with our switchgirl'.

Avoid Mr, Mrs or Ms

Unless you want to be particularly formal, avoid Mr, Mrs, Miss, Ms or similar prefixes. They serve little purpose except to draw attention (quite unnecessarily on most occasions) to private and personal differences. In business today, who really needs to know if the individual is single, married or somewhere in between? Most people today welcome being addressed by the first name, so (unless an individual objects) refer to everyone by name alone. If Terry Black has just been chosen as the new manager, say 'Terry Black has been appointed', not 'Ms (or Mr) Black has been appointed'. You don't specify Terry's race or religion; why mention whether Terry is male, female, married or single?

Do not suggest ownership of one person by another

Words or phrases that suggest that one person is a possession of — is 'owned' by — another of the opposite sex is particularly discriminatory; for example, 'Please phone and ask for my assistant, Miss Reagan'. Using a husband's first name in place of a woman's own first name suggests that hers is of less importance than his. Say 'Jean and Paul Baxter both won prizes' rather than 'Mr and Mrs Paul Baxter won prizes'.

- Discriminatory: While the Minister for Education, Mr Joyce, inspects the school, his good lady will be entertained at lunch by Mrs Ralph King, the Principal's wife.
- Non-discriminatory: Nadia Joyce and Aileen King will lunch together while Michael Joyce (Minister for Education) inspects the school with the Principal, Ralph King.

In the second example the style is correct and the meaning is clearer. Nadia Joyce is nobody's 'good lady', and the fact that Aileen is married to Ralph has nothing to do with the day's events.

Do not suggest that a member of one sex is behaving atypically

- The winning cake was cooked by *a man*, Mr John Smith.
- The highway was blocked when a truck, *driven by a woman*, hit another vehicle.

Describe the problem — not the people working on it

Your sex does not determine whether or not you can deal with a particular problem. Instead of 'Businessmen are concerned about the new rates' say 'The new rates are causing concern in the business world'. Instead of 'DANGER! Men at work', say what it is you want people to do or why you want them to take care: 'DANGER! Road under repair'.

Don't go over the top

Communication works best if you focus on what is relevant to the issue being discussed. In business what matters most is people, and they remain people regardless of their gender or other characteristics. Except in situations where an individual's physical wellbeing or safety is involved, personal characteristics are irrelevant and should remain where they belong — in the background.

Words by themselves do not cause discrimination. That is done by people who use them, because of the way they use them. Going 'over the top' by desexing every possible word, whether it discriminates or not, can harm the cause of genuine non-discrimination. The letters 'm-a-n' and 's-o-n' do not need to be wiped from one's vocabulary. Words like management, manufacture and manual are derived from the Latin word *manus* (hand); they have nothing to do with 'male'. Anyone can 'master' a problem without losing status, and few people are likely to be affected if a manhole remains that way rather than becoming a personhole.

Replacing traditional titles of power or honour such as 'Princess' or 'Lord Mayor' with unfamiliar terms could downgrade the honour bestowed by these positions. Individuals who have risen to the top in special fields are similarly honoured when described as, for example, a 'prima ballerina' or a 'senior statesman', and since their sex is already an established fact this does not discriminate against them as individuals.

Summary

1. Discrimination occurs when people express a preference for one item ahead of another. When the 'item' is a person, the basis for that preference becomes very important.

2. Not all discrimination is based on gender. Judgment based on race, religion, physical characteristics or handicaps is just as discriminating.

3. You can make sure that your communication is free of discrimination by following these seven methods: (a) personalise, (b) pluralise, (c) describe the occupation, not the operator (person), (d) refer to groups in terms of their common interest, (e) redraft expressions using different words, (f) use first names rather than Mr or Ms and (g) describe the problem, not the people working on it.

4. The 'person' solution (changing 'fisherman' to 'fisherperson') should be used only as a last resort. It weakens the style of your language.

5. Words by themselves do not cause discrimination; it's the way the words are used. Don't go 'over the top'.

Exercises

1. List five (or more) guidelines for avoiding discrimination when you write or speak.

2. Reword the following paragraphs to improve style and clarity, and to remove errors. You can change any or all of the original words as long as your answer conveys the same meaning. Your versions should be positive, active, free of discrimination and shorter than the originals.

   (a) It is imperative that each manager arranges for his staff to receive full training before any of the men commence actual usage of the new equipment.

   (b) A spokesman for the Master Builders' Guild said he expected more money to be made available to train Aboriginal draughtsmen next year.

   (c) The new chairman of the Manpower Resources Team is Ms Jill Lee, a recently arrived migrant from New Zealand. Her husband is a well-known newsman on TV.

   (d) When a new depot manager takes up his duties, he should always tell his secretary how he wants her to handle his calls. The switchgirls should be advised also.

   (e) We are pleased to advise that we have just opened a new branch of our firm, ACME Real Estate, in this town, and invite any local home owner who would like his property valued to kindly contact us.

   (f) Our new sales representative is Ms Laurena Lamb, a shapely 22-year-old female graduate from Queensland. With her looks, she's already managed to raise our sales figures by 10 per cent.

   (g) Ask your secretary what she thinks of the new PCR70 word processor, and she'll tell you it makes her job twice as easy.

CHAPTER 29

Having your say

Having your say in front of other people is a powerful yet simple way of communicating, and much easier to master than most people think. In this chapter the emphasis is on talking in a meeting, making a presentation, and knowing how to act and speak naturally in front of a group — skills you'll find more valuable than the ability to make a formal speech. However, once you can speak with confidence in front of a small group you'll find it no trouble to do the same in front of a large one.

> **Topics**:
>
> Preparing a talk
>
> Organising the shape and structure
>
> Presenting the talk
>
> Speaking techniques
>
> Practising and polishing
>
> Overcoming speaking fear
>
> Evaluation

Preparing a talk

All forms of public speaking should begin with thorough preparation. This involves thinking, planning and gathering ideas (researching).

Thinking and planning

The central theme

First select your central theme, your principal goal. What is the general aim of your talk? You may be

- sharing your views with others, to gain their support;

- presenting vital information on a problem;
- running a training session;
- demonstrating a product to a potential buyer;
- explaining a new procedure.

Write down your central theme in one short sentence. If you want to inform staff of a change, for instance, the central theme could be 'to inform staff about changes to the new system'.

Specific aims

Establish specific objectives; they represent the steps your talk will follow in support of the central theme. To persuade people to support the change rather than just accept it, these might include

- *informing* staff why the change is needed;
- *showing* how everyone will benefit;
- *explaining* how it will be introduced.

The central theme and specific aims tie the talk together. Outline the central theme as part of your introductory remarks, discuss each aim as a specific topic in the body of the talk, and conclude by focusing on the action needed.

Analyse your audience

Thinking about your audience is important. Be aware of the powerful relationship that can and should exist between you.

Find out about them in advance

It is better to talk *with* people rather than *to* them, and to do this you need to know something of their personal and business backgrounds. What are their special interests? Analysing your audience in advance helps you to decide what to say and how to say it.

Having your say

Identify with them

Speaking to a group is well recognised as one of the best of all ways of developing a team spirit and encouraging people to work together for the common good. Your future as a leader or organiser will certainly be brighter if you can talk to groups of fifteen, twenty or fifty people with clarity and confidence, but if you talk as an outsider rather than as one of them, it won't be the same.

Be positive

If you really do 'like' your listeners, your talk will be far better for it. A successful speaker works hard beforehand to develop a positive attitude.

Consider the size of the group

Slides or overhead projections have impact with a small audience but often fall flat with a large one.

Computer displays are not effective unless everyone in the group can get close to the screen.

Gathering ideas together — researching

Background research gives your talk depth. Collect cuttings; read books, journals and old reports. Gather ideas, not words. Do not even think of trying to write the text at this stage, but do make lots of rough notes. Expand your thoughts on the topic. To develop familiarity, talk about it with friends, argue about it with opponents. Discuss key points with business associates, find out their personal views and tune in to their relevant experience.

Collect extra material

Gather more material than you actually need. This gives you a broader perspective, and while you are talking you will be able to cover the same point in different ways, using examples from your store of extra information.

Add some original ideas

A talk that introduces new ideas is more colourful than a rehash of other people's. It is unwise, however, to build it entirely out of original thoughts. Mix old and new for best results. Chapter 14 listed techniques for generating new ideas when you write, and most of these work just as well in drafting a talk.

Look at both sides

Discussing issues on a 'for and against' basis adds colour and contrast. If there are two sides to an issue (and there usually are), look into both. Use techniques such as lateral thinking (see Chapter 11) to develop contrasting or alternative views.

Sit in the listener's chair

If you expect opposition, look particularly at the issue from an opponent's point of view. What kind of arguments might be raised in opposition to yours? You can, of course, 'help' an opponent by outlining the opposite point of view and then showing why this position is unsound. You will have already undermined the argument before anyone has a chance to present it!

Collect colourful examples

The more important the talk, the more it will require strong and dramatic information to hold attention. Colourful or unusual facts add life and interest. Use them to support more everyday material.

Organising the shape and structure

Organised ideas are easier to follow. Know *what* you are going to talk about, and *when* you will deal with each point. Arrange your information simply, clearly and logically, keeping in mind the words of an old bush parson — perhaps the best advice ever given on the construction of a public address, whether it be sermon, speech or sales talk:

> 'Every talk has three parts. First you tell 'em what it is you're going to tell 'em. Second, you tell 'em. And lastly you tell 'em what it is you just told 'em'.

A well-organised talk has three phases that mirror these guidelines:
- the introduction — say what you want to achieve;
- the body — give the facts, with logical persuasion;
- the action ending — summarise, and say what needs to be done.

A dramatic presentation can influence the outcome of a talk, but only if the content is well prepared and has an obvious structure. The more you plan, organise and practise, the more easily you will achieve this.

The first draft

At this stage you are ready to begin drafting your speaking notes. It is often easier to work on the body first and then to decide on the most suitable introduction and conclusion. The RIPPA formula is a useful guide for getting ideas in order.
- *Relationship*: Every talk needs at least one positive relationship message about caring, support or loyalty, or an emphasis on goals and interests that you and your listeners have in common. By telling people what they most want to know, you

show your understanding and empathy and your respect for the relationship you have with them.

- *Informing*: Share some useful information early in the talk to develop listeners' confidence in you. When you tell people something new, or something that they have been waiting to find out, they appreciate the time spent with you and will look forward to hearing more. Furthermore, if the information is confidential, this shows listeners that you trust them.
- *Point-by-point persuasion*: Aim your talk at a level that will build co-operation — gain support or approval; explain the advantages of co-operation.
- *Painting a picture*: Use charts, slides, posters or video tapes; write key points on a board or on sheets of plain paper on a stand. Any of these methods can raise the level of interest and understanding by 50 per cent or more. Do not rely on words alone, but when you do speak, choose words that paint clear and descriptive word pictures.
- *Action*: A successful talk must always close with a call for action. There are no other endings that work so successfully.

Speech outline

As well as your speaking notes, draw up a written outline, a short list showing just the main features and key ideas. See the outline (based on the RIPPA format) for a sales presentation on a new can-opener. The listeners will be a group of twelve purchasers from a large organisation, which could become a major buyer.

Because it is so much briefer than your actual speaking notes, an outline gives you a quick overall view and helps you to see if you have missed any important points.

Presenting the talk

The introduction

Your first task is to create a bridge between you and each individual in the audience. Rarely will everyone's attention be focused on you at the start; ways of getting attention vary from telling a humorous story to issuing a serious challenge.

Outline for sales presentation

Main aim
To get an order this week for at least 10 000 can-openers

Other aims
To build stronger personal relationship with every individual buyer
To set up an arrangement for repeat orders

Main idea	Key words
Introduction	
Switch on	Break-through in design Your firm can be first on market
Relationship	Your firm and ours work together — both benefit
Body	
Inform	Show new product List advantages Explain buying plan
Point-by-point persuasion	1. No opposition in market 2. Special discount to your firm
Paint picture	TV promotion 7 days from now
Action ending	
Sign order today	Order today, we can deliver direct to each of your stores on Friday morning

Don't reveal title or topic

Starting with the words 'Today I will speak on the new Myall Safety Release Unit' will not arouse interest. Listeners may know you are going to talk about safety equipment; many may from past experience be expecting a boring speech and be looking for an excuse to 'switch off'. Instead of announcing the title, begin with a startling or unusual announcement: 'While you were on your way to this meeting, ten Australian building workers spent the morning trying to kill themselves!' An unusual introduction arouses curiosity and catches attention.

Warn the person introducing you not to 'blow it' by announcing the title or topic in advance. If your talk is being publicised, to arouse curiosity further select an ambiguous name that could mean any number of things. A talk for sales staff on non-verbal communication could be advertised under the title 'Unspeakable Ways of Increasing Sales'.

'Switch on' techniques

1. Arouse curiosity.
Do something unusual or surprising. To open a session on time management, bring a plate of cereal, add milk and pretend to be having a rush breakfast. People wondering 'Why did the speaker begin like that?' are people who are listening.

2. Ask a series of short questions.
Issue a challenge. Pose a trick question that has more than one answer: What weighs 2 to 3 kilograms, starts work every day at around 6.30 am and is Australia's single most valuable asset? (A possible answer is given at the end of the chapter.)

3. Relate a dramatic 'scene setting' story.
This adds support to the theme of your speech. (See 'Paint word pictures', page 328.)

4. Wear something unusual.
Hats are particularly useful; an old digger's army hat can set the scene for a talk on loyalty or team building. A thoroughly out-of-date hat such as a British 'tiger shooter' sun helmet could establish the tone for changing out-of-date management methods. Take the hat off once you have made the point, though! It will distract people if worn for too long.

5. Get listeners to do something physical.
Tell the audience you are conducting a quiz or a poll; ask them to raise their hands or call out the answers. Start with specific questions ('Who comes from ——?'), but develop the range so that sooner or later everyone is involved. 'Who likes computers?' 'Who doesn't like computers?' Questions such as 'Hands up all the people who can't stick to a diet' work well, too.

6. Draw a contrast.
Describe the difference between conditions now and fifty years ago.

7. Use humour to help everyone relax.
Make sure, however, that you have everyone laughing with you and not at you (see page 331).

The more formal the presentation, the more it is appropriate to use an emphatic speaking style, but do not get too carried away or too theatrical. Drama is fine as long as it does not divert listeners from the real issue. For the same reason, do not use too many visual displays during the opening. Just make sure that you have explained your general aim.

The body of the talk

You can now develop the central theme of your presentation. The audience will find it easier to follow if they have an outline, so identify the main points and the order in which they will be discussed. Tell them

- how many points you will cover;
- when they can expect you to finish;
- what will happen afterwards (how long for questions);
- whether you plan to use visual material (explain how it will help).

Get everyone involved

Try to arouse every person's interest by explaining how all are personally involved with the topic. In a talk on quality control give facts to show that every employee is affected by high reject rates. Tell a story about a local figure to show how everyone's life can be touched by an issue such as road safety.

Ask questions, then answer them

Tie each listener into an issue by asking and then answering questions such as these.

- What is the chance of you or me as an individual being injured at work this week?
- How many people of your age group or in your occupation are injured annually in this community?
- How much do accidents at work cost the individual taxpayer? How much do they cost you and me?

Make it clear that you welcome questions. Never ask a group to 'hold the questions' until you have finished speaking. Instead, start the interaction early by asking questions of the group as a whole during the talk, or addressing particular questions to individuals. This is where the extra material you collected at the planning stage is so handy; it is also why (as explained below) it is better not to memorise a talk or to read from a prepared script. That only limits your flexibility when you need to deal with audience response. If you work from just short notes you can alter the presentation each time questions lead you in a different direction.

Paint word pictures

People remember things you show them. Use colourful and descriptive phrases to paint word pictures. Instead of a general statement such as 'There is too much waste on this project', explain how much money is being wasted each week. Dress facts and figures up by using colourful comparisons. A plain report on the first edition of this book might say that it was published ten years ago for use in management courses and has averaged sales of 4500 copies a year. In a talk, why not say 'Since 1981, when it was first published, this book has been read by over 45 000 Australian managers!'.

Tell a graphic story

If you need to present a controversial opinion or an idea that people may not readily agree with, begin by asking yourself 'What was it that made me accept this opinion? What did I see or hear that helped convince me? What did I feel at the time? Why was the experience so significant?'

Tell the story of this personal experience *before* you mention the idea you want to promote. Having heard your story, people will start to feel the way you do. When you finally state your point, you will be in the position of appearing to agree with your listeners rather than their agreeing with you.

Confirm your facts

If you are quoting facts and figures, be certain they are accurate. If you use data from books or periodicals, name the source in your talk (see 'Quotes, references and acknowledgments' in Chapter 18).

Use logical (point-by-point) arguments

Make sure that your reasoning is clear, logical and easy to follow. (Chapter 11 explains a number of ways of using factual information to support a logical argument.) Use specific examples rather than general statements. When you make a point,

spend the next few minutes hammering it home rather than moving on too quickly to the next one. Support and build on each key idea by talking about related topics.

Saying 'Thank you' — take care!

It is worthwhile in the body of the talk to thank the audience. Thank them for 'helping make the position clear' — or for doing whatever your talk is aiming to achieve. By all means thank them for supporting you, for inviting you to speak or for being so interested in the product you are demonstrating. But never thank them for *listening*, even at the end.

Know when to stop

The ideal talk should take no more than 15 to 30 minutes — that is the extent of the average person's attention level. If you have aroused your listeners sufficiently, they'll have many questions and will want to know how you will answer them. You continue to talk, but about points that are most significant for your audience. This will hold their interest more effectively than a 40-minute talk.

Action ending

There are two different kinds of action ending.
- The more common one follows immediately after the body of the talk. Then (after the applause has died down) you answer questions.
- The second is used if you expect a long (or heated) question session; in that case it is better to (a) give a brief action message to conclude the body of your talk, (b) ask for, answer and debate questions, and (c) deliver a powerful action ending.

Make sure that the person in the chair knows in advance which way you want to finish, otherwise you can find someone moving a vote of thanks (to you) following the question session, instead of you moving the audience with your real ending!

Action ending — guidelines

1. Summarise.
Your conclusion should reinforce the arguments

used to get the message across. Highlight your main ideas, even if you have stated them twice before (remember the old bush parson?). Restate the purpose of the talk, repeat one or two of the most telling arguments.

2. Don't introduce new ideas.
Keep moving towards the final action. Do not move away from the focal point of the talk.

3. Be positive.
Make the final recommendation or call for action as positive as you can. Avoid scare tactics. Talk about the benefits of your recommendations, not the faults of someone else's.

4. Call for action *now*.
Close by asking everyone to do something — not later, but now. Phrase your request so that what you ask can be done immediately: supporting a plan, voting on a motion or making a donation. If the topic warrants it, end with a direct call to 'Agree!', 'Reject!', 'Refuse!', 'Remember!' or 'Forget!'. At a conference, you can close with a call for everyone to 'Vote Yes' or 'Vote No!', 'Amend!' or 'Defeat!'. In a sales presentation, ask straight out for an order. Make a strong and specific call. Do not plead or ask for sympathy.

5. Start a movement.
As most top sales representatives know, when people make a physical movement that coincides with a mental one (applauding while agreeing, cheering while supporting), their commitment becomes more deeply implanted. The larger the audience, the stronger the effect. Your very last words should be aimed at getting the group to cheer, clap, raise their hands, stand up, say 'yes' — anything, so long as the whole group moves in unison the moment you stop talking. Every second's delay lessens the effect; if you want a contract signed, have it ready.

6. Do not end with 'That's about all I can say', 'That's it' or 'Thank you'.
These thoughts break the flow of ideas and audience energy towards the action you are calling for. Keep everyone's mind fixed on the response *they* should be making. Don't give the impression you are thankful you have finished, are grateful for the way the group have put up with you, or have run out of ideas.

Speaking techniques

A bright, outgoing approach is a tremendous asset and will help you to overcome many speaking problems. Be positive — express enthusiasm, show enjoyment, and above all make it clear that you like your audience and care about them. This also means keeping your talk down to a comfortable length — meaning comfortable for them, not for you!

1. Build a favourable climate for agreement between you and your listeners.
This is more likely to happen if they see you as a credible communicator, so try to sound confident or even authoritative.

2. Vary your speaking style.
In an informal meeting, put more emphasis on naturalness than on 'speech making' — informality is the key when you want to get through to people at work. On the other hand, the style is not that of ordinary conversation. Depending on the size of the group, your language can be a little more colourful and descriptive than in ordinary speech but less dramatic than in a formal address or a parliamentary-type debate.

3. Speak a little more loudly than in everyday discussions, but don't shout.
Your level of enthusiasm ought to be just a little stronger than in normal conversation, but not so much as to create an 'enthusiasm gap' between you and the listeners.

4. Show that you like 'being with' as well as 'speaking with' the group.
Use gestures — words alone seldom convey this clearly. Smile; pay them a sincere compliment. Show them that you trust them. One way to do this is to be completely honest with them — for instance, saying (if it is appropriate) that you are 'not really an expert' on the topic (which they would have worked out for themselves after a while, anyway).

5. Compare and contrast ideas.
Ask listeners if they want to succeed or fail, to choose A or B (having first made it clear why A is the better choice).

6. Link ideas or sounds (in threes).
Similar sounds repeated in quick succession add impact. 'Together we can win. Divided we are

destined for defeat.' 'If we think as a team and plan as a team, we can work as a team.' Yes, you would feel foolish talking this way in daily conversation, but in a talk it adds colour and emphasis, and strengthens agreement.

7. Pause after you make an important point.

The more important the point, the longer the pause should be. Give people time to think. Let your words sink in. *go into your head / understand*

8. Watch and listen to your audience.

Look around, maintain strong eye contact with as many people as you can. This gives an individual the feeling that you are speaking to her or to him personally and increases listeners' confidence in asking questions. Welcome anyone who disagrees with you — this gives you a chance to show the real strength of your argument.

Improving your style — guidelines

Every speaker can improve. Many faults are natural, and you may be unaware of them.

1. Respect your audience.

Perhaps you do know more than your listeners. If so, your task is to share your knowledge. Never criticise, and never preach. You may 'talk down' to an audience unintentionally if you fail to learn in advance the age and education level represented. A group of very mature students from an evening course (some years ago) still talk about the guest speaker who wished them all 'Good luck, as you go out into the world seeking your first full-time job'. Avoid a paternal or a 'Don't you worry about that' approach.

2. Be natural.

Relax. Be yourself. The more at ease you appear to be, the more your audience will appreciate your message. An overformal, flowery or unnatural speaking style suggests lack of confidence.

3. Choose an appropriate style.

People who have not been trained as speakers tend to copy speaking styles they have heard in the past. If many of your early listening experiences were with teachers and religious speakers, these are styles that you will be most likely to copy. Neither is appropriate for business speaking.

4. Say 'We' or 'You and I' — *never* 'You people'.

5. If you are nervous share your feelings.

Saying 'I'm feeling nervous' shows you are honest and open. Ask for support, but don't go on about it. Apologising for what you are doing draws attention away from what you want to say. Informing the audience that 'Some of you may find this uninteresting' marks you as an amateur.

6. Do not antagonise listeners.

Threatening people — or saying things that will arouse anxiety, fear or displeasure — is not a sound tactic. For a start, you'll lose their attention as they focus inwards on their negative feelings. If you have to tell people really bad news, do so as part of a team or a panel rather than alone.

7. Don't bluff.

If you do not know the answer to a question, say so. People appreciate this and will understand your position.

8. Make sure you know when to stop.

A talk that seems to you to be too short is probably just right for everyone else. How often do you hear people complain that a talk was not long enough? How often do you hear the opposite?

9. Don't read a talk.

On some occasions you'll need to use very precise wording — if, for instance, you are making a policy statement. In that case you'll naturally read the statement, but before you start explain why you are doing so. Otherwise, avoid reading from notes unless this is the only way you can be sure of completing the talk.

Visual display material

Imagine trying to explain to a builder what you want your new kitchen to be like without some kind of visual assistance! How successful would you be if you relied on words alone? Good speakers increase their chances of getting results by using visual displays to clarify meanings. Frequently this is the only way to be sure your listeners really understand you.

Visual displays are useful for highlighting, summarising, and illustrating relationships between ideas. They help to hold the interest of those whose attention-span for spoken words is limited. They are vital for presenting figures. And they make you appear as a more professional speaker. Simple items such as flip-charts, models, or actual pieces of equipment are all useful. If you are nervous, they can be life-savers by giving you something to talk about if you run out of words.

Using visual displays

- Work out at what stage in the body of the talk the material will have the strongest impact.
- Simple is best. Ordinary overhead projections can be more effective than something that is complicated or takes time to operate, unless someone else is available to help. You can lose your listeners' attention completely if you stop to set up a video or movie projector or spend time at a computer keyboard trying to put a message on the screen.
- Samples or photographs that can be passed from hand to hand add interest, but can also act as distractions. Be careful particularly of anything that has moving parts — an attraction that can distract attention from you and your talk.
- Spend time on a thorough hands-on rehearsal for at least half an hour with any machine before you use it 'on stage', to make sure that you are as practised in operating it as you are in speaking. Have spare bulbs and fuses on hand. If there is a power failure your visual presentation may collapse, so have a back-up script prepared to carry you through.

Printed hand-outs

Printed notes add valuable support to your talk. You can spend time on more interesting things if the notes are there to support what you say with facts, figures and illustrations. (They should be in addition to what you say; never give a copy of your actual 'script' to listeners.) There is, however, one problem if they are as interesting as they should be: people may read them instead of listening to you, so hand them out only after your main talk, just before question time.

If part of your talk needs to be recorded for publication in the media or as the terms of an agreement, then hand that section out in advance so that the audience can read it through with you.

Practising and polishing

Practising should be as realistic as possible. If you can, use friends or family as a stand-in audience. A

video camera or a tape recorder is, however, even more valuable as a practice aid because it gives you rapid and very honest (and unbiased) feedback in private: you can see and hear yourself as others do. This may come as a shock at first, but most speakers find that when they use a recorder regularly their choice of words, diction, tone, timing and style of delivery all improve rapidly. So does their confidence (see 'Overcoming speaking fear', page 332).

What to memorise

When rehearsing, concentrate on the opening and the action ending. As long as they are both well presented, your talk will be a success. In some cases it's important to memorise the entire opening if it involves a story or a punch line that should be delivered word for word. Memorise your closing lines too, so that no matter what else happens you will be sure of a polished ending.

What *not* to memorise

If you memorise the body of the talk as well, it will sound terrible. It is better to read it than to learn it off by heart — unless you have some ability as an actor, and a good memory. If you can achieve a relaxed delivery through good acting skills you can make a prepared speech sound spontaneous, but you will find that even this kind of presentation is better if you only learn key parts of the talk, and allow for off-the-cuff delivery in between.

Using cue cards

Instead of memorising, prepare a key or cue card for each main point. These work best if they are small enough to be held in the palm of the hand. Write key words or phrases in large, clear lettering so you can read them at a glance; keep the words to a minimum. Never write complete sentences. Numbering each card makes sure you find your place again, even if you get the cards out of sequence.

Using humour

Getting people to laugh with you is a real advantage, but unless you have a natural sense of humour, be cautious. Jokes must be chosen carefully and must not be of the kind that could offend sections of the audience. The story that had the whole group laughing at a party on Saturday is not going to win support at the sales presentation on Monday. Avoid sexist or racist humour. Do not make jokes about other people's embarrassment, failure or personal handicaps. The best jokes start without warning. Instead of 'Have you heard the joke about the new shop assistant who went up to the boss and asked if . . .', act as if you are describing an actual event or referring to a well-known member of the audience. 'I remember the first time I met Mike, just after he came to work here. He came up to me and asked if . . .'.

Overcoming speaking fear

Everyone probably has some fear of talking in public. It has been claimed, according to some surveys, that many Australians actually list public speaking as the thing they most fear apart from dying! If speaking holds any kind of fear for you, try looking at things from different angles.

Imagine you are talking to two friends, expressing your views on student fees. Are you nervous? Would you be upset if two other friends came over and joined you? Imagine, then, a couple more drifting over to listen. You are making good sense, they are interested, and they want to hear more. You are now speaking 'in public', but what is the difference? If you can talk to two people, you can talk to four. If four, why not ten? If ten, why not fifteen?

Suppose a stranger asks you for directions. Are you nervous as you explain? No, because you know you are helping someone who needs your advice. Your audience may be strangers, too, but as long as you are helping them by giving them useful information there is no need to be nervous about it.

Consider a well-known member of parliament making a speech. Do people praise the speaker's skills? Do they believe and accept everything in the speech because it was presented by an expert? Aren't many people inclined to be just as suspicious of a 'professional' speaker as anyone else? If a group asks you to talk to them it may well be because they want to hear from *you*, not from an expert orator.

If you still worry about speaking, the following techniques will help.

Before the speech

1. Practise in front of a mirror, or better still using a tape recorder (sound or video) as explained above. Speaking to these devices is remarkably like speaking to an audience, so you'll feel quite nervous at first. But if you make regular practice recordings, your nervousness will leave you and you'll discover the self-confidence to cope with a human audience.

2. Plan to talk about something that you know is true and that you believe in. The stronger your conviction, the easier it will be to talk. Your enthusiasm will rub off on your listeners.

3. Tightening and then slowly relaxing the band of muscles just under your ribs can help control nervousness. If necessary, do this for several minutes before speaking.

4. Keeping the same muscles tight, take a really deep breath. Breathe out and relax the muscles. Repeating this a few times immediately before you rise to speak helps to relax your vocal cords and boosts your oxygen intake. (If you do it more than ten times you may start to hyperventilate, so be careful.)

5. Estimate the time your talk will take. Then check the *actual* time during a practice run. Time seems to move very slowly when you are the speaker. You'll be surprised to find the time you need to complete your talk is usually *double* what you expected.

6. Speak a little more loudly, a little lower, a little more slowly and with a little more 'breath' than you do in normal speech. This will make you sound more confident — and in most cases also feel more confident. Develop the strength and volume of your voice by practising at different volume levels. One of the safest places to try this is alone in a car — try it on the way to work!

7. Remind yourself that to others you do not appear as nervous as you feel. If you can present a confident image, your nervousness may not even be noticed.

8. Most audiences are capable of giving tremendous support if you allow them to do so. They appreciate what you are going through. They want to help. All you have to do is to ask. As part of your introductory remarks, tell listeners that you need their help in dealing with a difficult topic. Even a hostile group will include some

who sympathise with you. If you are expecting to be criticised, say so; expressing vulnerability can reduce audience hostility, because you have been honest with them. But never 'rubbish' yourself or your topic.

Grammar problems — are you sure?

Fear of making grammatical errors is another cause of nervousness. Some people spend so much mental effort watching their grammar that they forget what they are speaking about! What they fail to notice is that in everyday conversation they make few (if any) grammatical errors. Ask a friend to listen to you talking to another person: if you speak correctly in conversation, it suggests that the part of your mind responsible for grammar and sentence construction is working well — so well, in fact, that it runs automatically. Imagine the danger if drivers constantly watched their feet operating the clutch and accelerator pedals! Similarly, if you are constantly watching your grammar and construction, your speech can run off the road.

If you maintain a conversational style when you speak in public, using short words and short sentences, your grammar sorts itself out and consequently your talk is more impressive; it's more likely to be correct, and you don't run the risk of a 'crash' caused by unaccustomed words and phrases.

Slips of the tongue

There are, however, a few errors that tend to slip in when you speak 'naturally', and which you therefore need to watch.

- Mixed plural and singular: 'Any employee (*single*) who wants to attend should write their (*plural*) name (*singular*) on this list'. It's correct to say 'Employees (*plural*) who want to attend should write their names (*plural*) on this list'.
- The plural 'you': The plural of you (one person) is also you (many people). There is no such word as 'youze'.
- Mixed past and present: 'This is (*present*) a problem that had (*past*) us worried'. Say instead: 'This is a problem that *has* us worried'.
- The split infinitive: Placing a descriptive word between the two parts of an infinitive weakens the verb. The construction, 'Staff need to carefully watch for these mistakes' sounds awkward. Say instead: 'Staff need to watch carefully for

these mistakes'. There are times when it is necessary to break this 'rule' to avoid ambiguity, but this should only be done deliberately and with good reason. You will be able to judge by the sound and the sense.

Evaluation

After it is over, check to see where your speech worked best and where it could have been improved. Immediate indicators of success are the amount of applause you receive and the number of people who afterwards comment or ask further questions. But don't just wait to be asked — approach and question those who do not come to you. Did they feel you covered the topic fully? Did you give enough emphasis to key issues? Could you be clearly heard? Enquire about the visual displays: were they easy to see?

Make a long-term evaluation as well. Look for feedback on the topic of your talk. A questionnaire circulated three to six weeks later is useful in discovering how you may have influenced listeners' views.

Summary

1. Establish clear objectives: know why you are going to speak and what you are aiming for.
2. Think about your audience and how you can use your talk to develop your relationship with them.
3. Research your talk. Collect ideas first, not words. Look at both sides of every question. Organise your ideas carefully.
4. The introduction must capture the attention of every listener (but don't reveal the exact title or topic at the start).
5. Give an outline; identify the main points and the order in which they will be discussed.
6. Confirm facts. If you are quoting figures, be sure they are accurate. If using data from publications, name the sources.
7. Repeat key points or key 'sounds'. Quick repetition (in threes) of similar sounds has a special impact. Pause after any important point.
8. There are two different kinds of action ending. One is to call for questions, before finishing the

talk; the other is to end the talk and then ask for questions.

9. Call on the audience to take definite and positive action. Never leave listeners up in the air, wanting to act but not knowing how.

Exercises

1. Draft an outline *only* for an informal 5-minute talk to your study group on any one of the following topics:
   - the greenhouse effect
   - public transport
   - lifestyles of poor and unknown students
   - noise pollution
   - censorship
   - music
   - advertising
   - smoking
   - addictions
   - a topic of your own choice

2. Discuss a newspaper cutting (that everyone in your group has read) on a controversial issue. Each of you should prepare a written outline for a brief (30–45 seconds) comment, either in support of the issue or against it.
   (a) Each person speaks in turn.
   (b) The issue is discussed in open debate.
   (c) Each summarises personal views (reached after the issue has been debated).

3. Prepare a written opening for a 2-minute talk based on a topic from exercise 1 or 2.

4. Prepare a written ending for a short talk based on the same topic.

5. Prepare short (about 2 minutes) speaking notes for the body of a short talk based on the same topic.

6. Discuss how each group member feels about speaking 'in public'.

7. Practise the techniques described in this chapter for reducing stress in speaking.

8. Read a prepared opening in front of the group.

9. Read a prepared ending in front of the group.

10. Give a short talk on a prepared topic.

Exercises like these introduce newcomers easily and naturally to the rewarding practice of talking to a group. Before extending the length of any talks, make sure that people with visual or tactile memories (see Chapter 6) are given
- the opportunity to write and practise their talks (have no impromptu speaking);
- free use of notes or visual prompts (such as an overhead transparency) while talking.

Avoid referring to any presentation as a 'speech'. Do not ask or expect all group members to give talks of the same length: fixed time limits suggest that those who finish early have failed. In the early stages of learning, speakers should be encouraged not to talk for more than five minutes; this will create the confidence needed to talk for longer periods.

Students with strong aural memories are the only ones who have a natural ability to give impromptu talks. To call on anyone to speak on a topic 'drawn out of a hat', or to talk without the use of prepared notes, is in most cases unwise. It is questionable, anyway, whether impromptu exercises 'teach' anything useful about public speaking.

Have you worked out the answer to the unusual opening lines (p. 327)? Australia's greatest asset is the human mind. The topic of the talk was 'Education'.

CHAPTER 30

Making meetings work

Most meetings are held to discuss and solve problems, so the typical business meeting is a semi-formal type of group communication. Depending on your job, you may be involved in meetings once a week or several times a day. Most community bodies also have regular meetings, so even your spare time can be taken up in this way.

This chapter looks at
- using committee meetings effectively;
- the way a well-run meeting is set up and conducted;
- how you can best participate in a business meeting;
- different ways of running a meeting.

Topics

Why have a meeting?

Different types of meetings

Planning and organising a meeting

At the meeting

Hidden agendas

The effective participant

Formal meeting rules

Why have a meeting?

Meetings offer many benefits to an organisation and its members. A well-run meeting
- encourages co-ordination — people can keep up to date with developments and changes, which means better planning and co-operation between sections;
- develops team spirit — staff involved in organising changes and introducing new functions,

whose advice and suggestions are accepted, think and act more as a team;
- encourages consensus — ideas can be developed and tailored as required;
- solves problems — many difficulties are better handled by a meeting than by individuals, and some can be solved only by group action.

Different situations require different kinds of meetings. Depending on the problem to be solved, the type of business to be transacted, the nature of the group and the style of leadership, you might choose
- committee meetings
- general staff meetings
- conferences
- formal board meetings
- informal decision-making sessions
- meetings to give instructions
- conventions
- training sessions

As Table 30.1 shows, if the reasons for a meeting differ, so should its structure and the method of control or leadership.

Chairing or leading?

Most business meetings do not need to be strictly controlled (in the fashion of parliamentary procedure) or to have just one person in the chair, but formal measures do become necessary if proceedings are heated or if a minority group attempts to force its views on the rest. For this reason, participants in even the most informal meeting should know
- how to formally bring an unruly meeting to order;
- how to participate in a formal meeting;
- how to control a hostile meeting from the chair.

Everyday meetings, however, in which one or several leaders encourage participation while still

maintaining informal control, are likely to be the more productive for business purposes. Provided all its members are skilled in group leadership *and* meeting management, a panel of two or three (representing, for example, both sexes) in the chair will help a meeting function more effectively than an individual leader.

Different types of meetings

In Table 30.1, meetings are classified according to their purpose; notice, however, that as the meeting's goals vary, so too does its structure. Leadership in these meetings ranges between chairing, telling, selling, joining, consulting, participating, and combinations of these styles.

Table 30.1 *Alternative meeting structures and leadership*

Purpose	Structure and leadership style
1. Getting agreement with minimal discussion	Leaders 'tell' the group what to agree on and how to agree. Direct influence is exerted by those who hold most power. Rules and traditional procedures are used to restrict the right of speech to 'approved' group members.
2. Getting agreement by majority vote	Analysis of facts and discussion is allowed, but only of 'approved' agenda items. Discussion is restricted by use of personal power, authority, formality, manipulation, pressure and other ways. Leaders 'direct' or 'chair' discussion. Resulting vote is not truly 'democratic'.
3. Reaching decisions and solving problems using consultative format	Open discussion is held, with unrestricted presentation of facts and opinions, followed by open debate. Leaders can vary level of control to help encourage or limit discussion. Leaders 'join' group as participative members.
4. Getting approval for decisions already made, but in which the team needs to give full support if the project is to succeed	Members put forward ideas and suggestions. This is where a consensus is most likely to be achieved. Leaders 'sell' the idea of teamwork and co-operation, but allow the group to play a part in deciding how the decision will be implemented.
5. Developing new ideas, encouraging creative thinking, planning, consulting and investigating	Open and informal discussions have few constraints other than time limits. Leaders 'consult' with the rest of the group. Leaders do need to work hard to make sure the group sticks to the topic.
6. Organising, getting the job done, delegating tasks	There is limited discussion, but wide opportunity for questions and answers on details. Those with the highest level of responsibility for results tend to control the discussion. Leaders 'tell' or 'sell', according to type of project.
7. Developing team spirit and goal-setting	Open and informal discussion centres on what the group should be aiming for. Leadership is still needed, but leaders should participate rather than dominate.

Committee meetings

Committees operate at all levels; their tasks range from deciding company policy and fixing major problems to making changes in daily routines at front-counter or shop-floor level. They can be among the most useful of all meetings or they can serve as a burial ground for ideas and initiative.

When to use a committee

A committee may be created to make a decision, to provide a list of recommendations, to generate ideas or to exchange information. It may be needed in any of the following circumstances:

- when a wide collection or coverage of information is needed before a sound judgment can be made;
- when the decision is so important that it demands the judgment of a group of qualified people;
- when regular and continuing co-ordination with different sections or groups is needed;

- when a problem requires airing and discussion at every level;
- when specialist decisions have been delegated to experts, and co-ordination is required to produce a balanced result.

Committee accountability

In every case, however, a committee should be responsible to a more senior group and should report regularly to that group. A committee is not a governing body and should not have an 'open cheque book', or authority to act without higher approval.

When not to use a committee

A committee should not be formed

- if there are no qualified people available to discuss and decide technical issues (don't form a committee out of the 'best we could find' — use outside consultants);

- if there are no clear goals in sight and no specific job for it to do;
- if time is short — a decision of higher quality than an individual's on-the-spot choice is of little use if urgent action is held up while a committee is formed and holds a series of meetings.

Selecting committee members – guidelines

How big should a committee be? It could have four, five, ten or (at the most) fifteen people. Anything larger than that is unwieldy and will not be effective.

1. Start with a small group.
If more people want to participate, invite them to attend a meeting. If they show they have something special to offer, ask them to join you.

2. Select people who are *not* all alike.
Pick people with different backgrounds and from different sections and levels of the organisation. Combine experts and non-experts. This will guarantee the widest possible range of views, and help to prevent groupthink (see Chapter 23).

3. Choose confident, assertive people.
This ensures that neither the person in the chair, nor any other single member can dominate the committee.

4. Choose energetic people.
Beware of anyone who is said to have 'plenty of spare time'. Someone else who is busy (but can make time) will often contribute more.

5. Choose people who *want* to be on the committee.
Interested people work hardest. A reluctant member cannot be a positive contributor. Watch, however, for people who like to be on committees for the honour and glory but are not prepared to share the workload.

Set clear goals

New members should understand the committee's background and past history, why it is important and, above all, what it is trying to achieve. Explaining this is one of the leaders' functions.

Review committees regularly

Committees can go stale. Look at the real purpose of the group regularly to see whether

- it is still doing what it was set up to do;
- its goals should be changed or revamped;
- the membership or structure needs to be varied.

Standing and temporary groups

A group such as a safety committee, which deals with the same issues over a long period and occupies a fixed place in the organisation structure, is known as a *standing* committee. Even so, the time will come when it needs updating. Members of any group, if allowed to become 'permanent', develop too much power. Keep rolling membership over.

A *temporary* committee might be appointed to handle the changeover from an old to a new system. It should be disbanded as soon as its task is completed, but members may be reluctant to see this happen and may even discover reasons why they should become a permanent group. Watch for this.

Suggestions for leaders

- Establish a friendly climate in the meeting room.
- Schedule meetings at a regular time so that members can plan ahead.
- Stress that the task and the final output are the group's joint responsibility.
- Encourage every member to bring up ideas, confident that they will be treated with respect.
- Tell members why they were selected; they will then know what, how and why they are expected to contribute.
- Share responsibility — identify specialists among members, or make each person responsible for carrying out specific jobs.

On-the-spot conferences

If there is a sudden breakdown on the shop floor, if the main computer blows up or if the store burns down, a whole range of decisions will have to be made in a matter of hours to get things going again. Temporary arrangements must be put in place immediately, standard procedures changed or relaxed, staff moved into emergency roles. This kind of situation can best be handled by an informal meeting called on the spot and attended by section leaders and supervisors of all affected areas.

Senior staff will usually lead the discussion and set guidelines. Middle and lower level front-line staff with special knowledge of the problem should be called in as needed. In emergencies they often know better than anyone the best and quickest thing to do.

The main thing at a conference like this is in fact to confer — to exchange ideas as quickly as possible. Informality is the key to success. Discussion should be free, dress casual, debate down to earth. The emphasis should be on co-operative pooling of ideas to promote constructive thinking, and the conference leader should use a wide range of questioning techniques. Chapter 23 lists many different ways of dealing with this kind of situation.

(Note that other gatherings are also called 'conferences', as in 'state conference'; to avoid confusion, these might be more appropriately called 'conventions'. This type of meeting is not covered in this chapter.)

General staff meetings

Problems that cannot be handled by any other method can be solved through a staff meeting. It often takes many minds and a large meeting to penetrate the core of a problem that exists across the whole organisation. What seems to be a large and universal issue may in fact be made up of many smaller ones, not all of which were previously evident.

A well-run organisation should hold a general meeting of all staff, from top management to cleaners, at least every half-year. Part-time staff should be included too. If the staff numbers thousands, section meetings of a similar nature should be held.

Smaller staff meetings for individual units should be held weekly or fortnightly and everyone in the section, at whatever level, should be encouraged to attend. Meetings of this kind help develop special advantages.

- **Team spirit and morale**
  If as many people as possible from all levels have a chance to express ideas, both individual and group morale is raised. Effective two-way communication in a staff meeting creates more interest in issues and makes staff more aware of the way other people function.

- **Pride in the organisation**
  Provided staff meetings are well run, regular participants develop a feeling of belonging and of pride in the organisation as a whole. Their aims broaden and their attitudes to issues such as client service are strengthened.

- **New ideas**
  By its very nature, a discussion in which everyone can join helps to stir up new ideas. The more people are encouraged to express their views without fear of ridicule, the greater will be the pool of information, and this in turn generates more ideas.

- **Shared problem solving**
  Staff meetings provide an ideal chance for individuals who thought they were alone in a problem area to become aware of others with similar problems. Solutions can be shared, too.

Requirements for a successful staff meeting

To achieve the greatest success, a staff meeting needs
- an experienced leader or leaders — the best are those who can define and clarify problems, and remain impartial (this is preferable to having high-ranking officials as leaders);
- the active interest and support of management — all participants must feel that they are supported by their superiors, and that management will take an active interest in the outcome of the meeting.

Planning and organising a meeting

Advance organisation

Choose the venue

The success of any meeting depends to a large extent on location and facilities. The venue should be as conveniently central as possible for the participants, but not too close to their normal workplace. People need to get away from daily activities if they are to participate fully. If it isn't possible to choose a room without a telephone, arrange to have all calls diverted until the meeting ends. The room chosen

should be quiet, and big enough for you to use charts and audiovisual equipment without anyone having to move in order to see them.

Book rooms and resources in advance

Rooms, tables, chairs, screens, recorders, players and videos for use during discussions need to be booked early. Test-run all equipment: it must work effectively. Preview all videos. Remember also that pens, pencils and notepaper are equally important. Run off extra copies of hand-outs and agendas (some people are sure to arrive without them).

Plan the room layout

Plan the positioning of tables and chairs, and physical resources. A neat, symmetrical layout looks efficient, but people relax more and contribute better if the surroundings are informal and they can

move furniture around to suit themselves. The worst arrangement is something that resembles a classroom.

Prepare name-tags and cards

Name-cards set around a large table enable you to place key individuals where you want them, and to separate people known to be either very friendly or unfriendly towards one another. (Put antagonists where they will find it hardest to look directly at one another.)

Notice of the meeting, and the agenda

Calling the meeting

Aim for a time that is convenient for everyone. Nothing gets a meeting off to a worse start than calling it without first consulting members about the timing. Key people should be consulted first, since the time may need to be fixed to fit in with them, and if necessary this should be explained (in advance) to the other participants. As soon as the time has been fixed, telephone everyone concerned. Follow this with a notice of meeting (in writing) and, if specific topics are already known, a draft agenda. Otherwise invite participants to submit items for an agenda, which will be sent out closer to the meeting time.

Make sure each person knows why he or she is being invited. This allows them to prepare their thoughts in advance.

The agenda

An agenda should give as much information as possible in advance. As well as actual topics, list in it the proposed goals of the meeting. Explain
- exactly where the meeting is to be held (room number, on which floor);
- why it is taking place;
- when it is to start and when it is expected to finish;
- what facilities are available and what members should bring;
- what background reading or other activities will best prepare people for the discussion.

At the meeting

Introductions

If you are one of the leaders, welcome people as they arrive. Hand out name-tags. Introduce members to one another as they arrive, using first names.

At the start of the first session, welcome everyone again. Mention special individuals or guests by name, calling attention to the special skills that each is able to contribute.

Encourage all members to participate fully. Outline the broad objectives, but do not indicate limits or make specific predictions as to what conclusions you expect the meeting to reach.

During the meeting

Once the meeting starts, leaders need to assume many roles. They can promote, lead, direct, inform,

interpret, encourage, stimulate, referee, judge, moderate and conciliate, as needed.
- Promote and stimulate discussion, but keep it to the point.
- Maintain an even distribution of discussion; control the overenthusiastic talker and encourage more reticent members to have their say.
- Restrict private discussion, and stop any 'ganging up' against individuals.
- Encourage lively discussion, but guard against it becoming too heated.
- Assist members to express their ideas, but don't do their thinking for them.
- Ask questions to provoke discussion and stimulate interest. Questions from leaders help to keep the discussion on track and can reduce the time taken to reach a decision.

Food and drink

Tea, coffee, iced water, other cool drinks and light food (nuts or mints, for instance) should be available at *all times*. Encourage people to help themselves whenever they wish, rather than to wait for breaks. If the meeting extends through a meal period, have food brought in (preferably nutritious rather than high-calorie items). Sandwiches — or anything that can be held in the hand — are better than food that requires plates and cutlery. The whole climate of the meeting and valuable discussion time are lost if the group splits up and leaves the room to eat elsewhere. (Consumption of alcohol during outside lunches does nothing to help the process, either.)

Subgroup sessions

Participants can become too comfortable. Any activity — even getting them to change seats — provides stimulation. Most meetings of more than eight people work better if at various stages they split into subgroups. If you plan to use this technique, arrange other rooms nearby where subgroups can meet. If you cannot do that, allow space in the main meeting room for chairs to be regrouped.

Subgroup sessions can give certain special advantages.
- They allow quieter members a chance to put forward their ideas through a more confident person, selected by a group to summarise its viewpoint.
- Instead of there being only one speaker at a time,

several people can speak simultaneously (each in his or her own group).

- Key figures who may dominate the main meeting cannot control discussion in small-group sessions, and this allows a wider range of views (including those opposed to the dominant opinions) to be heard.

Using hand-outs

Distributing too many loose papers during the meeting can be distracting. The best way is to have them bound in a single book and hand it out at the start.

Hidden agendas

Apart from the written or open agenda, which outlines the topics to be discussed, some people bring with them issues that make up their 'hidden agendas'. The term refers to issues raised in discussion which have no official place in the meeting but which relate to private or individual goals. In such cases individuals try to push through decisions that will benefit some people, but not the whole group.

Power plays at Power Holdings

The management team from Power Holdings is meeting to plan its budget for the next twelve months. Everybody knows that the company must economise, and that the goal of the meeting is to produce a budget that will restrict spending by individual sections.

Despite this, Mike, who is responsible for advertising, has come to the meeting determined to obtain a bigger budget for his section. His efforts to achieve this will detract from the overall objective of the meeting. His agenda item must remain hidden, since if it becomes obvious to the group, it cannot succeed.

While Mike is pushing his own goals, he cannot contribute fully to those of the meeting as a whole. He will be too busy watching for a chance to turn matters to his advantage.

Rae, from production, has recently been promoted and also has a hidden agenda. She wants to take every opportunity to impress Kem, the managing director. She will support everything Kem says, whether it is sound or not. So Rae won't be able to contribute fully to the meeting, either. Her hidden agenda, although different from Mike's, is just as harmful.

Identifying hidden agendas

Hidden agendas are present in almost all meetings, but are hard to identify. The best defence against them is constantly to be aware of their possible existence, to keep a sharp eye out for any sign that somebody might be pushing one into the discussion. A number of verbal and non-verbal background signals can be useful indications:

- one person regularly interrupting others while they are speaking, or disrupting logical discussion in other ways;
- two people supporting each other on every issue, especially if the support is personal rather than related to the topic under discussion;
- attempts to debate people's characters rather than the ideas they put forward;
- the amount of 'air time' commanded by one speaker — individuals who talk far more than they listen either see themselves as more important than others (a hidden agenda in itself) or may be trying to stop others having their say (Schein, 1969).

The effective participant

Go into a meeting with a positive attitude. Ask yourself 'What can I gain from attending?'. (This usually depends on what you contribute.) Be prepared to listen carefully, and to learn from others. Do not be afraid to speak out when you feel you have a worthwhile contribution to make.

Develop an approach that includes:

- respect for other group members and their opinions;
- understanding of the forces at work when people meet in a group;
- ability to speak clearly and to the point;
- ability to be an active listener;
- ability to think logically and to analyse ideas as they are presented;

- willingness to share speaking time with others and to help others to reach agreement;
- ability to help keep discussion on the right track and to encourage good ideas.

Not everyone enjoys meetings

Chapter 6 explained about different communication styles, and a mixture of these may be present in any meeting room. Remember the aural types? They will be much more interested in talking than the visual thinkers, who will be bored unless they have something to look at. The decisive types grow impatient if progress is not rapid enough, or else announce that they have only half an hour to spare so all decisions must be made by then. The polisher, of course, wants more time to discuss issues fully. Linear thinkers will prefer formal debate; feeling types want to stick with friendly discussion, and can become upset even by constructive criticism.

Accommodating these types and their conflicting preferences requires tolerance all round and skilled guidance, highlighting the value of team leadership rather than a single person in the chair.

Formal meeting rules

What is termed 'meeting procedure' is just a set of rituals and established codes of behaviour designed to

- allow one person only to speak at one time, yet give everyone a chance to be heard;
- allow the person or panel in control to maintain order and to direct the flow of business during the meeting;
- formulate ideas as motions, which are discussed and voted on in a democratic fashion.

Formal meetings that stick strictly to 'the book' are rare in the 1990s, since they seldom provide the fair and democratic procedure intended. In reality, many such meetings are controlled by whoever knows most about the rules and can turn this knowledge to advantage. Also, there are a number of different authorities on meeting procedure now observed, so the outcome may depend more on who is relying on which book than on any democratic process.

When do you need formal meetings?

Don't use formal procedure for ordinary meetings. It is slow-moving, and restricts the free flow of ideas. However, if a discussion gets out of hand or a minority attempt to take over a meeting, it is comforting to be able to move quickly into formal session and restore order.

Formal rules are also necessary at other times:

- in a meeting attended by over fifty people (and certainly if several hundred attend and all are angry and want be heard — for example, on a community conservation issue);
- when time is limited — for instance, if key members have to leave a meeting and important decisions *must* be made;
- when very controversial matters (such as dismissal of a key figure, legal action, or a financial crisis) have to be resolved and the decision noted in formal minutes;
- when a decision must be recorded as having been passed by a formal resolution (for instance, in company matters);
- when a group is polarised into opposing factions;
- if a group is being troubled by 'bush lawyers' or 'rule-book wavers' — people who are more concerned with showing their knowledge of the rules than helping to resolve issues informally and amicably.

Learning meeting rules

The basic rules can be observed by attending meetings. A handbook will provide you with a step-by-step list of procedures, but it is not easy to learn real meeting management from a book; for a start, the theory and practice of meeting procedure are often far apart. The most effective way to learn is to take part in practical training sessions in which members take the chair in turn while the remainder act as the participants. As the group's understanding of procedure develops, members can start trying to disrupt the meeting or confuse the person in the chair so that everyone has experience in handling a hostile group as well as a pleasant one.

This is the basis of the training game, *Chairman's Dilemma* (1986), which turns the learning process into a fast-moving team activity and provides hands-on learning experience in formal meeting control (see 'Additional resources and bibliography').

Summary

1. Both meeting structure and style of leadership should vary to suit the conditions and purpose of a meeting.

2. Of all the different types of meetings, committees are among the most useful. Committees should operate at all levels.

3. The more committee leaders understand about how a group meeting functions, and about meeting management, the better the group's chance of success.

4. The ideal size for a committee is from five to ten people. Groups of twenty or more are too unwieldy.

5. Select committee members from different backgrounds. Mixing experts and non-experts ensures a wider range of views and lessens the risk of groupthink.

6. Emergency situations can often best be handled by an informal conference called on the spot.

7. Organisations should hold regular general meetings of all staff. These improve morale and help to encourage teamwork.

8. The success of any meeting depends largely on the location and facilities available.

9. An agenda should give in advance as much information as possible about the topic to be discussed, the time and length of the meeting, and other details to enable participants to prepare.

10. Meeting leaders assume many roles. They promote, lead, direct, inform, interpret, encourage, stimulate, referee, judge, moderate and conciliate, and do anything else necessary for the group to achieve its aims.

11. Most meetings work better if at various stages members split into subgroups for discussions, subsequently reporting their views to the full meeting.

12. Items of hidden agendas are personal goals (not on the open agenda) which individuals (or subgroups) bring with them to a meeting. Hidden agenda issues are necessarily self-centred. Leaders who suspect such an issue is being raised should try to bring it out into the open.

13. Go to a meeting with a positive attitude. What you gain from attending depends on how much you contribute. Be prepared to listen and to learn from others. Do not be afraid to have your say.

14. Not everyone enjoys meetings. A mixture of different communication styles will be present in any meeting room. Be tolerant, and try to help everyone to benefit.

Exercises

1. List some of the advantages and disadvantages of establishing a temporary committee to look at a particular problem affecting your group or business.

2. You have been asked to form a committee to look at methods of improving efficiency in your group or organisation.

    What would you suggest were suitable types of people to act on this committee? How many people would you want? How would you arrange for members to be selected? How would you communicate with those selected and what would you tell them?

3. From your own experience, give examples of five situations in which committees could work effectively and five in which they would have less chance of success.

4. You are a member (but not the leader) of a committee. How can you best contribute during committee meetings?

5. You are one of three people appointed to organise and lead a meeting of sales staff to find out why a new product is not selling as well as was expected and to develop a new sales approach for the product. The meeting is to be held three weeks from today.

    (a) What background preparations would you make?

    (b) There are forty-five sales staff in three separate branches. You would prefer to limit the meeting to as few as possible. List the steps you would take to arrange for a balanced and participative group.

    (c) List the various items of written communication you would send to all those who are to attend.

    (d) Draft a copy of the agenda.

    (e) Draw a diagram of the room layout for the meeting. Why would you choose this layout?

(f) Briefly outline the remarks with which you will open the meeting.

6. You are a middle-level manager in a large manufacturing company. A sudden breakdown in the production plant will cause a two-day delay in delivery of urgent customer orders. Outline, step by step, what you would do to arrange a conference on the problem.

7. Discuss the following paragraph.

Each month on a night specially set aside, the natives would gather together to seek guidance from the Gods. Members of the group would speak certain words that had the power to ensure good decisions. After these ritual speeches, everyone would chant one of two magic words and the chiefs would decide which word was the louder. On some occasions the chiefs would ask everyone to wave their hands in the air, an even more powerful way of ensuring that the Gods helped them make sound decisions. Afterwards, the chiefs would announce to the group what the Gods had decided should be done.

Do meetings you attend have anything in common with the activities described above?

CHAPTER 31

Presentations, projects and submissions

Sooner or later you will find yourself working on a presentation — a project, a report or a submission — that is vitally important. It could be the final thesis that ensures your graduation. It could be a report that, if approved, will open up a new career, or a sales proposal which, if the client accepts, will make a considerable difference to your bank account. Whatever it is, you will want to use every available technique to present your material successfully. This chapter highlights further ways of making sure your efforts are rewarded.

Topics

Proposals, submissions and feasibility studies

Investigation and research

Experiments

Organising information

Strengthening your case

Proposals, submissions and feasibility studies

A submission, like a report, is a way of communicating in situations where it might otherwise be hard to make direct contact. You usually make a submission or present a feasibility study before you start a major project. Many submissions involve applications for loans or grants, but not all are concerned with finance. A government department may invite interested organisations to put forward proposals about changes in the way it serves the public. The public can make submissions (without being invited) about the way the government is handling community problems. These differ in several ways from ordinary reports.

- There is usually a clearly defined target reader (or readers) — perhaps an accreditation committee, a government department, a purchasing board or a college council. The submission will be directed solely to this group, whereas most reports have a broader readership.
- The overall approach, the language and the tone are more openly persuasive than in a report. Messages of this kind often face considerable resistance before they gain acceptance.
- A submission should be built around a strong central argument and must close with a specific proposal or statement that follows logically from that argument. It is not enough to give a list of facts and then leave it to your readers to work out a conclusion for themselves.
- People who read the document will be expecting you to present *your* point of view alone. There is not the need to include alternative views, as there is in a report. If you do mention an opposing argument, or product, it is more likely to be in highlighting its faults.
- While there is usually only one report written on a given situation, there may be many submissions — all competing for the reader's attention (and often the reader's dollar).

Organisation of submission topics

There is no standard format. It follows many of the conventions of a business report, as shown below, but there should be more specific headings.

Preliminary pages

- Cover (plastic, not cardboard)
- Title page
  Official or formal project title
  Name of organisation
  Branch, unit or individual responsible for project
  Time (month, year)
- Synopsis page
- Contents page
  Optional, but adds a professional touch (not needed in a submission of less than four pages)

Introduction

1. Outline
   Briefly explain the project or activity for which approval is requested. Summarise major points to be made in the pages that follow.
2. Aim of the project or proposed activity
   Set out the main goals or purpose of the proposed activity; program, project or purchase.
3. Benefits — value of proposed project or research program
   Detail the value of the proposed program, especially from the reader's point of view. Explain exactly what benefits will result if the proposal or project goes ahead.
4. Sources of information
   This section is often more detailed than in a report. Say how and where objective data was obtained, to maintain validity.
5. Historical background
6. Theoretical background — a theory or 'model' to show that your proposal or plan should work successfully.
7. Research method
   If research is involved, explain how results will be measured to ensure accuracy. Describe the test design or equipment, using appropriate headings:
   Technique A
   Technique B
   Technique C
   Location

Body of document

The current situation

- Give specific facts — presentation and content should be objective, similar to the findings section of a report. Readers may not agree with claims you make, so include evidence that proves the point.
- List numbers and amounts. Give measurements to back up your statements — figures are more effective than words.
- Use quotes or extracts — other research findings or reports can provide valuable sources of support.

The proposal

Describe in detail what is proposed. What will the project or research involve? Use diagrams to help make your case clear. If there are technical or statistical specifications involved, or if descriptions run to more than half a page, summarise only here and put the rest in an appendix. Whatever the topic, make your language as specific as possible.

- Timetable for stages in program
  Show clearly how long the project is expected to take. Be specific. Show the time set aside for each step (the plan in Table 16.1 is a good example).
- People involved
  Explain who will be involved and why they are well-suited for any special research.
- Funding requirements/budget
  Set this out logically, and in full detail. Be specific.

Central argument

Like the analysis section in a report, this section uses subjective material, but because it will meet stronger reader resistance, your argument will need to be logical, more detailed and more actively promoted.

Formal statement of proposal

Word this in such a way that there is no doubt about what the reader is actually saying 'Yes' or 'No' to. If it refers to several items (for instance, money, staffing, equipment or accommodation), list each separately.

Appendixes

Appendixes include any bulky items which would clutter the main document. For example:

Appendix A — Map of Avoca Park, showing project area

Appendix B — Copies of original statements by experts, as quoted in submission

Appendix C — Photographs, photocopies, maps and so on.

References or bibliography

List authors and titles as quoted in the submission document (see 'Quotes, references and acknowledgments', in Chapter 18).

Investigation and research

To be objective, both sides of an issue have to be clearly stated — the positive and the negative. A professional researcher selects not only the kind of information that reinforces his or her proposal, but seeks information that opposes as well. This maintains objectivity.

The purpose of research is to extend both your knowledge *and* your viewpoint. Most projects you work on will be related to issues of which you already have some knowledge; however, what you know may represent only one view. Your final presentation needs to cover the whole picture.

Most investigations involve research of both primary and secondary sources, so part of the initial planning for any project is to decide on the proportion of your work that will be given to each.

Investigation and research

Primary research

There are many advantages in using facts you uncover yourself. You can be more confident about the findings of your own investigation than those obtained from books or journals. The data that you count, measure or observe yourself is relevant to the local situation. It may also be more up to date than published research. On the other hand, investigation of primary sources takes more of your time and may be costly in comparison with the use of information waiting for you in secondary sources — books, journals and computer databases.

Direct observation — GASFY and RBWA

Most research programs will be seen as incomplete unless they include some direct investigation or observation. For example, if there is a problem in meeting deadlines, go and look at conditions in the section involved. Weigh up what you see, against data obtained from other sources. Many researchers include either a still or a video camera as part of their survey equipment. The well-known terms GASFY (Go And See For Yourself) and RBWA (Researching By Walking About) indicate the level of recognition accorded to direct observation as a means of discovering essential facts. (Research may also involve you in some 'detective' work. What you are shown and what you are told may represent only what others want you to see.)

Research interviews

Face-to-face interviews can produce essential facts, but even if they fail to uncover the data you were looking for they play a vital part in adding to your understanding of the topic. Information obtained in this way is not always reliable, but it can provide clues to more significant areas of investigation. What is unsaid may be more significant than the words you hear.

Often the facts are hidden among a maze of irrelevant information. What at first seems to be the cause of a problem can turn out to be only a symptom.

Interviews can be quite informal — just talking with colleagues and other employees — or can follow a structured format. Research interviews differ in some ways from the kind explained in Chapter 8.

Research interviews-guidelines
1. Talk to people who disagree with you.
Their points of view will add balance and depth to your study. A short interview with people who have recently left a firm may reveal information that current employees may not be so ready to share.

2. Ask interviewees, 'Is there anyone else you can suggest who could help me?'.
While the people mentioned may all hold similar views, the chances are that some might have vital bits of information you would otherwise have missed.

3. Follow up clues or leads.
Plan your questions in advance to give you control of the discussion, but tune in to any new or unexpected topics that are mentioned during the interview.

4. Use the telephone.
Telephone interviews allow you to talk to people who you cannot meet personally. As long as you are friendly and informal, and explain what you are looking for, people are usually willing to give information over the phone. But keep in mind the telephone barriers described in Chapter 22, and work to keep them as low as possible.

5. Use letters.
If you have to ask many people exactly the same questions, a letter is often as effective as an interview.

Consultants and technical experts

Talk with others who have had experience in the same area. The advice of a specialist or technical consultant can be vital in winning a tough business battle. (Consultants can, of course, help in many other ways.) The ideal person is one with wide experience in presenting proposals similar to yours and with special skills in the area. If you are concerned about the expense of using a professional consultant, you may find that a retired expert will be happy to help you for a lesser amount.

'Front-line' experts

If your research involves front-line issues, particularly 'people problems', some of the best (and cheapest) data can come from ordinary individuals who are familiar with your topic at the hands-on level: your own front-line operators — sales staff, trainers, delivery drivers, switch operators and repair technicians — all those who spend their time dealing directly with customers and clients. Also consult associates who have recently dealt with similar issues and have up-to-date information from their front-lines.

Technical tests

Information gained by scientific measurement has high credibility. If you are dealing with 'people' issues (for instance, morale or motivation) you may not find technical research so valuable, but in almost any other area it is worth using some form of test or measurement (see 'Experiments', page 353).

Surveys and questionnaires

Decide whether you are seeking facts or opinions, and don't mix the two in the same survey. Make sure you have a balanced sample by distributing the survey among a range of people representing the overall target population. If a college has 1000 full-time students attending on weekdays, 400 part-time students attending five nights a week and another 100 on Saturdays and Sundays, all these groups must be covered in roughly the same proportion in a survey on student parking. When surveying for factual data you can find out, for instance, what proportion of people travel by train or bus, drive, walk or cycle to college; but do not treat answers as precise — there will always be variations.

Designing a survey — guidelines

Questionnaires need to be carefully prepared to avoid leading questions — questions so phrased that they tend to suggest answers.

1. Use short, simple statements that cannot be misunderstood.

Decide whether you will get more accurate answers by asking people to tick boxes ('Yes', 'No', 'Not sure') or to mark a position on a line with contrasting words at each end.

4. Bus service 64A meets my present needs.

Agree I—I—I—I—I—I—I—I Disagree
        4 3 2 1 0 1 2 3 4

The linear method is generally more reliable provided you do not use emotionally weighted words such as 'very happy' or 'very unhappy'. Emotional words lead to less accurate responses. The linear scale discourages inaccurate mid-point responses suggested by words such as 'undecided' in a verbal scale. Few people want to announce the fact if they are uncertain, nor is uncertainty of necessity located in the middle of the scale.

2. Ask important questions twice.

Ask once in a negative and once in a positive form (but well apart), so that the two responses provide a check on validity. If a respondent says 'Yes' to both, it suggests either confusion or a lack of interest in giving accurate answers. Discount both responses.

3. Keep the number of questions to a minimum.

The easier it is for people to answer a questionnaire, the more likely they are to co-operate.

4. Avoid open-ended questions.

Instead, provide a number of alternatives covering a range of possible answers. Questions requiring long written answers produce inaccurate results. If you need general comments, allow a space at the end.

5. Always have a trial run.

Field-testing of your draft questionnaire is vital before you launch the main survey. Use a small sample group of twenty to thirty to make sure your questions are clear and that the words do not convey double meanings.

Surveys must be voluntary

Explain to respondents how co-operation may benefit them personally. For example, if you are seeking data on the leisure activities of managers, point out the use of such information to research into heart disease. Responding to surveys and questionnaires must never be compulsory, no matter how much you need the data. The only worthwhile answers come from people who feel they are co-operating or contributing. Thank respondents for their help; advise them how and when they can obtain details of the overall findings.

Interpreting opinion surveys

Someone says: 'Sixty-six per cent of answers indicate agreement with our present policies. That means two out of every three members want the rules left the way they are'. The speaker is misinterpreting the results. What happened was that two of every three of the people *who replied* ticked a 'yes' box beside a particular question. Ticking a box does not tell you whether people agree in their hearts, nor does it tell you how strongly they agree. It tells you nothing about the views of people who did not reply. Even if everybody who replies says 'yes', this does not prove the rules themselves are sound.

Treat opinion-survey results as opinions and nothing more. At best, they can provide a useful guide to trends or general viewpoints. Never treat figures or percentages from such a survey as though they represented factual data.

Running your own experiment

Sometimes the best primary research of all is to run your own experimental trial. This is growing in popularity in business; it works well provided that it is properly designed and that the people involved have what is called the 'freedom to fail' (see 'Experiments', p. 353).

Secondary research

Someone else's primary material already collected, sorted and indexed is certainly easier to work with than searching for yourself. Quoting expert data that reinforces your own case is an excellent aid to persuasion, and there are many sources.

Past reports and projects

There may be past records of surveys similar to yours, or a project or thesis on the same topic, but they may not be in the main library. Ask the librarian for lists of archive material. There may also be reports or general files at work dealing with similar topics. Ask your records section. Incidence of the problem you are investigating may be traceable for some time past.

Networks and organisations

Many other sources of information are worth looking into. If your study is concerned with political or social issues, such as conservation or discrimination, there will be a number of special interest organisations who will be able to put you in touch with up-to-date material, including research already completed. Often there is an information network already in existence on the subject, with its own library or computer database, and because these groups rely on public support they are usually happy to share their data and publications.

Commercial and industrial sources

People who sell and service a product will naturally be biased in the advice they offer about it, but this does not mean that they cannot give valuable information. For a start, they can tell you about faults in opposition products. Service technicians can supply facts about the technology behind their products that sales staff often don't want to discuss, and they appreciate being asked.

Industry-based organisations

Most industries have one or more associations or federations that collect data on the industry concerned. They are usually only too happy to share this with interested students. As long as you weigh advice from these sources more carefully than that from independent experts, the data can be extremely valuable.

Other sources

- Community groups: If you are looking for a topic for a study thesis or project, community bodies offer a fruitful area because most organisations like to be involved in studies by education institutions. Some even offer financial support.
- Conferences or seminars: Meetings of any kind conducted by any special interest group or organisation are a source of alternative viewpoints and the latest research findings in your area of investigation.
- Government departments: If there is a government department that deals with the topic you are researching, contact the departmental public relations office responsible for study material.
- Personal contacts: Friends and relatives can help by introducing you to other people they know with expertise in the area you're studying.
- Competitors: Don't forget the competition. Outlining what the opposition is doing in the same area that you are researching adds another facet to your work. Use information obtained by legitimate means only.

Library resources

Libraries are naturally among the richest of all sources of secondary material, including

- print media — books, journals, articles, magazines, technical reports and so on;
- audiovisual and graphic media — video tapes, tape recordings, films, slides and photographs, drawings and sketches;
- computerised databanks — in which you use key words to call up the precise data you want;
- general reference books — encyclopaedias, atlases, yearbooks, bibliographies, directories, and back copies of newspapers.

A major advantage of library research is that the information is already sorted and indexed. However, in using libraries look for more than just facts and figures. Discover opinions expressed and conclusions drawn by those who are authorities in their fields.

Classification systems

Libraries use recognised classification and cataloguing systems which are designed to cover all existing subjects and to allow for the addition of an infinite number of new ones. Any system exists to help you find the book, author or topic you want, so (although it may seem intimidating at first) it is worthwhile learning to use it. Librarians are happy to explain their systems, and most conduct regular training sessions. With a little practice, you can familiarise yourself with the way your library catalogues books and other media.

Apart from the speed with which a classification system allows you to find what you want, and the range of data available, there is another unique advantage. Once you have found the book you are looking for, you have found the place where other books on the same or similar topics are shelved. The result is a rapid expansion of your resource base.

Borrowing versus photocopying

The best way to make use of library resources is to take a number of books out on loan. If essential material cannot be taken out, photocopy the relevant pages on the library copier. This may cost you a few dollars, but you will then have plenty of time to study them. (Remember to copy the title and imprint pages, so you have the details needed for acknowledgment). Tables of figures or diagrams, once photocopied, can be cut out and pasted into your own text without retyping. However, remember that you may only photocopy a limited percentage of any one item at any one time (see page 307, 'Restrictions on copyright').

What if the book you want is not in your library, but you know it is available in a library in Melbourne or Perth? Membership of one library usually provides you with access to a system of interlibrary loans. Ask your librarian for details.

Audio, visual and computerised media

Today's technology makes it easy to present much important information on film, tape, compact disk, microchip and associated media. Some of the most up-to-date data are likely to be found on the most up-to-date media. Information in this form is also likely to be much easier to sort through using electronic scanning and sorting techniques, so do not restrict your library research to printed items.

Computerised databases

Imagine that you are researching the effect of participative management on productivity. Then imagine being able to pay a few dollars and receive a print-out giving the title, plus a short abstract, of every major book, journal or article in the world that deals with your topic — just by referring to the three key words: 'participative', 'management' and 'productivity'. This is a dream already approaching reality, as computerised databases continue to grow at a rapid rate. Many of them are now being linked to other bases by computer modem and overseas satellite links. Some you can tap into using your own personal computer and an ordinary telecommunication package, but the larger ones with overseas links may have to be accessed through a library computer.

Citation lists, abstracts and bibliographies

You can use a citation index or list of abstracts in much the same way as a computer database. Though hand-operated, such lists are still every bit as helpful with references on a given topic (and they cost nothing to use). As with any database the printed lists are indexed according to topics and titles, so you use key words to locate (manually) the title and publication details of hundreds of publications, including the latest journal articles, and other current media. A bibliography on a given topic is a similar and equally useful reference source.

Your librarian will tell you where these lists are and if necessary will help you to make the most efficient use of the index.

Experiments

A simple experiment can reveal more about a problem than a series of meetings or a logical but theoretical written analysis. However, keep your experiments simple. Do not get caught up in a university-level program if all you want to find out (as in the example below) is whether to have one or two people serving at a hamburger bar.

An experimental trial needs a sound, logical structure. A 'try it and see' approach is not good enough. Consider this situation.

> You have just started a part-time job running a hamburger bar for some friends who have gone overseas. They have always had one person, the manager (that's you, in this case), serving at the counter and two working in the kitchen. You decide to employ extra staff during the holidays to help you to serve. Your first assistant is a young student named Sandy. At the end of Sandy's first week you notice sales are up by 25 per cent. Sales are up 30 per cent the following week, despite factors such as weather conditions.
>
> What might be responsible for the rise?

Planning the trial

One way to find out if the extra counter staff is one of the factors responsible for increased sales is to run a number of trials, putting Sandy on at different times, on different days, during holidays and on slack days. You keep an accurate record of sales for each trial, and these figures become your test results. After a number of trials you can draw some initial conclusions: there may already be confirmation of your original view that having a second person serving helps to increase sales. But take care.

Interpreting results

To interpret the trial results you need to look at every factor that might have affected sales. Go back over your figures. Is it just the 'extra person' or is it specifically Sandy's outgoing and friendly personality that increases sales? To find out, you may have to run more trials using different people on the counter in ones, twos and even threes.

One obvious advantage of the trial method is that people find it hard to argue against the findings. The other advantage is that during the trial your understanding of the whole question of counter sales will grow. Test results like these can often tell you things about 'people' issues, such as over-the-counter selling, that you might not discover in any other way.

Freedom to fail

The experiment was meant to show that any two people working together on the counter would increase sales. If your later tests show that sales go up *only* when you and Sandy do the job together, has the experiment been a failure? No.

An important principle of modern (1990s) management is that trials like these should be seen as worthwhile no matter what the result. Negative results should be treated not as failure, but as an alternative set of data. There is often much to be learned from negative feedback (see 'Negative or error feedback', in Chapter 3). If people feel that they are 'not allowed' to fail they may not discover as much, their research will be the poorer for it, and they may even avoid trials altogether.

Using statistics

Preparing a winning case usually means that you will have to make some use of statistical analysis. Statistics can give powerful support to your case, but like any data, they need to be used properly. Statistical measurements must be valid and appropriate, and the results must be interpreted correctly. Tests such as 'T scores' and 'correlation coefficients' sound scientific and the results they produce may seem very impressive — especially to the novice — which means that they can be used (knowingly or not) to stop people arguing with findings. However, statistical tests do not really 'prove' results; they only serve to support real data.

If you do not understand a statistical technique, do not use it. Some tests have to be validated by other statistical checks before they can be accepted as reliable. Others only apply in special circumstances. If you have to use a particular test regularly, find out all you can about it. Get a good book on the method involved and keep it handy.

Organising information

To be persuasive, your information must be organised. The sequence of your argument must be apparent to your readers. Remember, from past chapters, the main rules for organising ideas:

- Group similar topics together — 'Five similar problems have been observed with this type of machine. They are . . .'.
- Keep topics of different kinds apart — 'The advantages of leasing are listed here. Disadvantages are discussed on page 5'.
- Follow familiar sequences where possible — 'The problem will be discussed in two sections: Part A deals with actual issues both past and present; Part B deals with possible future effects'.

Sequences for headings and subheadings

Different sequences suit different topics. Some useful arrangements are shown here, although there are many others. The simplest are often the best.

Order of time

This is used in any discussion related to the clock, calendar or time sheet. For example:
2.1 Installation of New Machines
2.2 Testing System in Use
2.3 Disposal of Old Machines

Order of location

A study of future markets for a product might look at the potential for sales in the city first, then in the country and then overseas.

Order of importance or rank

It is logical to list ideas in order of ascending or descending importance:

2.1 Discussions with Manager
2.2 Discussions with Sales Staff
2.3 Discussions with Drivers

Order of familiarity

Tell people first about familiar aspects of a situation before introducing new or unfamiliar topics.

Order of acceptability

If some proposals are likely to be less acceptable than others, start with the most acceptable.

Contrasting pairs

Understanding of a topic is increased when writers contrast opposite ideas:
3.1 Features of Old System
3.2 Features of New System
Other examples of pairing include question and answer, before and after, cause and effect.

Parallel order

There is usually more than one way of dividing a set of ideas. For instance, if you are investigating which of three different models should be purchased, it might at first seem a good idea to set out your findings this way:

2. RESULTS OF COMPARISONS AND TESTING
   2.1 Brand A
      2.1.1 Cost of purchase and running
      2.1.2 Maintenance and repairs
      2.1.3 Reliability
   2.2 Brand B
      2.2.1 Cost of purchase and running
      2.2.2 Maintenance and repairs
      2.2.3 Reliability

Is this the most useful way of presenting the facts? Anyone who wants to compare costs has to move from 2.1 to 2.2 to find the difference in price for brands A and B. Depending on the purpose of the submission, the arrangement below may be more effective.

2. RESULTS OF COMPARISONS AND TESTING
   2.1 Cost of Purchase and Running
      Brand A
      Brand B

2.2 Reliability and Accuracy
    Brand A
    Brand B
2.3 Maintenance and Repairs
    Brand A
    Brand B

Strengthening your case

Sound research and well-organised ideas are essential, but there is more than that to developing a winning case. Often there will be others presenting an opposing point of view, and part of their strategy may include a direct attack on your presentation. Be prepared for this. The stronger your argument the less chance they have, as the example below illustrates.

Giving credit where it's due

Three different submissions on credit management are being presented to the Executive Committee next week.

The first, which you are proposing, is from your own group (Sales) and argues for a change in credit policy. At present neither you nor your sales staff have any voice at all in the processing of customer-credit applications. You want your sales representatives to handle customer-credit interviews and be able to approve up to $1000 credit a month. Limits above that amount would be determined jointly by senior Credit Department officers and yourself.

The Credit Department opposes this. Their submission asks the executive to let it retain sole control over credit approval. Their argument is based largely on the claim that credit applications must be handled only by senior staff and need to be processed in strict confidence.

The Administration is putting up a third submission, which asks the executive to approve their employing three more office staff to handle the extra paper work which they claim your proposal will generate. Otherwise Administration will oppose your case on the grounds of the increased workload.

The following guidelines all serve to improve the quality of your presentation and to produce a proposal with the best possible chance of success.

1. State the outcome (result) in an appealing way.

In words that will appeal to the people who would say 'yes', define exactly what will happen if your proposal is approved. In this case:

> Allowing sales staff to process customer-credit applications may be more effective and may save time, but these two outcomes do not hold much appeal by themselves. Stress other results such as better customer relations, increased sales and higher motivation — outcomes that will appeal more to executive members.

2. Have verification on hand.

Business data gathered from the 'real world' makes a stronger case than theory or library research, particularly when you are trying to convince hard-headed managers. However, such information must be verifiable.

Suppose your sales staff have all had experience in finance and most have studied credit management and accounting subjects as part of their training. Have photocopies of their credentials and personal résumés on hand in case they are questioned.

3. Compare and contrast.

Comparing and contrasting strengthens your case. If others are contesting your claims, gather facts on the opposition's case. Reaching a decision on a complex issue is easier if you consider what *you* think are the advantages and disadvantages and also the points of view of opponents.

While you are comparing and contrasting, you'll start to think of answers to arguments that your opponents are likely to present:

> You know the Credit Department will bring up a 1986 case in which sales staff were allowed to approve credit on a trial basis. The firm had a total bad-debt figure of $10 000 in that year. Contrast this, however, with total sales for the same year of $1 900 000. Compare the 1986 bad-debt figure with the average bad debts ($7500 a year) from 1988 until now, during which period the Credit group has handled all approvals, but note that during the same period sales have averaged only $950 000 a year. (Is this because the Credit Department is too tough on potential credit applicants?)

4. Put analytical questions.

An analytical chemist gets answers by breaking

complex substances up into smaller units. Knowing just what a substance consists of increases understanding of it and makes it easier to work with. It's the same with many management and organisation issues, and the best way to break them up is to ask lots of questions.

Analyse successful credit-management techniques, and also some that do not work. You will understand better what it takes to know whether or not a customer will be a good credit risk.

Exactly what steps are involved when a customer applies for credit? What questions have to be answered? What skills and sources are needed to check a customer's statement? Is there a formula that relates an applicant's annual income or turnover to the amount of credit granted?

Like a fossicker searching for gems, you may have to turn over a lot of material, but usually you gather enough valuable information through analytical questioning to make the activity worthwhile.

5. What if . . .? Use your imagination.

Imagination helps you see connections between different ideas and solutions. People with fertile imaginations are often very successful in presenting a winning argument. Reasoning is not just a matter of logic; it can also involve dreaming up new and different solutions to old problems. The people who are best at reasoning are not always the most active thinkers, because they may fail to use their imagination enough.

Ask yourself: 'What if sales staff were to have a say in determining credit limits?' Visualise the probable effect on morale and sales. Imagine how the new system might work best. Which parts of the present structure would change?

Make a list of positive effects, but don't forget to look at the negative side. When a problem involves one group trying to break away from traditional or standard procedures, you will find (as in this case) that it is a good time for 'What if . . .?' or conditional thinking. If your opponents are using a negative version of the 'What if' approach — imagining what will go *wrong* if sales staff are involved in giving credit — beat them to the post by imagining the same thing. Then you will be more prepared for their arguments.

Imaginative, creative reasoning like this often produces some surprising answers and helps break

down long-established but unnecessary 'we've always done it that way' thinking.

6. Develop the central argument.

The core of any case is the point at which you connect all the main ideas. Clarify this central 'argument', starting with a series of conditions (as explained in Chapter 11, the 'if' statements). End with logical conclusions that support the aim of your proposal.

Condition 1: If sales staff are the people who know customers best,

Conclusion 1: then sales staff can also find out more about the customer's real financial situation than could a stranger from the Credit Department.

Condition 2: If sales staff make the credit investigations,

Conclusion 2: then customers will be more appreciative when they are granted credit,

Conclusion 3: therefore customers will feel a stronger bond with their sales representative and this will help maintain customer loyalty.

These conditions and conclusions then lead to one final condition, which reflects your original aim, and a final conclusion that suggests that the aim is worth supporting.

Final condition: If sales representatives are given authority to handle credit applications,

Final conclusion: then sales staff morale and motivation will increase, customer loyalty will rise, and sales will go up.

Your argument might not follow the same sequence as this example, but as long as there is a logical connection between the various conditions and their conclusions, and your ideas are organised, your case will be sound and correct. Use any of the types of argument described in Chapter 11 (inductive or deductive).

7. Test your proposal on home ground.

Find out who among your own team supports the logic in your argument (a process sometimes known as 'running the flag up the pole to see who salutes'). The answer does not necessarily make your case more reliable, but it can show whether the case is ready to present. If it lacks the quality called 'visibility' — if people cannot readily follow the line of your argument — it needs more work.

One of the best testing grounds is a team meeting, where all people involved (on your side) examine the case to see if it will stand up to opposition. Gaining support from a meeting can be frustrating and time-consuming, but no matter how well thought out your case may be, it has little hope unless or until your own team understands it. If they cannot or will not accept your reasoning, they cannot support it. They will be much more likely to give support, however, if they are allowed to help with the fine-tuning of the case, to assist in clarifying the parts of the argument they do not follow, and then to make the case stronger by adding their own contributions.

8. Put the proposal into an action format.
Your presentation ends at the point where you offer a logical and reasoned choice: your final conclusion.

However, a conclusion — no matter how strong — is still only an opinion or a prediction. To complete the process you need to project your conclusion to the point where it can be stated in terms of a decision. Suggest a set of step-by-step actions that can be approved to help put the policy into practice (see 'Recommendations', page 194).

RECOMMENDATIONS:

1. That sales representatives personally handle credit applications from new customers as part of their overall marketing strategy.

2. That sales representatives be given authority to approve credit applications from new customers up to a limit of $1000 per month.

3. That applications for credit above $1000 a month be approved only if agreed to by both the Sales Manager and the Credit Manager.

Summary

1. Most research will include some direct investigation or observation (primary research) and some reading of other people's primary research (your secondary research).

2. When researching information to support a proposal, seek data that opposes as well as that which supports your view so that you can be prepared to refute it if necessary.

3. Advice of a specialist or a technical consultant can be vital in preparing a successful submission.

4. A simple experiment can reveal more about a problem than a series of meetings or months of theoretical analysis.

Exercises

1. Who are front-line experts and why should you consult them when researching any important project or report?

2. What do the letters GASFY and RBWA stand for? What is their significance in terms of primary or field research?

3. List five guidelines for use in designing an opinion survey.

4. Why are libraries such a useful source of secondary source material?

5. What is the significance of the term 'freedom to fail' in regard to practical trials or experiments at work?

6. What are the three main rules for organising and classifying information in a submission or a report?

7. What is the 'What if ...?' approach? How do you use it to add strength to an argument for use in a submission?

8. What is the difference between primary and secondary research?

9. Kerry runs a test on three different plastics for use in the production of a new line of kitchenware, scoring the results on an index of 1–10. For acceptable quality, a minimum index of 7 is required.

Plastic	Test scores	Average score
A	7,8,7,9,8,7,7,8,8, 8,9,7,9,8,8,8,7,9,	142/18 = 7.88
B	9,8,6,4,7,8,8,3,6, 3,9,9,6,9,9,7,4,7,	122/18 = 6.77
C	8,9,4,9,9,5,9,6,9, 9,8,9,7,8,9,8,9,9,	144/18 = 8.00

Kerry works out the average score, and since C has the best average, recommends it. What mistake has Kerry made in interpreting the statistics?

10. Use your library to find and list six different references containing information on one of the following topics:
    - business writing
    - the greenhouse effect
    - client service or service management
    - intuitive communication
    - non-discriminatory or non-sexist writing
    - the evolution of management theories

Additional resources and bibliography

As well as acknowledging the following as the source of many important concepts, this list is recommended as additional reading on communication topics. Many are also excellent practical manuals for developing communication skills.

A note to the reader: In this edition we emphasise that information organised logically is more useful. We also say that identifying people by name — especially by first names — makes for better communication. With these points in mind, we felt that the following format would be preferable to a standard bibliography.

Books

General references — business communication

Beisler, Fran, Scheeres, Hermine & Pinner, David, *Communication Skills*, Pitman Australia, 1987.

Himstreet, William & Baty, Wayne, *Business Communication*, Holt Rinehart & Winston, Wadsworth, 1988.

Huseman, Richard, Galvin, Michael & Prescott, David, *Business Communication*, Holt Rinehart & Winston, Sydney, 1988.

McMaster, Michael & Grinder, John, *Precision: A New Approach to Communication*, Precision Models, USA, 1980. (Techniques to help ensure that business information is accurate, explicit and understandable.)

Maud, Barry, *Practical Communication for Managers*, Longman, London, 1974.

Pearce, Glenn, Figgins, Ross & Golen, Steven, *Principles of Business Communication*, Wiley, NY, 1984.

Taylor, Anita, Rosegrant, Teresa, Meyer, Arthur & Samples, Thomas, *Communicating*, 4th edn, Prentice-Hall, NJ, 1986.

Swanson, Richard & Marquardt, Charles, *On Communication*, Glencoe Press/Collier Macmillan, London, 1974.

Wrigley, Jim & Mclean, Paul, *Australian Business Communication*, Longman Cheshire, Melbourne, 1987.

Personal communication styles

Briggs Myers, Isabel, *Gifts Differing*, Consulting Psychologists Press, Palo Alto, Ca., 1980.

Harris, Amy & Harris, Thomas, *Staying O.K.*, Harper & Row, Sydney, 1985.

Williams, Linda, *Teaching for the Two-Sided Mind*, Touchstone, USA, 1984.

Zdenek, Marilee, *The Right Brain Experience*, Corgi, USA, 1985. [Because the study of personality and its effect on communication style is a relatively new discipline, titles are appearing all the time. Watch for those that refer to topics such as MBTI (Myers Briggs Type Indicator). The term NLP (Neuro Linguistic Programming) is often used in titles of works that discuss aural, visual and tactile (kinaesthetic) communication.]

Words, language and meanings

Casson, John, *Using Words*, Duckworth & Casson, London, 1981.

Smith, Gerald, *Hidden Meanings*, Celestial, California, 1977.

Developing empathy, co-operation and understanding

Bettinghaus, Erwin, *Persuasive Communication*, Holt Rinehart & Winston, USA, 1980.

Dainow, Sheila & Bailey, Caroline, *Developing Skills with People*, Wiley, Chichester, 1988.

Dick, Bob, *Helping Others to be Effective*, University of Queensland Press, St Lucia, 1984.

Egan, Gerard, *Exercises in the Helping Skills*, Brookes Cole, California, 1975.

Mellody, Pia, *Facing Codependence*, Harper & Row, San Francisco, 1989.

Smith, Shirley, *Set Yourself Free*, Transworld, Sydney, 1990.

Reading, studying and learning

Button, Leslie, *Discovery and Experience*, Oxford University Press, London, 1971.

de Leeue, Manya & de Leeue, Eric, *Read Better, Read Faster*, Penguin, New York, 1985.

Montgomery, Bob & Evans, Lyn, *You and Stress*, Nelson, Melbourne, 1984.

New Zealand and Australian Council for Educational Research, *SWOT (Study Without Tears)*, NZCER & ACER, Wellington, 1982.

Nutting, Rosamond, *Skills for Positive Living*, Pitman, Melbourne, 1985.

Packham, Gillian, McEvedy, Rosanna & Smith, Patricia, *Studying in Australia Using Australian Libraries*, Thomas Nelson 1984.

Percy, Diana, *Study Tactics*, Macmillan, Melbourne, 1983.

Thinking and reasoning

de Bono, Edward, *Opportunities*, Penguin, UK, 1983.

Golberg, Philip, *The Intuitive Edge*, Tarcher Inc., 1983.

Hewitt-Gleeson, Michael, *Software for the Brain*, Brain Users National Library of Australia, Victoria, 1989.

Mander, Allan, *Think for Yourself*, Ure Smith, Sydney, 1970.

Von Oech, Roger, *A Whack on the Side of the Head*, Angus & Robertson, Sydney, 1983.

Writing at work — letters and reports

Dumbrell, Laurel, *Becoming a Writer*, Allen & Unwin, Sydney, 1986.

Fielden, John, Fielden, Jean & Dulek, Ronald, *The Business Writing Style Book*, Prentice-Hall, NJ, 1984.

Flower, Linda, *Problem Solving Strategies for Writing*, Harcourt Brace Jovanovich, USA, 1985.

Houghton, Joy, *Round Holes — Not Circular Orifices*, London & Southern Gas Association, London, 1968.

Kerrigan, William, *Writing to the Point*, Harcourt Brace Jovanovich, USA, 1987.

Knott, Leonard, *Writing for the Joy of It*, Writers' Digest Books, Cincinnati, Ohio, 1983.

Getting the job you want

Nelson, Richard, *What Colour Is Your Parachute?*, Ten Speed Press, USA, 1989.

Read, Jean (ed.), *Résumés That Get Jobs*, Arco/Simon & Schuster, NY, 1963.

Stevens, Paul, *The New 'Win that Job'*, Centre for Worklife Counselling, Canberra, 1981.

Negotiating

Cohen, Herb, *You Can Negotiate Anything*, Angus & Robertson, Sydney, 1983.

Fisher, Roger & Ury, William, *Getting to Yes*, Arrow, London, 1988.

Karrass, Gary, *Negotiate to Close*, Collins, London, 1985.

Corporate communication, decision making and problem solving

Adair, John, *Effective Decision Making*, Pan, London, 1985.

Ansett, Bob, *The Customer*, Kerr, Melbourne, 1989.

de Bono, Edward, *Conflicts — a Better Way to Resolve Them*, Penguin, London, 1985.

Egan, Gerard, *Change Agent Skills A: Assessing and Designing Excellence*, University Association Inc., San Diego, Ca., 1988.

——, *Change Agent Skills B: Managing and Motivating Change*, University Association Inc., San Diego, Ca., 1988.

Irving, Janis, *Victims of Groupthink*, Houghton Mifflin, USA, 1973.

Kakabadse, Andrew, Ludlow, Rod & Vinnicombe, Susan, *Working in Organisations*, Gower, London, 1981.

Sanford, Edward & Adelman, Harvey, *Management Decisions*, Winthrop, USA, 1977.

Committee meetings and conferences

Schein, E.H., *Process Consultation: Its Role in Organisation Development*, Addison-Wesley, Massachusetts, 1969.

Making communication effective

Ansett, Bob, *The Customer*, Kerr, Melbourne, 1989.

Dick, Bob, *Helping Others to be Effective*, University of Queensland Press, St Lucia, 1984.

Johnson, David, *Reaching Out*, Prentice-Hall, NJ, 1972.

Peters, Thomas & Waterman, Robert, *In Search of Excellence*, Harper & Row, Sydney, 1984.

Public relations and mass media communication

Lewis, Gordon, *How to Handle Your Own Public Relations*, Nelson-Hall, Melbourne, 1976.

Having your say – public speaking

James, Brigid & Keaney, Leonie, *Talking Point*, AE Press, Melbourne, 1984.

International communication

Total Japan, Daikyo Inc., Japan, 1984.

Videotapes

The Art of Negotiating (26 mins), Rank Video.
Oh What a Lovely Report (27 mins), Rank Video.
Wipe Out the Jargon (24 mins), Seven Dimensions Pty Ltd, (Aust.).

Other resources

Downs Management, *Chairman's Dilemma*, Downs Holdings, Brisbane, 1986. (Interactive training game on formal meeting procedure and chairing a formal meeting.)

——, *Writing to Win*, Downs Holdings, Brisbane, 1987.

——, *Australian Business Letters*, Downs Holdings, Brisbane, 1987.

——, *Australian Business Reports*, Downs Holdings, Brisbane, 1987.

(The preceding three resources are structured programs of writing exercises and activities for use by trainers in business organisations. They cover the same areas as Chapters 14 to 20 of this book but in greater depth.)

Plazier, Tom, *Up and Down the Organisation*, Australian Communication Association, Sydney, 1981. (Dynamic group simulation game on formal organisation communication.)

The RIPPA Formula (copyright) and tables based on the formula are used in this text with the permission of Downs Holdings Pty Ltd, PO Box 1098, Stafford, Queensland 4053.

Index